DONCASTER SERMONS.

LESSONS OF LIFE AND GODLINESS

AND

WORDS FROM THE GOSPELS.

TWO SELECTIONS OF

SERMONS

PREACHED IN

THE PARISH CHURCH OF DONCASTER.

BY

C. J. VAUGHAN, D.D.

DEAN OF LLANDAFF, AND MASTER OF THE TEMPLE:
VICAR OF DONCASTER 1860—1869.

NEW EDITION.

𝔏𝔬𝔫𝔡𝔬𝔫:

MACMILLAN AND CO.

AND NEW YORK.

1891

[*All Rights reserved.*]

Lessons of Life and Godliness.
First Edition 1861, Second 1863, Third 1864, Fourth 1870.

Words from the Gospels.
First Edition 1863, Second 1865, Third 1875.

CONTENTS.

LESSONS OF LIFE AND GODLINESS.

SERMON I.
Twenty-third Sunday after Trinity, 11th November, 1860.
THE TALEBEARER.

PROVERBS XI. 13.—A talebearer revealeth secrets: but he that is of a faithful spirit concealeth the matter 1

SERMON II.
The Innocents' Day, Friday, 28th December, 1860.
THE INNOCENTS' DAY.

PSALM VIII. 2.—Out of the mouths of babes and sucklings hast Thou ordained strength because of Thine enemies, that Thou mightest still the enemy and the avenger 13

SERMON III.
Sexagesima Sunday, 3rd February, 1861.
THE DISREGARDED AND THE ACCEPTED OFFERING.

GENESIS IV. 4, 5.—And the Lord had respect unto Abel and to his offering: but unto Cain and to his offering He had not respect . 25

SERMON IV.
Quinquagesima Sunday, 10th February, 1861.
FEATURES OF CHARITY.

1 CORINTHIANS XIII. 5.—Charity doth not behave itself unseemly, seeketh not her own, is not easily provoked, thinketh no evil . 36

SERMON V.

Second Sunday in Lent, 24th February, 1861.

THE CAKE NOT TURNED.

HOSEA VII. 8.—Ephraim is a cake not turned 48

SERMON VI.

Third Wednesday in Lent, 27th February, 1861.

THE DANGER OF RELAPSE.

HEBREWS X. 38.—If any man draw back, my soul shall have no pleasure in him 58

SERMON VII.

Fourth Sunday in Lent, 10th March, 1861.

THE SECRET LIFE AND THE OUTWARD.

GENESIS XLIII. 30, 31.—And he entered into his chamber, and wept there: and he washed his face, and went out, and refrained himself 72

SERMON VIII.

Fifth Sunday in Lent, 17th March, 1861.

REVERENCE.

EXODUS III. 5.—Put off thy shoes from off thy feet, for the place whereon thou standest is holy ground 83

SERMON IX.

Third Sunday after Trinity, 16th June, 1861.

FAMILY PRAYER.

1 SAMUEL II. 30.—Them that honour me I will honour . . . 95

SERMON X.

Fourth Sunday after Trinity, 23rd June, 1861.

WAYWARDNESS AND WISDOM.

ST LUKE VII. 35.—But wisdom is justified of all her children . . 107

SERMON XI.

Sixth Sunday after Trinity, 7th July, 1861.

FAITH TRIUMPHANT IN FAILURE.

ST LUKE V. 5.—Master, we have toiled all the night, and have taken nothing: nevertheless at Thy word I will let down the net 120

SERMON XII.

Tenth Sunday after Trinity, 4th August, 1861.

FRIENDS AND FOES.

1 KINGS XXI. 20.—Hast thou found me, O mine enemy? . . 135

SERMON XIII.

Eleventh Sunday after Trinity, 11th August, 1861.

GREAT THINGS AND SMALL.

2 KINGS V. 13.—My father, if the prophet had bid thee do some great thing, wouldest thou not have done it? how much rather then, when he saith to thee, Wash, and be clean? . . . 149

SERMON XIV.

Twelfth Sunday after Trinity, 18th August, 1861.

ZEAL WITHOUT CONSISTENCY.

2 KINGS X. 16, 31.—And he said, Come with me, and see my zeal for the Lord...But Jehu took no heed to walk in the law of the Lord God of Israel with all his heart 161

SERMON XV.

Thirteenth Sunday after Trinity, 25th August, 1861.

THE COMMANDMENT EXCEEDING BROAD.

PSALM CXIX. 96.—I have seen an end of all perfection: but Thy commandment is exceeding broad.
Or (Prayer-Book Version), I see that all things come to an end: but Thy commandment is exceeding broad 173

SERMON XVI.

Fourteenth Sunday after Trinity, 1st September, 1861.

THE GOSPEL AN INCENTIVE TO INDUSTRY IN BUSINESS.

PSALM I. 4.—His leaf also shall not wither: and look, whatsoever he doeth, it shall prosper 186

SERMON XVII.

Fourteenth Sunday after Trinity, 1st September, 1861.

THE KING UPON THE HILL OF ZION.

PSALM II. 6.—Yet have I set my King upon my holy hill of Zion . 199

SERMON XVIII.

Sixteenth Sunday after Trinity, 15th September, 1861.

THE FALL AND THE RISING.

ST LUKE XXII. 61, 62.—And the Lord turned, and looked upon Peter. And Peter remembered the word of the Lord, how He had said unto him, Before the cock crow, thou shalt deny me thrice. And Peter went out, and wept bitterly . . . 211

SERMON XIX.

Seventeenth Sunday after Trinity, 22nd September, 1861.

USE AND ABUSE OF THE WORLD.

1 CORINTHIANS VII. 31.—And they that use this world, as not abusing it 225

WORDS FROM THE GOSPELS.

SERMON I.
Second Sunday after Trinity, 9th June, 1861.
IGNORANT PRAYERS.

MARK X. 38.—Ye know not what ye ask 241

SERMON II.
Third Sunday after Trinity, 6th July, 1862.
CHRIST EATING WITH SINNERS.

LUKE XV. 2.—This man receiveth sinners, and eateth with them . 252

SERMON III.
Sixth Sunday after Trinity, 27th July, 1862.
GOSPEL RIGHTEOUSNESS.

MATTHEW V. 20.—Except your righteousness shall exceed the righteousness of the scribes and Pharisees, ye shall in no case enter into the kingdom of heaven 262

SERMON IV.
Seventh Sunday after Trinity, 3rd August, 1862.
FOUR THOUSAND MEN TO BE FED IN THE WILDERNESS.

MARK VIII. 4.—From whence can a man satisfy these men with bread here in the wilderness? 273

Contents.

SERMON V.

Ninth Sunday after Trinity, 17th August, 1862.

MISMANAGEMENT OF ETERNAL INTERESTS.

LUKE XVI. 8.—The children of this world are in their generation wiser than the children of light 284

SERMON VI.

Twelfth Sunday after Trinity, 7th September, 1862.

THE DIVINITY OF WORK.

JOHN V. 17.—My Father worketh hitherto, and I work . . . 295

SERMON VII.

Sixteenth Sunday after Trinity, 5th October, 1862.

THE GRADUAL MIRACLE.

MARK VIII. 24.—I see men as trees, walking 306

SERMON VIII.

Nineteenth Sunday after Trinity, 26th October, 1862.

THE GOSPEL A FIRE.

LUKE XII. 49.—I am come to send fire on the earth . . . 317

SERMON IX.

Second Sunday in Advent, 7th December, 1862.

THE UNCHANGEABLE WORDS.

LUKE XXI. 33.—Heaven and earth shall pass away: but my words shall not pass away 328

SERMON X.

Third Sunday in Advent, 14th December, 1862.

THE OFFENCE OF CHRIST.

MATTHEW XI. 6.—And blessed is he, whosoever shall not be offended in me 340

SERMON XI.

Fourth Sunday in Advent, 21st December, 1862.

THE VOICE CRYING IN THE WILDERNESS.

JOHN I. 23.—I am the voice of one crying in the wilderness, Make straight the way of the Lord 353

SERMON XII.

Second Sunday after Christmas, 4th January, 1863.

THE GRACE OF MEDITATION.

LUKE II. 19.—But Mary kept all these things, and pondered them in her heart 364

SERMON XIII.

First Sunday after the Epiphany, 11th January, 1863.

YEARS OF PREPARATION.

LUKE II. 49.—Wist ye not that I must be about my Father's business? 375

SERMON XIV.

Second Sunday after the Epiphany, 18th January, 1863.

OBEDIENCE THE CONDITION OF HELP.

JOHN II. 5.—Whatsoever He saith unto you, do it 386

SERMON XV.

Third Sunday after the Epiphany, 25th January, 1863.

FAITH THE MEASURE OF HELP.

MATTHEW VIII. 13.—As thou hast believed, so be it done unto thee 398

SERMON XVI.

Quinquagesima Sunday, 15th February, 1863.

VAGUE PRAYERS.

LUKE XVIII. 41.—What wilt thou that I shall do unto thee? . . 409

SERMON XVII.

Second Sunday in Lent, 1st March, 1863.

FAITH TRIUMPHANT OVER REFUSAL.

MATTHEW XV. 23.—But He answered her not a word . . . 419

SERMON XVIII.

Third Sunday in Lent, 8th March, 1863.

THE DUMB SPIRIT.

LUKE XI. 14.—Jesus was casting out a devil, and it was dumb. And it came to pass, when the devil was gone out, the dumb spake 430

SERMON XIX.

Easter Day, 5th April, 1863.

THE LIVING SOUGHT AMONG THE DEAD.

LUKE XXIV. 5.—Why seek ye the living among the dead? . . 441

SERMON XX.

Easter Day, 5th April, 1863.

THE CHRISTIAN DOUBTER.

MATTHEW XXVIII. 17.—But some doubted 450

SERMON XXI.

Whit Sunday, 24th May, 1863.

THE COMPANIONSHIP AND THE INDWELLING OF THE SPIRIT.

JOHN XIV. 17.—He dwelleth with you, and shall be in you . . 463

SERMON XXII.

Trinity Sunday, 31st May, 1863.

TRINITY IN UNITY.

JOHN III. 9.—How can these things be? 475

I.

THE TALEBEARER.

Proverbs xi. 13.

A talebearer revealeth secrets: but he that is of a faithful spirit concealeth the matter.

BY *thy words,* our Lord said, *thou shalt be justified, and by thy words thou shalt be condemned. Every idle word that men shall speak, they shall give account thereof in the day of judgment.* I need not add anything more to excuse my calling your attention this morning to the verse just read to you, taken as it is from one of the Lessons selected for the Service for this day.

There is a prejudice in men's minds against what are called moral Sermons. And no doubt there may be a moral Sermon which is unchristian, Christless, and therefore miserable food for a Christian congregation. But it need not be so. I have heard Sermons on single points of duty, which I could never afterwards forget; Sermons for which I shall be grateful to my dying day. And I would desire, my brethren, as one very high object of my own ministry among you, to speak to you now and then upon special particulars of Christian conduct; praying God to make such Sermons not the least but the most stirring of all that are delivered to you; fruitful in humility, fruitful in vigilance, fruitful in self-knowledge, and fruitful in charity.

The Book of Proverbs, which is just now furnishing us with our Sunday Lessons, is a portion of Holy Scripture abundant in wise precepts. It is a miscellaneous collection of sagacious remarks, by one who knew the human heart well, and had had much experience of human life in its brighter and in its darker phases, and who unhappily had had in his own history but too many warnings as to the power of temptation and the miserable consequences of sin. The knowledge which we possess of the personal life of king Solomon, of his early piety, his singular endowments, his magnificent beginning and his melancholy ending, adds greatly to the interest of his writings. And yet, if we had known nothing whatever of him but his writings, we could scarcely have failed to regard him as one of the wisest and one of the most remarkable of men. What lessons does this Book contain for young men and young women; for persons whose course lies fresh and open before them, and who have still to form their principles and to point their aim in life. What solemn, what touching appeals to them as to refusing the evil and choosing the good. What earnest exhortations to think of the end from the beginning, and so to take heed to their ways at the first, that they may have peace and hope at the last. And then what lessons for men of mature life. What a storehouse of wisdom and prudence for the man of business. What grave admonitions as to the necessity of uprightness; that one chief virtue of the tradesman, and the merchant, and the agent or manager for others. Those oft-repeated, and in their sound almost obsolete, maxims about the false weight and measure—alas, is there no room for that precept in the world of this day? *The bag of deceitful weights* which we heard of, a few Sundays ago, in the prophet Micah, does that need much translating, or much adaptation, in order to make it suitable to the circumstances of some of those who hear me? Is the trickery of trade, its short measure and its light weight, a thing altogether of a past century?

But now let me come closely to my chosen subject. The talebearer revealing secrets, and the faithful man concealing matters. I dare say we have all heard this verse read many times, and thought but little of it. May God give us an ear to hear it to-day inwardly.

A talebearer. One celebrated nation of antiquity used to express this man's character by a very significant figure. They called a tale-bearer a 'seed-picker.' They gave him the same name which they used for a bird which goes about everywhere picking up seeds. The poor bird does it for its own support and for that of its young. I wish we could say as much for the tale-bearer. And yet it is no exaggeration to say that there are men in the world who live by their seed-collecting; by going about here and there, from house to house, from street to street, through a town large or small, and gathering together all the little stories which can be told or made about the neighbours who are (as last Sunday's Lesson expressed it) *dwelling* all the time *securely by them*, and ignorant of the calumnies by which they are assailed.

Yes, the 'seed-collector,' the man who goes about gathering anecdotes, great and small, about his neighbours, and retailing them again as he goes, is a common character everywhere. I wish that I could hold up the mirror to him for his own conviction. I am sure he would be ashamed, I believe he would be sorry, if he saw himself faithfully pourtrayed. If we endeavour to do so, it is for his good, with a view to making him a better man, with a view to showing him a more excellent way, with a view to bringing him to the Cross for forgiveness, and to the Spirit of Christ for cleansing. It may be that the giving up of one fault will be in God's hand the very saving of his soul.

A talebearer revealeth secrets. Things which have been confided to him, too often: things which a misplaced trust has put into his possession: things which a conscience ill at ease has deposited with him for its own relief: these things are sometimes betrayed by those who should have known better. Or else things which ought to be secrets: things which, even if true, are better not repeated: things the repetition of which can do no good either to religion or morality: things which it is a shame even to speak of, and which are only done, if done at all, in secret. Or else things which really are secrets; secrets even to the person who repeats them, inasmuch as they are mere guesses, chance shots, arrows winged at a venture, assertions founded on a mere suspicion, suspicions founded on a mere imagination. Yes, all these are examples of what we may understand by 'secrets' here. These are the things which are every day in every place being revealed: if true, a veil which was but decent is being rudely stripped off from them: if half true, if based only on truth, if mixed with but a grain of truth, if a mere fabrication, still worse is it then: the 'revealing' is then, in part or in whole, an inventing: and heavy is the responsibility, great the criminality, of him who so reveals secrets as to create what he discloses. Hence strifes and divisions among you: hence bitter heartburnings: hence deep resentments: hence misery in families: hence discords and separations between chief friends: hence blasted characters and blighted lives. Yet the talebearer sees not the ruin: he has borne but a small part in it ostensibly: he only picked up his seed, and dropped it again; *it* found its congenial soil; it sprang and grew up he knew not how.

What a mischievous habit! you all exclaim. And yet, my brethren, the tendency is in all of us. Many motives go to make up a talebearer. His character is not so odious, apparently, in its beginnings. Perhaps he is a witty man. He has what is called a turn for satire. His insinuations have much point in them. He can intimate, rather than express, a scandal. His representations of character are pungent. His imitations, his caricatures, of manner and of speech, are irresistibly comic. In society he is the life of his company. You scarcely think, and he scarcely thinks, of the effect he is producing upon the good name of others. It is not till he is silent and departed—perhaps not even then—that you begin to feel that there has been virtually a talebearer among you, and that he has been revealing unkind secrets.

Or, again, he may be a man in whose own conscience there is a sore place. He knows something against himself. He is conscious of some lurking, some secret, some bosom sin. And it is a relief to him to hope that others are not so much better than himself. He finds a solace in his wretchedness in making company for his sin. None are so bitter in their taunts, none are so credulous in their suspicions, as those unhappy people who are on the look-out for society in their degradation. To believe that others are even as they, to throw out the hint that they have reason to think evil, is a momentary palliation of the sting of an accusing conscience.

And there are others who cannot bear superiors. They do not like superiors in station: but superiors in character they cannot brook. To hear another praised is to hear themselves blamed. Everything which is ascribed to another is felt as though taken from themselves. Up to their own level, they can bear to see another lifted: but, above that, it is pain and grief to them. Their only comfort is in a general disbelief of virtue. A ridiculous story to tell of the eminently good is to them as a draught of water to the thirsty. If no one else is quite so good, we ourselves may perhaps not be quite so bad.

Sometimes it goes yet beyond this. A story is told—and I have seen it applied in this very sense—of a tribe of savages who believe that the strength of a slain enemy passes into his conqueror. Every man who kills his foe is not only ridding himself of a danger, but also possessing himself of a virtue. The speed, or the sagacity, or the courage, or the unerring aim of the dead man, all becomes instantly the property and the endowment of the victor. Is it not sometimes thus with our depreciations one of another? Is it not with us, sometimes, not only the taking down of that which towers above us, but also the elevation of ourselves upon its ruins? A man is often seen to be as eager in running down the merit of another, his goodness or ability, his uprightness, or his wisdom, or his kindness, or his devotion, as if he thought, like the wild Indian of whom we have spoken, that the denial of this or that virtue to another would be its ascription to himself.

Thus it is that the talebearer is formed. These, and many more, are among the motives which impel him to his mission. He goes on his way revealing secrets. He calls it himself by a very different name. Agreeable conversation, a quick sense of the ridiculous, a ready humour, a good-natured pleasantry, innocent and certainly not uncharitable mirth—it is thus that he denominates that which Solomon calls by the far less honourable name of talebearing, that which one greater than Solomon terms a tissue of idle words to be given account of in the day of judgment.

My brethren, do not imagine that he who is addressing you is able to look down from a high eminence upon the follies or the sins of others. He is seeking rather to impress his own mind as well as yours with the importance of the warning on which we meditate together. And as we have been compelled to dwell for a time on the dark side of the picture, so now let us turn it in our hand and view that which is brighter and more attractive: as we have sought to express to ourselves the character of the talebearer who revealeth secrets, so now let us think for a few moments of his opposite: *he that is of a faithful spirit concealeth the matter.*

The matter. He does not say what matter. But we may understand it to include two things: that which has been entrusted to him in the secrecy of confidence, and that which has become known to him to another's disparagement.

We all think ill, or at least slightingly, of one who cannot keep a secret. There are such persons. There are those whom the possession of a secret frets and irritates beyond endurance. They can only relieve themselves by telling it. Such persons do much mischief. They do mischief sometimes by what they actually divulge. It is hard upon those who have trusted them, that they should be betrayed. Perhaps it is their fault for making a bad choice of their confidant. But the mischief goes further. It shakes men's confidence in confidence. People are afraid to trust any one. It has become so much a matter of experience that confidences are betrayed, that we are obliged to keep to ourselves secrets which it would be not only a great relief but a great blessing to us to be able to confide to another. There are ways, we all know, of violating confidence without actual treachery. Sometimes we hint a secret which we do not tell out. Sometimes we take just one other person into our confidence; tell him our friend's secret; and can we wonder if he in his turn tells it to just one other? We ought, for the sake of the general good, as well as for the sake of guarding against individual injury, to practise ourselves in keeping secrets. *He that is of a faithful spirit concealeth the matter.* We may dislike, we may discourage, as a general rule we may refuse, confidences: happy is he who is the depository of none: but, if a confidence is accepted, if it is even forced upon us, then let it be sacred. Nothing can excuse its violation. Difficult as it may sometimes be to reconcile it with speaking truth, to guard our brother's secret without sullying our own conscience with falsehood, this is just one of the many difficulties of life—this adjustment of apparently conflicting duties to our neighbour and to God—and we must pray for His help in surmounting it. *He that is of a faithful spirit concealeth* certainly *the matter* which has been entrusted to him.

This may sometimes be, as we have seen, a difficult thing to do: difficult, in the only sense in which a Christian may use that word; namely, when the demands of conscience are ambiguous; when two things, each by itself, are right, and when to combine the two is a matter of perplexity. But to fulfil the charge in its second sense ought not to be very difficult; namely, to conceal the matter which has come to our knowledge in disparagement of another. It sometimes happens to a man to be unable to resist the conviction that another person has done wrong, has committed a particular sin or been guilty of some flagrant inconsistency of life. We all know what the talebearer does on such an occasion; an occasion which ought to be felt so painfully. He has picked up his seed, and he cannot rest till he has dropped it into some new soil. Whatever he may profess, or however he may flatter himself, the possession of this knowledge is to him not altogether painful. Whereas *charity rejoiceth not in iniquity, but rejoiceth with the truth;* is glad, not when another has sinned, but when another has either risen or stood upright; he, on the contrary, finds in every fall of another a rising of his own, and cannot rest till he has made his own knowledge the common property of his neighbourhood. I am not speaking here of those who, being set in places of public trust, make themselves *partakers of other men's sins* by the very fact of hiding them: there are cases in which discovery and even punishment are duties, and in which he who screens the sinner sins himself. But I am speaking of private life; of disclosures of fault or sin made, not reluctantly, for the purpose of cleansing away sin, but voluntarily, for the sake of divulging it to those whom it does not officially or practically concern. Of such disclosures, I say that they belong to the talebearer and not to the man of a faithful spirit. In such cases, he that is of a faithful spirit will conceal the matter. He will purpose, he will resolve, he will watch and pray, to do so. If he finds himself on the point of telling that which would be to another's injury, he will check himself by a strong effort of will and of duty ere the sentence has passed the door of his lips. He will gather strength, in doing so, to do so again. He will form the habit of *keeping his tongue as it were with a bridle* while they are present to whom his words would do injury by encouraging the present to despise or to condemn the absent.

My brethren, I cannot close my Sermon without expressing to you with all my power my sense of the importance of the subject. If we could only part for ever with the disposition of the talebearer, we should have parted with that which, more than anything else, confuses and perplexes and embitters human life. How peaceable should we be, if there were no talebearers amongst us; but, let me rather say—for it is the more profitable and the more Christian way of expressing it— if there were not within each of our hearts so much of the spirit of the talebearer. It is the crying sin of social life. We cannot meet for half an hour's friendly converse without taking away one or two characters. Of us, in reference to speech at least, the words of the wise man are too true, *They sleep not, except they have done mischief; and their sleep is taken away, unless they cause some to fall.* God give us all a better wisdom. Let us store our minds with things valuable, and meet one another to give out what we have first taken in. Let us talk less of persons. Constituted as fallen nature is, if we speak of persons, we shall be sure to speak ill of persons. If we must talk so much of persons, let us practise ourselves in speaking well of them. Let us see their good side when we can: and, when we cannot but see the evil, then let us go on our way and be silent about it. Above all—for here lies the root of almost every Christian grace—let us know ourselves a little better. Let us enter into judgment with our own hearts, and compare our own lives, outward and inward, with the standard of God's will and of Christ's example. I believe that, if we did this more, we should have little heart for scandal or for slander. We should be stopped, as by an audible voice within, when we were opening our lips to censure or to malign. It is the want of self-knowledge which makes us so keensighted. It is the want of acquaintance with Christ, as our Propitiation first, and then as our Example, which makes it possible for us to sit in the tribunal of judgment. O let us think what we are; let us call to remembrance our own sins, our own foolish, perverse, wilful, presumptuous sins, our own ingratitude to Christ, our own rebellion against God, our own hairbreadth escapes and our own shameful falls—O let us think what Christ is to us and has been; how gentle, how patient, how longsuffering, how forgiving, how slow to punish, how swift to bless—and well do I know that we shall have no heart left for triumphing over another, no pleasure in hearing of another's defeat, no sense of self-satisfaction in looking upon another's sin.

TWENTY-THIRD SUNDAY AFTER TRINITY,
November 11, 1860.

II.

THE INNOCENTS' DAY.

Psalm viii. 2.

Out of the mouth of babes and sucklings hast thou ordained strength because of Thine enemies, that Thou mightest still the enemy and the avenger.

THE special observance of the Innocents' Day in our Parish Church dates from the year 1675, when a small bequest was left, by the will of a resident in this Town, to secure its perpetual remembrance by an annual Sermon. I know not what particular circumstance may have led to the selection of this day from among so many preceding or following it, which might have seemed to possess a stronger claim to notice. It may have been—though I know not that it was the case— that some family event, the early loss of a child or grandchild, awakening a peculiar interest in the thought of the death of infants, guided the pious founder to the choice of the day on which we are assembled. At all events, for a period of almost two whole centuries, that will has been in force, and it has been the duty of those who have preceded me in this sacred office, as it has now become my duty, to use the festival commemorative of the massacre of the young children of Bethlehem as an opportunity of instruction and exhortation to so many of the people of this place as the call of local custom shall have succeeded in drawing together to hear and to worship. I have hoped that the selection for the first time of an evening instead of a morning hour, may enable a somewhat larger body of worshippers to avail themselves of this opportunity of edification.

All must have been struck, some perhaps perplexed, by the choice and arrangement of those Church festivals which follow immediately upon Christmas Day. There is no very obvious connexion between Christmas Day and the martyrdom of St Stephen; between the martyrdom of St Stephen and the life (protracted to extreme old age and to a peaceful end) of the great Apostle and Evangelist St John; between the commemoration of St John the Evangelist and the record of the cruel and untimely fate of the young children slain for Christ's sake at Bethlehem by the bloodthirsty king Herod. Various reasons have been discovered for this arrangement. Some have seen in the three days of which this is the last, the commemoration of three kinds of martyrdom; St Stephen's, a martyrdom both in will and deed; St John's, a martyrdom in will but not in deed; that of the Innocents, a martyrdom in deed not in will. They have seen in close attendance upon the feast of the Nativity the names of those who in different senses gave their very lives for Him who was then manifested in the flesh; those who may be conceived of as standing very near His throne in heaven, one for his martyrdom, another for his love, the third for their innocence; constituting in a manner the very first fruits of that work of redemption which the festival of Christmas presents to us in its marvellous origin and in its most comprehensive aspect.

There is perhaps something of fancy in all this. Perhaps we need not search very deeply for reasons why these three festivals, and not three others, or four or five others, should follow so closely in the wake of Christmas. Accident may have had its share in it, as well as design; more especially as, I believe, there was a difference of date in the institution of the three festivals; St John's Day having been consecrated at a later time than St Stephen's, and the Innocents' Day having been originally associated, not with Christmas, but with the Epiphany. Reasons may be found for many things afterwards, which had no share in causing them.

Our business now is with one only of these three days; that which commemorates the fact recorded in the second Chapter of St Matthew's Gospel; namely, that, when king Herod found that the wise men who had come from the East, under the guidance of the star, to enquire for the birthplace of the infant King of the Jews, had departed into their own country another way, instead of exposing themselves, and the young child also, to the risks of his rage and malice, he sent forth and slew all the children that were in Bethlehem and in all the coasts thereof, from two years old and under, that he might be quite sure to include amongst them Him whose rising power he ignorantly feared. A cruel and shameful, as well as impotent, endeavour: but what was there here, we might ask, which could either entitle these little children to a place in a Calendar of Christian saints, or furnish us with any spiritual lesson, beyond, indeed, that new proof which is here afforded of the folly as well as wickedness of presuming to fight against God? Jesus was already by God's providence withdrawn into Egypt, when the terrible decree went forth for that indiscriminate and barbarous slaughter.

We must look for our answer to these questions to the Services appointed for the day. In particular, we shall turn to the Collect for the day; in which we shall find (as the name itself perhaps implies) the doctrine and principal instruction of the occasion collected into a brief and comprehensive form, and made the subject of direct prayer to God through His Son Jesus Christ.

The older form of the Collect for the Innocents' Day was to this effect:

O God, whose praise this day the young innocents Thy witnesses have confessed and showed forth, not in speaking, but in dying: mortify and kill all vices in us, that in our conversation (conduct) our life may express Thy faith, which with our tongues we do confess; through Jesus Christ our Lord.

At the last Revision of our Liturgy, in the year 1661, the Collect assumed its present form:

O Almighty God, who out of the mouths of babes and sucklings hast ordained strength—quoting from the 8th Psalm the verse read as the text—*and madest infants to glorify Thee by their deaths;* didst by Thy permitting and overruling Providence bring it to pass that even little children should give their lives unconsciously in behalf of Thy Son, satisfying that fury of the oppressor which would else have sought far and wide for its intended victim, and giving him to imagine that in that slaughter of the innocent he had actually cut off Him whose life he sought; *mortify and kill all vices in us, and so strengthen us by Thy grace, that by the innocency of our lives, and constancy of our faith even unto death, we may glorify Thy holy name*, that is, may show forth what Thou art, *through Jesus Christ our Lord. Amen.*

My brethren, the Innocents' Day is practically the commemoration of departed children. It is the festival which we keep in remembrance of all who have died in infancy; taking as their sample and firstfruits the martyred children of Bethlehem. It is the festival on which we recount God's teaching by children; showing forth what we know, from Scripture and from experience, of their possible effects, by word and act and suffering, upon the hearts of men; treasuring up the memory of all those who have safely died in the arms of Christ's redeeming love even before they knew or could understand it; asserting the same hope which the Church entertains and expresses concerning them, that *children who are baptized, dying before they commit actual sin, are undoubtedly saved;* and, for ourselves, deeply pondering the lessons which the thought of them ought to teach us, that we, following their example in the points in which it is so distinctly instructive, may inherit the blessing of Him who said, *Except ye be converted, and become as little children, ye cannot enter into the kingdom of God.* The young children of Bethlehem were a type of redeemed children in every age of the Church; and of the whole body and Church of redeemed children as it now is, or hereafter shall be, safely housed in heaven.

This then is a festival which recommends itself very strongly to what I may almost call our Christian instincts, and which ought to be especially dear to all those Christian parents who are either now fostering the infancy of their little ones, or have already laid it to rest in Jesus in the sure and certain hope of a future glorious resurrection.

Out of the mouth of babes and sucklings hast Thou ordained strength because of Thine enemies, that Thou mightest still the enemy and the avenger. Thus wrote the inspired Psalmist in days before the Gospel; and One greater than he quoted the passage, on an occasion towards the close of His earthly life, described by St Matthew in these words: *And when the chief priests and scribes saw the wonderful things that He did, and the children crying in the temple, and saying, Hosanna to the Son of David! they were sore displeased, and said unto Him, Hearest thou what these say? And Jesus saith unto them, Yea; have ye never read, Out of the mouth of babes and sucklings Thou hast perfected praise?* The love of Jesus for little children was indeed, as we all know, strongly marked during His ministry. It is not without reason that the stress of Scripture proof with reference to the Baptism of Infants is thrown by our Prayer-Book upon that most elementary yet most significant of all intimations, His receiving the little children that were brought to Him, taking them up in His arms, putting His hands upon them, and blessing them. He who once did this, and who also took a little child as the one specimen of those who shall be greatest in His kingdom, may well be trusted, now that He is gone away from us, with the spiritual and eternal charge of those little ones who are dedicated to Him in His own ordinance of Baptism; yes, and with the charge also of those little ones who have early passed from a world of sin and sorrow into the dwelling-place of peace and love.

In proportion as we more learn of little children, we rise higher, our Lord Himself teaches us, in the scale of His heavenly kingdom. What then are some of the ways in which we should learn of them? In what respects do they teach a lesson of Christian wisdom to older men?

1. The Collect for this day shall be heard first, in answer to this question. It says that little children teach us a lesson of innocence. *Mortify and kill all vices in us, and so strengthen us by Thy grace, that by the innocency of our lives, &c.* And so the Baptismal Service, commenting upon the passage already referred to, reminds us how Christ *exhorteth all men to follow their innocency.* We need not shrink from the expression. Innocence, freedom from hurting, from harming, from wrong-doing, is the blessed attribute, even since the Fall, of little children. They inherit a fallen and corrupt nature; but Christ has taken away the guilt of it by His redemption, and they cannot yet choose the evil, or act the evil, for themselves. They are in a happy pause, a blessed interval, could it but continue; washed from original sin, and not yet involved in actual sin; cleansed once, and not yet defiled; safe from the old Adam in the new, and not yet, of their own freewill, going back from the freedom of the latter into the bondage of the former. Who that has grown up even to boyhood, much more to middle or advanced age, may not well envy, may not earnestly pray to recover, the innocence of the little child? True, there is a higher

state than innocence; that of a tried and disciplined godliness: innocence regained is a more glorious attainment than innocence not lost; the position of the young man in Christ, who has overcome the wicked one, than the position of the babe in years, who has never yet been called to encounter him. But innocence not yet lost is a better state than sin, than committed transgression, than forfeited integrity, than stained and sullied purity. If you would shame a young man walking in the way of his own heart in the indulgence of vanity and lust, bring him face to face with a little child: let him look on that clear eye, on that open brow; let him listen to that simple prattling tongue; and, depend upon it, if he be not utterly hardened, there will stir within him, unavowed but not unfelt, the breathing of regret and sorrow, if not of godly repentance, as he looks on this picture and on that; here on the spectacle of what he is, and there on the spectacle of what he was. It is something to be taught, however late, the lesson of innocence; the desire to regain if it were but the vestige of that state in which no wrong has yet been done to the soul or the body of another, no affront consciously offered to the holiness of God, to the blood of Christ, to the grace of the Spirit.

2. There is another lesson never so taught as by a child; the lesson of simplicity. In a very little child there is no guile, no artifice, no affectation, no self-consciousness. What he is, he seems: what he seems, he is. His real wishes are those which he expresses. He does not say one thing and mean another. He does not seek to gain unavowed ends by crooked and circuitous means. His wants are few, and what he

wants he cries out for. Simplicity is in many cases the first thing *lost* by a child; before purity, before innocence. Self-consciousness soon comes in, in some natures, and spoils the whole beauty of the first creation. But this only marks simplicity yet more strongly as the peculiar possession of the little child. Some retain it long, others lose it early; some regain it afterwards, some part with it for ever: but, none the less, in every case, simplicity is the virtue of the very young child.

Simplicity. What a grace. How beautiful, how attractive—yet ceasing to attract the very moment that it desires it. O how far are most of us gone from it. The poor sometimes, to our eye, show it wonderfully: but it is not so with all even of them: they too have their guile, though it is not the same precisely, in its workings, with our own: they too have oftentimes things which they feign, and things which they dissemble: they too have oftentimes unavowed objects to gain, and they seek those objects by crooked means. But in other stations of life how rare, how extremely rare, is a perfect candour, a true simplicity; not degenerating, as we sometimes see it, into rudeness, into harshness, into faultfinding, into disregard of feelings, but kind and gentle as its Author, sincere in every profession, and straightforward in every act and purpose.

3. There is yet another lesson taught us by the little child; and that is a lesson of trust. Our Lord tells us that God has hidden His truth from the wise and prudent, and has revealed it unto babes; to those, that is, who are like little children in this respect, that they receive with affiance and faith that which one older and wiser than themselves communicates. A little child

is no arguer, no caviller: it has an instinctive reliance upon the truth and love of its parents, and never suspects that they would mislead, deceive, or betray. It is a cruel mockery to tell a young child that which is deceptive. It is painful and shocking to see the faith, the credulity if you will, of a child, trifled with. That first dawning suspicion in a child's mind of the truthfulness of an informant, who has gravely asserted something which he does not intend to be accepted as a fact, is no pleasing spectacle to a right-minded observer, though it is but the commencement of an experience which that child must afterwards complete painfully amidst the thousand lies and deceits of the world into which, if he lives, he must enter.

It was said of simplicity that it is that virtue which a child oftentimes first loses: we may say of trust, of credulity, that it is generally the longest kept, the last forfeited. It is not indeed till a little later than the age of infancy that it can be said, in this form, to be brought into exercise. The little child—like those of Bethlehem —*of two years old and under*, has little receptive faith to practise. Still it is in him a quality, if not exercised, only dormant: it is there—in him above all—only waiting for the touch which is to awaken it.

And is not this a quality which we all greatly need to learn from him? this simple trust in One wiser and better than ourselves? Is not this the history of all error in Christian doctrine, that we have parted with the character of little children; have set up for ourselves as wise and prudent, and therefore must see to ourselves altogether, apart from Him who is our Wisdom as well as our Righteousness?

4. I will add one other quality of the little child; and it is closely connected with the last-named: the quality of submission. The last was submission of the mind; this is submission of the will. The Collect prays, *that, by the constancy of our faith even unto death, we may glorify Thy Holy Name.* It regards the little children of Bethlehem as examples, though involuntary and unconscious examples, of this sort of submission. God's Providence, overruling a cruel decree, accepted, as it were, the sacrifice of those young lives as glorifying Him in His Son Jesus Christ.

And is not this sort of submission one of the special characteristics of the little child? He is in the hands of one who was the instrument of his very being. He lies passive in those hands. Food or medicine, rest or exercise—nay, God's own ordinances of day and night, cold and heat, summer and winter—are all ministered to him through another, and to resist the appointments of that other would be for him not unreasonable only but impossible. The little children of Bethlehem were obliged to give their young lives to the executioner: the power of resistance is the endowment of a later age: they are at another's mercy, and whithersoever he will he may carry them.

My brethren, our prayer is, that, what a little child is in the hands of its parents—what those little children were in the hands of an absolute king—that we may learn to be in the hands of God. *Even unto death:* that is the limit of our submission. He who gives his life gives all. In God's hands: yes, that is our proper place: and, let me add, that is our place of safety, and that is our place of happiness, and that is our place of dignity. To be in God's hands absolutely, is the glory of God's creatures. Christ came to bring us back into those hands; no longer as the hands of a ruler only, but as the hands of a parent too; of One who gave us being, and who desires only our good. What He gives, we will receive: what He denies, we will forego: what He takes away, we will part with. While He bids, we will stay here: when He bids, we will go hence. Ours shall be the mind, ours the life, of the little child, who subjects himself in all things to another and a wiser will, and out of whose mouth, in the language of a perfectly resigned and submissive heart, God evermore ordains strength and perfects praise. Thus it is that He stills the enemy and the avenger. By the faith of His little children, He puts to silence the ignorance and the hostility of foolish men. Men marvel at them, and, in spite of themselves, sometimes enquire the secret of their constancy. Then they hear that it is because Christ lives that they live also. Then they understand the meaning of the inspired words, *Persecuted, but not forsaken; cast down, but not destroyed: always bearing about in the body the dying of the Lord Jesus, that the life also of Jesus might be made manifest in our body.* His strength is made perfect in their weakness: insomuch that the words are daily verified, *When I am weak, then am I strong.*

THE INNOCENTS' DAY,
Friday, December 28, 1860.

III.

THE DISREGARDED AND THE ACCEPTED OFFERING.

Genesis iv. 4, 5.

And the Lord had respect unto Abel and to his offering: but unto Cain and to his offering He had not respect.

THERE are two things which distinguish the Bible from every other book; even from some of those books which profess to derive their teaching from the Bible. Two things, which, when all the arguments which infidelity can bring against the Bible have been exhausted, will still stand their ground, vindicating for it everything which is really included in the term Inspiration, and making it in its completeness—the Old Testament and the New Testament together—the great storehouse for ever of human wisdom and of human hope. These two things are—if only two must be spoken of—the view given us in the Bible of man, and the view given us in the Bible of God. The one so human, the other so Divine. The one so exactly consistent with what we ourselves see of man, the other so exactly consistent with what we ourselves should expect in God; in other words, with what our own conscience, which is God's voice within, recognizes as worthy of God, and ratifies where it could not have originated.

The explanation and enforcement of this general remark might of itself fill my Sermon. But for to-day it must suffice to ask you to apply the remark itself to the brief and familiar narrative from which the text is taken.

With what rapid strides does the history of the world advance through these first chapters of the Book of Genesis. What a wisdom shines in the brevity. What an indication of the purpose with which God sends His Word; not to gratify curiosity; not to anticipate and not to stifle science; not to supersede human labour and not to indulge human speculation; but simply to instruct man in the things which he could not find out for certain without God; just to give the great leading strokes which it needs a master hand to put in, and then to leave him to fill them up, for himself, yet under their sure direction, with the lesser lines of reflection, of inference, of application, and of experience. The Creation, and then the Fall, and then the reign of sin unto death —these are the real primeval records, and they have their confirmation in everything that we see around us and in everything that we feel within.

We might have thought that, if sin did enter, it would enter by slow degrees. We might have expected that, for some few generations at least, there might have been a lurking alienation of heart from God, a growing reluctance or indifference to worship, and a diminution of natural kindness on the part of men one towards another, without any violent or fatal outbreak of the very worst passions of a tainted and corrupted nature. But no: the first paragraph which follows the history of the Fall is the history of a murder, the murder of a brother by his own mother's son. Surely this is instructive: it tells us how man's only safeguard—literally his only safeguard—is in God: it tells us how near we are to the very worst crimes: it tells us how acts, of which, on their first hearing, we should exclaim, *Is thy servant a dog that he should do this thing?* may yet, under altered circumstances, be not only possible to us but easy; meditated and done and even slept upon; thought of afterwards, not only without true repentance, but even without remorse and horror. I repeat it, there is no safety for any one of us but in God; in His constant upholding, sought of Him by constant prayer. There may be some young man, or some child, in this congregation, little aware of the career opening before him, little aware how soon the relaxation of Christian habits may be followed in his case by sin and shame, by crime and punishment; little aware how short is the step from quitting God's presence into openly defying Him, from losing the light of love within to trampling upon it in some fearful deed without. Let us run back into our one refuge, if we have quitted it; the refuge of God's fatherly hand, of Christ's patient love, of the Holy Spirit's quickening and protecting grace.

And now we will approach somewhat more closely to the historical fact before us, and seek by God's blessing to draw from the text one or two thoughts suitable and profitable to ourselves.

The Lord had respect unto Abel and to his offering: but unto Cain and to his offering He had not respect. Whence this distinction? Each of these worshippers brought an offering suitable to his occupation. Cain was a tiller of the ground: it was of the fruit of the ground that he brought his oblation. Abel was a keeper of sheep: and he brought of the firstlings of his flock and of the fat thereof. Was there anything in the material of the two offerings, which made the one acceptable and the other offensive? Have we any right to say this, apart from the express language of Scripture? any right to say, as some have said, that by bringing an animal in sacrifice Abel showed a clear perception of the true way of atonement, and that by bringing of the fruits of the earth Cain proved himself a self-justifier, a despiser of propitiation—proved himself, as some one has strongly expressed it, *the first Deist?* I think that in all this we are somewhat in danger of adding presumptuously to the record of Scripture. We are nowhere told that worship by sacrifice was a primeval ordinance of God. If God enjoined it upon our first parents; if He even intimated to them (as some have imagined) by the *coats of skins* with which He clothed them, that the sacrifice of animal victims was the acceptable mode of approaching Him; then indeed the offering of Abel was in itself an act of obedience, and the offering of Cain, in its very form, a proof of presumption. We must be contented to leave this part of the enquiry where the Word of God has left it. In the absence of express guidance there, we dare not assert with confidence that it was in the material of the two offerings that God saw the presence or the absence of an acceptable principle. In proportion as we lay the stress of the difference more upon the spirit and less upon the form of the sacrifice, we shall be more certainly warranted by the inspired Word, and more immediately within the reach of its application to ourselves.

We read in the Epistle to the Hebrews the following description of the offering of Abel. *By faith Abel offered unto God a more acceptable sacrifice than Cain, by which he obtained witness that he was righteous, God testifying of his gifts: and by it he being dead yet speaketh;* not only at the time of his death, when the accusing voice of his blood cried unto God from the ground on which it had fallen, but still—still after many centuries —testifying to the one distinguishing principle and the one supporting hope in which God's people from the very beginning have all been one. It was by faith that Abel offered a more acceptable sacrifice than Cain. It was because of the presence of faith in Abel that God had respect unto him and to his offering. It was because of the absence of faith in Cain that to him and to his offering God had not respect. Here we are upon sure ground. Here we are speaking only where God, and so far as God, has spoken first. God saw in Abel a spirit of faith: and in Cain God did not see a spirit of faith. Therefore Cain and Abel were our examples, not by a forced or a remote application, but by a direct and immediate likeness. The test to which they were brought, all those ages ago, is the very test to which we are all subjected. We too bring offerings. Every age and every land has tried to do so. The heart of man in its furthest estrangement is conscious that God has a claim upon His creatures; and, if it were only to pacify conscience, something must be brought and something must be done to satisfy this claim. We cannot live without worship. At least, it takes a long time, and many struggles—yes, struggles —as many struggles, almost, as, if properly directed, would make a man a Christian—to enable any one of us to live without God and not be fearful of the consequences. Therefore most of us offer something. A daily form of prayer, however brief and hurried; a weekly attendance here, however spiritless and perfunctory; all of us give this: it is our offering. Cain brought his offering as well as Abel: Judas brought his offering as well as John: we bring ours. And there is no fault, perhaps, to be found with the nature, with the material, of the offering. We are not sure that there was any fault of this kind in Cain's offering. We dare not say for certain that, when Cain brought his basket of fruit or his sheaf of corn to present it before the Lord, it was a sin in him not to have begged or bought one of Abel's sheep, that so the sacrifice might be one of a typical life's blood, and not of mere gratitude or mere self-denial. Certainly in *our* offering there is nothing wrong externally. God is a Spirit: and they who worship God now must worship Him as a Spirit; worship Him with spiritual offerings, not with gifts either of natural produce or of sacrificial blood. The human tongue, with its divers utterances of praise and supplication, is the instrument by which we must worship; and we have brought no other. Or, if another, if in one single instance, as on this day, we do bring, besides, a little offering of a visible oblation; if, kneeling at that table, we do, in that one service, ask God to accept, not our alms only for His poor, but also our oblations—His creatures, as it is afterwards said, of bread and wine, to be eaten and drunk in His presence; yet is this in obedience to an express command of our Saviour Christ, who instituted this as a perpetual commemoration of His precious death for sin, to be continued until His coming again. Here too, here above all, none can find fault with the material of our offering: here therefore again we have to look at the instructive example proposed for us in the text, to see whether in any sense it can be hoped or feared, with respect to different members of this congregation, that God has respect to one of us and to his offering, but to another and to his offering He has not respect.

It was by faith that Abel offered to God, and it was by want of faith that Cain failed to offer to God, an acceptable sacrifice. And so it is now. The bodies of us all are here: and the right sounds issue from our lips; right sounds, and the same from all: what then can be wanting? Why is the worship of one accepted, and the worship of another disregarded? Why? Because one has faith, and another has no faith. And what is faith? *Faith is*, as the Chapter just referred to tells us, *the substance of things hoped for, the evidence of things not seen.* Faith is, the looking not at the things which are seen, but at the things which are not seen. Faith is a spiritual sight of things spiritual; let us rather say, of Him who is invisible and eternal. In daily life, faith is the setting God always before us; the walking before God; the doing and saying and thinking all things as in His presence; the having Him more powerfully present to us than the attractions or the temptations or the provocations of things below; the being able to say, and to act upon the resolution,

This will I do, for I fear God; and again, *How can I do this wickedness and sin against God?* More especially is it, the consciousness of Christ; the being assured, the remembering, and loving to remember, Him who died for us, and rose again; and the actual endeavour to set our affections on things above, where He sitteth at the right hand of God. This, carried into its consequences, is the daily life of faith.

And now what is it in worship? How does faith enable, or the want of faith forbid, a man to offer an acceptable offering? How was it that Abel offered? how was it that Cain did not offer? Surely, the worship of faith is the concentrated energy of the life of faith. In worship a man who has faith is not only remembering God as a check upon sin, or as a motive to diligence, or as an encouragement to hope, or as a stimulus to watchfulness; not only thinking of Christ as One who is, and is all-powerful to help, and all-sufficient to make reconciliation, and longsuffering to our infirmities and our backslidings; but also, making application to Him as such; entering into His presence as such; communing and interceding with Him as such; making use of his sonship and of his redemption; gaining new supplies of grace and strength, from Him whom he knows as his Father, through Him whom he knows as his Redeemer and as his High-Priest in heaven. This is faith as exercised in worship. Where God sees this, there He has respect to our offering: where God sees not this, to that person and to his offering He has not respect.

My brethren, this suggests a very serious question. It is right that we should come hither, as on this day, to praise and to ask of God: but it is not certain that in so doing we are doing more than Cain did: he brought of the produce of his ground, and stood before God with it as a worshipper and as an offerer. Yet to him and to his offering God had not respect, because he offered not in faith. He did not realize God's presence as his Creator, his Benefactor, his Owner, and his God. He did not feel towards God, as a creature, owing everything to Him, ought to have felt. His worship was a mere homage, empty and ceremonial: and God, who looks on the heart, saw in it nothing. He had no respect to the offering: He could not regard it as having any value or any meaning. And Cain was angry at this: not penitent, not ashamed, not sorry: he did not pray and struggle for a better mind: he was very wroth, and his countenance fell. O what a picture of the natural man in all times. The disregarded, the refused, the unrespected worshipper, goes away angry: he never sees the cause of the refusal in himself: he never admits that the reason of his rejection lay in the worldliness, or the sinfulness, or the unbelief, of his own spirit: no, he thinks it hard that he should have humbled himself to worship, and not been noticed; that he should have taken the trouble to kneel and to respond, and God did not regard him. *He was very wroth, and his countenance fell.* O, my brethren, let us learn a better lesson from the truth before us. Let us acknowledge that without faith it is impossible to please God, unreasonable to expect to please Him. He that cometh to God must believe that He is, and must approach Him in the one way which He has marked out.

And how shall we know whether God has respect to us and to our offering? How shall we know, each one of us, as we kneel this morning at Christ's holy Table, whether we, we personally, are among the regarded or the unregarded worshippers? Cain knew it, we may suppose, by the absence of the heavenly fire which consumed his brother's sacrifice. When Abel offered, the flame of God fell, and consumed the offering; attested the faith of the suppliant, and crowned it with a visible acceptance. When Cain offered, all was still: the fruit or the grain lay there upon the earth-built altar; lay, and was disregarded: the worshipper himself might fetch it away: He to whom it was nominally presented did not want, did not notice, did not care for it. These signals are of the past. The fire of God is now, like His sacrifice, spiritual: it is only in the heart within that the one is presented or that the other is vouchsafed. Yet is there such a thing as a sense of acceptance; such a thing as the Spirit of God witnessing with our spirit that we are His sons; a comfort of love, and a confidence of communion, to testify that we are heard, and to send us on our way rejoicing. These things may still be looked for, and expected, and prayed for, in our worship: if we have no consciousness of being heard, none ever, we have reason to enter into judgment with ourselves as to the cause of this want: may there not be some secret thing kept back from the Lord, or some attempt to mix together heaven and the world, or some culpable remissness and carelessness in worship, interfering with the brightness and with the directness of the spiritual vision? These things we may fear: these things should be looked into: lest perhaps our worship itself should be nugatory, lest our very prayers should be turned into sin. But, after all, the proof of acceptance lies yet more decisively in the after than in the present results: do we, when we go hence, find ourselves, if not comforted, yet at least strengthened? do we find that we have received something of real help against sin; something which has made us more successful in realizing to ourselves God and Christ, more earnest to fight the good fight of faith, or more loving in our spirit towards those who thwart us, or try us, or provoke? If we have this, we can almost dispense with the other: strength is better than comfort: at all events we can wait God's time for His comfort, if He only gives us His strength: he who finds himself a little more earnest, a little more serious, a little more consistent, in consequence of worship, can afford to endure patiently the delay of a bright hope or a positive assurance.

And yet, why not both these things? Why not both comfort and strength? Surely *the Lord's hand is not shortened, that it cannot save; nor His ear heavy, that it cannot hear. Ask, and ye shall have: knock, and it shall be opened.*

SEXAGESIMA SUNDAY,
February 3, 1861.

IV.

FEATURES OF CHARITY.

1 Corinthians xiii. 5.

Charity doth not behave itself unseemly, seeketh not her own, is not easily provoked, thinketh no evil.

WE enter this week upon a season of humiliation. Our thoughts are to be turned to the special subject of sin and repentance. Is it quite by chance that the Epistle for the preceding Sunday is the 13th Chapter of St Paul's First Epistle to the Corinthians? Or is there not something, in this choice, of preparation, designed preparation, for the special work of Lent?

I do not suppose that there is one of us who can listen unmoved to the description of charity, or Christian love, as it is here set before us by St Paul. And when we see the importance which he, under the guidance of the Holy Spirit, attached to this particular grace; when we hear him say that all spiritual gifts are valueless without it; when we hear him say that prophecy is nothing, and knowledge is nothing, and faith itself is nothing, without charity; when we hear him say that even self-denial, self-devotion, and self-sacrifice for the good of others, is nothing, unless there be also in the heart, as the motive of all, the spirit of a living charity; then surely the thought must press upon us very heavily, what is charity? and, have I charity? have I that particular grace or fruit of the Spirit, which is something distinct from faith, distinct from piety, distinct even from almsgiving and from the service of the poor? have I, in my heart and in my life, *that most excellent gift of charity, without which whosoever liveth is counted dead before God?* Thus we are led, first to the searching of the Scriptures, and then to the examination of ourselves: and I am much mistaken if the result of this process will not be to awaken anxiety and even alarm, lest perhaps, after a long profession of faith, after *doing many things and hearing gladly*, we be found destitute of the one Christian characteristic, in the day when God shall judge the secrets of men by Jesus Christ.

I have selected for consideration this morning just one verse of the Chapter, containing four brief clauses. Each of these clauses adds one feature to the portraiture of charity. We shall look at each separately.

1. First, *charity doth not behave itself unseemly.* The expression in the original is still shorter. Its first meaning is this: *is not shapeless, is not misshapen, is not indecorous, rude, or unmannerly.* A strange element, we might think, in the composition of charity. Not indecorous, not rude or unmannerly—what has that to do with charity? Reflect a little, and you will perceive that this also is no small thing to mention, and that it bears very directly upon the grace spoken of.

In this, as in other cases, we see a thing best by its opposite. Have we ever noticed such a thing as indecorum, unmannerliness, rudeness, in persons claiming to be Christians? Yes, it is sometimes made a part of religion so to be. There are those who make what they call faithfulness the one virtue. They are so fearful of disguising their own convictions, and so fearful of encouraging carelessness or false security in others, that they run into an opposite extreme, and would obtrude upon the notice of every passer-by those truths or those feelings of which the whole value is in their depth and in their humility. It may be that there are some to whom God has given a peculiar power of startling others into conviction by a mode of presenting His truths which on other lips would be simply offensive and repulsive. There may be such persons, and He who has peculiarly endowed may peculiarly bless. But for others, for Christian persons generally, it is not safe to forget the special warning which Christ has given (in His own emphatic figure) against *casting pearls before swine*, or the remarkable feature here presented to us by this Apostle in the delineation of the grace of charity, that it is never unmannerly. To ask a stranger, casually and suddenly, whether he is a converted man, whether he has the love of Christ in his heart, whether he is on his way to heaven or hell, &c., is the language of impertinence rather than of duty, with regard to which the words of the text may warn us that true charity doeth not so; knowing that, for one person driven by these rough means into the path of peace, many will rather be diverted and deterred from a religion so indifferent to the rules of propriety and of good taste.

True Christian charity is deeply concerned about the souls of men, and would count no labour and no sacrifice too great if she might but save one. But charity is not rudeness, not impertinence, not self-sufficiency, and not arrogance. One part of charity is courtesy. And, depend upon it, courtesy, which is consideration for the feelings of others, will in the long run win more souls to Christ than rudeness. Where we are sure that courtesy is genuine; not timidity, not time-serving, not a mere wish to please, but a delicacy of perception and a tenderness of feeling; there nothing is so attractive; attractive, not only in the sense of conciliating personal regard, but even in the sense of recommending godliness and drawing minds and hearts to Christ.

I am not counselling silence at all times upon the concerns of the soul. There are persons charged with a ministry, who must be instant in season and out of season. There are affronts offered to Christ in the world, which require of those who love Him that they speak out, even to protest, even to reprove. There is such a thing as compromise. There is such a thing as cowardice. There is such a thing as being ashamed of Christ before men. And we know who has said that of such persons He will Himself be ashamed when He returns in glory. If charity is not rude, neither is she cowardly.

And, if charity has to guard against rudeness in the things of God, much more will she abhor it in the things of self. For one person who is unmannerly in Christ's behalf, a thousand and ten thousand are unmannerly, obtrusive, pushing, and impertinent, in their own behalf. Let these see in the words before us a grave reproof and a serious warning for themselves. If it is wrong to be indecorous for a heavenly Master, much more must inconsiderateness and coarseness of feeling be repugnant to charity when destitute of any such excusing or atoning motive. *Charity doth not behave itself unseemly.*

2. Secondly, *charity seeketh not her own.* We have already seen something of a reason why this clause should follow closely upon the former. The courtesy of charity must not be selfishness. A man might seem to be mindful of the charge not to be unmannerly, and yet be wholly regardless of the next caution, that he be not selfish.

All seek their own, St Paul complains, *not the things which are Jesus Christ's.* How true a saying. How prevalent, how almost universal, is the spirit of self-seeking. When man, in the Fall, broke loose from God, he broke loose also from his brother. The natural man is not ungodly only; he is selfish too. In fact, it is only in God that hearts can really meet. It is only so far as it succeeds in turning both alike to God, that any ministry can be effectual (to use the language of the last verse of the Old Testament) in *turning the heart of the fathers to the children, and the heart of the children to their fathers:* they meet in Him as their common centre.

My brethren, when we speak of selfishness, we can only lay ourselves in the dust, and mourn together. Who is not selfish? selfish in common things, in little things, in the things of everyday life? Who does not grudge trouble? or, if not all trouble, yet trouble of any kind which is not self-chosen and self-imposed? Who does not dislike being put out of his own way; having his plans for the day broken in upon; having his few moments of relaxation and refreshment curtailed yet further by some unexpected and unwelcome call? But we might go further, and say, Whose religion, whose charity, is not somewhat selfish? Is there any one who really desires, in doing good to others, their good more than his own? How many of us, in visiting the poor, are really aiming at gratitude, really seeking, if not the applause of lookers on—and do not be absolutely sure that there is not a little even of this feeling lurking within—yet at least the thanks and the love of those to whom we are ministering, instead of the result itself; the good, in soul or in body, of the person benefited or served. In this case, charity herself is seeking her own.

And in another sense too. In serving others, we may be thinking of ourselves, even without aiming at gratitude We may do it as a duty, as a means of gaining good for ourselves, of promoting our own salvation, or even with some lingering relics of an idea of merit. Do not think that I would strain too far the demand of a disinterested motive. It is well for the world that charity should work in it anyhow, from any motive. And it is far better, even for ourselves, that we should be diligent in the service of others, whatever the imperfection of our motive, than not diligent. And we may pass through lower motives to higher; gradually purifying our work from the dross of selfishness as we go on and get forward. Still I think that it is good for us, both as an exercise of salutary humiliation, and still more as a means of casting out evil from our hearts and lives, to contemplate the diviner form of a real Christian charity as it is set before us in the pages of Holy Scripture: to remind ourselves, for example, that then only is charity perfect, even as its Source and its Inspirer is perfect, when in no sense it seeks its own; when neither the desire of human applause or human gratitude, nor even the desire of self-improvement, much less of self-approval or self-justifying, has any place in it, but the heart has learnt something of that most sublime of all exercises of self-forgetfulness and self-sacrifice to which St Paul had risen when he wrote the memorable though sometimes misunderstood sentence, *I could wish that I myself were accursed from Christ for my brethren.*

Charity seeketh not her own. Charity is altogether unselfish. Just so far as self enters even into our best deeds, in that same degree we are without charity. And if the best of men have deplored to the end of life how wanting they were in the grace of an entire self-forgetfulness, may we not, here also, apply the subject to some persons, in this as in every congregation, who never know what it is even for a moment to seek any one's good or any one's pleasure but their own, and urge them, by the love of Christ and by the hope of heaven, to practise themselves, ere it be too late, at least in little self-denials, if perhaps a better spirit may by degrees be formed in them, and they may rise at last to something of that mind which was in Christ Jesus?

3. In the third place, the text tells us that *charity is not easily provoked.* I fear we must confess that the word *easily* is no part of the verse as St Paul wrote it. Whence it crept in, I know not. Whether it was really felt that the rule was beyond human reach without it; or whether some mere accident occasioned its insertion; these questions are comparatively unimportant: but I fear that we must read the words without modification, *Charity is not provoked.*

It is not said that charity is never angry. On the contrary, we read of our Lord Himself that on one occasion He looked round upon an audience *with anger, being grieved for the hardness of their hearts*. And the same holy Apostle, whose words are now before us, writes elsewhere, *Be ye angry, and sin not*: implying that all anger is not sinful. It is right to be indignant at some things: we may well wish that there were more amongst us than there is of righteous indignation at things mean and shameful, acts of revenge and lust and cruelty. St Paul says of himself, *Who is offended*, that is, caused to offend, hindered and injured in his Christian course, *and I burn not*, that is, with holy anger on his behalf?

Charity is not provoked refers to different matters. It follows closely upon, and indeed springs directly out of the foregoing particular, *seeketh not her own*. Selfishness, self-pleasing and self-seeking, is the common cause of provocation. If we had no self in us, we should not be provoked, no, not once in a thousand times, as we now are. How seldom does provocation really arise out of a disinterested care for the good of others. How seldom are we, like our Lord, simply grieved because of the hardness of another's heart; simply concerned to think of the dishonour done to God, and the risk brought upon a brother's soul, by unbelief, ungodliness, and sin. Or, even if there be something of this motive for anger, yet how mixed is it with lower regards; with vexation, perhaps, because we can make no impression; with irritation at the perverseness which will not see aright; or with weariness in the disappointment of efforts to correct and to improve. And how true is it, that when once charity is provoked, it ceases to be of any avail; ceases to influence, because it ceases indeed to be charity. O, if we would be of any use one to another; if we would move in the world as Christ's witnesses, whether among equals or among inferiors; we must pray without ceasing for a gentle and a loving soul; even for *that ornament of a meek and quiet spirit, which is in the sight of God of great price.*

4. In the fourth and last place, it is said, *Charity thinketh no evil.* This is a different thing from *Charity believeth all things,* or *hopeth all things,* of which we read below. *Thinketh no evil* is, properly, *reckoneth not that which is evil.* In other words, Christian charity is shown in not keeping an account of injuries or of unkindnesses; in not registering and recording acts or words of neglect, contempt, or wrong; in not entering such things in the tablets of memory, as if for a future day of human reckoning or of divine retribution. Some minds, my brethren, are strangely tenacious of such things. It is in vain to remind them—in vain do they remind themselves—of shortcomings and offences of their own: in vain do we say, O bring not upon yourselves the judgment of the unmerciful servant. O provoke not God, by your harsh, uncharitable, unforgiving spirit towards men, to remember your far greater debt of sin towards Him. O be willing, when you remember how wrongly, how ungenerously, how suspiciously, and how contemptuously, you have yourself often spoken or acted towards others, to forgive and to forget a few such acts and words when they have injured or wounded *you.* In vain, I say: for charity is the gift of God only: *Send Thy Holy Ghost,* we pray, *and pour into our hearts that most excellent gift of charity:* charity is the gift of

God, given by His Spirit, given in answer to earnest prayer, given as the fruit of many watchings and strivings, of many struggles with ourselves and many conflicts with Satan: no wonder therefore if they who ask not and believe not are not charitable, do not love.

Charity reckoneth not evil; preserves no record of it, keeps no account against it. There was an expression in ancient times, denoting one of the great boons promised to the populace in a revolutionary crisis. That boon was called *new tablets;* new account-books: in other words, the cancelling of the old; the abolition of all outstanding debts. In that application, however attractive in its sound, however expedient at certain times in order to prevent worse consequences, it was not an act of justice, and it was a dangerous precedent. But, in the sense in which I now use it, it involves no danger, and, on the whole, taking one side with another, no injustice. If we have all something to forgive, have we not all something also to be forgiven? Let us have new tablets this Lent. Let us agree to cancel all outstanding debts. Let us turn our thoughts from earthly dues to heavenly; from things owing to us to things owing by us; yes, owing by us both to man and God. Let us start afresh. Let charity reckon no evil: let charity destroy her old account-books, and forget the past. We cannot deal with our own sins, till we have done with those of others. *If thou bring thy gift to the altar, and there rememberest that thy brother hath ought against thee,* or thou thyself (might we not venture to add?) against thy brother, *leave there thy gift before the altar, and go thy way: first be reconciled to thy brother, and then come and offer thy gift. Forgive us our trespasses, as we forgive them that trespass against us.* More than that we do not even pray for: can we look for more?

Charity is not rude.
Charity is not selfish.
Charity is not provoked.
Charity reckons not the evil.

Such are a few of the features of that divine grace. There are others, and we should study all. But even these few have humbled us. Even these few enter into judgment with us, and condemn us. Let us not be satisfied with recording the sentence, and thus flattering self-love with a dream of great humility. Let us rather see how arousing, how stimulating, yes, how invigorating, if rightly used, is the word which humbles. We must pray, and we must struggle, for the grace of Christian courtesy, that we may be wise to win souls; not insolent, not arrogant, not awkward, not repulsive. We must pray, and we must struggle, for the grace of Christian unselfishness; beginning to practise it in little things, and passing on by degrees to greater. We must pray, and we must struggle, for the grace of an unprovokable spirit; remembering how we have provoked God, and yet He has been patient. We must pray, and we must struggle, for a short memory in evil; for the power, not to forgive only, as men too often count forgiveness, but to forget also; the power to sponge well every night the heart's tablets, that they may preserve no mark of bad impression until the morrow. This if we do, seriously, daily, and in God's presence—on our knees, with the windows well open towards the heavenly temple—He will help us. God is nearer to us than we think: and in His presence is strength.

QUINQUAGESIMA SUNDAY,
February 10, 1861.

V.

THE CAKE NOT TURNED.

Hosea vii. 8.

Ephraim is a cake not turned.

THE language of Scripture is largely borrowed from common life. Most often, from natural objects; fields and trees, sea and sky, the means and processes of vegetation and agriculture. But sometimes in-door life is laid under contribution for spiritual illustration. Sometimes it is a feast, with its bright lights, its good cheer, and its merry guests within, in contrast with an outer darkness and a sad exclusion. Sometimes it is a humbler matter still; a lost piece of money, and a woman sweeping the house till she finds it. Sometimes it is one of the processes by which food is prepared for strengthening man's heart, and the poorest man or woman is taught how to find profit for the soul out of an occupation which seems to be wholly confined to things sensible and earthly. You would be surprised, if you looked into a Concordance of Holy Scripture, to see how large a space is occupied by the word *bread*. We might almost say that bread has been consecrated by the Bible, the Old Testament and still more the New, to *such an excellent mystery* that by it is typified and represented the work of grace in the heart of man.

Now of this character is the figure employed in the text. *Ephraim is a cake not turned.* Ephraim, in its original meaning here, denotes the kingdom of Israel or of the Ten Tribes. But I am sure I need not say that that which is written of a rebellious and perverse nation has its exact counterpart in the individual; nay, that it was only because true of individuals that it was ever true of a nation; and that human nature, fallen human nature, is of one stock and of one blood in all times, so that, if we get below the surface (God's Word guiding us) with reference to one man in one age, we are quite sure to find the same thing true of the depth of some other heart in some other age—yes, in germ at least, true of every other heart in every other age. Ephraim, being interpreted, is man. At least, he is many a man, under circumstances at all similar to those of the Israelites at the time spoken of. In other words, the character ascribed in God's Word to Israel of old is the character of very many persons to whom God has spoken, whom He has brought within the pale of His covenant and of His Church, and striven with through long years by the inward pleadings and remonstrances of His Spirit. Ephraim, so understood, is compared in this passage to a cake not turned.

English history has treasured among its anecdotes of a favourite royal hero, one which tells us of a cake not turned. The disguised sovereign, occupied with graver cares, forgot the duties of the task which he had assumed, and left the countrywoman's bread to spoil for lack of turning. Such is the very emblem here employed by God's Prophet. There is something in the character of some men which resembles a burnt loaf; a cake left too long with one side exposed to the fire, till it has caught and been scorched, while the other side is still mere dough. So condescending is the language of Divine Revelation, when it seeks to show us to ourselves as we are. A little accident, familiar to every cottage and to every kitchen, is seized by the wisdom of God, and made the vehicle of correction and instruction in righteousness. May He help us so to use it.

The character described is easily legible. It is that in which there is a too much and a too little. One side is overdone, the other is underdone. There is nothing even and equable in the compound. It is in pieces and patches: here a lump of dough, and there a cinder: here that which must be cut off because it is too dry and too black for mastication, and there that which must be left upon the plate because it is too moist and too sticky for digestion. I am sure, my brethren, if we think of it, we all know such characters. Some of us, who look closely within, may perhaps be constrained to confess, Certainly I know one such.

It is intended, you know, that the grace of God, or by whatever other term we designate the thing spoken of, should go through and through the whole of us. The comparison slightly varied gives us the leaven which is hid in the meal till the whole is leavened. Just so is it in the baking. That which has been first thoroughly mixed, and then thoroughly leavened, must last of all be thoroughly baked. Every part of the mind and life—the principles and the affections, the temper and the spirit, the motives and the conduct, the feelings towards God and the feelings towards man—ought to be alike and equally influenced by the presence of the Holy Spirit within. The cake is imperfectly mixed, imperfectly leavened, or imperfectly baked, if it be not so. The whole man ought to move together in God's love and in God's service. It is the want of this unity, this coherence and consistency of parts, this combination and harmony of all elements in one whole, which makes the words true of any human character, *Ephraim is a cake not turned.*

And this might be exemplified in many ways.

1. There is, first, the case which the context seems to point to; an inconsistency arising from too much of voluntary intermixture with the world. *Ephraim, he hath mixed himself among the people:* he hath mingled himself among the surrounding heathen, and learned their ways: *Ephraim is a cake not turned. Strangers have devoured his strength, and he knoweth it not: yea, grey hairs are here and there upon him,* testifying to a loss of strength, to a decay of vigour, *yet he knoweth not.* A very graphic picture of the life of many. Certainly some are very arbitrary in their definitions of the world. They do not understand the difference between the heathenism which surrounded Israel of old or the Christian Church in its first beginnings, and the nominal Christianity which is about us on every side now. We have no right to ignore Baptism and Communion, profession of faith and attendance on ordinances. These things are not unimportant. For good or else for evil, they make a distinction between him who has them and him who has them not. Still for

practical purposes, as a matter of Christian prudence and of Christian consistency, we must put a difference now between some and others even of our fellow-worshippers. A brother who walks among us disorderly, who is either notoriously sinful in his life, or whose influence, at all events, is entirely adverse to religion, cannot be regarded by us, nor ought he to be, as a fitting friend or companion for one who desires above all things to save his soul alive. And there is such a thing in these days as a man *mixing himself among* such persons, and becoming by that intermixture like a cake unturned. His religion may become in that way rather an incongruous adjunct than a pervading leaven. He may still have a religion: he may still think himself religious: he may continue a worshipper, he may continue a communicant: he may have prayers in his family, and prayers in his chamber: but his life is not religion; his day is spent away from God; his prayers are isolated from his occupations and isolated from his interests; his heart is in the world, whatever his professions or even his occasional wishes be.

2. Or, again, there is the still sadder case, if it be possible, of one who is tied and bound by the chain of some evil habit. How much that is beautiful and apparently hopeful in a character may coexist, for a time at least, with a sin. In the end, no doubt, the forcible words of this Prophet are made good in every instance of a life of sensuality, *Whoredom, and wine, and new wine, take away the heart.* Fearful are the exemplifications of this saying—of the heartlessness of the sensualist—in human life. They meet us everywhere: patent among the poor; discernible, doubtless, to a

closer inspection, in the homes of the wealthy. But this, in its full developement, belongs to a late stage of sin. In its beginnings there may be a great mixture of good. Sometimes there is a considerable amount of piety, of religious feeling I mean, in a character which has its dark spot all the time. Often there is in it what I may call a pathos and a plaintiveness very touching and even attractive. If the strong man despises, the humble Christian cannot but pity, may almost love. That profound sense of sinfulness, that exceeding bitter cry which rises in the hearing of God or man from a self-condemning heart, that deep humility, that tenderness in judging, that consideration for the feelings and faults of others—all which are sometimes characteristic of a man vainly struggling rather under than against a prevailing evil temper or victorious evil lust—are things not to be witnessed without compassion even by one who cannot, for his Master's sake, be indifferent to the guilt, or blind to the danger, of the sin which thus reigns. The words of the text may well recur to us as we contemplate such a case. O that the whole man were what a part of him is. O that that inconsistency could be reconciled. O that that tenderness and that humility could but have been combined with purity, or that generous warmth of feeling with some command of speech and of temper. How beautiful then might have been the compound, where at present we can but admire a few separate ingredients. Would that God's grace might even yet bring unity into that confusion, casting out that which is evil, and claiming for His own that which is good. He has done so, for a few at least, even in this most perilous and fatal case of all:

He has, here and there, given a man the victory even over a sin which had long led him captive: often enough to forbid despair, though not often enough to preclude deep anxiety.

3. But the subject is still far from being exhausted: I feel rather that we have as yet scarcely sounded its depths. The peculiar point in it is the imperfect diffusion of good through the whole man; the exaggeration of some parts to the disparagement of others; the one side overdone, and the other scarcely touched, by the fire of truth and grace. How applicable is this description to some characters to which we can scarcely deny the title of religious; some which perhaps most confidently arrogate that title to themselves. How often have we seen in such persons zeal without tenderness; energy without repose; eagerness for what they deem truths, without charity towards those whom they count in error; a distortion, for themselves and others, of the whole proportion and balance of the Gospel, by pressing one truth as if it were all the truth, and casting into the shade of practical disregard other things which a more impartial reader of God's Word would see to occupy a primary place. And great dishonour is done to Christ oftentimes by such distortions and by such onesidedness. Great injustice is often done to personal merits of a different and less obtrusive order. Men are regarded as far behind in the Christian race, who in all save the loudness of their profession or the narrowness of their view may be far forwarder than their judges. And, what is worse, many honest struggling men are so discouraged in their estimate of themselves, and so deterred by the representation thus made to

them of Christ's Gospel, that they are really thrown back in the race, or diverted into some erratic course the end of which can scarcely be recognized as the Christian's heaven. Such are some of the evil results of that imperfect blending of Christian graces, that disproportionate developement in one character of the various elements of true perfection, which we have so often to deplore even in religious persons, and to which no figure of comparison could be more appropriate than that drawn for us in the words of the Prophet, *Ephraim is a cake not turned.*

4. And, if applicable thus far to Christian men, what shall we say of the bearing of the subject upon persons who have not yet taken a decisive step towards Christ's service? Is there no inequality, no jar, no disorder, in their being also? What if in many of them conscience is at variance with practice, conviction with conduct? If you are not inwardly convinced that there is something in Christ which is not to be dispensed with and not elsewhere to be found, why are you here? I would fain believe that that which is indicated by your presence among Christ's worshippers is in reality the very deepest and truest part of your being. It is not that I would teach you that you are guilty of hypocrisy or false profession in coming hither. That is dangerous language, and not more dangerous, I believe, than false. Rather would I urge you to cherish that habit, of coming to hear Christ's Word read and preached, and of joining in His public worship, as one of the links which still connect you with the realities which lie above, and which lie within, and which lie before you. But then, my brethren, if you are not to discontinue

worship, let it mean something. It will not do to have two parts of you entirely severed and at variance. Your faith in Christ, which you express by worship, must not be confined to worship. If you call Him *Lord, Lord,* you must also try to do the things which He says. O, if there be in you but one thing which He disapproves, be assured that it will be for your happiness to part with it—certainly it will be for your happiness to *have* parted with it: make the effort in His name and strength, and He will enable you. And, not less, endeavour to carry the thought of Him into your daily life in all its parts. Try to understand, and try to exemplify, what is meant by even eating and drinking to God's glory—by temperance and by thankfulness—by using moderately what He gives, and by praising and remembering Him in your hearts over it. You will never be really happy until your life is at one. The *cake not turned* is a spoilt and damaged thing; good neither for food nor show: men cast it out. Pray and strive that it be not a figure descriptive of you. Let your prayer, and the prayer of all of us, be that of the inspired Psalmist, *Unite my heart to fear thy Name.* Yes, bring all its scattered parts into one whole. Reason and conscience and will, judgment and affection, energy and enjoyment, thought and speech, soul and spirit, mind and life, let each in its office serve Thee, and let the whole be Thine. *Then are they glad, because they are at rest: and so he bringeth them unto the haven where they would be.* In God alone is the rest of man: he that findeth Christ findeth peace.

Unity is happiness, and unity is strength. If you see that the Lord is God, follow Him; follow Him whithersoever He goeth. If you hear the voice within, saying, *This is the way, walk thou in it;* if conscience tells you that a particular thing is right, because Christ commands it, or a particular thing wrong, because it might lead you or another into sin, into some occupation or some indulgence which Christ in His Gospel has forbidden; let that be decisive: an hour later you will be glad of it. No man can serve two masters; God and the world, Christ and self, Christ and sin. It is misery to attempt it. They are the wretched men of this world, not who live entirely for the world, not who live entirely for God, but, who have just light enough to prevent their forgetting Him, and not decision enough to be His wholly. They are the wretched men: others have the world to enjoy, and there is some enjoyment in it so long as men can forget the last end: and others, again, have God to enjoy, and His service is perfect freedom, and in it is nothing to be forgotten: but *they* have *neither;* they miss both worlds: and a weary bondage they suffer. Well may the text say to each of us, Be one man, not two: make up your mind, and let mind and life move together. *God is one:* let him who is God's be one also.

SECOND SUNDAY IN LENT,
February 24, 1861.

VI.

THE DANGER OF RELAPSE.

Hebrews x. 38.

If any man draw back, my soul shall have no pleasure in him.

THOSE of us who have ever had to do with sickness know the serious import of the word 'relapse.' 'What we have to guard against is a relapse' is the expression of a most pressing anxiety: the tidings, 'He has had a relapse,' must sound in every ear with much of the awfulness of a death-warrant.

It is my purpose to-night to speak to you of that which is analogous to this in the soul. 'The danger of relapse' is our subject. I would address myself to it, not so much as the physician, but rather as the friend or the relative of the patient; nay, as one compassed himself with every danger which can beset or befall the weakest and the most sinful.

It is not obvious to every one, on first hearing the word, that 'relapse' is synonymous with 'backsliding.' It is the Latin form of that English word. And yet it seems to convey to us a more real and tangible sense. Backsliding is a term appropriated to religious subjects: relapse is a term of wider use, applicable to bodily as well as spiritual matters, and, in the same proportion, as it appears to me, more natural and more significant.

In either case, you will notice that the force of the word lies in its indication of a gradual process. A relapse is a gliding or slipping back. There is nothing in it of suddenness or of violence. Whatever the result may be, however unexpected or however fatal, the word denotes that the process and progress towards it has been easy and perhaps imperceptible. And we shall readily understand that in that particular point lies the main risk and peril.

To give something of clearness and definiteness to the remarks now to be made upon it, we may separate the two cases, of act, and of spirit; of particular habits and tendencies, and of the general mind and life. In each of these there may be either a progress towards recovery, or else a relapse: and the danger of relapse will be sufficiently evident when we draw out into a few serious thoughts the thing which that word indicates.

1. And first in its reference to particular acts and habits.

All of us have known, either for ourselves, or in those near to us, what it is to fall into a bad habit. Habits are of all kinds: it is a word which we use indiscriminately with reference to small things and great; to bodily, mental, and spiritual acts; to matters which are mere tricks of manner or gesture, as well as to grave moral concerns on which the life or death of the soul may hang.

A great part of early education, in the nursery and

the school-room, is taken up with the prevention or correction of bad habits. Little faults of deportment, mere awkwardnesses and rudenesses of tone or posture, give early teachers much trouble, and we are deeply indebted to those who will take that trouble with us. Again, in our childish or youthful lessons, certain tendencies early show themselves towards particular mistakes: special defects, of natural talent, or of attention and industry, lead to a perpetual repetition of the same error; only to be overcome, if at all, by an equally incessant struggle, on the part alike of the teacher and of the taught. And, once more, how obstinate, how wearisome to ourselves and others, are those faults of temper which form the first battle-field of the child with indwelling sin; faults of pride or of passion, of irritability or of sullenness, as the case may be; which, if left uncorrected, will be the torment of a lifetime, and which, with all the care and pains that can be bestowed upon them, are seldom perhaps so entirely eradicated as to give no trouble at all even to the grown man, even to the established Christian.

Now, taking these very simple and elementary experiences as illustrations of three kinds of bad habit; the first concerned mainly with the body, the second with the mind or understanding, and the third with the spirit or soul; we can all see in them, though on a very humble scale, what is meant by the danger of a relapse.

It sometimes happens that this early home-training is temporarily interrupted. Perhaps a mother, whose whole time is given to the care of her children, is laid aside for a time by sickness, or called from home by some demand of duty. A few weeks pass, during which she has been compelled to leave her children in the hands of servants, or of some person less wise or less keenly interested than herself in the true discipline of those concerned. How often, under these circumstances, do we hear of what in reference to graver or later faults we should have to call a relapse. Tricks of manner, once corrected, are again as bad as ever. Inattentions and carelessnesses and slovenlinesses over lessons are all come back, and the combat must begin afresh. Bad tempers of whatever kind, irritable, morose, passionate, have resumed their hold, and the work of faithful and judicious discipline is felt to be thrown back by weeks or months, and to require to be absolutely begun again. There has been, in all senses, a relapse: and in the judgment of a true educator and a true Christian a relapse is always and at every age a matter of great anxiety and of great danger.

But there comes a time when this danger is terribly aggravated, and the everlasting state of a soul comes to be bound up in it.

The life of home, we will suppose, is for the present ended, and the boy or young man goes forth to a place of far less constant, less tender, and less anxious watching. He is left to form for himself—and it is needful that sooner or later he should do so—his own habits of good or evil. And even if he still remains under his parent's roof, he will yet have to do this. An age comes, at which self-management and individual responsibility become, in the order of God's Providence, the burden of each one of us, and to attempt to bear it for one another can end in nothing but disappointment and injury. It is a very serious time, and it sets vividly before us the anxieties of that probation which is our lot below. I need not and cannot trace in detail the thousand influences which begin to affect life, inward and outward, at this stage. It is enough to say, as one speaking to those who know it, that multitudes—I dare not institute any comparison of numbers, so as to say what proportion, or anything like what proportion, of human characters may thus be described—but multitudes, at all events, do fall under most injurious influences, in conduct and habit, at the entrance upon mature life. Sinful and vicious habits, learned from without or springing from within, do lead captive many a young life. In many instances, the sin and its consequences are incurred almost or quite unawares. There is no positive consciousness of either, until the poison has been drunk in. The life of many a young man is thenceforth a life of disquiet, of unrest—happier if of conflict. Many fight not at all, but yield to their sin day by day. Many repent of it every morning, and before night, as regularly, are again fallen. Some—many, we are sure, these also—are awakened, under some one of those many providential influences for good which are always counterworking the snares and mines of evil, to a deep sense of the sinfulness of sin, and to an earnest and effectual repentance, shown, as true repentance is sure to be, by a recovery, under God's grace daily sought and cherished, from the dominion and bondage of their sin. Though life can no longer be ignorant of evil, or (in one sense) innocent of evil, it may yet be cleansed and purged from evil; graver, sadder, than once it was, but not therefore disconsolate, and not therefore unblessed, and not therefore inoperative for the highest and noblest good. If a young man *cleanse his way, by taking heed thereto according to God's Word*, he may still do a good life's work, and be owned by Christ at His coming.

But, alas, how great, in every such instance, will be the danger of relapse. When sin seems to have been entirely put away, how quickly, how suddenly, does it reappear, nay, how close by us it seems to have been standing all the time. *Who can say, I have made my heart clean, I am pure from my sin?* Sin once admitted seems to have a sort of claim upon us: it returns ever and anon as to its own house, and rather demands than asks admittance. It has been said, and too truly, that a man's besetting sin will be such to the end of his life: it is one of the strongest arguments, could its strength but be felt beforehand as it is felt in the retrospect, against harbouring sin at all, against suffering any inducement to make us part with the integrity of an unstained life. He who has once admitted into his life or heart a definite form of sin, may cleanse himself perhaps from it for a time, may remain for three years or five years free almost from its solicitations, and yet again it shall come back upon him, in the thoughts of his heart if not in the very act itself, and he shall find himself, if he ever relax his watchfulness, as much its slave as ever, and the house from which it went out shall have been as it were but swept and garnished for the hour of its return.

It is needless to carry the matter one step further, and speak of the dangers of a relapse in the case of the formed and matured habits of later life. There are two sins, more particularly, which have exemplified again and again the fearful risk of a return to evil. Of one of these I will not speak. From the other, the sin to which we commonly restrict the term intemperance, it is painful but not impossible to draw the illustration. Alas, how dreadful is our experience of it in the dwellings of the poor. What a raging monster is drunkenness; how utterly hardhearted; how dead to the call even of natural affection, even of humanity, even of self-love. And what a tyrant is it; how resolute its rule over the soul once enthralled. Neither entreaties nor resolutions, neither shame nor remorse, neither fear of God nor regard for man, avail anything against its iron grasp. How it exemplifies too the saying of the Book of Proverbs, *Wine is a mocker*. Now and then it seems as though it would relax its hold: the voice of conscience has been heard within, awakened by some dispensation of God's Providence, or quickened into energy by some conviction or persuasion of God's Word: for a time we hear the glad tidings that he whom Satan has so long bound has struggled into freedom: the home of poverty smiles again, and cheerfulness, if not plenty, is seen where all was gloom and wretchedness: alas, again and again even this fair hope has been disappointed: there has been a relapse: the later darkness is more absolute than the earlier; the evil spirit has come back, as though with seven others more wicked than himself, and the last end of that man is even worse than the first.

2. We turn now to the latter part of the subject, and would speak of the danger of relapse in reference to the spiritual state generally, rather than to particular habits of life.

I need not say to any one here present that there is an inward life for each one of us; real and definite, though not visible; a life which we live towards God, and by which God judges each of us from day to day. If we are not conscious of any relation to God; if we can live without Him in the world; if, for us, the words faith and hope and love, as towards God, are unreal and unmeaning; all this does not prove us to have no inward state, no spiritual condition, but only to be in a state of the greatest possible risk and danger, a condition of living death, carrying about with us everywhere not only a deeply diseased but an actually dead soul.

We who are here this evening are not, we may hope, quite in this state, any of us. We have a spiritual existence, and a spiritual history, every one. As we look back upon the years that are past, we can see that there has been a thread running through them, connecting each with each, and all with God: we can probably, if we examine them, say with regard to one period, *I was then making some effort to be religious*, and of another, *I was then walking carelessly*, and of another, *I was then under a particular influence operating strongly upon my character in this direction or that*: it is perhaps on the whole, for many of us, a painful retrospect, but not the less necessary on that account: there can be no repentance without a retrospect, and I think there is no retrospect which does not testify quite as strongly to God's patient love as to our perverseness and sinfulness.

But every glance cast backward upon the things behind, must have one effect at least amongst others;

that of showing us the precariousness (humanly speaking) of the Christian life; its slow and intermittent growth; its liability to reverses and relapses; its exposure to innumerable influences and accidents; its wonderful fluctuations and its too frequent vacillations. If on the whole its course were progress; if, viewing it at intervals, we could see distinctly that we were in advance now of the position which we had attained then; the result would be less saddening and less discouraging. But I fear that many of us have to confess that our spiritual history has not been so much a progress with drawbacks, as a mere oscillation; a swaying to and fro; a pendulum limited in its range by two extremes which it cannot pass, rather than the hand of the clock advancing by a steady though almost imperceptible progress to the completion of its hour. This it is that makes our hearts misgive us when we look forward. Is it to be so always? Is every apparent advance to be made up for, as it has so often been, by an equal or greater decline? Is our Christian life to be always lived within barriers which at its best it cannot surmount? Am I never to get into a higher region of experience, a purer air, a brighter light, and a more expansive freedom? We all know how to reply to these questions: we can all say, *Ye are not straitened in God, ye are straitened only in yourselves;* straitened in your own expectations almost as much as in your own endeavours. It is true, and we do well to remember it, and to rebuke ourselves even sharply for our weakness of faith and our faintness of hope. But we need also some serious counsel: we need at some times a very bracing, if at other times a soothing treatment: and I am persuaded that both for ourselves and for others we are all too apt to shrink from it.

I wish that for this night we might be enabled by God's grace to lay well to heart the few words given as the subject of meditation, *the danger of relapse*. If we felt this as we ought, it would lead us to take the proper precautions against it. And in the soul, however it may be in the body, there is properly no such thing as accident: our spiritual state is the result of influences the effect of which we can to a certain extent calculate, and which conscience, the Word of God, and the Spirit of God, will, if duly listened to, teach us how to direct.

Ye are idle, ye are idle—well might it be said to us—and then lay upon human infirmity, or else almost upon Divine appointment, the blame of a result which you could have foreseen and with which you are chargeable. O, my brethren, we do not take the pains with our souls which we ought. It would be a daily miracle if our bodies were kept in health without food: why should we expect a like thing in the soul? Which of us is not more or less guilty of starving his soul? Which of us gives his own soul either proper food or proper exercise or proper rest? These things are all alike found in communing with God: and which of us knows as he ought what that is? O let us say to ourselves each morning, so many of us as have any fear or love of God at all, *I am at a certain point now, whatever it be, in my soul's life: twenty years, or thirty years, or fifty years, of my probation are ended, and soon, soon at the latest, my destiny will be determined: at present, though under the care of God, I am in an enemy's country: many things will this day arise which will try my faith:*

temptations will come, offences will come, and it is my business to meet and to surmount them: but, most of all, and at all events, I know that I shall be influenced by things seen and temporal to relax my hold upon things unseen and eternal: and it may be that from within also, out of the sins of the past, some definite root of bitterness will this day spring up to trouble me: it is of the utmost consequence that I should not fall, that I should not go backward: I am behindhand enough now; let me not, by my carelessness or by my wilfulness, or by my presumption, make my case yet worse: O let me remember, while it may yet avail something, the importance of overcoming, of standing fast, of not drawing back, of not relapsing: and let me now come with all my heart to Him who is able to keep me from falling, that He may help and protect me all the day: may, as it is written, hold up my goings in His way, that my footsteps slip not. Such thoughts, carried out into their natural consequences, first of earnest prayer, and then of watchful living, will be our safeguard in the time of trial: God will be in our daily life, and He will not suffer us to be greatly moved.

The subject which has engaged us is one of melancholy tone and sound: but every word of God has its bright side also. The danger of relapse is great and formidable: no one in this life is exempt from it. Rich and poor, high and low, learned and unlearned, old and young, all are in danger of sliding back, of becoming backwarder than now in the Christian race, of actually drawing back unto perdition. We hear of it from time to time as a danger realized in sad experience. We receive sometimes from dying lips the confession, *I was once what I am not now: in my youth I was converted: I began to serve God: I came to the Lord's Table, I attended religious and devotional meetings: I thought all was well with me. But I fell away: the cares of life, or the unkindness of others, or the discovery of hypocrisy in some whom I had thought Christians, or*—it may be—perhaps, if we knew all, yet more often—*some subtle bosom sin, insinuated itself and ate the heart out of my religion: by degrees I gave up my profession; I ceased to communicate; I ceased to pray; I went with the multitude: and I lie here a backslider; afraid and ashamed to lift up my eyes unto heaven; the source of prayer dried within, and the ear of God closed.* Such is the reality of the danger in its last and most fearful developement. But the sense of danger, realized betimes, is not a terror but a caution: it is given to us that we may be both warned and armed against it: and the same Scripture which tells us of the danger tells us also how to counteract it.

When our Lord had been delivering to His disciples the discourse which we still read in the sixth chapter of the Gospel according to St John, on His relation to them as the bread of life; and when, in answer to the cavils of those who would not understand, He had gone on into language still more difficult, and had spoken of eating His flesh and drinking His blood as the one condition of spiritual life; it is recorded that *from that time many of His disciples went back, and walked no more with Him.* In their case, it seems to have been the depth and spirituality of His teaching which was the cause of stumbling; just as in other cases, it has been the holiness of His teaching, and the necessity of choosing between our sins and Christ; the impossibility of keeping sin and yet being saved from it; of being cleansed from guilt without being washed from sin. The effect is the same: a relapse from Christ's service into some other, whatever the precise form of that other service be. *They went back, and walked no more with Him.* Then He turned to the twelve disciples, those whom He had specially chosen to be with Him and to be His friends, and He said to them, *Will ye also go away?* Are even ye not to be relied upon? must I see you also one by one turn away, and leave me alone? *Then Simon Peter answered Him, Lord, to whom shall we go? Thou hast the words of eternal life.* The danger of relapse was only a reason, with him, for flying more earnestly to the source and spring of life. To take shelter in Christ with redoubled faith and love was his remedy and his comfort. May it be ours. If we are in danger of relapse, yet, remember, that danger is not an accident, and it is not a fatality: it is not a danger which need take us by surprise, and it is not a danger which must prevail against us. Say to Him whose we are, to Him who came to die for us, and who now lives again for us, *Lord, I see the danger: I feel myself powerless: O keep me. To whom can I go? If I turn away from Thee, I turn only to restlessness, to darkness, and to despair. Thou hast the words of life: O grant that neither the world, the flesh, nor the devil, neither temptation nor infirmity, neither neglect of duty nor tampering with evil, may draw me aside from Thee. Any one of these things is stronger than I: but in Thee is almighty strength. O keep me near Thee; keep me with Thee;*

when I faint, revive me; when I stray, recall me; when my faith fails, strengthen it out of Thy fulness; and, when some earthly idol would usurp Thy place within, give me grace to dethrone it, cost what it may. So praying and so trusting, we shall not be confounded. *Cast not away therefore your confidence, which hath great recompence of reward. For ye have need of patience, that, after ye have done the will of God, ye might receive the promise. For yet a little while, and He that shall come will come, and will not tarry. Now the just shall live by faith: but, if any man draw back, my soul shall have no pleasure in him. But we are not of them who draw back unto perdition, but of them that believe to the saving of the soul.*

THIRD WEDNESDAY IN LENT,
February 27, 1861.

VII.

THE SECRET LIFE AND THE OUTWARD.

Genesis xliii. 30, 31.

And he entered into his chamber, and wept there: and he washed his face, and went out, and refrained himself.

THE whole of that history from which the text is taken is a picture of human life. Not indeed in its details of circumstance: for the life of Joseph was one marked by stranger vicissitudes than fall to the common lot of man. But in its truth to nature; to the feelings of nature, good and bad; to the jealousies of nature, and to the selfishnesses of nature, and to the cruelties of nature; and again, on the other side, to the sensibilities of nature, and to the humanities of nature, and to the tendernesses of nature; the history of Joseph is a living picture still of man and of human life, and it will be read to the very end of time as one of the thousand indications of the naturalness of the Bible, as well as of the deep insight of God who made us into the wills and ways and woes of man.

I have selected for this morning's meditation one single point in this delineation of human life; the contrast exhibited by the text between the secret life and the outward life of each one of us; between the chamber and the banqueting-room; between the man whom God sees and the man whom the world sees in each one of us. I have not done so for the sake of a beautiful sentiment, or a poetical dream; but for a practical purpose, which I trust will be evident to all of us as the course of remark unfolds itself.

Joseph made haste; for his bowels did yearn upon his brother: and he sought where to weep, and he entered into his chamber, and wept there. And then he washed his face, and went out, and refrained himself, and said, Set on bread. Is it not a true account of many a life? Have not many of us, perhaps all of us at some time or other, had this double part to play; this weeping in the chamber, and this refraining of ourselves below; these heart's griefs known to God only, and this necessity of taking part, notwithstanding all, in the busy world of duty and of society?

The heart knoweth its own bitterness: and a stranger doth not intermeddle with its joy. There is a grief which can talk; but we never think of that grief as the sorest or the deepest. Most of us, perhaps, have or have had a grief of this kind; a grief patent and avowed, for which others could pity us, and for which we let them pity us. Of such a kind are the commoner disappointments of life, its obvious privations, most of its losses, most of its bereavements. With these things others can sympathize: they have known something like them: at least they can appreciate the things in question; they can imagine what it would be to undergo, if they have not yet themselves undergone them. In these things, if there be a weeping in the chamber, there is no need to disguise it below:

it is expected of us that we should feel them: not to feel them would be a sign of insensibility rather than of fortitude.

But these things, except in cases rarely fortunate, do not make the whole or the worst part of life's real sorrows. For all these things there is a remedy, if in all there is a smart: the assurance of a loving purpose in chastisement, of the benefit of a mixed or even bitter cup below, the prospect of a future compensation for life's troubles, of a future reunion with life's lost relations, is of itself not a nominal but a real solace under such calamities; and many, we trust, are they who find it.

It is rather to the thought of secret sorrows that the text directs us; sorrows of which the world, perhaps our nearest friends, know little or nothing in us; sorrows which, however keenly felt in secret, must be disguised and suppressed in the company of others.

It is not necessary or desirable, even in the way of general description, to strip off the veil from such distresses. A very few words will characterize and classify them: and then we may turn intelligently to those aspects of the subject which are entirely useful and practical.

1. The trouble of Joseph on the occasion spoken of in the text was one of the heart or affections. There was a beloved brother before him, whom he had not seen for many years, and to whom he could not yet unbosom himself with the full warmth of natural feeling. The pent-up love was overwhelming: it could only be relieved by a burst of tears: he sought where to weep; he entered into his chamber and wept there. How many

of those who hear me can feel with him. Where is the house in which affection is not the source of some secret trouble? How many a sister has had her youthful years entirely clouded by the coldness of a brother. What anguish does God witness in a thousand secret chambers from this one cause—love, natural love, unreturned, unacknowledged, unaccepted. What pangs may be inflicted by a very little selfishness, a very little inconsiderateness, on the part of one fondly loved. It is easy for those who go out from home into the varied interests of a busy life, to forget or even to be ignorant of sorrows which have no such chance of dissipation. It is easy (to adhere to the same illustration) for a brother to think that he gives all he ought, discharges every Christian obligation, if he is tolerably obliging and good-tempered to the inmates of home when chance brings him there, and occasionally recognizes the tie of nature by a letter in his absence. And perhaps long experience, long patience, and long self-discipline, may at last make those acquiesce in this amount of affection, who find that they must expect no more. But to all young people in this congregation I would take this opportunity of saying very seriously, Be well aware of the possible existence in others of a tenderness of feeling which is not your own: be well aware of the risk of overlooking or trampling upon such affection: be quick to notice the effect of your conduct and manner upon those with whom God in nature has allied you; and count it a great inhumanity, and therefore a great sin, to allow either temper or indifference or preoccupation of mind to make you add one jot or one tittle either to the dulness of an uneventful home-life, or to the burden of an over-charged spirit.

This on the one side; to those who have it in their power to wound. On the other side, to the weaker and perhaps younger, to the sister disappointed in her brother's affection, and even to the wife wounded sometimes by a husband, I would say in all tenderness, and simply with the view to the promotion of happiness, Be not (for your own sake) too expecting or too exacting: school yourself to patience: be prepared to find less than a home here: learn to look higher for your rest; even to One who always loves more than we love Him, One who loved first and will love last too. Your trouble is a real one: loneliness of heart, unrequited love, is a calamity: God sees it, God pities it: but be brave, in His strength, to face and to endure it, and do not put aside, in perverseness or in self-will, that offer of divine love which in the long run will be worth all else to you.

2. I have taken one example of a secret sorrow, as the text seemed to suggest, from the natural affections. And it is but a step from this to the next example, that of anxiety about the souls of others. Here again, we have only to look round, even if it were in a comparatively small congregation, and be quite sure that some heart echoes the words, and that some chambers, even of our own, could bear witness to the severity of the grief thus described. Are there not, for example, some Christian parents whose whole life is embittered by a secret misgiving as to the spiritual or even the moral well-being of a favourite son? Do we not know such cases; cases in which perhaps a singularly engaging and endearing nature was alloyed by faults of temper, faults of feeling, faults of conduct, growing with the growth and strengthening with the strength, until at last they

are developed in mature life into some definite habits of immorality and of ungodliness? Or cases in which a wilful childhood and a disobedient youth has ended in a total severance of all possibility of intercourse; in which the only chance of recovering a lost position has been the removal into a distant land, where nothing from home could follow the exile, save a mother's daily yearnings and nightly prayers and tears? Or, to take another example with which the slightest acquaintance with humble life must make us too familiar, are there not amongst us, even between wives and husbands, instances of a constant, wearing, never ending, ever fresh anxiety, which can neither be avowed nor yet calmed? What is it to see signs of incipient intemperance, or of intemperance returned to? signs of an evil spirit holding possession, or else of an evil spirit temporarily dispossessed only to return back with seven others? What must it be, not to stand by and watch (as a disinterested spectator might do) such a case, but to have to live with it, to have to be involved in it for good or evil, or, far worse—for love is not thus selfish—to see it creeping or hurrying to its own destruction, and feel oneself powerless to help or mitigate? What words could more aptly designate such a life of anxious watching, than those which speak of a weeping in the chamber and a refraining oneself below; a couch watered with tears, yet a face which must smile by day that it may not tell its tale? Yes, well is it written of such a sufferer, that he went out and refrained himself; held himself in (for such is the figure) as with bit and bridle, that he might not reveal, that he might not betray.

3. Unrequited love, undivulged anxiety, have fur-

nished two examples of secret sorrow: the third and last illustration must be taken not from the heart but from the soul: and we must think of those distresses which come to us from the inward strivings of sin; from those restless workings of inward corruption, which make the life of so many one long toil and conflict. These too, these above all, are secret things. I speak not of sin yielded to and indulged: in this there may be little weeping in the chamber, and little refraining of oneself below. But O how little do they know of the heart of man, who are at a loss to understand the meaning of a weeping and mourning for inward sin. There must be indeed, in such a case, something of better desire, some longing after God's favour, some aspiration after the freedom of holiness. It is not the careless, the worldly-minded, the simply decent and moral, who can be expected to enter into these sorrows. But between the total slavery of sin and the perfect freedom of holiness there lie many long and dubious stages; between the dead sleep of natural indifference and the entire wakefulness of Christian maturity. All through that intermediate region the saying of the text may be realized in a thousand ways and degrees. More and more in proportion to the advance once made in the life of God, and to the extent of a subsequent declension from it. More and more in proportion to the keenness of the spiritual insight, and to the feebleness of the obeying will. More and more in proportion as conscience is strong and resolution weak; the sense of duty accurate, and the habit of self-government loose and intermittent. In such cases, the chamber may well be a scene of weeping, though the life below and the life abroad may bear few traces of it. The sad condemning retrospect of sinful indulgence, even if that indulgence has been but in heart, and has not actually stained the life afresh with sin; those *bitter thoughts of conscience born* which *with sinners wake at morn;* the plain direction of duty, yet the experience alike and foresight of departure from it; these things recurring every day are enough to make life very wretched; most of all—the point now before us—do they account for much discomfort and much agony in that secret communion with God, which (strange though it may appear, yet with a truth beyond gainsaying) may still be maintained in some sense even by the unstruggling or scarcely struggling combatant. Nor is it he only who weeps, and has cause to weep, in his chamber. Where is he amongst us who does not in many things offend? Where is he who has not every night to repent of shortcomings, and every morning to dread his own unfaithfulness? All probably, of those here present—and certainly of the best Christians amongst us it will be the most true—have had occasion to go softly and even to walk mournfully before their God on account of the repeated inconsistency between their profession and their life, between the thing which they prayed for, and the thing which they attained. These are among the secret sorrows of life. We tell them not, in detail, to our dearest friend. We trust to his taking them for granted: we dread the certain inaccuracies of human confession, and we dread the possible flatteries of its reception by man. These things are our secrets: but they exist. They make a large part of our own existence, and we have to refrain ourselves not to show them.

Let us hear the brief conclusion of the subject. It will have two parts.

i. To some—to those who need the caution—I would say, Do not nurse your secret sorrows. They are not fancies in themselves, but they may be made fanciful. Sorrows of affection grow by pondering. They are loud calls to work. If this world cannot be what you would have it in enjoyment, take care at all events not to miss its object. It was never given to you to rest in: that belongs to a different life; a life, moreover, which you will miss altogether if you do not apprehend the object of this life. Your griefs will not be allayed, they will be fostered, by hugging them to your bosom. Make up your mind, by stern resolution, that this is evidently not to be a world of rest to you, whatever it may be to others. Then carry your sorrows out: take them with you to the house of God; perhaps you will leave them there: take them with you to the abodes of poverty, of sickness, of misery; there you will be ashamed of them; there you will be half inclined to call them fancies, when you look upon those palpable hideous forms which are buffeting and torturing the mortal life of others. These people who are in the hands of want, of disease, of vice, of cruelty, have no time to think of sorrows of sentiment or of the heart: learn a lesson from them: it will alleviate if it cannot cure your griefs.

And even as to those sorrows which are in no part fanciful; sorrows springing out of an unselfish and a just anxiety; still even these, so far as they are mere anxieties, can do no good: turn them from cares into prayers, and then they will be altogether salutary; salutary to yourself, salutary (may we not believe, however hopeless in man's judgment?) to him for whom you are in anguish.

Nay, even your struggles with indwelling corruption may be helped by the charge to forget (in some sense) the things behind, and to reach forth to the things before. To lash yourself for your offences, to prognosticate their repetition, if it stop there, is idle and unmanly. Call upon God, and there is meaning in it, and hope. Say to yourself, *I am not the creature of chance, I am not the sport of destiny: I am a man: I have a God: let me for this day fight like a man and trust in that God. Am I weak? yes, far more weak even than I know: but have I not heard that there is strength in God? Let me try. One day of hard fighting, of real struggling, will at least be bracing, if it be not decisive: God help me, for His Son's sake, by His Holy Spirit, and I will not yield without a struggle. While I lie here on the ground, mourning for the past, I am losing precious time: confess thyself, my soul, to the Lord: invoke His help as a real living thing, and get thee back to thy conflict: soon the night cometh, when no man can work, when no man can fight.*

ii. Finally, to stronger men, who have no such experiences of secret sorrow, whatever its cause and source, I would say, Beware of disregarding and despising those who have. Make room for others—make room even for the weak, the fanciful, or the morbid—in this capacious world of ours. Live, and let live. Be tolerant, for Christ's sake, of moral feebleness. Be gentle, for Christ's sake, to the erring and the sinful. This in general. But, in particular, the subject on which we have dwelt says to you, and to all, Recognize the existence of secret sorrows as an explanation of many phenomena of character. Is the temper of one with whom you live less than perfect? Is there an inequality of spirits, is there an absence of mind, is there a heaviness and a silence, which displeases and irritates you? Be merciful to it. Perhaps, if you knew all, you would perceive in that bosom a lurking care, disappointment, or self-reproach, enough, and more than enough, to account for what you witness. The cheerfulness which there is may be all a self-refraining: the chamber may have a sadder tale to tell; of tears and watchings, of tormenting doubt or distracting fear. Respect what you see not. Jesus Christ bore our griefs and carried our sorrows: bear ye one another's, and so fulfil the law of Christ. In a spirit of consideration, of deference, of silent yet intelligible sympathy, of tenderness towards another's untold trials, of pity for another's undivulged temptations, in these things is the love of Christ well-nigh perfected: they who practise these things have learned of Him. And they who learn of Him partake also of His power: in His school you will yourself become *a son of consolation:* and sorrowful wounded hearts will take knowledge of you that you have been with Jesus.

FOURTH SUNDAY IN LENT,
March 10, 1861.

VIII.

REVERENCE.

Exodus iii. 5.

Put off thy shoes from off thy feet, for the place whereon thou standest is holy ground.

THE text is a call to reverence. I need hardly say how much that duty is dwelt upon in Scripture, both in the way of precept and of example. *Let us have grace, whereby we may serve God acceptably with reverence and godly fear: for our God is a consuming fire...Serve the Lord in fear: and rejoice unto him with reverence... The Lord reigneth; let the people tremble: He sitteth between the cherubims; let the earth be moved...God is very greatly to be feared in the council of His saints, and to be had in reverence of all them that are round about Him...Tremble, thou earth, at the presence of the Lord, at the presence of the God of Jacob; who turned the hard rock into a standing water, and the flint-stone into a springing well...The Lord is in His holy temple: let all the earth keep silence before Him.*

We must all have been struck with the feeling expressed towards God in the Old Testament. What a profound awe, what a prostrate yet loving adoration, what an admiring sense of His goodness, what a longing, what a hungering and thirsting, after the knowledge, after the sight, of Him. Take only the example of him of whom the First Lessons for to-day and for some following Sundays contain the history. I know nothing more wonderful, nothing more touching, than the mind of that great and holy mediator of the first Dispensation towards the God whom he served. What profound humility, what entire and absolute self-devotion, what a sense of the necessity of God's presence, what deep submission to the stroke of chastisement for sin, what a single desire that God's work should be done, whatever might be man's portion. I can scarcely conceive of the mind which is not affected by the record of his character as it is incidentally disclosed in the Books which bear his name. And how noble a supplement to those records is that 90th Psalm, which is headed, as you remember, *A prayer of Moses the man of God;* that well-remembered Psalm which many of us have heard read over the bodies of friends and relatives, *Lord, Thou hast been our refuge from one generation to another: before the mountains were brought forth, or ever the earth and the world were made, Thou art God from everlasting, and world without end...O satisfy us with Thy mercy, and that soon: so shall we rejoice and be glad all the days of our life...Show Thy servants Thy work, and their children Thy glory. And the glorious majesty of the Lord our God be upon us: prosper Thou the work of our hands upon us, O prosper Thou our handywork.*

My brethren, I must appeal to you whether there is amongst us at this day anything of this spirit of reverence. Where do we see it? Is it shown in our conduct? Is it shown in our language? Is it shown in our use of God's Word? Is it shown in our meetings for God's worship? Order there is: decency there is: God forbid it should be otherwise: but is there amongst us, even in this house of God, that deep awe, that heartfelt reverence which the text prescribes? *Put off thy shoes from off thy feet, for the place whereon thou standest is holy ground.* Translate this charge from its oriental form into its spiritual sense, and what does it say to us?

Some have laboured, and, as I think, foolishly, to reintroduce under the Gospel a sort of exaggeration of that local reverence which belonged rather to the Law. They attract attention by their gestures and postures, their bendings of the head and knee, in Church, and more particularly at the Lord's Table, and imagine themselves in so doing to be either exercising or else learning a spirit of reverence. If they think so, we would not grudge them the help which they deem useful: but we would rather point out to them a more excellent way; one in which they may walk unostentatiously and simply, and perhaps attain that substance of which the other is at best the shadow.

What is reverence? What are its ingredients, its component parts? What hinders and what helps it in us? And what are some of its blessings? God Himself aid us in the endeavour to speak in His name upon some of these points.

1. I need not say—for all agree in it—that Gospel reverence must be a thing of the heart. It seems to be compounded of two things; the knowledge of God, and the knowledge of ourselves. It is the contact between the sinful and the sinless. It is the access of a conscious transgressor to One who is altogether holy.

It is the mind of a created being, who has also fallen, towards One whom he desires above all things still to belong to, still to return to, still to be with, and still to serve. I do not think it necessary to say more in the way of definition. O, my brethren, would that I could impress upon you my own deep conviction of the desirableness of this mind. How dreadful it seems that we should not all possess it. When the thought of God forces itself or breathes itself upon our hearts, how dreadful does it seem—I might almost say, how impossible—that we should trifle before Him, and trifle with Him, as we do. I am sure the remembrance of our Sunday worship—though it is perhaps the best thing we have to show in the way of reverence—will be a very bitter thing to many of us some day. O these wanderings—O these vanities—O these murmurings—O these idolatries—which seem not only to hang about us here, but really to be more at home with us and more tyrannical to us here than anywhere—what shall we think of these things when we look back upon them with eternity open? Do you suppose that Moses the man of God worshipped in this way? Do you suppose that he who said, *I beseech Thee, show me Thy glory*, and meant what he said—he who prayed, *Let the beauty of the Lord our God be upon us,* and meant as well as uttered the prayer—knelt before God as we do, with the world all about him, with the flesh and even the devil busy in him while he prayed? And yet it ought to have been said, *Among all that were born of women there was not a greater prophet nor a more holy man: notwithstanding he that is least in the kingdom of God is greater than he.*

I know that it is a matter of great regret and great sorrow to many of you that this should be true. And be assured that we can all feel for one another, and feel with another, about it. How happy should we be, if a few plain words spoken by a fellow-sufferer and fellow-sinner might assist any one (for is not that the use of preaching?) in seeking and cultivating that good spirit of which we must all lament the rareness.

2. The hindrances to a spirit of reverence lie on the very surface of our life. Things that are seen obscure the things that are not seen. We cannot help feeling earthly things to be very real. What can be so real, we all say to ourselves, as this work, this person, this house and garden, this bright sun, this fair world, which is here before my eyes? Compared with these things, all other knowledge, we think, can be but guessing. The reality even of the Maker is put out of sight by the thing made.

This is general. Then there is an early habit of inattention or of half-attention even in religious worship. I do not see how it is to be altogether avoided, but there is no doubt that children's prayers, and still more children's attendance at Church, must be, in part, of this character. The outward habit has to be acquired before the inward, the formal before the spiritual. Then there is no marked moment at which the child's prayers turn into the man's prayers; at which the inattention which was once a want of understanding has become an inattention consciously culpable: and thus, unlike St Paul, we do not, in this respect, when we become men, altogether put away childish things: we keep the two together: and the same man will often exemplify the sad combination, of an intellect mature and vigorous, and a devotion absolutely puerile and childish.

Irreverence is fostered also by everything approaching to unreality of expression in prayer. It is one of the many advantages of our Church Prayers that they are for the most part extremely simple, and (what is not less important for a mixed congregation) perfectly level to humble spiritual attainments. There is little or nothing in them which it is hypocrisy for a very humble Christian to use. An advanced and devoted Christian finds them enough for him, but a backward and very failing Christian can use them without feeling them unreal. There is something perhaps in the mere fact of their being prescribed to us which gives us confidence in using them. It is not so always with other prayers. It is not so always even with our own private prayers: we are apt, some of us, to use expressions which, if we examine them, we shall find to be beyond our mark; beyond the mark of our desire, I mean, and not only of our experience. All such prayers are irreverent. They do not express the mind of a poor sinner kneeling before his holy God. They are more or less the prayers of one who thinks wickedly that God is such an one as himself, and can be misled by words, when the heart is not in them.

Amongst other causes of a want of reverence, I must not omit the mention of an excessive indulgence of what is commonly called a sense of the ridiculous. In moderation, that is no fault: it has many advantages: it keeps a person from many follies: it is often the companion of a very sound judgment, and of a great capacity for good counsel. But where it is allowed full scope, without a restraining hand of piety and of charity, a sense of the ridiculous may become a very serious fault and risk. There are some people who can see only the ludicrous side of things. Human life itself has for them no grave aspect. They can turn everything into ridicule; until, at least, one of the great tempests beats upon them themselves. Then they feel. But that feeling is then selfish. And the predominance of the other, the opposite feeling, has perhaps by that time eaten out the very heart of reverence within. A man may lie on the ground, and lash himself for his sins, and sigh and cry for his sorrows, and yet not possess one spark of reverence for God, or even of real consciousness of His being and presence. Reverence, to be learned at all, must be learned by effort and by patience.

And I may add one special caution with reference to the intrusion of levity into sacred subjects. A man's heart ought to have one sanctuary. Even if he is not yet a devoted man, he ought to keep just one spot in his heart (as it were) clear for God: he ought to allow nothing else to possess it, even if God has not yet taken up His abode there. Whatever else he jests about, he ought to keep the name of God, and the Providence of God, and the Word of God, and the servants of God, safe from profanation. The letting in of common light upon this province; the admission of profane words or thoughts into that which ought to be a holy subject; is not only a decisive mark of present irreverence, but it is also a bar to future reverence: he will not find it easy, even if God should give him repentance, to recover the strength of his religious instincts or the purity of his religious regards. This is one of those ways in which a prudent man makes provision for future contingencies: he will not fling away the chance of wanting God hereafter, even if he can dispense with Him in the time that is.

3. I have said that we, all of us, more or less, mourn over a want of reverence. There are times when we terribly miss it. I am sure we some of us feel that, if we could only know what a holy awe of God is, we would submit patiently to a want of comfort and to a want of confidence. There is nothing so real as godly fear. It introduces us into that which is within the veil. A sense of God's reality, a sense of God's nearness—of His power, of His holiness, of His right over us, of His concern for us, of His future judgment—is the foundation of all piety and therefore also of all peace. How miserable, how consciously condemning, is the want of this. To kneel down, knowing that we are in need, in weakness, in darkness, in sin, and yet not to be able to feel that we are before any one; not to be able to find the throne of power, much less the throne of grace; to lie there prostrate and grovelling, yet by ourselves—no light above or within to mark the presence, much less to indicate the will to hear—this is very wretched: and I know that it is no fiction, no fancy: it is the case with many: not only have they no Saviour, they can find no God: they have let themselves alone, they have let themselves drift and go, too long, and now they are being filled with their own ways and eating as it were of their own perverseness.

But God would not have even these left here, left thus. Reverence may, by His gracious help through

Christ by the Holy Spirit, be gained—yes, regained. We bless Him for that hope. We do believe that He desires not our death but our life: O let us come to Him. We must practise reverence, as well as pray for it. We must always recollect ourselves thoroughly before we begin to worship. In private, we must, if I might so express it, meditate and study God's presence. We must not begin our prayers without trying to set God clearly before us as a living Person to whom we are coming, to whom we are about to speak. *When I pray*, said a poor person well instructed unto the kingdom of heaven, *I tell God what He is, and what I am, and what I want, and what He has promised, and what He has done.* No account of prayer was ever more thorough. And for the present, think of those first words, *I tell God what He is:* I count over, as it were, the particulars and items of His character: I set Him before me as what He is: I make quite sure of my ground by a preliminary recollection of the almighty power, the boundless mercy—but, yet before these, the living presence—of Him to whom I am about to address myself.

And then, everything which we know or can learn of God may be made a help to reverence before Him. We ought to reflect and meditate upon His qualities as they are set before us in Scripture; not only in a summary and combined form, but in items and particulars: we ought to make these things, in their full and ample expanse, a subject of meditation, so that they may impress us as they ought, and dwell with us, even as we treasure up in our inmost hearts the features of the face, and the beauties of the character, of some loved friend, never weary of recounting them to ourselves, and gathering from the repeated survey of the whole a sense of the reality of the living man, over which even absence, even separation, even death itself, has at last no power.

And thus we pass from that help to reverence which is found in setting God fully before us, on each particular occasion, as the object of prayer; and from that help to reverence which is found in the occasional study of His character and attributes in detail as they are revealed to us; to a third and last consideration; the help which a spirit of reverence will derive, above all, from repeated personal acquaintance and intercourse with God Himself. The man who is most reverent will be the man who knows God best and has seen most of Him. Where there is anything of unsoundness in a character, anything concealed and glossed over, anything of mere manner and profession and false appearance to recommend it, there, of course, increased knowledge is fatal to respect. There the only hope for a person is distance, and familiarity does but breed contempt. But it is not so with true characters, even amongst men. There are those, and many, we thank God, are they, whom the more we know the more we honour: persons, sometimes, of less attractive form or manner, but who are true to the backbone, and whom the most intimate knowledge only serves to exalt immeasurably in our esteem. If this can be ever so with men, what must it be with God. The only thing that can ever make God less than reverenced by His creatures is ignorance of Him; ignorance involuntary or wilful; that ignorance which is the want of knowledge, or that still commoner ignorance which is the rejection and contempt of knowledge. In proportion as you see more of God; in proportion as you extend and multiply your opportunities of deep and hearty converse with Him; in proportion as you add a little (with a loving and earnest heart) to the length or the frequency of your daily times of prayer; in the same degree will you find that you are growing in reverence for Him, appreciating more justly each feature of His character, and learning more happily to harmonize each with each.

4. I end with two brief remarks.

Reverence is the pervading tone of heaven. It predominates over every other characteristic, save love alone. And even love itself needs reverence to solemnize without chilling it. *I saw the Lord sitting upon a throne, high and lifted up, and His train filled the temple. Above it stood the seraphims: each one had six wings; with twain he covered his face, and with twain he covered his feet, and with twain he did fly.* Four wings for reverence, but two for flight. It is a true parable. Reverence for unworthy objects is the curse of earth: reverence for Him who deserves it all is the very perfection of heaven.

Lastly, reverence was characteristic on earth of our Lord Jesus Christ Himself. What an awe of God filled and sometimes overwhelmed His soul. Trust, obedience, submission, love, unwearied zeal, unwearied prayer—yet, amongst and above all these, what a paramount and pervading reverence. *Father—my Father—my Father which is in heaven—your heavenly Father—my Father and your Father, my God and your God*—what a tone of reverence breathes in the very sounds. In His recorded words addressed to the Father; in His sense of the necessity of repeated and prolonged intercourse with His Father; in those long nights of prayer in the desert or on the mountain, after long days of toil in the city or by the way; what a token do we see, what an infallible sign, of reverence and godly awe. Well might it be written of Him, that *in the days of His flesh He offered up supplications and prayers with strong crying and tears, and was heard in that He feared—heard* (as it might be given) *for His reverence*. Now He has gone back into the invisible, the inaccessible glory: and it is ours to approach Him with the same reverence with which He on earth approached God. *That all men should honour the Son even as they honour the Father...He that honoureth not the Son honoureth not the Father, which hath sent Him.* Now the earlier adoration, *Holy, holy, holy, Lord God Almighty, which was, and is, and is to come,* is supplemented and completed by the ampler doxology of the Gospel, *Blessing, and honour, and glory, and power, be unto Him that sitteth upon the throne, and unto the Lamb for ever and ever.*

FIFTH SUNDAY IN LENT,
March 17, 1861.

IX.

FAMILY PRAYER.

1 Samuel ii. 30.

Them that honour me I will honour.

THIS is God's rule. Them that honour Him He will honour. Let a man make it his object in life, to bring to God all the honour that he can; to show that he remembers Him and regards Him and reverences Him, even when it is not likely to be noticed, even when it is inconvenient to himself, even when there might be many excuses found for postponing, or omitting, or forgetting it; let a man live thus, and God who is thus honoured by him will in turn, as it is here written, honour him. He will cause men to see that a life of remembering God is, on the whole, in the long run, a happy life and a successful life and an honoured life. In early years such a man may have gone through much: he may have been overlooked, he may have been passed by, he may have been despised; or again, he may have been pointed at, he may have been opposed, he may have been ridiculed: but, let him have held on his way quietly and stedfastly, let him have held his principles firmly, spoken the truth in love, and above all things kept manfully to his great object, that of bringing to God Himself all the honour that he can; and you will find that the path of that man has been ever a smoothing and brightening path; whatever his youth may have been, his mature age has been respected, his hoar hairs honoured, and his dying day bewailed. *Them that honour me I will honour.*

And we all know how the opposite half of the truth has been made good in every generation. *They that despise me shall be lightly esteemed.* There are those whose whole life has been one continued despising of God. They have gone on as though it were quite certain that no one of God's words was true. They have lived as if this world were all. And not only so, but as if, even with regard to this world, even with regard to such happiness as can be found below, God knew nothing, and might be entirely disregarded without fear of consequences. To what particular acts of folly or disobedience they may have surrendered themselves, is of less moment: that has depended upon a thousand things; inclination, influence, rank, wealth, companions, circumstances: but one thing has not varied: they have disregarded God, they have practically despised God: they have said in their hearts, either that He cared not, or that He knew not, or that He was not, and have lived from day to day on that supposition, on that principle. Has not the advancing life, has not the old age, has not the death-bed, has not the memory, of those men, proved, over and over again, the truth of the saying, *They that despise me shall be lightly esteemed?* Has not the respect of men been found to a remarkable degree to come and to go along with the approval of God? Not uniformly, not perfectly; or the judgment of human actions would be present, not future; exercised by the world that is, instead of waiting for the world that shall be. But still, when we read in Scripture of sinners awakening from the dust of the earth to shame and everlasting contempt, do we not feel that there is a foretaste for them of that contempt below? that, even in this life, there is an instalment of despite for them that have despised God, and an anticipation at least of that shame which is hereafter to be the portion of those who have here been ashamed of Christ?

These remarks are perhaps too general to have found their way into the conscience. I proceed to a special application of the subject, for the sake of which I have chosen it from one of the Lessons for the day. The topic of my Sermon this morning is Family Prayer. I have reason to fear that it is one which will come home to some hearts in this congregation with reproof and conviction. Let them not therefore cast it from them. Let them listen seriously to the few words now to be spoken, and, according as they shall judge, so let them act. God grant us all grace to listen in this practical, honest, and earnest spirit.

I need not spend a moment in explaining what is meant by the words, Family Prayer. They mean that prayer which is offered to God by an assembled family or household. Such devotion occupies an intermediate place between private and public worship. It partakes in some degree of the character of either. It is carried on at home, but not in the chamber: it is carried on with others, yet not in the congregation. It has about it much of seclusion, but it aims not at secrecy. The worshippers are not all of one age, or capacity, or station, or descent: but they have all something in common: they form together one household, one society, one community, combined together partly by ties of nature, and partly by those of service required and service rendered. It is a great mistake to suppose that the union of a family, even with reference to those members of it who are not made so by birth, is a slight or feeble bond. It is a connection, not only of mutual advantage, but also, where it is rightly understood, of great kindliness and of strong attachment. When a united family kneels down to pray to God—parents and children, master and apprentices, mistress and servants, together—it is not a mere collection of isolated units: there is a reality in the connection, there is a unity in the aggregation, and therefore also there is a meaning in the worship incommunicable to any other.

I may take it for granted, further, that family worship has its well-understood and (in all main features) uniform course. The reading of some portion of God's Word, with or without comment; and then a prayer read or uttered aloud, either from the heart of the master of the family, or from our Church Prayer-Book, or some other manual of devotion such as is everywhere to be met with; this is the common order of such worship, and, however it may differ or vary in its details, its general tenor may be assumed to be the same for all.

Now let me suggest a few plain reasons for establishing and maintaining this sort of worship in every family.

1. And let me place first, as the text teaches us to do, this paramount consideration: *family worship honours God.*

We are far too apt, all of us, to leave out of sight this object of worship. We ask, and we do well to ask, What can I get by prayer? How can I make it most profitable to my own soul? *What shall I have therefore?* And prayer is meant to do us good; to bring back an answer; an answer direct, personal, and substantial. But this is not all: and perhaps I might say, this is not the highest office of prayer. The Lord's Prayer itself begins with three petitions concerning God, His name, His kingdom, His will, before it says one word of our wants; of daily bread, of forgiveness, of deliverance from evil. It is a very great and a very high object to keep up the remembrance of God upon earth: to see that each member of every family, however much he may neglect private prayer, shall yet be reminded of God's reality and of God's truth every day: to provide that in every home (if it might be so) in a particular parish or town there should be, as it were, an altar built to no unknown God, and the fire of a periodical sacrifice kindled upon it in the sight of all who dwell therein. Family worship is an honour due to God from those who are living together upon His bounties, and who, collectively as well as individually, have a state and a life before Him. When the bell rings for worship at the appointed time, breaking off other occupations, and silencing other sounds, we recognize in it a voice which says to us, *God is, and is your God: Christ is, and is your Lord and your Saviour: the Holy Spirit is, and is your Sanctifier and your Comforter.* Thus, if not otherwise, twice in each day, is the call of conscience made audible to the careless, and the reality of things unseen proclaimed to men tied and bound by the material and the temporal.

2. Again, *family worship elevates and consecrates and (in one word) Christianizes family life.*

What a poor thing, taken in itself, is the work which fills our day. I will put aside now the thought of a statesman's life, which may seem to be really engaged in great matters, and the thought of a clergyman's life, which has to do directly and constantly, so far as its great object is concerned, with the souls of men. I will speak rather of the occupations of business (commonly so called) for men, and of household affairs for women. What an expenditure of time and thought, of capacities and abilities, upon subjects trivial, transitory, perishable. Which of these things will be of importance, which of these things will be in existence, ten years, or perhaps ten days, hence? And yet they must be done. Much depends, for present comfort and for present well-being, upon a punctual discharge of worldly business, and upon the conveniences and decencies of a nicely ordered home. Let no man despise the occupations of a man of business or of a domestic woman. In these things we live: only a fool despises them. But yet, my brethren, but yet, how poor, if this were all; if there were no God for the soul to serve in these things, or no future world for which this is but the porch and the vestibule. Now in family prayer this background of faith is made for the time the foreground. When those who have been toiling through their little carnal domestic duties sit together to hear a portion of God's Holy Word read, and then kneel together to ask for His forgiveness, His help, His blessing, and His Holy Spirit, how are they reminded of the elevating and consecrating principle which pervades, or ought to pervade, human life in all its parts; how are they reconciled to common duties, when they see, above, behind, or within each, that thing which makes the mean great, the common sacred, and the earthly heavenly; how cheerfully do they go forth again to the appointed tasks of time, in the sure and certain hope of an immortality of rest, of blessedness, and of glory.

And there is another point also. Who that has lived, as all have lived at some time, in a family, can be unaware of the various little jars and collisions which the coexistence in one household of various tastes, tempers, and characters must necessarily, constituted as we are, involve? Every day brings with it some experience, expected or unexpected, because old or new, of contrarieties of wish and will between different inmates of one home, which must either be endured by an effort of principle, or combated with discomfort, dissension, at last perhaps with dislike and enmity. It is only amongst persons very imaginative and very unreal in their notions of life, that family coexistence is treated as if it were all peace or all sunshine. It is not so: and, to speak of one important portion, more particularly, of every large household, its inferior members, its dependents, its servants, could it be expected to be so? Gathered together, in that case at least, from various quarters, to perform together a stated hired service, what is there to make it probable that all their likings and dislikings will be harmonious, or that, if not so, they will feel pleasure in sacrificing their own to another's? We expect too much in looking for these things to come naturally. We ought to recognize the difficulty, and in a Christian spirit to meet it. And again I would ask, What expedient is so likely by God's blessing to operate powerfully towards the Christianizing of a family—for that is what we mean when we speak of diffusing a spirit of kindness and mutual forbearance throughout it—as that gathering together, night and morning, before the throne of a common Father, in the name of a common Saviour, and with prayer for the inward grace of a common Spirit? Often, as they there kneel, will those who have a little forgotten themselves (as we speak) towards one another feel themselves to be silently reconciled, and some early opportunity will be seized of performing one of those little acts of mutual kindness which are often the pledge, better than words, of a restored harmony and a forgiving spirit.

3. I will add a third reason. *Family worship has God's promise, and will draw down God's blessing.* It is not only an honouring of God, and it is not only beneficial in what may be called its indirect effects upon the social life of a household, but it is itself an act of real communication with God, commanded by Him, and sure of His blessing.

Wherever two or three are gathered together in the name of Christ, there is He in the midst of them. That which is taken for granted with regard to private prayer is expressly promised and asserted of social prayer; as though it needed a stronger encouragement, or as though (might we not almost say it?) it were in itself a yet higher act of faith. Let us never lose sight of the direct effects of prayer in the indirect. Prayer has a thousand minor and collateral uses: but it has one primary meaning, and one definite object. It asks for something; and it expects an answer. Even thus it is with the particular mode of prayer which is now before us. If family prayer is worth anything, either as an honour to God, or in its influence upon a household, it must be because it is prayer; not only a thing bearing that name; not the repetition of a few lifeless sounds, as a propriety and a decency, at certain stated hours, by a family calling itself Christian; but the confession of real sins, the avowal of real wants, the outpouring of real desires, to a God believed in and reverenced, through a Saviour known by those who are present, and trusted in. It is not altogether unnecessary, I well know, to enforce strongly this obvious consideration. The direct object of family prayer is, God's blessing. O who shall measure the full compass of that brief phrase—God's blessing? Who does not know the difference between wealth and God's blessing? between prosperity and God's blessing? between domestic love and God's blessing? To feel, within the limits of one's own home, that God's blessing dwells there; that He in whom, whether as friend or foe, we must live and move and have our being, is not an enemy but a Friend; that whatever we have, His smile rests upon it; whatever we do, He precedes and follows it, He approves and He prospers it; that the life which is lived within the sacred precincts of home is a life crowned with His favour, and therefore sweet, therefore happy; this indeed is a comfort worth praying for, and this is that which family prayer daily invokes, and which (I fear we must add) without family prayer can scarcely be. *The blessing of the Lord, it maketh rich: and He addeth no sorrow with it.*

I am firm in the hope, my brethren, that the mention

of this subject to-day, as I know that it is not unseasonable, so will be followed by some marked results in the week which shall follow. Let it not be for nothing that your family will have heard this charge to-day laid upon you, that you institute for them an opportunity of united worship. Let it be a help to you to be aware that they will themselves expect it of you. You know that your conscience has not been altogether easy in the neglect of this duty. A little shyness—very intelligible, very natural, but still not to be yielded to—is all that has, for some time past, stood between you and the establishment of family worship. That shyness has only been waiting, I trust, for some outward appeal to demolish it. To-day you have heard it. Now therefore I will ask you to lose no time in acting upon the call. Life is short: sudden death is too common amongst us to be called a shock or a surprise: set your house in order, for, very soon, soon at the latest, soon whatever be the notice, soon you shall die and not live. Do not have on your conscience any neglected or (which is much the same thing) any postponed duty. It will lie very heavy on you then. Do not have to feel then that, in addition to any personal sins you may have to answer for—slackness in private devotion, acts of injury to your own soul secret or open—you have also to excuse yourself for an habitual neglect of the souls of your family, for having starved them by a denial of the means of grace, whether as ministered in the congregation, or as provided by yourself at home. These are thorns in dying pillows: take heed lest yours be strewn with them.

I anticipate many blessings from an increase of this

family religion amongst us. I do not indeed confuse the terms *family prayer* and *family religion*. There may be punctuality in the one, and no life in the other. But, without the one, the other can scarcely be. If the family are not gathered for worship; if there is no recognition, in any particular house, of God as the God of the family; then consider how greatly you are aggravating the risk of the separate members of the family not worshipping God, not serving God, for themselves. Personal religion is a distinct thing, in some senses, from family religion: we can imagine a family in which its separate members served God in secret, but which nevertheless had no public recognition of Him: and, even on that least formidable of all suppositions, we should feel that there was a want, a defect, a fault, in the community, though it was well covered and to a certain extent redeemed by the individual spirit of devotion. But how improbable is that supposition. It is very easy for a careless master to say, *I have no family worship, but I hope we all serve God equally well in private:* has that master ever seriously reflected upon the opportunities which his household enjoy of serving God in secret? Has each child, has each apprentice, has each servant, his place for private worship, and his time for private worship? Are you ignorant that in many cases there may be interruptions offered, by other inmates of the same chamber, to the exercise of individual worship? that in all cases there are temptations, strong temptations, to neglect it; work beginning at an early hour, and hours of rest too short already to leave much margin for secret prayer night and morning: and, when the day has once begun, and the tasks of the day have set in, and each one is hurrying to and fro to discharge household duties, or is a close prisoner in the shop or in the counting-house, with scarcely leisure so much as to eat, it is a mockery to talk of moments being spared for devotion, unless the piety, unless the charity, unless the humanity, of the employer secures them for all by making it a rule of the house that at certain times all shall assemble for worship? Then, while all other sounds are hushed in the one office of reading the Word of God and of prayer, there will be secured at least one brief interval, two brief intervals, in each day, for self-recollection and for communing with God: and, if the hearts of any should wander away to vain things, you, at least, will be blameless: or if, on the other hand, the hearts of any should seize that period of quietness for a deeper and more personal self-recollection than the words which are in his ears, and which are designed generally for all, could furnish, still He who seeth in secret will accept the offering which gives what it has and does what it can: and yours, in any case, will be the happiness of feeling that you, by word and by example, have made that prayer possible which else would have been impracticable; you have smoothed the path of life for one who might else have missed it; you have drawn down upon your house and upon your heart that promised blessing, *He that watereth shall be watered also himself...Them that honour me I will honour.*

THIRD SUNDAY AFTER TRINITY,
June 16, 1861.

X.

WAYWARDNESS AND WISDOM.

St Luke vii. 35.

But wisdom is justified of all her children.

THE preaching of our Lord was extremely simple. Always grave, always reverent, always, in the best of senses, dignified, it was yet, at the same time, always level to human capacities, just because it disdained not to address human nature and to draw its illustrations from human life. Processes of husbandry or of domestic economy, occupations of poor people and of working men, operations of nature and of Providence, incidents of fortune and instincts of the heart, all were used by Him as illustrations of divine truth, and nothing regarded as too mean or too common to be elevated and consecrated into a vehicle of holy doctrine.

The context affords a singular example of this sort of adaptation. There the very games of children are laid under contribution for a sacred purpose. The pastimes of childish leisure, and the whims and caprices which are sometimes to be noticed in them, are used as an illustration of the temper and conduct of the men of that age towards God and His dispensations.

I beg your attention for a moment to the passage itself; one not entirely easy of explanation, nor always rightly understood.

Whereunto shall I liken the men of this generation, and to what are they like? It is as though the all-wise Teacher were Himself for the moment at a loss how to characterize the disposition of His generation. It is like the question which He sometimes put to His disciples before working a miracle. *From whence shall we satisfy these men with bread here in the wilderness?... And this He said to prove him;* to test the faith of a disciple; *for He Himself knew what He would do.* And thus in the passage before us: though He asked for a comparison, yet He Himself knew what He would say. *They are like children sitting in the marketplace, and calling one to another, and saying, We have piped unto you, and ye have not danced; we have mourned to you, and ye have not wept.* We have tried all ways of pleasing you, gay and grave, and you would accept none. We played you a lively air, and you would not dance; a pathetic dirge, and not a tear fell. We offered to play at marrying, or to play at burying; we would imitate a wedding festivity, or else a funeral solemnity; you would have neither: so unsociable, so unaccommodating, so wilful, so crossgrained. Even thus is it with you grown-up men. You are towards God just what these little perverse wayward children are to their companions. God has tried with you all methods. He sent you one messenger, who was all austerity, all gloom: *John the Baptist came neither eating bread nor drinking wine:* he was a man of the wilderness, expressing by his own garb and deportment the severity of the message with which he was sent to a self-righteous and a self-pleasing age: and you, instead of recognizing the fitness of that character, instead of being awed by it into attention, reverence, and obedience, instead of saying, *God hath done all things well, teaching as much by the demeanour as by the doctrine of His messenger*—instead of this, *ye say, He hath a devil;* you ascribe the isolation of the prophet to moroseness, and moroseness to possession. Again God speaks to you, and, this time, speaks in His Son. He adopts now a different channel for His utterance, and invests with a different character the person of His representative. *The Son of man is come eating and drinking:* He who comes with tidings of salvation, He who not only calls to repentance but offers forgiveness, He whose mission is to human life as a whole, that He may raise, that He may transform, that He may consecrate it all to God, must mix in that life: He must not summon men out of the world to speak with Him in the wilderness, but rather visit them in their world, and show them by His own example how they may be in the world yet not of it: He therefore *came eating and drinking*, mingling with men in those hours of relaxation in which yet more than in business or in devotion they speak as they feel and show themselves as they are. But with what result? Did those who cavilled at the austerity of the Baptist hail the more genial freedom of the Saviour? No, the caviller cavils still, and says, as he sees the Divine Teacher seated at the marriage-feast in Cana, or eating bread in the Pharisee's house, *Behold a gluttonous man, and a winebibber, a friend of publicans and sinners.* Thus it is, and thus it will ever be, with the unregenerate heart of sinful man. He has his excuse always ready for putting aside the call of God. If he cannot quarrel with the message, he will find fault with the messenger: if the words are undeniably sound and wholesome, he will find something to impeach in the dress or the deportment. Meanwhile there are those who judge a more righteous judgment. *Wisdom is justified of all her children.* The wisdom of God in each and all of His dispensations is justified, that is, recognized, felt, and owned, on the part of all those who are truly children of wisdom. The wise justify God's wisdom. They see that in all that He does He does well and He does wisely. They quarrel not with the roughness of the Baptist: they suspect not the gentleness of Christ. They see that each in its place suited the work of each. The presence of an Elijah would have been incongruous at a banquet: the home of the Redeemer could not have been in the desert. God placed each where each was fitting: and they who had gone forth with tears of repentance to be baptized of John in Jordan confessing their sins, returned to listen, seated at the feet of Jesus in the temple-courts or in the home of Capernaum or of Bethany, to the gracious words which told of life for sinners and of a God well pleased for His sake with man.

My brethren, I have thought that the passage thus brought before us in one of the Lessons for the day contained some good and seasonable instruction for us who are here assembled before God. May He by His Holy Spirit bring it home to our hearts.

We have here a contrast presented. There is on

the one side the perverseness, the waywardness, of man; his disposition to cavil at all God's appointments, especially at those which concern religion, revelation, and the soul; his readiness to complain of each as inappropriate, inadequate, inconclusive, or unreasonable; his proneness to say of each, If it had been thus, and not thus, it would have been more satisfactory, more impressive, or more convincing; I should have felt it so, and God, if He had sought my good, would have thus arranged it. On the other side, there is the sympathy of wisdom with wisdom; the kindred and affinity which exists between the voice of God in His Word and the voice of God in the heart and conscience of His creatures; the certainty that what God speaks, and the way in which He speaks—the persons by whom and the circumstances amidst which He speaks—will commend itself to those who are wise indeed, wise in the humility of a true self-knowledge, wise in the genuine insight of an illumination from above.

The waywardness of which our Lord here speaks is more or less in all of us. In some it is a prevailing and predominant habit of mind. We have seen it in its working towards men. There are those—and they are the torment of families—who are possessed by that unhappy temper which takes everything wrong. They are always imagining slights and suspecting insults. They can receive nothing in a simple, straightforward, natural sense. They are always annoyed that this has not been done, rather than that. If they have not arranged a thing themselves, they can perceive nothing but faults in it. They give it to be understood that, if they had had the doing of it, it would have been differently and far better done. Without speaking their thoughts plainly, they wear a look of offence, which is far more trying to others than any anger or any censure. These are the wilful, the wayward, the perverse characters, as shown in human life towards human persons. But that which we all dislike, and feel the discomfort of, in human intercourse, we are all, more or less, guilty of towards God.

We show it in reference to all God's appointments. We have long thought, If I had but this, I should be happy. If I could but gain this one object, this one step in life, this one position or emolument or affection, I should be fully satisfied, I should want nothing more. It comes—it is given—the wish is gratified: do we want nothing more? O, behind the first reach of that mountain summit, there stretches yet another and another and another: to have gained the height which we saw from below, is only to come in sight of a second, and then of a higher still, and yet a higher: he who begins to climb must climb on, or he can but despise the earlier ascent which once seemed so important. Nay, do we not hear of something worse than new desires growing out of old attainments? Who has not known what it is to find the character of an object changed as we grasp it, and to pass from charging God foolishly for not giving, into a yet more sinful murmuring against Him for having listened to our desire? The wayward mind is never satisfied: great need have we, even with regard to earthly matters, to say, Not my will, O Lord, but Thine be done. There are those who, in reference to outward things, justify God's wisdom instead of setting up their own. There are those who say, He has judged better for me than I could have judged for myself: this which He has denied would never have made me happy: this which He has given is the very best thing: it must be so: for has not He, my Father, ordered it?

But it is far more distressing, and scarcely less common, to see the wayward spirit running on into the affairs of the soul. It is impossible to conceive anything more painful than the feeling which some persons cherish as to God's treatment of them morally and spiritually. How often have we heard a young person complain of the strength of particular evil tendencies felt within, as though it were a proof of God's want of love, almost of God's injustice. We have heard that person refer in no submissive tone to the more favourable religious circumstances of another. Not only in reference to the superior character of parents, friends, or companions; to the better example daily witnessed, or the more abundant advantages of Christian instruction. No, the natural constitution of the character has been made a ground of complaint. An irritable or morose temper has been laid, almost in terms, at God's door. An excitability of temperament which makes certain temptations more powerful, or a languor and indolence of habit which makes all manner of exertion more toilsome, than is the case with others, has been expressly charged upon Nature: and what do we know of Nature, save that it is God's order? Men have excused themselves for their faults by their faults. They have found an apology for sins in tendencies to sin. They have said, If I had had the amiable disposition of this person, or the cold temperament of that person, I should have had no trouble in being good. And perhaps that other person may be saying—you, if that regret or that wish of yours had been listened to, would probably have been saying now—If I had the energy of this nature or the fire of that, this indomitable spirit or that impatience of repose, I should not suffer as I do from the difficulty of being an earnest and a zealous Christian. There is no end to these things; these fruitless wishes for a different moral constitution, or these recriminations upon Nature for our faults and sins. It is not only that they are vain: it is that they are perverse, and it is that they are ungrateful. Each one of them can be inverted; and instantly would be so, if the opposite were our condition. These complaints from human hearts are ever rising into the ear of the Lord of Sabaoth, and they sound there like the caprices and irritabilities of little children, whose companions say of them that nothing will satisfy; the grave and the gay are alike distasteful: *We have piped unto you, and ye have not danced; we have mourned unto you, and ye have not lamented.* The wise in heart view all these things in a different spirit. They know that no one is free from tendencies to evil, and no one free from hindrances to good. They know that in these tendencies and in these hindrances lies man's earthly struggle: through these things resisted he must serve God; through these things vanquished he must enter heaven. They see also—or, if they see not, they can trust—that God has ordered the spiritual affairs of His creatures with all justice and judgment; that a principle of compensation runs throughout them, as through their physical and mental circumstances; that what is denied here is given there, and what seems in this point to be an unfairness of disadvantage is made up in that point by some countervailing preponderance of good. And if in some cases they can neither see this, nor see how it can be so, still they trust God's justice through all, and not only silence but satisfy the involuntary risings of doubt within, by the great elementary question, *Shall not the Judge of all the earth do right?* For themselves, they are quite sure that it is so; and they acquiesce in that all-wise appointment which has commanded that their particular battlefield should be situated here and not there; in a character tending (as the case may be) to an excess of warmth or an excess of languor, to irritability or else to torpor, to sensitiveness and its accompanying unreasonablenesses, or else to coldness and its probable shortcomings and deficiencies. They know that their business lies with that which is, not with that which might have been: they set themselves in God's strength to do the work which He has made theirs, and not to imagine how, under altered circumstances, they might have done better that work which He has made another's. Thus is the wisdom of God justified by its children.

We approach yet more nearly to the original use of the context, when we add a few concluding remarks upon the perverseness of man in reference to God's revelations of Himself. The waywardness which is here expressly rebuked was exhibited in the manner in which the Jews of that time received the mission of the Baptist and the mission of the Saviour. They settled with themselves how God ought to speak, and judged accordingly with regard to that which He did speak. When He sent them a reprover, in the befitting garb of austerity and of isolation, they attributed to a diabolical agency those manifestations of the character of the message which he conveyed. When He sent them One who was to bring God's love into everything; to raise what was low, and to sanctify what was common, in human life, by coming Himself into the midst of it to show, not by precept only but by example, what it might be made; then they said that it was self-indulgence which prompted the intermixture, and that one who really came from God would never associate on equal terms with the earthly and the sinful. Thus, whatever God did, was just wrong. If He spoke severely, it was unloving and morose: if He spoke gently, it was a compromise with evil.

My brethren, there are those who judge in much the same manner now of God and His revelations. If He says what we know, or think we know, already, it is superfluous: we do not want a revelation to teach us that. If He says one word beyond what nature or reason might have taught us, it is irrational: the word must be brought to the bar of a pre-existing faculty within, and whatever that faculty does not instantly ratify, must be condemned as a fancy or an imposture. One of the plain declarations of the Bible is pronounced to be inconsistent with probability, another with some human authority, another with the Divine justice, another with Christian charity: one is harsh, one is sweeping, one would lead to mischief, one is extravagant, one is unattainable: all these things must be cast aside as not suiting our preconceptions of God's character or of God's truth. And, as it is with the contents of God's Revelation, so is it also with the proofs and evidences of its Divine origin. One person does not like miracles, another cannot accept prophecy: one says, it is unworthy of God to suspend His own laws; another, it is unworthy of God to dignify human persons by the prediction of their names and deeds; a third finds nothing so convincing to himself as what he calls the internal evidence of truth, the testimony of his own conscience telling him of the goodness of the word spoken, or the comfort of his own heart in the exhibition there made of the holiness and the love of God. And what each one does not like in the way of evidence, he directly casts aside as valueless, and perhaps goes on to demonstrate to be hollow and delusive. Such is man's treatment of God's revelation. And if there be something, in all this, which is presumptuous and shocking; something which offends a sound judgment as irreverent towards God and unthankful for means of conviction largely and variously vouchsafed; might we not apply also to this subject the language now before us, and say that there is also in such reasonings something unworthy and puerile; something which may remind us of the little children sitting in the marketplace, whom nothing can please, who are dissatisfied with every endeavour to charm them from their waywardness and ill-temper? What would they have? What can God say to them which they will not find some excuse for quarrelling with? How can He support His disclosures by such proofs as they will accept as satisfactory? We shall find, I fear, in too many cases, that the real dislike is to Revelation; that the real repugnance is to the idea of being taught anything from above; that the ground of the refusal of this and that as an item of truth or as a mode of demonstration is in fact an overweening estimate of the power and sufficiency of man; insomuch that, whether the heavenly music be gay or grave, it will alike in either case be unresponded to; whether the messenger be the Baptist, he will be said to have a devil —or the Saviour, He will be accused of companionship with the sinful.

Meanwhile, here also, wisdom is justified by her children. They whose hearts are softened by a true self-knowledge, and enlightened by a real communion with God; they who are wise in that wisdom of which the condition is humility, and the beginning the fear of the Lord; will see wisdom in that which to the caviller is folly, will recognize a Divine harmony where all is discord to the self-confident, and own an abundance of resource worthy of the All-wise and the All-merciful, in that variety of evidence which affords to different minds, and perhaps to different ages of the world, their appropriate as well as conclusive reason for believing. The very things which others calumniate are to them indications of wisdom. They see how the message of the Baptist and the habits of the Baptist—the office of the Saviour and the life of the Saviour—are severally harmonious and of a piece. They see how exactly God adapts His means to His end, and His messenger to His message. Where they do not see this, they yet trust. Not blindly, nor in the dark: for they know Him whom they have believed, and judge of that which they discern not by that which they have already known. Thus they live: thus would they die. They cannot part with what they have, till they have found something better. They cannot cavil at God's Word, till they have discovered something more wise, more durable, and more supporting. When the question is put to them, *Will ye also go away?* their answer is, *Lord, to whom shall we go? Thou hast the words of eternal life.*

FOURTH SUNDAY AFTER TRINITY,
June 23, 1861.

XI[1].

FAITH TRIUMPHANT IN FAILURE.

St Luke v. 5.

Master, we have toiled all the night, and have taken nothing: nevertheless at Thy word I will let down the net.

THE Miracles of our Lord are Parables too. Not that we are to lose the fact in the doctrine. Not that we are to say, as some have presumed to say, that the allegorical is either the whole or the primary sense of a Gospel miracle: each miracle is a fact first, and out of the fact flows the doctrine. It is because the record is literally true, that it is also spiritually instructive. It is because the narrative is true to fact, that it is true to life, true to nature, and true to the heart. It is not by deceptions and it is not through illusions that the God of truth leads His creatures into the light of life.

The history from which the text is taken is the account of something which actually occurred. The two little boats lying empty on the shore; the fishermen washing their nets; the request of our Lord for the loan of one of the boats; the discourse held from it with the people on the beach; then the command to let out the

[1] This Sermon was preached also in Westminster Abbey, at the last Special Evening Service of the year, June 30, 1861.

nets, the answer given in the text, and the miraculous draught which followed; these things are all true, they all happened: they are as much matters of fact as is this evening's concourse, as real as that the sound of a human voice is now in your ears. Equally true, as a matter of fact, is that memorable incident which followed; when Simon, suddenly convinced of the superhuman presence in which he stood, threw himself at the feet of Jesus, a man before the Son of Man, and said, *Depart from me, for I am a sinful man, O Lord.* Equally true is it, as a matter of fact, that he received on that occasion a reply which changed the whole course and current of his life, a reply uttered by human lips, but conveying a promise which it was beyond mere human power to fulfil, *Fear not: from henceforth thou shalt catch men.* The after-life of Simon and his companions was the acting upon that command, and the performance to them of that promise. Fishers of men, throwers of the Gospel net upon the world's waters, with results real and palpable; results which have changed the face of history—have made a large part of the earth a totally different scene from that which it else would have been—have altered, have reversed, have inverted human lives, and stamped men with characters the very opposite of those which otherwise they would have borne; results which have either endured, or else been constantly renewed and repeated, through long ages; this is what the disciples here spoken of became and did: this is what Christ's word made them, and He has glorified Himself in them.

Very wonderful and very instructive are the lessons contained in this latter part of the narrative. But I would speak to you this evening on the one verse read as the text; on the answer of Simon to the command to launch out and let down his nets: *Master, we have toiled all the night, and have taken nothing: nevertheless at Thy word I will let down the net.*

Which was the more probable time for catching? Which of the two would the fisherman choose for the exercise of his calling—night, or day? the shaded or the glaring light? the stillness which precedes or the stir which follows the dawn? We need not to be told this: and therefore we can enter into the force of the words, 'All the night we were toiling and caught nothing;' yet now, at Thy word—though it be against experience, against custom, against calculation and expectation—at Thy word I will again let down the net. Thou speakest as with authority: Thy tone is not that of a mocker: if Thou commandest, I cannot think it vain: I have already seen something of the power that is in Thee, when at Thy bidding one of my household rose from a bed of sickness: yes, though all things be against it, yet at Thy word I will let down the net.

My brethren, Sermons have been preached, solemn, earnest, touching Sermons—touching in themselves, and touching in the time and circumstances of their delivery—on the two topics, *Faith triumphant in doubt*, and *Faith triumphant in death.* I would ask you to-night to ponder with me a topic, full of interest, I am persuaded, to many souls here present and open before God, *Faith triumphant in failure:* All the night we have toiled in vain; we have spread the net, and it has enclosed nothing; we have looked in the morning, and, behold, our time, our pains, our patience, had been thrown away; yet, for all this—notwithstanding past discouragement, disappointment, and failure—nevertheless, at Thy word we will once again let down the net.

The terms *success* and *failure* have a large range in human life. Some men are born, we say, to succeed. There are certain qualities which we feel to have a direct bearing upon the realization of objects. A clear conception of the thing aimed at, and a resolute look towards it; a just calculation of distances, and a wise allowance for impediments; a concentration of thought upon means, and a perpetual recollection of ends; amidst and above all, an immovable purpose, and an indefatigable perseverance; these are qualities, or powers, call them which we will, from the possession of which, in any particular instance, we confidently prognosticate success, and the absence of which we deem a certain prophecy of failure, in the race of life viewed only with reference to the interests of this world. And yet even in this matter we are but imperfect judges, fallible prophets. There are failures, even with all these gifts. Perhaps there are successes—it is just possible—without any of them. Nothing that man possesses can guarantee results. After all, *promotion cometh neither from the east nor from the west: God putteth down one, and setteth up another.* Circumstances which man controls not, changes which he cannot foresee, and chances which he cannot regulate, have a wide operation, wider perhaps than ought else, and under their influence it is seen again and again that *the race is not to the swift, nor the battle to the strong;* failure comes where success was certain, success where every one foresaw failure.

And no one can be insensible to the importance, for a human being, of the alternative thus described. It is a very grievous thing for a man to feel at the end of life that life itself has been for him a failure. No one can know, without experience, what the sense of mercantile or professional failure is to a man; what it is to have to confess to oneself that time and strength, the years of education and the years of activity, have been devoted to one work, and that that work has failed; that we have toiled all day and all night, and have taken nothing; nothing that was at all equivalent to the exertion used, the sacrifices made, and the hopes perhaps once fostered.

Happy are they, my brethren—and they are sometimes to be found—who are able to comfort themselves under the consciousness of earthly failure by the sense of a higher and a better success. If a man has found heaven, he may bear to have lost earth. But is it not true that failure has place also in this higher work? Are there no spiritual senses in which the words of the text are true? Is there no such thing as a toiling all the night and taking nothing, in the matters of that world which is of the soul and of eternity?

The history of the Church of Christ is full of answers to that question. What long dark nights has it had to toil through as a body. Have there not been whole periods in which its real work seemed to be going back rather than forward? periods at the end of which the condition and prospects of the Gospel must have appeared even worse than at the beginning? And, on the whole, has not this been the true account of the cause of Christ on earth during the eighteen centuries of its warfare, that it has been, more often than not, apparently stationary; making no visible progress; taking no strides, certainly, towards universal empire; just holding its own by the patient labours of its faithful few, but scarcely seeing one new indication of the approach of the promised day when the kingdoms of the world shall have really become the kingdom of our God and of His Christ? And have not the great advances of the Gospel, when they have come, been irregularly and fitfully bestowed? now and then a whole country opened at once to the inroad of the truth, and then again a generation or two passing without one event which could possibly be called a victory won for Christ? These things have been: and we scarcely know how much of them we ought to ascribe to the order of God's Providence, and how much to the indolence and faithlessness of man. But of this we are sure, that the long toil of the night, however little rewarded, was essential to the marvellous success of the morning; as essential (we cannot say more so) as the faithful letting out of the nets, when morning came, in obedience to the special call of Christ. The attitude of the true Church on earth has ever been characterized by the brief words selected as the topic of this sermon, *Faith triumphant in failure.*

And how shall we say, my brethren, that the case stands now—stands for us? Are we living in a night, or in a morning? Are we of this generation toiling through long hours and taking nothing, or are we rather living in one of those glad and encouraging moments, at which the risen Lord stands at daybreak on the shore of our sea, and says, *Children, have ye any meat?* and when we answer, *No*, goes on to direct us by His own authoritative and loving voice, *Cast the net on the right side of the ship, and ye shall find?* It is not easy to answer that question. It is not for us to seek to answer it while we are yet among the toiling. But it is very important for us not to be deceived; deceived with that sort of deception which mistakes seeming for reality, and counts means instead of weighing results. Nothing is so opposite to faith as vanity. It is far better to be labouring in the blackest night, than to fancy ourselves gathering with Christ when we are indeed scattering without Him.

I hope that it is not thus with us. I hope that there is much, in the Church of this day, of that quiet, steady, faithful plodding, to which the promise is sure, *In due season ye shall reap, if ye faint not.* This, in every age, is the real strength of the Church. It is given to few persons, and at rare intervals, to have magnificent triumphs. St Paul himself, who wrote, *Thanks be unto God who always causeth us to triumph in Christ,* wrote in the very same Epistle of affliction, of anguish, of many tears, of a sentence of death felt in himself, of a restlessness of spirit in anxiety for others, which forced him even to turn aside from a door opened to him of the Lord. The real work of the Church, I would say it once again, is done, in every age, by those who are as willing, if so it be, to toil all the night and take nothing, as they are, at their Master's call, to let out the net for an abundant draught. We think it a great thing—and no one ought to despise it—to have originated some great enterprise of good, some new way of winning souls, some mission, perhaps, to a land hitherto uncared for, or some novel mode of proclaiming the Word of God at home. And it is right to try every way: we are far too fainthearted, and far too unenterprising, and far too uninventive, in this one field alone: *the children of this world are in their generation wiser than the children of light;* and it is dishonourable to our faith and zeal that in the highest and grandest of all works we should be contented to go on in that drowsy and torpid spirit which in matters of business, of science, or of research, would be regarded by all as ruinous and disgraceful. But yet, my brethren, be we well assured that the condition of success in heavenly things is still, as it ever has been, not ingenuity, but devotion; not hurry, but patience; not self-confidence or presumption, but quiet toil, earnest prayer, and invincible faith. All can, by God's grace, labour through the night and watch for the morning: all cannot, upon earth, see that morning break, or hear the joyful summons to let out their nets for one last, one crowning success.

Such thoughts can never be long absent from the hearts of those whose office it is, whether in our own or distant lands, to be fishers of men, watchers for souls as they that must give account. It is theirs to spread the net upon the waters, ignorant whom in particular that net may enclose; ignorant indeed whether in the day of that final drawing ashore, in which the ministers shall be not they but God's Angels, there shall be found within its folds so much as one soul tracing back its eternal life to their instrumentality. It is theirs to spread the net widely; and in prayer, in faith, in patience, to await its gathering. They look not at the agency employed: they desire never to be suffered (in the Prophet's words) to *sacrifice to their net:* they would rather toil through their night, and look solely to His blessing who alone can give the increase. God grant that that increase may be largely, may be abundantly, bestowed. Yet, even if it come not, faith shall still triumph amidst failure—still, at Christ's word, shall continue to let down the net.

We wonder oftentimes, and who can help it? that, if the Gospel be indeed God's, more success is not vouchsafed to it. And, though the reasons for its failure are not few nor far to seek; reasons wholly of man's neglect and indifference and inconsistency; still we wonder on, and in moments of darkness could almost suffer wonder to pass into murmuring. But this I think we can say—and, if it is no answer to the general question, at least it may speak to us as individuals—that it is but little of success which any of us can safely bear. Where is the man whose highest life is not somewhat injured by success—whose soul does not prosper most in failure? Yes, my brethren, the remark has a wide compass: I know not whether we may not almost carry it into the inward as well as the outward work of man. But of the latter, at all events, we may say it; that then is a man's soul safest and most healthy, when he is not borne along on the highest wave of a triumphant success. Look at the life of one who has devoted himself to the ministry of Christ's Gospel. Do you suppose that there is no danger to that man's soul from seeing himself followed, listened to, admired, by a crowd of persons assembled rather to hear than to worship? That, you will say, and most truly, deserves not to be called success: the object of the ministry is to win souls not to man but to God; and it is not until man is forgotten that God is found. But go further: there are men, and in these days women too, who have an evident power granted to them over the souls of others; when they appear, there is respect; when they speak, there is attention; when they reason, there is conviction; when they remonstrate, there is shame; when they persuade, there is change, there is obedience, there is reformation. Well may they thank God, and take courage for further conflicts. But do we not feel also that out of this power over others arises a risk for them? Is there not to be seen a tinge of self-complacency, self-gratulation, at last almost of self-confidence, in the very language of humility and self-abnegation in which they publish their successes to the world? Yes, indeed it is true not least in spiritual things, that *man being in honour hath no understanding:* we can all bear comparative failure better than marked success: and I doubt not that that faith which triumphs over failure is oftentimes a purer and a brighter quality than the faith which gives thanks, or forgets to give thanks, over success.

No one can overestimate the qualities which are demanded for a steady triumph over failure. Mark the man to whom that grace has been given. I have seen such a man in a country parish, remote in place, unattractive in scenery, uninteresting in every characteristic of its population. He came there in early years, endowed with gifts of intellect, fresh from academical honours, and he established himself there deliberately for life. He was the friend of his people in health, their physician in sickness, their counsellor in life, their comforter in death. The Word of God was his study and his meditation: week by week, and day by day, he was unfolding its stores to such as would listen. For nine and forty years he lived thus: he carried his plan of life to its completion, and died where he had laboured. And yet that man never knew what success was. He had no striking, no marked, triumphs. He spent and was spent; he offered himself day by day upon the sacrifice and service of his people's faith; and yet he felt, all the time, that, the more abundantly he loved, the less he was loved. This never shook him from his purpose. If he toiled all the night and caught nothing, still his faith was proof even against that failure. At last he rests from his labours: and now, no doubt, his works follow him. No doubt, others are entering into his labours, and reaping what he had sown. So would he have it. He served a faithful Master, and he will be quite satisfied, when he awakes, with His likeness. Which of us, in the retrospect, cannot see that that life was a safe life and a blessed one? Dull and uneventful, monotonous and unremunerative, when weighed in an earthly balance, was it not a noble one when weighed in the balance of God's sanctuary? Noble, just because it was far-reaching and deep-sighted; noble, because it showed a wonderful superiority to the influences of things seen and temporal; noble, because he who so lived was able to say, and to act upon the declaration, *Master, I have toiled all the night, and have taken nothing; nevertheless at Thy word, I will* again and yet again *let down the net.*

And is it not even so, though it be in humbler measure, with all those who have cared deeply for the souls of others? Has not the parent whose heart has been deeply exercised with anxiety for the salvation of her children, found in that long watching, that fervent intercession, that occasional agony of apprehension, a seriousness, a sobriety, a devotion, a nearness of access to

God, which might else have been distracted by meaner cares, or drawn downwards by lower attractions? There is perhaps no greater triumph of faith than that which has been won over and over again amidst the apparent failures of this anxious conflict. When the very child in whom earthly hope centres can be truly resigned into the hands of God; when the disappointment of prayer itself only makes prayer the more earnest; when a career of indifference, folly, or sin, while it wrings the heart with anguish, can yet be watched through and prayed through in the strength of an invincible trust in the mercy and faithfulness of an Almighty Saviour; then, even more than in self-denying works of charity, is the victory of faith won: and may we not believe that in the most unpromising case there is a virtue in that fervent prayer which shall at last make it effectual? that Christ sees in that toiling through the long night a trust which is altogether acceptable, and will crown it, even after death, with the very boon for which it waited?

But, my brethren, it is not only in reference to others that faith in Christ has to combat and to conquer failure. And I believe that it is when we come to our own case that we shall feel, not least but most deeply, the truth on which we have dwelt.

Where is he amongst us who, looking back upon the years that are past, can count his spiritual history altogether a success? I should almost doubt him if he declared it so. The Christian life is often called a warfare: is that warfare always a victory? I know that it ought to be so. St John writes that a Christian *cannot sin, because he is born of God;* that he *keepeth himself, so that the wicked one toucheth him not.* Those are words which have caused misgiving to many a serious heart: how could it be otherwise? For indeed we feel, my brethren, that the Christian of whom such words could be spoken is scarcely one of us. We know that it ought to be so: we know that, if a Christian sins, it is because he is, so far, not a Christian; because he has forgotten his Saviour, and looked off from his God. But, for ourselves, what can we say? O, if the hearts of this congregation were laid open, where would be he amongst us who could come forward to claim the victor's wreath? I know better than to suppose that there is one here present to whom the sense of failure is not more familiar than the experience of triumph. What is our day made up of, but a succession of failures? What is *the time past of our life* but a long retrospect of defeats? Duties left undone; relations unfaithfully fulfilled; Bibles left unread, prayers often left unsaid and oftener left unprayed; a testimony for God rarely borne with the lips and often contradicted in the life; affections set not on things above but on things of the earth; that is one part of the record: I do not suppose that any one will gainsay that charge. How is it with another? Sins, not of omission only; definite bad habits; unkind, envious, resentful thoughts; unkind, mischievous, irreparable words; yes, and worse things still than these—whose history is entirely free from darker stains? I know there are those who are so: let them thank God far more than themselves if it be the case: let them thank Him for a natural disposition, perhaps, which pointed not towards some iniquities: let them thank Him for controlling circumstances which have stood between

Faith triumphant in Failure.

them and some transgressions: let them thank Him for that diffusion of general light which in a Christian land makes some crimes all but impossible in some stations: but let them not fail to acknowledge that in them, that is, in the natural heart, dwells no good thing: let them not deny that in all of us there is the germ at least of every sin: and, if they have little of outward open sin to answer for, then let them carry the question further, and see how it has been with sins to which they were prone; let them ask whether, on the whole, success or failure in the great spiritual warfare of life has been for them the more frequent: and I shall expect to hear that these too find themselves condemned; that these too must look back upon a long night, if of toiling, yet of taking nothing; of incessant defeat in whatever was for them the spiritual conflict; of countless disappointments in whatever they did prescribe to themselves as their bounden duty and service.

My brethren, *nevertheless* let faith triumph over failure. I know that every failure is a proof of the want of faith. I know that, if faith were present, failure could not be. But there is such a thing as faith, after defeat, returning to the charge: and it is in that returning to the charge that the test of our Christianity lies. A man who can come back to Christ, and say, *Lord, I have slept at my post—Lord, I have let my oars drop—Lord, I have often left my net unmended until it could enclose nothing—Lord, I have suffered weariness to make me indolent, and long disappointment to make me hopeless—I have done all this—but yet—even now—even thus late—I will, once again, at Thy word let my net down, and wait Thy blessing* —that man may have many faults, he may be much behindhand, he may be full of infirmity and of sin, but he has the root of the matter in him; he has a little faith, and according to that faith shall it be to him. That man knows something, however little, of a faith triumphant in failure. He, if he tries it, shall triumph too. Christ watches not for our halting but for our rising. It is not in Him that we are straitened. O suffer not yourself to fall finally—it has been the case, alas, with many—just because you would have it that you were not a Christian. Arise, call upon Christ, and be assured that He will give you light.

May His blessing, which is life and strength, be upon us all. He stands, as He stood of old, upon the shore, and asks us of our welfare. He enters, as He entered of old, into the little vessel which contains our fortunes: He feels for its frailness, He will guide its flittings, He will steer it for us into the haven where we would be. Hitherto we may have toiled and taken nothing: but if, at His word, we will now let down the net, He will bring into it that which shall be sufficient for us, and man's failure shall be Christ's success.

SIXTH SUNDAY AFTER TRINITY,
July 7, 1861.

XII.

FRIENDS AND FOES.

1 **Kings xxi.** 20.

Hast thou found me, O mine enemy?

SOME of us may have read of battles in which there has been a mistaking of friend for foe. Whether owing to mist or darkness, to unexpected positions or to intentional disguises, assailants have been hailed as supporters, or friendly succours attacked as hostile reserves, and the error, on whichever side it occurred, has decided the fortune of the day, turning defeat into success, or victory into discomfiture. It is above all things necessary in fields of battle to be able to distinguish between friends and foes. And it is regarded either as a terrible misfortune, or (more often) as a gross mismanagement, if, in these late days of the world, when the science of war is well understood, and the dearly bought experience of ages has prepared men for all chances and for all manœuvres, any such error is allowed to find place as must cause a wanton sacrifice of human life and make havoc of the wisest plans and the most sanguine hopes.

Thus it is in the warfare of flesh and blood. How is it in that warfare which is not carnal but spiritual? Is there in that warfare which is waged by the soul—

that warfare on the result of which, for every one of us, depends hell or heaven—any such thing as a mistaking of friend and foe? Is it possible that any one of us might hail as a friend one who is really a sworn and deadly foe, or receive a true and trustworthy friend with the question of the text, *Hast thou found me, O mine enemy?*

We read this morning of a case in which such a confusion actually occurred. A wicked king had selfishly coveted the vineyard of a subject. He offered terms for it, and they were refused. Deeply offended and bitterly vexed, he yet felt that there the matter ended. If Naboth would not sell, Ahab could not buy. If Ahab could not convince Naboth of the desirableness of the proposed exchange, Naboth must keep the inheritance of his fathers, and Ahab must go without it. But there was a counsellor at home, more bold and more unscrupulous. When Ahab is lying on his bed, like a peevish child, with his face turned to the wall, refusing to eat because something has thwarted and crossed him, his wife Jezebel comes in to rebuke his faintheartedness, and to remind him that, for a king, might is right, and what cannot be got by persuasion may yet be taken by force. *Dost thou*, she said, *now govern the kingdom of Israel? arise, and eat bread, and let thine heart be merry: I will give thee the vineyard of Naboth the Jezreelite.* The rest of the sad story is soon told. By false evidence an innocent life is sworn away, and Jezebel comes back to her husband with the triumphant tidings, *Arise, take possession of the vineyard of Naboth the Jezreelite, which he refused to give thee for money: for Naboth is not alive, but dead.* Without scruple and without remorse, Ahab avails himself of the opportunity thus procured. He goes down at once to take possession of the now vacant vineyard. But God has looked on, and marked every step of the guilty process. God does notice these deeds of violence and oppression, and, if a man will not turn, He must whet His sword. He sends His Prophet to meet Ahab in Naboth's vineyard. The words of the text are Ahab's greeting. *Ahab said to Elijah, Hast thou found me, O mine enemy?* It is thus that sinners regard God's messenger. He is their enemy. He may be discharging a solemn duty; reluctantly, unwillingly, with great pain to himself, with all kindness in his heart; it matters not: if he comes from God, if he carries God's message, if he speaks the truth, if he loves righteousness, he is regarded as an enemy by one who will not be saved.

Human nature is not altered by lapse of years, nor by change of circumstances. This mistaking of friends and foes is inherent in us all. God grant us grace to meditate on the subject to-night, for correction, for conviction, and for conversion.

Hast thou found me, O mine enemy?

God's messengers to us are various. Sometimes He sends a man to us; addresses the sinner by a human voice, and confronts him, face to face, with the minister of righteousness. That is, in one aspect, the office of the Christian pastor. If he takes any pains to acquaint himself with the state of his flock—and without knowing its state how can he hope to do anything real and true? he will find, in no long time, cases, patent and notorious, of actual immorality among those committed to his oversight. The frightful disregard, in a town like this, of God's law of marriage; the perpetual discovery of lives lived in adultery; of men leaving their wives, and women deserting their husbands, to form new connections; and the terrible shamelessness with which such lives are excused or even justified, either by the commonness of the example, or (in some cases) by the provocation received; these things constrain a Clergyman, if he would not shut himself up at home in a sinful indifference, to speak in God's behalf, again and again, to persons sunk in sin, and to warn them, as they would escape the wrath to come, to cleanse themselves, while they can, from that which is provoking God's judgment every day. But, when he seeks to do this, how is he reminded, in his own experience, of Ahab's speech to Elijah. What endeavours does he observe to evade him, to avoid his visit, to keep him off the subject. What an obvious reluctance to be found at home. What excuses of business, of haste, of an inconvenient time. What vague general remarks. What cold unmeaning admissions. What an affectation of unconcern, of self-satisfaction, or else what idle hopeless expressions of an intention hereafter, at some remote day, to reform. However various the form of the reception, how clear is it that the person addressed is determined to regard you as an enemy. How little are you recognized as one who has at heart the good of a sinner; who would fain carry comfort only; who, if he wounds, wounds but to heal.

Nor is it only in these extreme cases, where there is a definite cause of irritation, and a natural temptation to repel advice, that a Christian minister finds himself received as an intruder and a foe. Wherever God is not honoured, the messenger of God must be unwelcome. Not, indeed, if he will drop that character, and enter only as a complaisant visitor. How often is he tempted to be this and nothing more. There is such a manifest wish to keep him within these limits; such an evident anxiety to prevent his coming to close quarters, or being, in such a visit, at all what he is in the Church; sometimes such a nervous restlessness in avoiding topics which might lead on to matters of religion; that he is perpetually reminded of the conditions on which alone he is received, and made to feel that there is no real cordiality towards him in that which ought to be his true character, however friendly his acceptance while he forgets or lays it by.

Have we not seen the same thing in chambers of the sick, beside beds of the dying? There lies one who has shirked through life the responsibilities of a Christian: one who has been irregular as a worshipper, grudging as a giver, infrequent or unknown as a communicant: one who has lived to himself and for himself, immersed in this world's business, or engrossed by this world's pleasures. At last the end is come; or the beginning of the end: and the Clergyman who has been disregarded in health must go to minister to the sickness. Twice or thrice, perhaps, he calls without admission: the sick man is weary, or he is sleeping, or he is not equal to exertion, or the physician has enjoined quiet: at last, excuses are exhausted, and without actual rudeness admittance can no longer be refused. But even then how little may have been gained. *Hast thou found me, O mine enemy?* may be the language of the manner, if not of the lips: hast thou taken advantage of my misfortune to disquiet me with unwelcome reflections? I know all that thou wouldest say: I have my own thoughts and my own devotions: why come to torment me before the time?

But God's messengers are not all men: and the chief power of the human messenger lies in his close connection with another, not of flesh and blood. It has been difficult to speak of the one without introducing the agency of the other. If the visit of a Clergyman, in the midst of sin or of sickness, has in it anything formidable, anything which can suggest the idea of hostility, it is because the thoughts which he comes to awaken are already lodged in the conscience of the sinner. Elijah would have been little to Ahab—certainly he would not have been his enemy—but for his connection, in Ahab's mind, with the remembrance of good left undone and of evil done. As soon as he saw him, there rose before his mind's eye the ghost of the murdered Naboth; the spirits of the Lord's prophets, by him, or with his connivance, slain with the sword; the remembrance of sins against God, and of sins against His people, which could not always be forgotten, and which had still to be accounted for. The Prophet was his enemy just because he was in concert with an enemy. The real enemy was not he, but conscience.

O, my brethren, who shall describe the ways of men towards their conscience? What a wonderful thing it seems, what a proof (did we need it) of our fallen state, that we should allow such an ordinance as that of conscience to be a hindrance to us and an offence. The instinct of an animal is his guide and his protection: the appetite of the body is the stimulus to self-preservation: how comes it that that thing within us which was so evidently designed to teach us what to do and what not to do, what to avoid beforehand and what to regret afterwards, is, not trusted, not followed, not cherished, not welcomed, but disliked, disregarded, thwarted, evaded, at last dreaded and hated? What a proof not only of the danger, but of the unnaturalness, of a life of sin. If it puts us at variance within, if it makes us try to smother and to extinguish within us that which ought to be the very lamp of our feet and light of our path, surely it cannot be good for us, surely it cannot bring us peace at the last. It cannot be well with any man who has to say to his own conscience, *Hast thou found me, O mine enemy?*

And yet so it is. Once let a man break loose from God; once let him give himself up to his self-will, lead him where it may; and forthwith, increasingly, at last utterly, he will find his conscience his foe.

Sometimes conscience will say to him, in the darkness of night, in the stillness of solitude, There is a certain duty which you are neglecting. There is a certain trust to which you are unfaithful. There is a certain relation of life—the relation of a son, or the relation of a parent—the relation of a husband or wife, the relation of a brother or sister—the relation of a servant, or the relation of a master—which you are not fulfilling but in some known point neglecting. Or there is some one whom you have injured, and you have made no restitution. Or there is some one with whom you are at variance, and you are taking no pains, making no exertion, nay, perhaps, actually refusing, to be reconciled. In business, you are not scrupulously honest: in conversation, you are not watchfully charitable: this man or that you have spoken evil of, perhaps needlessly, perhaps falsely. There is that poor person, known to you, whom you have failed to look after: there is that sick friend whom, in idleness or unkindness, you have shrunk from visiting. These remonstrances of conscience ought to be trumpet-calls to duty. We ought to thank God for admonishing us of forgotten claims, and bringing to our remembrance definite obligations which cannot be disregarded without risk of ruin. But is that our feeling? Who has not looked upon these workings of conscience rather as the stabs of a foe?

Even more is it thus when conscience does not so much awaken to duty as rebuke and punish for sin. There are sins, definite sins, upon many of us; far past it may be, or else perhaps quite recent; nay, possibly still lived in, still habitual. And for the most part we may be able, by long use, to sin, and sin again, and sin on, without very great misery. It is the tendency of sin to drug conscience. The most sensitive conscience is the most innocent: even we, when we were children, were agitated and tortured by the smallest fault in a way now unknown to us even after heinous sins. But the sleep of sin itself has its visions and its nightmares; its dreams of punishment, its anticipations of judgment. Never, till sin has actually wrought death, is conscience entirely and always silent. Conscience is God's minister in life: after death it will be God's executioner. At present, it is charged with an office of mercy, to the most wicked: it is our friend, however severe, however stern, however alarming. Even in those terrible pangs by which conscience sometimes stirs to its very bottom the heart of a transgressor, there is a gracious purpose, a loving aim. Conscience is the voice of God Himself, saying to the sinner, *Why wilt thou die? I have no pleasure in the death of him that dieth:* repent, turn, and thou shalt be forgiven, thou shalt be accepted, thou shalt be saved. But so we will not have it. We will have it that conscience is an enemy: in other words, that God, if He loved us, would let us sleep on, and at last die, in our sins; would give us our brief lifetime, uninterrupted and unmolested, to waste or to abuse it at our pleasure, and at least not meddle with us, not send messages to us of rebuke or warning, till the earthly day had run out and the long night of eternity had closed in.

But, if it seems strange that any one should count his own conscience an enemy, when he ought to know that the only object of conscience is to warn, to benefit, and to save, is it not yet more wonderful that the same feeling should ever be shown towards the very Gospel of grace, towards the Saviour of sinners Himself? We all think it a proof of unnatural wickedness, that persons living on earth when Jesus came should have been able to resist the power and wisdom, the tenderness and love, which were shown alike in His words and in His deeds. The names of Judas who betrayed, of Pilate who condemned Him—of the chief priests, the scribes and Pharisees, who accused Him of encouraging sinners, of irreverence, of presumption, of blasphemy—are by-words of shame and reproach: it never occurs to us that we by possibility could have done even as they. We all agree to call Him by the reverent and loving names of our Lord, our Saviour, our Mediator and Redeemer. We cannot understand how, even in the dread of a Divine presence, any one could ever have said to Him, like Simon Peter, *Depart from me.* We read of it as an infallible mark of possession by an evil spirit, if the organs of human speech were ever used to utter the sounds, *What have we to do with thee, Jesus, Thou Son of God? art Thou come hither to torment us before the time?* And yet, my brethren, I repeat that multitudes of persons—yes, even of respectable, even of church-going persons—pass through life regarding our Lord Jesus Christ as an enemy. They are afraid of Him; afraid of what He might bid them to do and not to do, if they were to connect themselves closely with Him; and therefore they keep Him at a distance: they do just enough as it were to pacify or propitiate Him: they know that they will one day want Him: but they almost deliberately defer seeking Him till the late hour of a death-bed repentance.

My brethren, these are the *enemies* of the natural man, of the fallen, the sinful, the unbelieving man: God's minister, conscience or God's voice, Jesus the Divine Saviour. And let me say that to have these for enemies involves having many other things as enemies which need not be so. When adversity comes, whether in the shape of difficulties or misfortunes in business, or in that of deficient or failing health, or in that of separation, loneliness, and loss of friends, then to each of these the man who is living apart from God has to address himself in the words of the text, and say, *Hast thou found me, O mine enemy?* And yet his neighbour, ten times more troubled and distressed than he in outward things, yet, in the confidence of an unshaken faith, may be discerning in each circumstance of anxiety and sorrow the hidden hand of God, confessing that he not only merited but needed each stroke of chastisement, and assured that behind every cloud of a frowning Providence there lies concealed an unerring wisdom and a stedfast love. Most of all is this so when death approaches. O how does the worldly man fight death off. How does he put away from himself upon others each warning—and they are many—of his certainty, of his nearness, of the possible suddenness and surprise of his coming. How does he veil from himself the tokens of advancing age, and catch at every instance of an extension beyond the common limit of man's threescore years and ten. And, when at last he finds himself tracked and hunted down by the footsteps of the pursuer; when the weakness of age has made itself felt, and the sickness which must be final has at last laid its grasp upon him; can we not hear him exclaim, in the bitterness of his soul, *Hast thou found me, O mine enemy?* thou who art to snatch me from everything loved or believed in, and to hurry me whither I know not, whither I would not? O how unlike the language of him for whom even death, *the last enemy,* has already lost his sting, and who can even welcome his coming, however formidable in itself, as the means of carrying him, safely and surely, into the very haven where he would be; into the presence of that Almighty and All-merciful Saviour whom not having seen he loves.

Hast thou found me, O mine enemy?

Is there any person, or is there any thing, whom we ought thus to address? Yes, my brethren. We spoke, at the outset, of the risk of mistaking friends for foes. Human nature addresses as its enemy weariness and sickness, poverty and bereavement; shrinks at the touch of pain, and is in bondage throughout life to the fear of death. And fallen human nature, fallen and unrenewed, addresses as its enemy the man who brings with him a message from God, conscience which is God's voice within, and Jesus Christ Himself who comes to save us from our sins. Thus its warfare is wholly misdirected: every blow is aimed at some disguised friend, and every plan and every watchword is betrayed to some disguised enemy. What can come of this but defeat, rout, carnage? Human nature, and each several partaker of it, has an enemy: but it is just that one thing which counterfeits the voice and professes the interest of a friend. That one enemy is Sin. *We wrestle not against flesh and blood, but against principalities, against powers, against the rulers of the darkness of this world, against spiritual wickedness in high places.* When we say, *Hast thou found me, O mine enemy?* we ought to mean, *I am in the presence of a strong temptation:* we ought to mean, *My adversary the devil, as a roaring lion, walking about, seeking whom he may devour, has come hither also, and he seeks my life:* we ought to mean, *That evil thing to which I am most prone, that particular evil temper, evil passion, or evil lust, which is, of all, the most potent with me, is at this moment soliciting me, and bids me yield even if I die for it:* we ought to mean, *Now is a crisis of the spiritual life: shall I fight, or shall I fly? shall I tamely succumb to this false bidder, who tells me that he wishes me to be happy, tells me that this thing is happiness, tells me that I cannot dispense with it, that I must have it, let who will forbid? or shall I boldly say to him that he is a foe in disguise, and that I will none of him? God help me to count him my enemy, even because he is His enemy; and to answer, in the name of God, Thou hast found me, O mine enemy: but thou hast found me watching, not sleeping; armed of God, and therefore not defenceless.* If Ahab had said to Jezebel, when she came to tempt, *Hast thou found me, O mine enemy?* he would have had no cause to say it to Elijah, when he came to judge.

God grant, my brethren, that we may less and less have occasion to use the words of the text in their yet sadder sense, not of the presence of temptation, but of the commission of sin. O that bitter waking to the consciousness that we have yet again fallen, when we have to say not to the tempter only, but to the sin itself, *Hast thou found me, O mine enemy?* found me, not watching, not armed, not praying, not looking upward, but careless, supine, self-confident, self-complacent, and therefore unstable as water, nay, even like the house swept and garnished for the evil one. Whose life bears not the impress of some such sad experience? Happy they who still, even amidst much weakness, many falls, and many sins, yet retain so much at least of a Christian purpose, as to hate their own sin and count it their enemy. These, surely, whatever others do, will betake themselves to their refuge. These, surely, whatever others do, will feel that in God, in Christ Jesus, in the Holy Spirit, is their one hope, their one safeguard, their one chance of escape; and will be able, at last, by God's grace, not only to ask St Paul's question, *O wretched man that I am: who shall deliver me from this body of death?* but also to answer it, in St Paul's words of gratitude, trust, and faith, *I thank God through Jesus Christ our Lord.*

TENTH SUNDAY AFTER TRINITY,
August 4, 1861.

XIII.

GREAT THINGS AND SMALL.

2 Kings v. 13.

My father, if the prophet had bid thee do some great thing, wouldest thou not have done it? how much rather then, when he saith to thee, Wash, and be clean?

SUNDAY after Sunday, in reading the Lessons taken from the Old Testament history, we have the remark forced upon us, How true is Scripture to human life. How entirely is the God of the Bible the God of Providence and the God of Nature. How exactly are we ourselves and the men amongst whom we move—our own hearts, and theirs—our own infirmities, and theirs—our own temptations, and theirs—pourtrayed and mirrored in these narratives.

Is it not so to-day? Read the account of Naaman the Syrian. He is one of those persons, of whom we have so many examples now, who have every blessing that heart can wish, except just one; or who are exempted from every trouble and trial, except just one; who are men, perhaps, of high position, of affluent means, of popular manners, of talents made for success, and yet have one little ingredient in their cup, which poisons all the rest. He was *captain of the host of Syria*...he was *a great man with his master, and honourable*...he was also *a mighty man in valour*...BUT *he was a leper*. And with that drawback what was all else? Wealth, honour, military fame, what were they, with such a sorrow added? At last a ray of hope enters. A little maid, brought away captive out of the land of Israel, tells of a prophet there who possesses a charm even for the plague of leprosy. The news reaches the king, Naaman's master. He concludes that the powers of the prophet of Israel must be at the command of the king of Israel, and sends Naaman to him with a letter simply stating that he comes to be recovered of his leprosy. The king of Israel regards this strange request as a mere pretext for a quarrel. But, when the prophet hears of it, he recognizes this as an opportunity of making the name of God known, and desires that the stranger may be sent on to him. We can see the pomp and circumstance with which the visit is accompanied. *With his horses and with his chariot*, the foreign general, so great a man at home, drives to the humble dwelling of Elisha, and expects a reception suitable to his rank and fame. Instead of this, he receives a mere message, affronting in substance and affronting in manner, bidding him go and wash seven times in the paltry stream of Jordan. The pride of Naaman takes fire instantly. He had expected that at least the prophet would come out to him, and, with all the proper parade of invocation and enchantment, conduct the process, in person, of an elaborate cure. If washing in a river is all that is needed, he can do that at home. *Are not Abana and Pharpar, rivers of Damascus, better than all the waters of Israel? May I not wash in them, and be clean? So he turned and went away in a rage.*

It is at this point that the words of the text occur. *His servants came near, and spake unto him, and said, My father, if the prophet had bid thee do some great thing;* if he had prescribed a long and a severe course of treatment; painful abstinence, or nauseous medicine; the pursuit of health by long journeys or difficult exertions; *wouldest thou not have done it?* wouldest thou have regarded anything as too burdensome or too wearisome to be endured as the condition of a perfect cure? *how much rather then* mayest thou obey him, *when he saith to thee* this only, *Wash, and be clean.* The timely and respectful remonstrance, the rational and unanswerable argument, had its due effect. Naaman saw the folly of his anger, and set himself without delay to act upon the simple prescription. *He went down, and dipped himself seven times in Jordan, according to the saying of the man of God, and his flesh came again like unto the flesh of a little child, and he was clean.* No words and no gifts could then adequately express his gratitude. Into the sequel of the story we do not now enter: that might be the subject for a Sermon of its own. It is with the remonstrance of the servants, and the lessons to be derived from it, that our present concern lies.

If the prophet had bid thee do some great thing, wouldest thou not have done it? How true is this even in reference to matters of bodily health. How often has a person suffering from continued indisposition, or from some troublesome special ailment, refused the suggestion of a remedy, not because it was too severe, but because it was too simple. It is ridiculous to suppose that such a thing as that could do me good. Nay, so much is this recognized as an infirmity of human nature—this tendency to be affronted by the simplicity and facility of a proposed means of cure—that physicians themselves are sometimes compelled to humour it, and, even where they see that nothing is required but a small change of diet, or the application of some perfectly obvious medicine, find it necessary, nevertheless, to wrap up the case in a certain degree of mystery, or to compound the efficacious drug with a certain quantity of harmless but unmeaning adjuncts, in order to satisfy the patient that his malady is duly respected, or that he himself is treated with the honour due to his position.

How true is the remark also in reference to the life of families. There is a brother or sister, a wife or a husband, really devoted to the person with whom they live; ready, not in name only but in truth, to give all they have, to give their very life, for another; and yet they who can do the greater thing cannot do the less; cannot promote the comfort, in little things, of those to whom in theory they are devoted; cannot give up their own will to another's in small matters, for the sake of peace and happiness; cannot correct the thwarting temper, cannot stifle the provoking taunt; cannot, in short, make those little sacrifices which are required of them, though they would cheerfully make those great sacrifices which are seldom necessary, perhaps never possible. They cannot enter at all into the force of the argument, If some great thing had been required of thee, wouldest thou not have done it? how much rather then, when all that is asked of thee is so small, so easy.

These things, in bodily matters, are innocent if foolish weaknesses. In social life, they become more important: the peace of families, and the happiness of individuals, is often wrecked upon them. But they are shown also in spiritual things, where nothing that is wrong and nothing that is foolish can enter in without real mischief, perhaps actual ruin, to the soul.

1. We see it in reference to the ordinances of the Gospel.

If the prophet had bid thee do some great thing, wouldest thou not have done it? How many persons are there, sufficiently desirous of salvation to have been tolerant of a very burdensome ritual, had the Gospel prescribed it, who yet find in the fewness and simplicity of its authorized observances an excuse for disregarding them altogether. I do not doubt that there are many here present, who, if they had been commanded to perform certain acts of worship seven times in a day, to undergo great privations and make great sacrifices in order to accomplish a very wearisome round of ritual ceremonies, would have found in the mere difficulty of compliance a motive for obedience. There is evidently something in human nature, not only which is roused by difficulties, but which is flattered by demands. Let a man suppose that heaven is to be won by punctuality of observance, and he will count every added ceremony not only a fresh stimulus but a new honour. And yet the same person cannot be brought to regard with proper respect the moderate and quiet services of his own Church, the humble instrumentality of preaching, or the two Sacraments which Christ has ordained. If you wish to gain his attention at all, you must add to these true and just requirements a multitude of others which rest but on opinion or fancy. He cannot be brought to see that a simple ordinance like that of Christian Baptism can derive any importance from the fact of Christ's institution, of Christ's command. He cannot understand how there should be any connection at all between *the washing of water* and the condition of a soul; between *the putting away*, as St Peter expresses it, *of the filth of the flesh*, and *the answer of a good conscience toward God*. If he brings his child to the font, it is in compliance with the world's custom rather than with the Saviour's word. He cannot see that the very simplicity of the sign is rather an argument for than against its Divine origin. If man had had the ordaining of it, certainly it would have been something more difficult, more cumbrous, and more costly. In the same way, he refuses to believe that there can be anything beneficial to the soul in eating a morsel of bread or drinking a few drops of wine at the table of his Lord. He asks again, What can be the connection in such matters between the body and the soul? How can the food of the body be in any sense the strengthening of the soul? He can understand that what he calls a good life, or even a devout and pious spirit, may be an acceptable offering; but he cannot believe—he will almost say so in words—that it can be a matter of the slightest moment whether or no he performs that outward act of communion which nevertheless he cannot deny to be distinctly ordained and plainly commanded in the Gospel. If the prophet, if the Saviour, had bidden him to do some great thing, he would certainly have done it: but he cannot bring himself to believe and obey, when the charge is that simple one, to wash and be clean.

2. The same tendency is exemplified in reference to the doctrines of the Gospel.

If we rightly read the Scriptures of the New Testament, they tell us that the way to salvation is through faith. And they tell us further that faith is a very simple thing; that, great as its effects are, and great as its consequences are, the thing itself is nothing more than taking God at His word; believing that what He says is true, what He says He has done He has done, what He says He will do He will do, what He promises He is able also to perform, what He offers He is not able only but willing to bestow. And thus we find that, as the basis of all His dealings with us, He has made an atonement for our sins through the blood of His Son ; has laid all our sins upon Christ ; has made Him, who knew no sin, to be sin for us ; has given Him to be the propitiation for our sins, and not for ours only, but also for the sins of the whole world. We find that He calls upon us simply to believe this, and, believing it, to act upon it : to act upon it by accepting, by apprehending, by grasping, the assurance thus conveyed ; by receiving into our hearts the comfort, and the strength, and the blessing, contained in the doctrine of a free forgiveness; by throwing ourselves with our whole weight upon the declaration, *Behold the Lamb of God, who taketh away the sins of the world.* Now, when this Gospel comes to us, how often do we see it evaded. Nay, my brethren, let us look at ourselves : how many of us have accepted this revelation, and are living as forgiven persons; in the calm, peaceful, vigorous state, of mind and of life, which is the natural consequence of being consciously at peace with God through Jesus Christ ? It has become almost the fashion to smile at this simplicity of doctrine, as though it were the badge of an ignorant and unreasoning party, instead of being, as I believe, the very hope, and strength, and test also, of the true Church and of the true faith of Christ. Many are they, both among ministers and people, who dare not take this truth in its simplicity: they must fence it against misconception, and guard it from abuse, by explanations and cautions and conditions on the right hand and on the left, until the Gospel of St Paul, and the Gospel of St Paul's Master, is drained of its very virtue, and has lost all its divine power to renovate and to save. And is it not thus also with the other half, if we might so describe it, of the heavenly Gospel; the offer of the Holy Spirit of God to all who ask Him? The words of the promise, as we read them in Scripture, are plain and express beyond the reach of doubt: but how are they encumbered and overlaid by man's misplaced conditions, until the promise which a child can read has become a remote and an ambiguous possibility which is far beyond and far above, even out of our sight. And thus it comes to pass, that they who would have done some great thing will not do that which is less; they who would be willing to toil on under hard conditions, to go heavily all their days in the bitterness of their soul, to walk mournfully and fearfully along the path of life before the Lord of hosts, if haply they might at length attain, by pains and cares and tears, to the resurrection of the just, will not accept the tidings of an accomplished forgiveness, will not close with the offer of a positively promised Spirit; and thus fulfil, again and again, the description of the text, *If the prophet had bid thee do some great thing, wouldest thou not have done it? how much rather then, when he saith to thee, Wash, and be clean.*

3. We may add yet another illustration; drawn from the requirements of the Gospel.

So long as a person is walking altogether in darkness, the demands of the Gospel give him little trouble. He heeds them not. They may be light, or they may be grievous, the commands of God are for him as if they were not. If he keeps any of them, it is by chance; it is because natural disposition runs, in that respect, for him, in the groove of right, in the track of duty. But when, if ever, he begins to feel that he has a soul to be saved; that God has a will concerning him, which it is life to obey and death to contradict; how often is it seen that, in the pursuit of some great thing, in the search for something arduous and something new, he loses altogether the duty and the blessing which lay at his very door, in his very path, could he but have seen them, and shows, unknown to himself, a spirit of self-will and self-pleasing at the very moment when he seems to be asking most humbly what is the will of God concerning him.

Examples of this error are always at hand. We have seen a man, to whom God's Providence had assigned some other work, some calling of common life, a business or a profession, innocent and useful in itself, but not commonly called sacred—we have seen him, as soon as God's Holy Spirit has really touched and changed his heart, become impatient of all common duties, and think that nothing can be called God's service save one thing, the ministry of the Word, the direct office of guiding and saving souls. With little aptitude, it may be, for preaching, with no suitable education, with habits of mind and life all turned in another direction, he has set himself, in mature age, to learn and to unlearn everything; just because he could not see that everything is clean which God's Providence has ordained, and everything sacred on which God's blessing has been invoked. Too often, if the ranks of the regular ministry of the Church are closed against him; if he is too poor or too ignorant to seek admission into the clerical office in its constituted form in this land; he will ordain himself to the preacher's office, and find in some unauthorized and disorderly mode of ministration that sphere which he conceives to be destined for him. Is not this because he is unaware how wide is the area of God's true service; how needful in common callings are the zeal and devotion which too often are thought to be appropriate to one only; how important it is that in the lay business of life there should be men of faith, of charity, and of consistent godliness; because, in short, he has not rightly attended to the counsel of the text, *If God had bidden thee to do some great thing for Him, thou wouldest willingly have done it: how much more when He only saith to thee, Wash, and be clean?*

Whole systems of religion have been founded upon the forgetfulness of this principle. Men have either gone out of the world, or sought to render themselves and others miserable in it, just because they thought it necessary to *do some great thing* in order to please God. What is monastic life in all its forms and degrees, the endeavour to escape from the temptations of society and to anticipate heaven by a life here below of uninterrupted devotion, but a neglect of the principle suggested by the text? And what is asceticism in all its forms and degrees, the refusal to oneself of life's simple comforts, the prohibition of marriage and the commanding to abstain from meats, the substitution of a system of self-torture for a spirit of temperance and of thankfulness, but a neglect of the same wise and wholesome caution, that what God looks for in us is, not the doing of some great thing, but the endeavour to be pure and holy in the performance of common duties and in the use of lawful enjoyments? And how true is it, in all these cases, that the easy thing is not always the small thing; that to some natures it is far more attractive to have a high thing, a great thing, a novel thing, proposed to them, than a level, an ordinary, or an old duty, pressed upon them; insomuch that he who would have exalted himself to the one cannot humble himself to the other, and he who would have buried himself in a cloister, or foregone every luxury and every amusement, without murmuring or complaint, cannot bring himself to be an exemplary man in life's common or natural relations, cannot set himself vigorously to that which brings with it neither applause nor self-gratulation, the fulfilment, as in God's behalf, as in Christ's service, of the little everyday duties of kindness, of self-denial, and of charity, the careful walking in a trivial round, the punctual, loving performance of a common task.

Alas, my brethren, *the heart is deceitful above all things...who can know it?* When shall we have tracked all its mazes, or learned indeed to see ourselves as God sees us? What an amount of self-will, of waywardness, of perverseness, lurks in each of us. What a dislike of imposed duties; what a readiness to choose duties and to change duties, for ourselves. Who is there amongst us who simply enquires at the beginning of each day, What is that which God sets me to do for Him in these coming twelve hours? not, What can I find to do which shall be interesting to me, which shall be striking and pungent, which shall be important and noticeable, novel or original? but, What comes to my hand, in the course of that Providence which guides my life and which is God's arrangement? Let me say of nothing, It is mean, it is poor, it is unimportant, it is beneath me: it cannot be so if God's Providence has assigned it. Let me say of nothing, It is common or unclean; there is nothing religious in it, nothing sacred, nothing heavenly, nothing for Christ: this cannot be true of it, if God's Providence has brought it to me to be done. It is in the little things of life that God is, not least, but most honoured. He that is faithful in the least thing is faithful also in the greatest: it matters not in which of the two God tries and tests, employs and owns him. Thus it is that the apparent inequalities of life are redressed and rectified. There is an eye upon us, which marks the spirit in each act: there is a judgment before us, in which the awards will be according to the motive. He who here has done God's will, whatever it was for him; done it as a man forgiven and blest, done it in faith, done it in hope, done it in love; that man—it matters not whether he had a great work, as man judges, or a little work, as man judges, set him to do—that man shall hear in the day of account the joyful summons, *Well done, good and faithful servant: thou hast been faithful in a few things: enter thou into the joy of thy Lord.*

ELEVENTH SUNDAY AFTER TRINITY,
August 11, 1861.

XIV.

ZEAL WITHOUT CONSISTENCY.

2 Kings x. 16, 31.

And he said, Come with me, and see my zeal for the Lord...But Jehu took no heed to walk in the law of the Lord God of Israel with all his heart.

IT is a melancholy record, which these Books of the Kings contain, of human character. One sovereign after another passes rapidly across the stage, to be dismissed with the brief but fatal epitaph, *He did that which was evil in the sight of the Lord, according to all that his fathers had done.* That is all that remains, in many cases, of a long life. There may have been power, and wealth, and martial fame: there may have been vigour, and popularity, and success: nay, there may have been the original elements of much good; intelligence, and instruction, and conscience; perhaps a childhood of innocence, and a youth of promise; amiable affections and right impulses, and many lawful and proper acts: but He who looks on the heart in its source, and reads the life as a whole, and characterizes it (amongst many ambiguities and many contradictions) decisively for good or evil, has declared of that man that *he did evil in the sight of the Lord;* his right acts were done with no good motive, from no good principle; the self-will reigned in him over the will of God; he did not deny himself to do good and to eschew evil; and therefore, when he falls on sleep and is gathered to his fathers, the testimony of his life as a whole has been against God and not for Him; he has done evil, if not in man's sight, yet in the sight of the Lord, and goes down to future generations not as an example for imitation but as a beacon for warning.

These cases are dark and saddening: but I know not whether there is not yet a sadder case beside them. When we read of characters wholly evil, we are prone to regard them as belonging to a different category from our own. There is an unreality in the conception of unmixed evil, as of unmixed good, on earth, which removes it out of the reach of an application to ourselves. But it is otherwise when we read of mixed characters; of a good man with many faults, or of a bad man with some virtues. Then we feel that we are in our own world again. That is just what we see everywhere every day. From such cases we can learn: and such cases are the commonest of all in Scripture. Bad men with some good points; good men with infirmities, faults, and sins; these are the staple of Scripture as a record of character, and therefore it is that Scripture comes home to us as it does, both for correction and for encouragement.

A character of which we have been reading in the Old Testament lessons of last Sunday and this, has suggested this remark. Jehu is not in any sense an interesting person. He is presented to us as a sort of scourge of God to punish apostasy and idolatry in Israel. He is an energetic and bold man; prompt in action, determined and thorough-going, unfeeling and unscrupulous; well-fitted for his particular work, which was rough and stern and sweeping, a work of judgment upon those who had sinned beyond mercy. But, though Jehu's is no interesting or attractive character, we must remember that he had a Divine commission, and that he executed it faithfully. In softer days we read impatiently of acts of severity, even when done in God's behalf, or by God's command. We do not feel sin as we ought, and therefore we often cherish a kind of morbid sympathy with the sinner; a feeling, not only—which is right—of grief for him, not only—which is right—of instant tenderness towards his repentance, but even—which is not right—of dislike and disapproval of that suffering for sin which is either mercifully remedial or needfully retributive. The same God who now visits sin chiefly by its consequences, by those miseries which grow out of it and which in fact are but the sin itself developed, was pleased in earlier ages to punish it sometimes by human instrumentality; an instrumentality not more questionable, when God's command was clear, than is that of the civil magistrate who now pronounces a sentence of death upon a great offender. Such was Jehu's office, and he discharged it well. He could say with truth, as he says in the former part of the text to Jehonadab the son of Rechab, *Come with me, and see my zeal for the Lord*. It was not here that he failed. His zeal for God was thorough in act, and perhaps sincere in intention. The fault was, that, while he had a real zeal, he had no true obedience. He could enforce God's law upon others, but he could not obey it himself. *The Lord said unto Jehu, Because thou hast done well in executing that which is right in mine eyes, and hast done unto the house of Ahab according to all that was in mine heart, thy children of the fourth generation shall sit on the throne of Israel. But Jehu took no heed to walk in the law of the Lord God of Israel with all his heart.* He had destroyed the worship of Baal, the open idolatry of Ahab and Jezebel: but *he departed not himself from the sins of Jeroboam who made Israel to sin.* He maintained that political expedient, of symbols of worship placed in his frontier cities, by which the first king of the ten tribes had sought to keep his people from being attracted back to the house of David in Jerusalem: he continued the worship of the golden calves that were in Bethel and that were in Dan, though he had broken down the image of Baal, and the temple of Baal, and destroyed his worshippers, in Samaria. And therefore, *in those days,* even in the reign of him who had done such good service to the cause of God in his earlier years, *the Lord began to cut Israel short;* and Jehu himself is handed down to us not as an example but rather as a warning, while upon his tomb we stand and read the condemning inscription, *Zeal without consistency: zeal without obedience: zeal without love.*

My brethren, I doubt whether in these days we are not in danger of too much disparaging zeal. Zeal is the same word as fervour. In its forcible original meaning, it is the bubbling up of the boiling spirit, whether in the excitement of some human emotion, or in the jealousy of a devoted heart for God's honour. It is the opposite of an impassive, a cold-hearted and a cold-blooded indifference. It is the opposite of that disposition which can stand tamely by while man is oppressed or God dishonoured. It is the outburst of that generous indignation which cannot endure to see right trampled underfoot by might. It is the overflowing of that gratitude, of that devotion, of that love, towards God, which counts no toil irksome, and no suffering intolerable, if it may but express its own sense of His greatness, of His goodness, of His long-suffering in Christ, and draw others, by its example, to know and to speak good of His name. It is the glowing warmth of that divine humanity which would willingly spend and be spent in snatching but one or two brands from the burning; in turning, if it were but one soul, from darkness to light, and from the power of Satan unto God. This is what we mean by zeal. The zeal of Jehu was of a lower order than this. This zeal can scarcely be without obedience. It is inconceivable that there should be a real, an active, a self-denying concern for God's honour and for the souls of others, where there is no care to walk watchfully before Him in holiness. We have parted company therefore with Jehu and with his direct example, when we speak of zeal in its higher and nobler workings. Yet even Jehu may reprove. We all know what the boiling up of the spirit within us is or may be: but which of us has ever known it save for himself; in the assertion of his own rights, in the vindication of his own honour? Which of us, I repeat the question, knows the ebullition of a righteous indignation in behalf of other men, or of a pious earnestness in the cause of God? Would to God, my brethren, that we saw more of this, that we felt more of it. It is a great sorrow and a great shame to us, that we know it so little. It is our daily complaint against ourselves, that we are so little stirred to emotion by the sight and hearing of sin, so little roused to eagerness by the thought of what God has done for us, and of the way in which man neglects and despises Him. O let us pray more for zeal. We are becoming too much used to sin. We are learning to treat it as a thing which must be. We are losing heart and losing hope in striving with it. We are acquiescing in sin and its consequences as necessary evils, instead of facing it in the name of God; instead of mourning over it as a raging plague, and instead of going forth, as Christians, into the midst of it, to stand as it were between the dead and the living till that plague be stayed. I would to God that there were more of us—must I say, that there were any of us—who could say in any true sense, like Jehu, *Come with me, and see my zeal for the Lord.* Any zeal for God, even an ignorant, even a mistaken, even a rash zeal, were better far for us than none.

Instead of it, what have we? What is there in the world or in the Church now which approaches even remotely to the grace of zeal? It is scarcely possible to answer that question seriously. We have established for ourselves a moral law by which we regulate ourselves and by which we judge others. Need I say that our law—the law, I mean, by which society acts and judges in a Christian country—differs very widely from God's law? We have one law of morality for men, and another law for women. We have not only degrees of penalty for degrees of departure from the law of God, but we treat some departures from the law of God as altogether venial, and only some as heinous or reprehensible. There are some sins which only a clergyman has to be ashamed of: the Christian community (so called) has transferred to its ministers the burden of some of God's commandments to be borne for it by proxy. And a zeal for God—if that sacred name can thus be parodied—is shown chiefly by the infliction of arbitrary and most disproportionate punishment upon offenders not against the moral law of God but against the moral law of the world. Where God has spoken, man may sin and scarcely suffer: where the world has spoken, no sorrow and no suffering, no lapse of time, no sincerity of repentance, and no consistency of amendment, is allowed to replace the erring man or the erring woman within the pale of a human sympathy or even of a Christian charity. Such is zeal for God, when debased and disfigured by the modifying hand of man. Of such zeal it may truly be said, as it cannot be said of the other, that it is most commonly found, as it was found in Jehu, altogether divorced and dissevered from obedience.

And this brings us, in the second place, to apply to ourselves, in the way of counsel and warning, the unfavourable part of the character before us. Jehu had a zeal for God, but Jehu nevertheless took no heed to walk in God's law with all his heart.

There is great force in that word, *took no heed—observed not*, as the margin renders it—to walk in God's way. We all know what heedlessness is in a child. We know the trouble it gives in teaching, when we cannot get what we call attention; the stretching (as it were) of the muscles and sinews of the mind to the subject proposed, to the task in hand. And we know the vexation, the irritation, which is caused in supervision, by finding the same awkward trick, the same bad habit, the same troublesome fault, fallen into again and again, in spite of oft-repeated warnings and punishments, just because no heed was given; because a sufficiently deep impression could not be made upon the light and shallow soil of that young mind to secure the permanence of a right recollection or the practical efficacy of a general wish to amend. Alas, my brethren, in the things of religion, in the ways of God and of the soul, we are all too much children. We are inattentive to God's teaching: we are heedless under God's discipline. It is astonishing, we say to ourselves in moments of remorse or penitence, how I could forget that precept again; how I could fall again into that oft-laid snare; how I could utter again that uncharitable or that unthankful or that irreverent expression; how I could cherish again that sinful train of thought; how I could, in spite of warnings and resolutions and prayers unnumbered, believe again the lying voice of the tempter, when he said to me that I might commit without fear that old sin yet once more, that I need not be too scrupulous, that there would be time enough afterwards for repentance. And surely, when we look back upon even a short lifetime, we must marvel at our slowness of heart to take in God's lessons of wisdom. How often have we been brought down by the stroke of His chastisement, whether in the form of sickness, or of sorrow, or of disappointment, or of bereavement; how often have we seemed for the moment thoroughly humbled, completely subdued, finally softened, sobered, and changed; and yet no sooner has the hand ceased to smite, no sooner has the pressure been relieved, no sooner has light broken in upon us and the sun shone again, than the old carelessness, the old levity, the old presumption, the old audacity, has returned, and we are even as we were; only a little harder, a little more obstinate, a little less impressible.

Such is the heedlessness of human nature, and most of our sins may be traced up to it. Jehu took no heed —we take no heed—to the will of God. We think we know all about it: or we think that a little deviation will not be noticed, will not be punished, certainly will not be fatal: we admit into our lives little irregularities, into our hearts little dark places, and think that the general tenor may still be acceptable, that the general colour may not be dark but bright. And then we find by bitter experience that the beginning of sin, like the beginning of strife, is as the letting out of water, hard to restrain when it has once been suffered. And then we find by bitter experience that the conscience within is a delicate as well as powerful instrument; that its sensitiveness is soon destroyed, and along with it its use whether as a guide or a reprover. And thus we are taught—happy if it be not quite too late—that there is no safety for a Christian but in careful walking, in watchful living, in observing, in taking heed: *Wherewithal shall a man*, young or old, *guide and cleanse his way? even by giving heed thereto according to Thy word.* And thus, when we are tempted to think that perhaps this or that little indulgence might do no great harm; that perhaps for this one morning it may do no great harm to give up reading the Bible, or for this one evening to intermit our prayers; that perhaps this little duty may be slightingly performed for once, or for once left undone, and God not be displeased; in all these things we learn at last that there is no safeguard for us but in punctual, minute, exact obedience; that there is no end to concessions once begun, no limit to inaccuracies and inattentions once indulged; and that, for us at all events, happiness as well as safety will depend upon absolute consistency, upon unintermitted watchfulness, if perhaps God may give us at last His grace of a perfect and an upright heart, established in His truth and devoted to His service.

Yes, my brethren, the text adds, *with all his heart. Jehu took no heed to walk in God's law with all his heart.* Is not this the fault in our service, the cause of our heedlessness, that the heart is not given to God; not whole with Him, as it is written; not right with God? Therefore it was that Jehu gave zeal, but could not give obedience; gave zeal, but could not give consistency; gave zeal, but could not give love. And therefore it is that we too often give neither zeal nor obedience, neither zeal nor love.

My brethren, these histories of the Old Testament may not seem at first sight to have much of the Gospel in them: you may almost count them dry subjects for Christian souls. But is not the root of the Gospel in them? for us, at all events, who can read them by the light of the New Testament? Is not to-day's a Gospel subject? It is our own fault assuredly if for us it is dry or lifeless. But I hope and believe that we have not found it so. It is not because a subject is reproving, or because it is arousing, that it is not a Gospel too. True tidings from God, whatever be their sound, are always good tidings also, if they be heard in time, and if they be listened to. It is self-deception, it is delusion, it is falsehood, which is our real enemy. Nothing is so unlike the true Gospel as that which says to us, Peace, Peace, when there is no peace. Anything which awakens us from sleep, anything which arouses us from death, is a Gospel; a note of the Gospel. So may this be. It says to us, Never think anything of zeal, in yourself or in another, except in so far as it is a fruit of love, an utterance of sincerity, the consistent expression of a devoted heart, of a watchful life. It says, Never take credit to yourself for declaiming against the sins of others. Jehu did more: he executed punishment, God's punishment, upon the sins of others: and yet he took no heed, himself, to walk in God's law. Be especially suspicious of yourself when you find words of condemnation, of contempt, or of abhorrence, most familiar to your tongue. Christian zeal, like Christian faith, worketh by love. *The wrath of man worketh not the righteousness of God.* If you are tender to the suffering, if you are plain with the sinful—yet both alike in humility and in all kindness—then you may hope that your zeal has something in it of Christ. But most of all look within. Look to the heart. See whether there is any love of God there. You can tell, if you will. You have no difficulty in saying whether you like, whether you love, an earthly person: do you seek to be with them? are you happy in their company? do you miss them in absence? do you long for their return? Even thus is it with him who loves Christ, with him whose heart is in God's service. He loves prayer: he feels himself dull and desolate when he has been long kept from it: he flies back to it as his solace: he rests in it as a chief joy. And how is it with you in the matter of attention to

God's will? If you love an earthly person, how minutely do you carry out his wishes; how little do you grudge toil and pains in doing so; how do you reproach yourself if you should find that he misses something which he had asked for, or sees repeated that which he has complained of. Even thus is it with him who loves Christ, with him whose heart is whole with God. He disregards no duty because it is small: he refuses no duty because it is difficult. He desires that God should be always with him: he sets the Lord always before him: there is no part of his life, public or private, which he tries to keep out of God's sight: there is no part of his heart, however secret, on which he does not desire that God's light should shine. O, my brethren, so long as ours is a grudging service, it will also be a thankless one: so long as we weigh and measure our acts for God, they will be burdensome, and they will be unproductive. Give all, and all will be happiness; because all will be unity, all will be peace. In this one sense, if in no other, the whole is less than its parts: to give a part is burdensome—to give the whole is light. *Do this, and thou shalt live*, was a condition of salvation too heavy for man: but thousands and tens of thousands have found rest and healing and joy in obeying the Gospel call, *My son, give me thy heart.*

TWELFTH SUNDAY AFTER TRINITY,
August 18, 1861.

XV.

THE COMMANDMENT EXCEEDING BROAD.

Psalm cxix. 96.

I have seen an end of all perfection: but Thy commandment is exceeding broad.

Or (Prayer-Book Version),

I see that all things come to an end: but Thy commandment is exceeding broad.

WE have all felt the relief of escaping from a close and crowded room into the freshness and freedom of the open air. With some of us, that close and confined room may have been the chamber of sickness; and to escape from it is to be restored from the compulsory inactivity of illness to the liberty and vigour and power of health. With some men, though not, thank God, with us, that close and confined room may have been a prison; and to escape from it is to be released from the restraints of a penal seclusion into the freedom of will and action which is the privilege of those who are unstained by crime.

One of the words which St Paul sometimes uses to express suffering is borrowed from this sort of experience.

He speaks of anguish under the figure of *narrowness of space*, of straitness of room, of the pressure arising from confinement within too close limits. And we have abundant examples also in Scripture of the use of the opposite figure to express a condition of relief, of deliverance, and of happiness. Thus, when the patriarch Isaac, after a succession of struggles with the Philistines for the possession of wells of water, at last found one well for which they strove not; one which was obtained without dissension and might be enjoyed without fear of contradiction; he called the name of it *Rehoboth* (*room, space, breadth*); *for now*, he said, *the Lord hath made room for us, and we shall be fruitful in the land.* The Psalmist more than once uses the same figure of freedom and amplitude of space, to denote a condition of mental and spiritual comfort. *Thou hast set my foot in a large room...I called upon the Lord in distress: the Lord answered me, and set me in a large place...I will run the way of Thy commandments, when Thou shalt enlarge my heart.*

Something of the same contrast is observable in the words of the text. It describes the difference between everything that is of man and everything that is of God. The one has limits, has an end: the other is exceeding broad. Human perfection of all kinds has a visible term and bound: human excellence, human power, human knowledge, human life itself, comes to an end, and is not: but God's commandment, that which God has ordained, that which God has taught, that which God has made known, or is willing to make known, of Himself, of His will, of His truth, of His character, of His glory, is exceeding broad: there is an amplitude in it, and a grandeur, and an abundance, and an expansiveness, which forbids any feeling of straitness or of stint or of cramping: a man may walk and run, as far as he will, in any direction, and he will never find himself at a fence or a boundary: the truth of God, the revelation of God, the character of God, is infinite like God Himself, and it is His will that we should expatiate in this domain without let or hindrance, without prohibition and without coercion.

The thought thus suggested is a very glorious one, and I propose it for your meditation this evening. *I see that all things* else *come to an end: but Thy commandment*, Thy revelation, *is exceeding broad.* The contrast is that between man's narrowness, in every sense of that word, and God's amplitude, God's grandeur, God's large and satisfying magnificence. We must reflect upon this contrast in some of its particulars.

1. *I see that all things come to an end: but, Thy word endureth for ever in heaven.* What an impression is forced upon us, by the progress of life, of the poverty of man and all that belongs to him, in point of duration. What a dream is earthly ambition, earthly consequence, earthly rank and wealth and honour. We ourselves have lived to see men pass through greatness into nothingness. We have flocked to look upon the form of some great general or statesman or potentate, who is now dust and ashes. We have hung upon the lips of some eloquent orator, speaking of things concerning national interest or interests greater still; interests of the soul, secrets of eternity; and those lips are now for ever closed and silent. Others are now the powerful men, the admired men, the revered men: and we are curious,

for a day, about them: it is their turn: soon it will be the turn of yet another: soon will the stage be occupied by a new set of actors, and gazed upon by a new set of spectators. *I see that all things come to an end.*

And it is not only as observers that we feel this. We feel it in ourselves. How fleeting are our own possessions, our own treasures, our own topics of absorbing interest. How did we, when we were children, boys, or young men, set our hearts upon this and that, which we must have, we thought, or be miserable. It came: it was given: and, behold, it was a shadow: or it came not: it was not given: and we survived the disappointment. Over and over again the desired thing has changed, for us, and been superseded: now we would give nothing for what was once, in our eyes, so precious: we marvel at the inexperience which could alone have made us thus distort and miscalculate, or at the stupidity which could alone have made us thus call evil good and good evil. And yet, perhaps, we are doing it again; doing it now. Perhaps we are even now calling something good which is really evil; desirable, which, if granted, would be ruinous. Certainly, to judge by the past, to judge even by an experience already our own, our present objects will hereafter appear to us insignificant. From the other world we shall look back upon them with contempt, if not with abhorrence. *I see that all things come to an end;* not least human wishes, human aims, and human ambitions.

How comforting then, how satisfying, ought it to be to us, to know of just one thing which will not thus fail and terminate. *Thy commandment, Thy word;* that which God has spoken, whether in the way of disclosure,

xv.]   *The Commandment exceeding broad.*   177

or of command, or of warning, or of promise. That endures; *endureth,* as the Psalmist says, *for ever in heaven.* The march of centuries affects not that. Human opinion, worldly change, the fluctuations of thought or fashion, the rise and fall of men and of nations, work no alteration there. That is still right which God has commanded; that is still wrong which God has forbidden: that is still true which God has revealed; that is still false which God has contradicted. The law of moral duty given in the wilderness of Sinai more than three thousand years ago, to a different nation from ours, amidst every circumstance of contrariety to our own, is still unchanged: it is read Sunday by Sunday in our churches as the unaltered and unalterable rule of conduct: it changes not as we change, because it is God's utterance to man's reason and to man's conscience. It is so with every part of His Word. There is not a place where Christ is named, not a congregation in which His creed is professed, in which conscience is not stirred, repentance quickened, and faith made fruitful, by the repetition of those well-known words, handed down not more in Scripture than by the living voice of parents and teachers, which reason with us of righteousness and temperance and judgment to come, till the sinner trembles inwardly and resolves at least, if it be at some distant day, to call for the Apostle and for the Saviour. These things are the same in all generations. These things partake of that permanence which is an attribute of God only. It is a strange thing, we might say, knew we not the cause, that the same Book should be appropriate to the case of every individual of every age; should never need to be re-written or re-worded;

should be intelligible in its practical parts to every mind, and impressive in its leading disclosures alike to every kind of human character. I see that all things come to an end: human works, human writings, are for one nation only, for one age, far more often for one year, not for another: they refer, for the most part, to matters of passing concern, of limited or even local interest: if in a few, a very few cases, they survive into another age, and are prized by students of various race and character, still even these are bounded in their range by certain conditions of intelligence, of taste, of character: but the Word of God, spoken once with the voice, and now preserved by writing from adulteration and from decay, endures for all time, and is vocal to all sorts and conditions of men: in every land and age, he that is of God heareth God's Word, and finds in it, whosoever he be, a light to his mind and a lamp to his steps. *Thy commandment is exceeding broad.*

2. *I have seen an end of all perfection.* That which has been said of human life may be said also of human character. We have spoken of man's limits in point of duration: he and all his—enjoyments, projects, interests, attainments, glories—are essentially short-lived and transitory: but the other version of the text seems to extend the remark to a further point; that human excellence, human goodness, has a bound, and a narrow one: if you sound it, you reach the bottom: if you measure it, you can take its compass: there is an end of all human perfection, as there is an end of all human duration.

The text speaks not of bad men only, but even of the good. It supposes that a man has excellence, has something which may even be called perfection: it only says that there is an end of it, a limit to it. Sadly, painfully true is this, oftentimes, in its worst sense. Again and again has human goodness in the long run broken down. A man who not only seemed to be in the right way, but who, as an Apostle expresses it, was running well, has been hindered by some adverse influence that he should not to the end obey the truth. One who not only thought himself to be standing, but was standing, has failed to take heed: he has grown secure: he has been high-minded instead of fearing: he has counted himself to have apprehended, and then, from some untoward accident, his out-stretched hand has been diverted from grasping the prize. He has suffered some little root of bitterness to spring up inwardly and defile him: he has allowed himself in some doubtful indulgence, and awakened only to find himself its slave: he has forgotten the exhortation which reminds us that no man can serve two masters, and has hoped to succeed in combining the two incompatible services, of Christ and the world, of time and eternity, of the pleasures of sin and the recompence of the reward. Thus at last the eye of men, even as the eye of God all along, has seen an end of his perfection. He has fallen, fallen away, fallen in mid course, fallen finally: and men of God who looked upon his tomb could only exclaim over it in sorrow and godly fear, *Alas, my brother! I have seen an end of all perfection.*

But the words are true in a sense short of this worst and saddest: they are true even of men who fall not away, but of whom we may well hope that they are *true and faithful, partakers of the benefit.* How often do we observe a limited where there is no fallacious perfection.

How much are we disappointed oftentimes in good men; in men whom we thought and still think good. How do they break down, oftentimes, under the test of trial. What weaknesses come out when we, or, more frequently, when circumstances, probe them. How does temper fail under provocation, or humility under neglect, or unworldliness under temptation, or thankfulness under disappointment. How do we find, when we go to them for counsel, that they have no resource; or for encouragement, that they have little faith and less hope. How do they grieve us by their harshness towards the erring in life, or by their unfairness towards the erring in doctrine. How do we miss at every turn the mind which was in Christ Jesus; the entire wisdom, the absolute truthfulness, the perfect charity. We go away with the confession wrung from our hearts, *I have seen an end of all perfection:* there was sincerity, but there was no wisdom; there was a general good intention, but there was no minute, no exact performance. And then have we not turned with relief to that character, that mind, that word *exceeding broad*, in which there has been no risk of reaching the end, of sounding the depth, or exhausting the fulness? that character, even the mind of God revealed in Christ Jesus, in which there is perfect purity together with perfect patience, perfect truth with perfect charity, perfect wisdom with perfect love? that mind in which is no variableness neither shadow of turning; no fickleness, and no impulsiveness; no one-sidedness, and no narrowness; no exaggeration, no weakness, and no one part dark? Surely, if in one sense with awe, in another and a higher sense with comfort, we look off from man's littleness to God's greatness, and learn to say, not with humility only but with thankfulness, *I have seen an end of all perfection: but Thy commandment is exceeding broad.*

3. The breadth of God's Word, in contrast with the narrowness of human doctrine, is a topic full of interest. How does the Bible comprehend, and gather into one, all the good parts of all the human systems of theology that were ever framed. Every form of error within the Christian community in any age of the Church has arisen, not from the invention of a falsehood, but from the distortion of a truth. Some clause or some chapter of the New Testament has been fastened upon: it has been fetched away from the rest of the New Testament; perhaps forced from its context: it has been stereotyped, it has been microscopically examined, it has been logically dissected, reasoned upon, argued from: and then a whole sect has taken it for its watchword, and made it, for itself and for others, the one test of truth. Meanwhile there lay in another part of the same holy Book, perhaps very near the former, a statement of another and a different kind: if the one passage spoke of Christ's humanity, the other as strongly asserted His divinity: if the one dwelt upon the sovereignty of God's grace, the other enforced no less earnestly the responsibility of the free-will in man: and, while one party takes the former as its sole criterion of sound doctrine, another party no less vehemently insists upon the supreme dignity and importance of the latter. The Church of Christ rings for half a century with the tumult, and a permanent breach and schism may be the consequence. The asserters of free-will, and the asserters of sovereign

grace, can no longer speak of each other with charity, or worship the one God in union. And yet in their first rise both were in the right: Scripture sided not with one but with both: each had a fragment of the truth of God, and the error of both lay only in asserting that that fragment was the whole. They should have allowed, each of them, that there was that in the Bible which seemed to favour their opponent: they should have remembered this, and they should have moderated their tone in the recollection: they should have understood that, with reference to the revelation as well as to the Providence of God, there is ever room for the application of the saying, *What I do thou knowest not now, but thou shalt know hereafter.* The time for reconciling the various disclosures is not yet come: at present we must be contented to hold them all in combination. We must make room within our system for opposite aspects, for unreconciled sides, of God's whole truth. Unless we do so, we must be wrong, however right we are. We may be right, we must be right, in asserting the truth of whatever is really found in God's Word: but we may be wrong, and we must be wrong, in denying, forgetting, or disparaging, the truth of any other thing, however apparently diverse, which is also really found in God's Word. We ought to be able, even now, to rejoice in the thought that God's revelation is *exceeding broad;* very large, very simple, very comprehensive; large enough to give a standing-place for all who are truly sincere, truly in earnest, in studying and in learning from the words which Christ and which God has spoken. It is they who can only take in one mutilated portion of xv.]   *The Commandment exceeding broad.*   183

His truth, and who exclude and denounce every other portion of it, who are really the presumptuous, really the erring, really the heretical.

It is a delightful thought, that one day we shall know as we are known; that one day, if we only walk now in faith and in charity, we shall be enabled, in the full light of God's presence, to perceive the consistency of things now disjointed, the harmony of sounds now discordant. Meanwhile, as we love our souls, we must be willing to wait, and we must be candid in receiving. *Thy commandment is exceeding broad:* our doctrine, if it is true, must be able to stand this test. Is it the whole, or is it only one part, of the whole counsel of God as revealed to us in Scripture? Does it embrace within its compass all that God has said; so far, at least, as to exclude and to deny, to force and to mutilate, nothing? Few indeed are those ministries, or those schemes of doctrine, of which this can be said: God grant us the wisdom to aim at it and to attain to it, in some measure, in our own. The importance of doctrine is great : by it souls must be nourished, or left hungry; by it lives must be regulated, or left wandering. O, my brethren, learn to love your Bible for its breadth of teaching. Admire its comprehensiveness. See how it urges the responsibility of man, and yet gives God all the glory. See how it sets forth the sinfulness of sin, and yet magnifies the mercy of God towards the sinful. See how it takes within its ample fold every sort and condition of man as he is, and offers to feed each with the very food convenient for him; the food of wisdom and of tenderness and of strength and of hope and of love ; that food from which the most cultivated mind may derive profit, and the saddest and most sorrowful and most sin-burdened heart comfort and relief. All things else come to an end; meagre in their supplies, narrow in their views, limited in their compass, barren in their consolations: but the revelation of God as made by Himself is exceeding broad, and the largest of minds and hearts can find room for themselves within it. O what a blessing is it, to feel ourselves in contact with the infinite; the eternal in duration, the unbounded in extent, the unsearchable in depth, the inexhaustible in satisfaction; to know that we are but on the margin of that sea of God's counsels which no human foot has yet tracked, and which no length or profoundness of search will ever render less wonderful or less glorious. *Thy' righteousness standeth like the strong mountains: Thy judgments are a great deep....O the depth of the riches both of the wisdom and knowledge of God! how unsearchable are His judgments, and His ways past finding out!...For of Him and through Him and to Him are all things: to whom be glory for ever.*

It remains only that I briefly press upon you the question, Is the Word of God your study, your meditation, your delight? O learn more, from what has been said to-night, of its dignity and of its grandeur. O believe that it is worth your study, and will repay it. It is *exceeding broad:* there is room, on its ample platform, for every capacity, for every gift, for every desire and every want, of man: let it not fail to find room for you. It has a blessing for each one of us: but we must come, and come betimes, to receive it. If we come not while the day of grace lasts—and its length, for any of us, who can tell?—there can be for us but a closed door and an outer darkness. *Ye know how that afterward, when he would have inherited the blessing, he was rejected: for he found no place of repentance, though he sought it carefully with tears.*

THIRTEENTH SUNDAY AFTER TRINITY,
August 25, 1861.

XVI.[1]

THE GOSPEL AN INCENTIVE TO INDUSTRY IN BUSINESS.

Psalm i. 4.

His leaf also shall not wither; and look, whatsoever he doeth, it shall prosper.

MORE than fifty years ago, in the fourth year of the century, a small bequest was left by a native of this Town (to whose munificence the poor of the place are largely indebted) to secure an annual sermon in our Parish Church, on the first Sunday in September, on the following subject: *The genuine tendency of the Christian Religion to lead its professors to industry and diligence in business.* A very noble topic, my brethren, if it might be rightly handled. And a topic, also, common as it may sound, not always presenting itself to our thoughts, or urged in our churches, with the force or the attractiveness which ought to belong to it. God grant His blessing to the consideration of it to-day.

There is a large choice of texts in Holy Scripture bearing upon this point directly and indirectly. Some of them will occur readily to any student of the Bible.

[1] This Sermon was preached, in accordance with the requirement of Quintin Kay, before the young men apprenticed under his charity.

XVI.] *The Gospel an Incentive to Industry.* 187

But, upon the whole, my choice has been directed to that beautiful and well-known Psalm which stands at the head of our sacred collection of inspired Hymns, and which has been used in our service on this day, which happens to be not only the first Sunday but also the first day of the month.

Without further preface, I will make a few plain remarks upon the sound and salutary doctrine of the Psalm itself. This will lay a good foundation for the more special work entrusted to me to-day.

Now we will say, first of all, with reference to the general aspect of the Psalm, how important it is that all worship, and all religion, should recognize the essential difference, not only between good and bad acts, but between good and bad men. We are very apt, not only to break down the barrier, for ourselves, between that which is right and that which is wrong, calling things by false names until we really lose all strong sense of their moral complexion; but also to remove and obliterate utterly, with regard to others, the landmark between the righteous and the wicked, the godly and the ungodly, the holy man and the sinner. It is spoken of by the prophet Malachi as one of the results of a coming day of judgment, that this displaced landmark will then at last be restored to its position. *Then shall ye return, and discern between the righteous and the wicked, between him that serveth God and him that serveth Him not.* It is a question often asked by children of their parents, *Is he a good man?* expressing a sort of intuition as to this matter; an instinctive feeling that the difference between the good and the bad is not so shadowy and evanescent as we are sometimes tempted to make it, but that, however little man can fathom or ought to seek to fathom the mystery, *the Lord*, at all events, *knoweth them that are His*. My brethren, while we check and correct this tendency; while we refuse to characterize decisively, for good or evil, the various characters and the various persons crossing our path in life; yet let us remember, for our own warning at least, that there is a difference between one and another in the sight of God; a difference as wide as between acceptance and rejection, between acquittal and condemnation, between heaven and hell. That is the great elementary truth to which the first Psalm bears testimony. And I say that it is well that it should stand there at the very head of the Psalms, as a sort of direction and finger-post to the path of life and to the path of death.

Again, I would ask the attention of my hearers to-day—and more especially the attention of those young persons who are amongst us—to the description here given of the life and character of each of these two classes.

1. The good man is described first by negatives. What is he not? *Blessed is the man*, as the Bible Version gives the words, *that walketh not in the counsel of the ungodly, nor standeth in the way of sinners, nor sitteth in the seat of the scornful.* There are three kinds of persons whom he avoids. Walking, or standing, or sitting, he refuses to do so by the advice or in the company of certain persons, described successively as *the ungodly, sinners, the scornful.*

i. He will not walk in the counsel of the ungodly. If a man has no regard for God, if he shows by his words or by his actions that God is not in all his thoughts, then he cannot be a good adviser. The man who would be really happy must decline his counsel. My young friends, mark well your companions. Not in uncharitableness, still less in self-righteousness, but, to speak plainly, in self-defence, in the exercise of a sensible as well as religious concern for your own safety, you must (and you easily can) observe the character and the principles of those amongst whom either education or business throws you. And, if you are compelled to say to yourself, That young man, or that older man, whatever else he may be, does not fear and does not love God ; then you must not walk in his counsel ; that is, you must not take his advice, or follow his direction, as to what you shall do or not do. If you do so, you will some day bitterly repent it. That is the first point.

ii. Again, the man who would be happy must not stand in the way of sinners. As some men are *ungodly*, so some men are *sinners*. As some men have not God before them, so some men live sinfully. You may not always be aware of it. You may be deceived about it for a time. But in the long run a man of this sort will betray himself to those around him. At all events he must betray himself if he would draw you, his companion, into actual sin. Now, whenever or in whatever way you find him out as a sinner, this Psalm says you must not stand in his way. You must not stand about, you must not wait or loiter, in the road or the street by which he passes to his sin. That is the figure. Do not let him find you hanging idly about when he passes by. If he does, you will be in danger of being induced to go with him. O, my brethren, in this Town we might take the advice thus given almost literally. Is it not oftentimes in your roads and in your lanes, at the mouth of your yards and at what the Psalmist calls *the thievish corners of your streets*, that temptation first assails you? Take heed how, in that most literal of all senses, you be found standing idle in the way of sinners.

iii. But, once again, besides the dangers of walking and of standing, there is a danger also in sitting. The man who would be happy must not sit in the seat of the scornful. The Psalmist, under God's holy inspiration, knew us well. He wrote for all times, not only for his own, when he spoke of the seat of the scornful. Who is meant by the scornful? What is the character thus designated? It is the same which is elsewhere described as that of the *scoffer*. He is the man who mocks at everything, even at sin. *Fools make a mock at sin.* He is the man who turns everything into a jest; even holy things. He is the man—alas, his name now is legion—who carries the habit of joking into all matters; sees nothing serious in human life, nothing sacred in divine truth, and nothing formidable even in a future judgment. You know that there are such persons: some of you may have suffered from them: is it possible that any one of you may be of them? may be what the Psalmist calls a scorner? *Blessed is the man*, he says, *who sitteth not in the seat of the scornful.* The ungodly may walk; the sinner may stand; but the scornful sit: they occupy a position of dignity: they are the world's censors; in our days they are the world's judges: their cutting words, their sharp sayings, their insolent and arbitrary sentences, decide the fate of books, the conduct of rulers, the characters of men: in humbler life, they give the law to social circles, and exercise a fearful tyranny over the acts and habits of youthful associates. O sit not thou, the Psalmist says, in the seat of the scornful. Aim not, if you love your soul, at the reputation of a censor, a jester, or a wit. More than this: avoid the seat where such men are enthroned: they will overbear your better judgment; they will insensibly lead you to think and to judge even as they.

2. These three are the good man's enemies; his, because God's. These things are what he is not; what he avoids and dreads. Now, what is he? Can we look within, and see where the secret lies, of his character, and of his life? Yes, the Psalmist goes on to say, *But his delight is in the law of the Lord: and in His law doth he meditate*, or, as the Prayer-Book Version gives it, *exercise himself, day and night*. The Word of God is his counsellor. That advice, which he will not receive from the ungodly, he takes, and he seeks, from God Himself. His delight is in God's law, in God's Word. It is not, to him, a closed book. It is not a mere Sunday duty to read a chapter in it. No, it is his delight. *Thy testimonies*, he can say, *are my delight and my counsellors. Day and night*, in hours of business, of recreation, and of repose, he meditates in God's law: when he cannot be reading it, it is still dear to him, still treasured in his memory, still cherished in his heart. It guides his life, it directs his judgment, it breathes in his spirit, even when it is not in his hand, and not upon his lips.

3. And then, after viewing the good man in these two aspects—what he is not, and what he is—what he eschews, and what he loves—we are briefly told, in the third and last place, what his course is, and

what his end. *He shall be like a tree planted by the rivers of water, that bringeth forth his fruit in his season: his leaf also shall not wither; and whatsoever he doeth shall prosper.* God's blessing is upon that man. There is no mistake as to his being under a divine benediction. Everything is, with him, orderly and seasonable. There is a regular process of culture and of fruit-bearing: nothing miraculous, nothing marvellous perhaps, in his condition or in his progress: we are not surprised by a sudden gathering in midwinter, or by a harvest that precedes the sowing: we only see that, in him, as in a duly cultivated and well-watered garden, all things come in their season: the work of grace within goes on we know not how, but there is a growth, we see, a progress, and a maturity: even sorrow and affliction, like that *digging and dunging* of which a well-known Parable speaks, have their place in his training, and yield afterwards the peaceable fruits of righteousness in him who has been exercised thereby.

His leaf also shall not wither: and look, whatsoever he doeth, it shall prosper.

My brethren, it is the special object of this Sermon to exhibit *the Christian Religion*, that is, the Gospel of our Lord Jesus Christ, in one of its many beneficent operations; in its *tendency*, its *genuine* (that is, real and not merely nominal) tendency, as the terms of the bequest express it, *to lead its professors*, those who, like all of us, profess and call themselves Christians, and who, in so doing, are no hypocrites, *to industry and diligence in business*. I have sought thus far to show you what manner of men the true professors of Christianity are. I have drawn my text from the Scriptures of the Old Testament. But the character of the godly man, in the points touched upon, has been the same under both of God's great Dispensations: it scarcely matters, in these respects, in which of the two mirrors we reflect his image. The general character is the same: but the Gospel added not a little to the inducements of godliness.

Take the particular point now before us. See what that Gospel of Jesus Christ did for the promotion of human industry and diligence in business, in the three particulars, of precept, of motive, and of example. A very few words must suffice upon each of these topics.

i. Open the New Testament where you may, you will find something bearing upon the duties of common life. There is no encouragement given in it to desert those ordinary duties, on the plea of greater devotion to religious contemplation and worship, or on any other. These excuses, where they have been made, have been made in despite of the Gospel, not out of it. I might fill many pages with precepts of a directly opposite kind. Our Lord's discourses, wherever they touch upon duty (and where do they not?) represent human life as a time of work, and God's call as a call to work. The very imagery of the Parables is drawn, not from the amusements of a fashionable trifling, but from the occupations of a busy industry. What is the Parable of the sower, of the tares, of the mustard-seed, of the leaven, of the hidden treasure, of the pearl of great price, of the net cast into the sea—to run through the contents of one whole chapter of Parables—but a picture, again and again presented, of human activity in the discharge of a life-long labour? What is the Parable of the labourers in the vineyard, but an indication of the sort of calling wherewith Christians are called; a calling to work and to endurance, to perseverance and to patience, to a day of labour and an evening of recompence? What, above all, is the Parable of the talents, but a solemn warning as to the demand of God upon human energy amidst opportunities few or many; an earnest correction of the common mistake, that it is only they who can do much who are required to do anything; a gracious assurance that everything which we possess is a memento of God's care and regard for our service, and that every man shall receive in the end, be he great or small, honoured or despised, upon earth, according to his own honest, hearty, self-denying labour? And, if we pass from the Gospels to the Epistles, we find the latter full of exhortations such as these few which follow. *Not slothful in business, fervent in spirit, serving the Lord....Let us not be weary in well-doing; for in due season we shall reap, if we faint not...Not with eye-service, as men-pleasers; but as the servants of Christ, doing the will of God from the heart...Study to be quiet, and to do your own business, and to work with your own hands, as we commanded you; that ye may walk honestly toward them that are without, and that ye may have lack of nothing...Even when we were with you, this we commanded you, that, if any would not work, neither should he eat: for we hear that there are some who walk among you disorderly, working not at all, but are busybodies: now them that are such, we command and exhort by our Lord Jesus Christ, that with quietness they work, and eat their own bread.* There is room in the Gospel for every kind of work: there is room for the sick, there is room for the aged, there is room for the suffering: but there is no room for the idle. They must repent of their wasted time, and set to work earnestly; or Christ's Gospel will be for them a dead letter, an empty sound.

ii. The Gospel has not only added precepts to those which went before it as to the duty of labour: it has also furnished industry with new motives. *What reward*, it bids us ask, *shall I render unto the Lord for all His benefits that He hath done unto me?* What can I do to express my thankfulness to God, not only for creation and preservation and all the blessings of this life, but above all for His inestimable love towards me in my redemption through Christ Jesus, in giving me so many means of grace and so sure a hope of glory? And the answer lies beside the question. *He hath showed thee, O man, what is good;* what is right and acceptable before Him: *and what doth the Lord require of thee, but to do justly, and to love mercy, and to walk humbly with thy God? Whatsoever thy hand findeth to do, do it with all thy might, as to the Lord, and not unto men;* and He will accept, He will bless, thy stedfast and thy loving labour. Christ redeemed thee from the curse of guilt, from the power of sin, that thou, by quietness, by sobriety, by useful and Christian industry, mightest show forth the praises of Him who called thee out of darkness into His marvellous light. Redemption itself is work's new motive. The love of Christ constraineth me to labour, lest any reproach, of idleness, of uselessness, or of disorder, should fall upon Him who loved me and gave Himself for me.

iii. Finally, the Gospel of Jesus Christ has enforced industry by a new example. Yes, my brethren, we will pass upwards from Christians to Christ; through Apostles and Prophets, through saints and martyrs, who all lived and died in toil for their Master's sake, unto Him who is the Apostle and High Priest of our profession, in whose strength they all served their generation, in whose tender mercy they all, one by one, at last fell asleep. We will pass upwards through them to Him, and learn the duty of *diligence in business* from Him who is the one Example, as He is the one Saviour, of us all.

My brethren, there are many ideas utterly incompatible and incongruous with the thought of our Lord Jesus Christ. Everything that is an imperfection, a moral infirmity, a questionable tendency, in man, is repugnant and abhorrent to our conception of Him. But I will venture to say that no one defect is more absolutely inconceivable in His perfect character, than that of idleness. Our Lord Jesus Christ was, above all men, diligent in business. He had a calling upon earth, and He followed it. In early years, yes, until the age of thirty years, He worked as a carpenter in a shop at Nazareth. His own hands contributed to the support of an earthly home and a human family. O the depth of that condescension! *Being in the form of God...He made Himself empty* of that glory, *and took upon Him the form of a servant, and was made in the likeness of men;* yes, made in all points like as we are, save only sin. Who can complain, after this, of the humility of his position, or of the irksomeness of his work, on earth? The Saviour, who was also the Creator, occupied a mean village dwelling, and wrought in a workshop with His own hands, during thirty precious years of that precious life. And when at last the fulness of the time was come, and He emerged from that profound obscurity to exercise the glorious office of the Prophet and the Revealer of God amongst men, was there any difference then in this particular? Was life then for Him a period of greater ease or refinement or repose? Nay, my brethren, it was a life without rest: when He rested at all, it was not so much for sleep as for prayer. Read the record of a single day of that holy life, as it is preserved for us in the first chapter of the Evangelist St Mark. It was a sabbath-day; a day, to others, of relaxation and of intermitted toil. What was it to Him? First there is the work, no light one, of teaching in the congregation. That teaching is broken in upon by a scene of excitement and terror; the outcry of a poor demoniac, who says, under the possession of an unclean spirit, *Let us alone: what have we to do with Thee, Thou Jesus of Nazareth?* and who, by the power of that almighty word, is instantly relieved, emancipated, comforted; restored to the government of reason and conscience, and to the peaceful occupations of a safe and useful life. As soon as He quits the synagogue, and enters into a house, new toils and new duties await Him. There is a fever to be healed, and another life thus given back by the intervention of its Lord and Maker. Then, *at even, when the sun did set,* and when others were thinking of that repose which belongs to the season, He, on the contrary, had to see *all the city gathered together at His door*, bringing to Him *all manner of sickness and all manner of disease*, to be separately enquired into, separately ministered to, separately healed and blessed. Long hours thus passed before rest could come. At last, we may suppose, He lay down to sleep. But the night which labour contracted at the one end, devotion shortened at the other. *In the morning, rising up a great while before day, He went out, and departed into a solitary place, and there prayed.* Even thither He is pursued by the importunity of man. *Simon and they that were with him followed after Him: and when they had found Him, they said unto Him, All men seek for Thee. And He said to them, Let us go into the next towns and preach there also: for therefore came I forth.* O, my brethren, look on that picture of *industry and diligence in business*, and go forth from the contemplation, if you can, to be indolent, self-pleasing, idle, useless men.

FOURTEENTH SUNDAY AFTER TRINITY,
September 1, 1861.

XVII.

THE KING UPON THE HILL OF ZION.

Psalm ii. 6.

Yet have I set my King upon my holy hill of Zion.

WE considered this morning a Psalm of a very general character. It spoke of the righteous and of the wicked: of the happiness of the one—of his conduct in doing and in avoiding—of what he loves and what he abhors—of the secret of his strength and of his peace—of his orderly progress from the planting to the fruit-bearing—of the permanence of his produce, and the success of his endeavours. *His leaf also shall not wither: and look, whatsoever he doeth, it shall prosper.*

To-night I would direct your thoughts to another of the Psalms for the day; a Psalm of a very different nature. As the first Psalm is of a general kind; one which deals only with religion as a life of piety towards God and of well-doing towards men; so the second Psalm has much in it of the spirit of prophecy, and can only be intelligently read in the light of the Gospel of our Lord Jesus Christ. I am not speaking to-night to unbelievers or what are commonly called freethinkers—though indeed no term was ever more incorrectly applied than is that of freethinkers to men who, even more than others, think within bounds, and very narrow bounds, upon every subject which has to do with Christ and the Gospel; to-night, I say, I am not speaking to such persons—and therefore I shall not stay to vindicate the Christian character of this Psalm, which seems to me to breathe in every line of it, and to be only got rid of by a sophistry far more irrational than any credulity. Taking the Psalm in that sense in which fair criticism, almost as much as Scripture authority, teaches us to understand it, we will ask God's blessing upon the study and application of it with reference to ourselves and our own state and wants.

The twelve verses of the Psalm seem to fall naturally into four divisions, each consisting of three verses.

1. The first of these sets before us in a bold and striking picture the opposition of men to the kingdom of Christ and of God. There is a raging multitude gathered together, whole nations of the earth, with their rulers and kings, for the avowed purpose of shaking off the yoke of God and of His Anointed. I need not mention that *the Anointed One* is the translation, in English, of the terms *Messiah*, or *Christ*. When this passage from the second Psalm is quoted in the fourth chapter of the Acts of the Apostles, it is in this form: *The kings of the earth stood up, and the rulers were gathered together, against the Lord and against His Christ.* God's Christ is God's Anointed One; that Person whom God, as it is said in the tenth chapter of the Acts, *anointed with the Holy Ghost and with power* for the glorious threefold office of His Prophet, of His Priest, and of His King. Now the representation here made is, that there is a general rising

of the world against the yoke, that is, against the restraining will and word, of Christ, and of Him from whom Christ came. There is a general cry rising from the earth, *Let us break their bands*, the bands of God and of His Christ, *asunder, and cast away their cords from us*. This has been true in all times, less or more. *The carnal mind*, St Paul says, *is enmity against God; for it is not subject to the law of God, neither indeed can be*. It is only they who are, as he expresses it in the same passage, *not in the flesh but in the spirit*, by having the Holy Spirit of God dwelling in them, who are delivered from this enmity, and enabled to yield a willing service, of heart and life, to the God who made them, and to the Saviour who redeemed them with His most precious blood.

This has been always true: and we have some reason to think that it will be more signally manifested as the end draws on. It is not easy for one generation to compare itself accurately with any that have gone before. We are prone to exaggerations, both for good and evil, when we ourselves are concerned. But still, I think, we can discern some indications, in our own time, of a growing insubordination to the authority of Christ. There is less, within that nominal Church which for us is almost coextensive with the world, of a sluggish and torpid acquiescence in truths unrealized and disregarded: there is more of positive life—and we would thank God for it: but is there not also, on the other hand, more of a definite and outspoken infidelity? Are not things said now, and written, against the Gospel and against the Divine nature of Christ, which certainly some years ago would not have been written and spoken by persons similarly circumstanced and of similar character? Is there not something of a ranging and marshalling of the hosts, as if for decisive combat, which the eye of faith may recognize as a token of the approach of that day of which the Prophet Joel has written, *Multitudes, multitudes in the valley of decision: for the day of the Lord is near in the valley of decision?* If this be so, is it not a matter of vital importance for each one of us, that we should take our side, and take it rightly, against that day? We know not how soon the final struggle between truth and error, between faith and unbelief, may be coming upon us: we know not how powerful, or how insidious, may be, for each one of us, the persuasions of that lying vanity which seeks to seduce men from their Saviour. O, is it possible that there may be, even amongst us, even amongst the worshippers and professed servants of Christ present here this evening, any who are saying in their hearts, *Let us break their bands asunder, and cast away their cords from us?* Yes, if there be one who is living in sin; if there be one who is cherishing any secret, any bosom sin; if there be one who is using his influence over others for a bad purpose; if there be one who is a lover of sceptical or immoral books; if there be one who laughs at good men, or who is living himself without prayer and without communion; that person—and dare we hope that he is not amongst us?—is saying of Christ in his heart, if not with his lips, *Let me break His bands asunder, let me cast away His cords*, His cords of love, *from me.*

2. We turn to the second section of the Psalm before us. It extends from the fourth to the sixth verse. It tells us how God regards this insurrection of earth against His Christ. *He that sitteth in the heavens shall*

laugh: the Lord shall have them in derision. If God is to speak to men, He must speak in man's language. It is not really that the sin of man, his devotion to his own ruin, his obstinate rejection of mercy, or his foolish warfare against the truth, is a matter viewed lightly, or treated with ridicule, in heaven, in that place where all is truth and all is reverence and all is love; but this is the figure which best expresses the utter futility, the utter folly and helplessness, of a struggle between man and God, between the thing formed and Him that formed it. O, my brethren, it is no exaggeration of the simple truth. What must our arguments and our discussions, our limitations and our concessions, appear in that place where all is seen as it is, and where the inhabitants of the world are counted as grasshoppers? How trivial yet how serious, how harmless yet how suicidal, must there appear those attacks upon God and His Revelation, which in this lower world pass for wit or for wisdom, for ingenious novelty or for deep discernment. *Then shall He speak unto them in His wrath, and vex them in His sore displeasure. Yet have I set my King*—thus He speaks—*upon my holy hill of Zion.* The silence of God is at last broken. *God is a righteous Judge, strong and patient; and God is provoked every day. If a man will not turn, He will whet His sword.* The contrast is that of St Paul's address to the Athenians: *The times of this ignorance God winked at: but now commandeth all men everywhere to repent; because He hath appointed a day in the which He will judge the world in righteousness by that man whom He hath ordained.* The kings of the earth may set themselves, and the rulers take counsel together, against the Lord and against His

Christ...*yet have I set my King upon my holy hill of Zion.* What a solemn, what a formidable testimony against all who resist or impugn the truth. None the less for them—none the less because they gainsay or ridicule—none the less because they in words oppose or in works deny Him—*God has made this same Jesus, whom ye crucified, both Lord and Christ...The Lord shall send the rod of Thy strength out of Zion: rule Thou in the midst of Thine enemies...Yet have I set my King upon my holy hill of Zion.*

3. And now with the third section of the Psalm there is a change of Speaker. *I will declare the decree: the Lord hath said unto me, Thou art my Son; this day have I begotten Thee.* We are taught in the New Testament to see the fulfilment of this *decree* not in the eternal sonship, and not in the incarnation, of our Lord Jesus Christ, but in His resurrection from the dead. In St Paul's discourse at Antioch in Pisidia, we read, *And we declare unto you glad tidings, how that the promise which was made unto the fathers, God hath fulfilled the same unto us their children, in that He hath raised up Jesus again; as it is also written in the second Psalm, Thou art my Son, this day have I begotten Thee.* The resurrection of Jesus was the fulfilment of the words, *Thou art my Son, &c.* Even as we read again in St Paul's Epistle to the Romans, *Concerning His Son Jesus Christ our Lord, who was made of the seed of David according to the flesh, and declared to be the Son of God with power, according to,* or, *by the operation of, the Spirit of holiness,* the Holy Spirit, *by the resurrection from the dead.* It was the resurrection of Jesus which declared Him to be the Son of God according to the *decree* here spoken of in

prophecy. And thus also in the Epistle to the Hebrews we read, once again, *So also Christ glorified not Himself to be made an High Priest, but He that said unto Him, Thou art my Son, to-day have I begotten Thee.* The investiture of Christ with the office of our great High Priest was the fulfilment of the prophetic announcement, *Thou art my Son, &c.* And upon that office of the High Priest of man He entered by resurrection. On earth He was the Prophet: not till He had died had He any atoning blood with which to present Himself, when now He lived again to do so, before the presence of God in the most holy place of the eternal temple.

And, as the priesthood of Christ, so also His kingly throne, was founded upon His resurrection. *Ask of me,* so the Divine decree continues, *and I shall give Thee the heathen for Thine inheritance, and the uttermost parts of the earth for Thy possession. Thou shalt break them with a rod of iron: Thou shalt dash them in pieces like a potter's vessel.* How exactly is this account of His entrance upon His kingdom the language of His own prayer to the Father in the immediate prospect of the completion of His earthly work by crucifixion: *I have glorified Thee on the earth: I have finished the work which Thou gavest me to do. And now, O Father, glorify Thou me, with Thine own self, with the glory which I had with Thee before the world was.* That glory was to be entered upon through resurrection. And in accordance with this prayer in the foreview of His sufferings was the language of our Lord to His disciples when those sufferings were surmounted, and when, in the fulness of risen life, He says to them, *All power is given unto me in heaven and in earth. Go ye therefore, and teach all nations.* The priesthood and the kingdom, like the Sonship out of which both spring, are the results of the resurrection.

My brethren, I cannot pass on without saying, in one brief word, how little like the Gospel, as our Lord and His Apostles delivered it, must be any system which teaches men to disregard or to disparage the crowning miracle of the resurrection. The resurrection of Christ is the very keystone of the Gospel arch: they who remove it must get themselves a new Gospel: they can never patch up the old Gospel without it. God give us all grace to hold it fast, and to live by it. *If Christ be not risen, then is our preaching vain, and your faith is also vain...If Christ be not raised, your faith is vain: ye are yet in your sins. Then they also which are fallen asleep in Christ are perished.*

4. One last section, also of three verses, yet remains. It is a word of application; the suitable close of the truths just declared. *Be wise now therefore, O ye kings: be instructed, ye judges of the earth.* If no efforts of yours can shake the throne of Christ; if God has certainly invested Him with universal dominion; if the uttermost parts of the earth are by sure anticipation given Him for His possession, and if, consequently, all who will not have Him to reign over them must in the end be discomfited and brought to nought; what is it which prudence dictates to you? Surely, to be humble in time. Surely, to learn, while you may, a lesson of reverence and godly fear. *Serve the Lord with fear, and rejoice with trembling.* What a word of divine wisdom is that, for each one of us. *Rejoice with trembling.* Rejoice: for the Gospel tells of a free salvation; forgiveness for the guilty, cleansing for the sinful, hope for the desperate, life

for the dead. But forget not the added caution; *with trembling.* How shall we escape if we neglect, if we abuse, if we trifle with, so great salvation? The greatness of the salvation is the measure of their danger who hear of it without listening, or listen to it without obeying. *Kiss the Son,* in token of submission and of homage, *lest He be angry, and ye perish from the way, when His wrath is kindled but a little.* The words are very remarkable; yes, my brethren, very salutary. It is as if it were said, Do not think to say in your hearts, I may go a little way in sinning; Christ is merciful, and, if my sin is not very great, He will deal gently with it: beware, rather, lest His wrath be kindled against you ever so little; for, if it be kindled but a little, it is formidable, it is terrible, it is a consuming fire. O beware lest you, beginning from small departures, have in the last day to combine those two most opposite ideas, and call upon the rocks and mountains to hide you from *the wrath of the Lamb. Kiss the Son* betimes, *lest He be angry. Blessed are all they that put their trust in Him.* There is no other safety: there is no other hope.

My brethren, the caution is not needless. God give us grace to ponder it. There is not enough of Christ in our thoughts even of religion. There is not enough of Christ—I often deeply feel it—in our sermons. Hence a vague, dreamy, purposeless religion. Hence a cold, dry, unpersuasive Gospel. Hence a want of purely Christian faith; and, let me add, strongly conscious of it, a want of Christian reverence and of godly fear. We greatly need the thought of Christ in His atonement. Without it, we grovel on in our sins, and never get them dismissed. That is the very meaning of the *remission* of sins: it is, their dismissal: it is, the having them put away, sent away, discarded, banished, done with, by a sentence of entire absolution. That, I say, is one want. But we much need the thought of Christ also in His greatness; in His present exaltation, in His kingly glory, in His universal and irresistible dominion. We greatly need that awe of Him of which we read as resting on the minds of His disciples when they saw Him after He was risen: *None of the disciples durst ask Him, Who art Thou? knowing that it was the Lord.* It is very sad that we do not love Christ more; that we do not more sincerely trust in Him; that we do not more eagerly seek and more tenderly cherish the thought of His propitiation, of His sacrifice, of His intercession, of His priesthood. But I am not sure whether, when we think of it, it is not even more dreadful that we have so little fear of Him. Really, if the Gospel be true, if this Psalm be true, we have great cause to fear Him. That sort of indifference, that sort of disregard, that sort of boldness —I can call it by no other name, that sort of audacity— which is so common amongst us, concerning the Lord Jesus Christ; an audacity shown in disobeying Him, an audacity shown in discussing Him, an audacity shown in going on as if He were not, as if every word which He says of Himself were at least an open question, if not a false claim; and this, not during a few weeks or months of anxious questioning, but all through life; in combination with a Christian name, with a Christian profession, with a Christian worship, and even with a Christian communion; all this is indeed a very grave matter, when we come to think of it: and dare I say that none of us are chargeable with it? Can I hope that none of us who are here assembled are guilty of the sin, of the impiety, of daring the anger of Christ (as this Psalm expresses it) at least a little? of walking carelessly, of walking confidently, of walking presumptuously, before Him, if we have not gone altogether astray, and counted the blood of the covenant an absolutely unholy thing?

For these and such like diseases of the soul I know of no remedy so potent as the kind of revelations contained in this Psalm. What we need is, to have the position of Jesus Christ reasserted and reestablished amongst us His professed people. We want to have Him set forth before us in all His tenderness, as though crucified amongst us. We want to have Him set forth before us in all His greatness, as though enthroned, as though crowned, as though reigning, amongst us. So He is. *He ascended into heaven*, we say Sunday by Sunday, *and sitteth on the right hand of God the Father Almighty; from thence He shall come to judge the quick and the dead.* Is that true? Are those three particulars true—His ascension, His session, His return? If they be, then *out of thine own mouth will I judge thee*, thou wicked, thou slothful, thou unfaithful servant. *Yet have I set my King upon my holy hill of Zion.* You may band yourselves together to disregard or to dethrone Him: you may leave Him out of sight in your plans, you may modify or annul His laws, you may say, *Where is the promise of His coming?* you may begin to doubt whether indeed He ever died for you or ever rose, you may treat His word with irreverence, with suspicion, or with contempt: BUT He that sitteth in the heavens is above your reach—His foolishness is wiser than your wisdom, and His weakness stronger than your strength—He will be when you are forgotten, He will still reign when you are dust. And then, at last, the sign of the Son of God shall be seen in heaven, and the light of His presence, shining from the one end of the earth even to the other, shining into the graves of the righteous and into the graves of the wicked, shall be the answer, decisive and final, alike to the misgivings of doubt and to the gainsayings of unbelief. God grant to each one of us who are now present before Him, that we may so humble ourselves before His truth while the day of grace lasts, that we may see Him with joy and not with grief when He exchanges the throne of mercy for the throne of judgment. *O taste and see that the Lord is good: blessed is the man that trusteth in Him.*

FOURTEENTH SUNDAY AFTER TRINITY,
September 1, 1861.

XVIII.[1]

THE FALL AND THE RISING.

St Luke xxii. 61, 62.

And the Lord turned, and looked upon Peter. And Peter remembered the word of the Lord, how He had said unto him, Before the cock crow, thou shalt deny me thrice. And Peter went out, and wept bitterly.

SUCH, my brethren, is the after-taste of sin. Such is the awakening from that sleep of the soul, to which the tempter has successfully presented one of his bright seductive visions. I wish you to ponder with me this evening an example of the process of temptation, as it has been witnessed ten thousand times in every generation since the fall of man. We shall have to notice three things: the sleep, the dream, and the awakening: or, to speak more plainly, the state of the soul before the sin, during the sin, and after the sin: the condition of which the tempter avails himself, the mode of his operation, and the condition in which he leaves us. God grant, not only that the subject may be (as I am sure it is) seasonable; but also that our consideration of it may be serious, earnest, and profitable to many.

[1] Preached on the Sunday before the Races.

1. What I have called the sleep of the soul, or its condition before the sin, may be briefly described as a state of security. Not of safety, but of security; that is, of supposed safety, of imagined strength. When our Lord, at the last Supper, so mercifully warned His disciples of the approach of danger, it was Peter, you remember, who repelled the warning by an eager assertion of his own resolution and constancy. Take the account of what passed from the Gospel now before us. We have to look but a few verses back from the text itself. In the 31st verse we read: *And the Lord said, Simon, Simon, behold, Satan hath desired to have you*, or, more exactly, *Satan begged for you, demanded you, that he might sift (winnow) you as wheat*. Observe, the pronoun *you* here, as elsewhere in Scripture, is plural: it includes all the disciples: then it turns to the singular. *But I have prayed for thee, that thy faith might not fail: and, when thou art converted, strengthen thy brethren.* The words are a little more precise: *and thou at some time having turned*, or, *and thou having at length turned, strengthen thy brethren*. These words, coming from their Lord Himself at so solemn a crisis, ought surely to have startled the disciples; and especially that disciple to whom they were addressed. Only consider for a moment what was contained in them. Was not their purport plainly this? 'A great danger is before you. It is as if Satan himself, the great enemy of souls, whose work it is to ruin men, and whose joy it is when he can succeed in doing so, had asked God for you; had begged you of God; had made a special request that your souls might be put into his hand for a season, even as the body of one of God's servants in old time, the

patriarch Job, was consigned to him, when *the Lord said unto Satan, Behold, he is in thine hand; but save his life.* The object of Satan, in making that request, was to sift the very heart and soul of that good man. He wanted to show that Job's obedience was all self-interest. *Doth Job,* he said, *fear God for nought? Hast not Thou made an hedge about him, and about his house, and about all that he hath on every side? Thou hast blessed the work of his hands, and his substance is increased in the land. But put forth Thine hand now, and touch all that he hath, and he will curse Thee to Thy face.* And then, afterwards, when the loss of all that he had, and of all that he loved, had failed to produce this effect, Satan said again, *Skin for skin, yea, all that a man hath will he give for his life. But put forth Thine hand now, and touch his bone and his flesh, and he will curse Thee to Thy face.* Thus he desired to have him that he might sift him as wheat; that he might probe every secret of his soul, every principle of his life, and bring to light his real unsoundness, his deep hidden falseness and worthlessness. Even so it is now. Satan would fain try his whole power, by God's permission, upon you. He will do so. But for one of you, in particular, I have made an earnest prayer to my Father in heaven. I have prayed that his faith may not fail, may not utterly vanish and disappear, in that fearful encounter. If it must fail for the time, yet may there be a reawakening and a recovery, a conversion and a turning back to God. And when this, in answer to my prayer, is so, let him make it thenceforth his life's work to strengthen his brethren; to feel for their dangers from the experience of his own, and to strive by word and act to keep them in their integrity and in their stedfastness.' My brethren, if our Saviour had addressed these remarkable words to any one of us, might we not have expected that we should hear them at least with alarm? What then was Peter's answer? It is given in the 33rd verse. *And he said unto Him, Lord, I am ready to go with Thee, both into prison, and to death.* He spoke earnestly, but he scarcely spoke humbly. He knew that he had love, and he knew that he had zeal, and he thought those two things must suffice for constancy. He made no allowance for altered circumstances. He remembered not how differently things appear in prospect, while they are at a distance, and in experience, when they are close upon us. And, therefore, however sincerely—and he was entirely sincere—he yet spoke ignorantly, rashly, in that spirit of self-confidence which is always utter weakness. And our Lord answered yet once more, and said to him, *I tell thee, Peter, the cock shall not crow this day before that thou shalt thrice deny that thou knowest me.* Peter was silenced, but he was not convinced. His Master had spoken plainly, but he still thought that he knew better.

My brethren, the same sort of security, of self-reliance, of false confidence, is our chief bane also. Even Christian people are liable to it. Even persons who call themselves miserable sinners, and say in their prayers, as we all said last Sunday, *The frailty of man without Thee cannot but fall*, are exposed to the same peril: the peril of self-confidence, of relying upon their own good intentions, good resolutions, or good principles, and of forgetting the solemn charge given to us all by our Master Himself, *Watch and pray, lest ye enter into temptation: the spirit indeed is willing, but the flesh is weak.*

2. We turn now to the temptation and to the sin. We have seen the condition of him who is about to enter into temptation: now let us mark the sort of disguise under which the offence comes. The disciple had already had a warning of the truth of his Master's words. He had not found it quite so easy as he had expected, to be firm and resolute. True, in the first excitement of the apprehension, he had used the sword but too readily: he had struck a hasty blow, and, but for Christ's instant interposition, might have brought upon Him the reproach of resisting force by force. Immediately afterwards, Peter, like the rest of the disciples, forsook Him and fled. This surely might have taught him wisdom. This surely might have shown him that he was not so bold or so constant as he had thought himself. But no: worse was to follow. At a distance, a long and timid distance, he had followed the band which led Jesus away. And now he has cautiously entered the high priest's palace, and seated himself there at the fire among the servants *to see the end.* He thought himself unknown and unnoticed, and hoped thus to combine the two objects, interest in his Master's fate, and freedom from personal risk of sharing it. He was mistaken. A certain maid—St Mark says, one of the maidservants of the high priest—saw Peter warming himself at the fire, and, after attentively observing him, said, *This man was also with Him;* or, *Thou also wast with Jesus of Nazareth.* The temptation came, as usual, suddenly; and the first impulse was that of self-preservation. *He denied Him*—denied his loved Master and Lord—*saying,*

Woman, I know Him not. How sad, how shameful, yet, alas, also how natural. Even this fall did not awaken conscience effectually. He moved his position; left the hall, and went out into the entrance; it might be, to escape further questioning. But the temptation was not ended. *After a little while another saw him, and said, Thou also art of them;* thou too belongest to the company of this man's disciples. Again Peter answered, *Man, I am not; denied,* St Matthew says, *with an oath,* saying, *I do not know the man.* Space was now given him for reflection. An hour passed, and he may have thought that now, however shamefully, his trial was ended. But *about the space of one hour after, another confidently affirmed, saying, Of a truth this fellow also was with Him: for he is a Galilæan. And Peter said, Man, I know not what thou sayest.* Or, as it is expressed still more strongly in other Gospels, *Then began he to curse and to swear, I know not the man.*

Temptations, my brethren, are very various. We know that sometimes they assail us, like the first temptation of all, through the body, through some appetite or passion to which we are all liable, and which carries us along, as if tied and bound, to its gratification. But the narrative before us not only represents the sudden and unexpected manner in which all temptation assails us, but shows us as in a glass the likeness and the very image of a whole class of temptations to which we are all exposed; those, namely, which derive their power from our sensitiveness to the opinion of others; from our dislike of being singular; from our desire to stand well with our neighbours, both in what we do, and in what we do not. We speak of *the world* as one of the

Christian's three enemies; and this is just what we mean, or ought to mean, by it. The world, which, as Christians, is one of our three enemies, does not mean always the great world, the world of high fashion or of unapproachable rank: it means our world: it means the men and the women who surround and who influence us: it is a very practical thing; and for this reason; because it varies with station and circumstance: the poor man has a world, which is his enemy, just as much as the rich and the great have a still more glittering and powerful world, which is their enemy. O how many of us, my brethren, are slaves of their world, be it what it may—the world of the rich man, or the world of the poor man. Which of us dares—yes, I ask the question of many men not destitute of firmness and courage in a bodily sense; of men who would stand out boldly against the attack of a robber, or repel with spirit the accusation of a slanderer—which of us, I repeat the question, dares to do exactly what he thinks right, without regard to what other men will say of it? Peter, an Apostle, a warmhearted, loving, earnest man, a man who afterwards gave his body bravely to the agonies of the cross, yet, at the time now spoken of, allowed himself to deny Christ rather than be laughed at by a few servants. O what a picture of human nature in all times. What a picture, my brethren, of us, in our little timidities about the world's opinion. Peter's world at that moment was the high priest's kitchen: it looked as large, to him, for the time, and as important, as the king's court has looked to men of rank and fashion: the world was his enemy, and the question, *Art not thou also one of this man's disciples?* put by a maidservant, was enough to make havoc in him of every resolution and of every principle. May God write the lesson deeply upon our hearts. The essence of the warning lies in this: that we are always exposed to a very peculiar risk of denying Christ, that is, of disclaiming our connection with Him, of saying, or acting as if we said, *He is not my Master, and I am not His servant*, for the sake of avoiding a moment's ridicule or a moment's reproach: and that this is a temptation; this is a solicitation of the devil; this is what brings us under the operation of that solemn sentence of our Lord Himself, *Whosoever shall be ashamed of me and of my words, in this adulterous and sinful generation, of him also shall the Son of man be ashamed, when He cometh in the glory of His Father with the holy Angels.*

3. In the case before us, the prayer of Jesus, though it prevented not the fall, yet secured the rising. *When thou art converted*, is said of one who shall first have wandered. The faith shall fail, but not utterly, and not finally. Scarcely had Peter uttered the third denial, with all its sad and grievous aggravations, than that sound was heard, which his Lord's prediction had connected with the sin—*immediately, while he yet spake, the cock crew*—and, at the same moment, his Lord, standing before His judges, exposed to every sort of insult and mockery, yet retaining amidst His sufferings the same care for His disciples which He had ever manifested, *the Lord turned, and looked upon Peter*. Not a word was spoken, or could have been heard amidst the uproar then ringing through the palace: but no word was needed: that look, such as we can picture it—full of sorrow, full of pity, full of tenderness—recalled the sinner instantly to himself, and brought after it such a

flood of grief, of self-reproach, and of misery, that he could hide his feeling no longer, but straightway *went out, and wept bitterly.* There, in that anguish, he is left by the Evangelists, until they have to tell how, on the morning of the resurrection, he was one of the first to run to the sepulchre; one of the first to whom Jesus showed Himself risen: and how he who had so lately thrice denied, was invited by his forgiving Master thrice to declare that he loved Him, and invested afresh, and in express terms, with that apostolic commission which he might seem for ever to have forfeited.

If any of us, my brethren, have ever, like St Peter, been led to deny Christ; if we have ever been induced, by fear or affection, to say of Him, in our conduct at least, *I know Him not, I am none of His;* may we, like St Peter, bitterly lament such cowardice and such ingratitude, and hasten back to Him with tears of penitence and earnest prayers for His forgiveness. To some, no doubt, a terrible fall has been salutary, yes, saving. Some can look back upon an act of sin, revealing to them their own weakness, and convincing them of their need of a Divine Saviour and Sanctifier, as the very turning-point of a life. Happy are they of whom this is true. But O, for one of these, how many thousands have found their first yielding the very *letting out of water*—the commencement of a course and life of sin, from which they have never afterwards been emancipated to this day. And therefore, while we would thank God for the encouragement given us in St Peter's bitter tears and in his restored acceptance and apostleship, we have need to lay well to heart the lessons taught us by his shameful fall.

You can imagine why this subject should have come into my heart for the present time. I can have no secrets with you, my brethren; no reserves, and no evasions. Your ministers could not possibly ignore the excitement which this coming week must bring with it. And you yourselves would be the first to despise them, if, being conscious of the fact, they did not dare to mention it.

It is a great pity, and, I think, a great error, when the whole of religion is practically made to turn upon abstinence from one or two particular amusements. Such statements you will not hear from this place. But there are certain things which a minister of the Gospel, if he would be faithful to his trust, is bound to say, and which his hearers, if they are true-hearted and honest men, will not only bear with, but respect. I shall close my Sermon with two or three words, as I hope and believe, of this nature.

i. There is a right and a wrong in all things. Whatever it is in your own power to do or not to do, it is your business to judge whether you ought to do or to forego. And, if you cannot decide this question, in a particular case, for yourself, you are bound to ask advice upon it from older or wiser or more experienced men.

ii. The duty of all persons under authority is absolute obedience. Children are commanded in all things to obey their parents, and servants their masters. What they bid you do (if not directly contrary to God's law) becomes on that very account your clear duty, and to disobey them is to disobey God.

iii. A thing which is wrong in itself must always be wrong for you: but even a thing which is not wrong in itself may be wrong for you. If by a particular act of yours you should wound the conscience or hinder the well-doing of another, then it is your duty to abstain from that act, not for your own conscience sake, but for the sake of the conscience of that other. This is the Gospel rule, as laid down for us briefly by our Lord, and explained more at large by His holy Apostle St Paul.

iv. The Gospel of Jesus Christ allows no Saturnalia. It does not permit one week, or one day, in the year, to be regarded as a time of licence. Whatever Christian duty is, whatever Christian obligation is, whatever religion is, whatever holiness is, at one season, that it is at another and at all seasons. Some men say, 'I cannot expect this week to be like a common week. It is a very peculiar, a very unusual week. The whole place is transfigured. Everything is in a whirl and in an uproar. Every one is beside himself. God Himself, under these circumstances, will make some allowances. A little more levity than usual, a little more frivolity, a little more indulgence, than usual—nay, some little concession, if it should be so, to sinful practices, to carnal lusts—is only natural, is quite venial, in a week like this.' My brethren, that is not the language of the Gospel. And why not? Because the Gospel, because He who gave, because He who brought, because He who died for, the Gospel, loves us too well to speak thus to us. That language, about a time when it is not necessary and not possible to be good, is the language, not of God who loves, but of the devil who hates you. It is the language of an enemy, wanting to throw you off your guard and then to destroy you. It may be more difficult at one time than another—it is always difficult enough—to be what we ought to be: but never say that it is unnecessary, and never say that it is impossible. *With men it is impossible, but not with God: for with God all things are possible.*

v. In the next place, and for the same reason, we must say this: Whatever you find by experience to be bad for you, injurious to you personally with reference to your religious state, that you must avoid, that you must flee from, that you must give up, at any cost. We do not say what this thing, or these things, may be in your case. But, though we do not prescribe, you can judge. Is there any amusement, is there any society, which does harm to your soul; which makes prayer more difficult, the Bible more distasteful, heaven more distant to you? Then that amusement, then that society, you are bound to give up. I say again, we judge not for you: *I speak as to wise men: judge ye what I say.*

vi. Once more: there may be difficulties, there may be temptations, which, with all your wish to do right, you cannot get rid of. Through no fault of yours, this coming week may be a time of difficulty and of trial to your faith and constancy. Then I would urge you to a more diligent use than ever of God's appointed means of grace. Shall you find it unusually difficult to maintain a serious and a Christian mind? Shall you be more than commonly pressed and burdened by the cares and interruptions of life? Will temper be especially irritated, and tranquillity of mind ruffled? Then take heed lest, in proportion as your dangers increase, your safeguards be diminished. Take heed lest, as is so often the case at such times, you be tempted to abridge your prayers, to intermit your reading of Scripture, to seek or to make for yourself no quiet moments for thought and meditation, when each one of these things will be so peculiarly, so more than commonly, needful for you. Many a man, I doubt not, and many a woman, has been able to trace back a decided and a fatal declension from good, to a week of special excitement like that which begins to-day. God give us all grace to escape that dreadful experience.

vii. Finally, my beloved brethren, I would say to each one of you, Remember the end. When next Sunday comes, for those of us who are spared to see it, this week, with its trials and its interests, will be ended. Nothing will then remain but the recollection. O let not that retrospect be bitter and condemning. Do not have to confess then that the demon of gambling, or the demon of drunkenness, or the demon of lust, has made havoc of soul and body during these six days which follow. God forbid. But, that it may not be so, you must indeed, more than ever, watch and pray during them. The spirit may be willing: to-day you may be saying with Peter, *Though all men should deny Thee, yet will not I.* But the flesh is weak. Even Peter, with all his zeal and with all his love, first vowed, and then fell. God keep each one of us from that presumption, and from that fall. But O, *if* you fall, God grant you—for it is indeed His gift only—the grace of that recovery.

May He be so with us, that, in all humility and in all patience, in all earnestness and in all love, we may bear each one his own burden, and every one that of others also. May He establish us and keep us from evil. May He, according to the words heard already in this evening's service, may He, the God of peace, beat down Satan under all our feet shortly.

I shall end with a few words, not of man's but of Christ's; of Him who is our Saviour, of Him who shall one day come to be our Judge. You have heard them already in this day's service.

Then said Jesus unto His disciples, If any man will come after me, let him deny himself, and take up his cross, and follow me. For whosoever will save his life shall lose it: and whosoever will lose his life for my sake shall find it. For what is a man profited, if he shall gain the whole world, and lose his own soul? or what shall a man give in exchange for his soul?

SIXTEENTH SUNDAY AFTER TRINITY,
September 15, 1861.

XIX.[1]

USE AND ABUSE OF THE WORLD.

1 Corinthians vii. 31.

And they that use this world, as not abusing it.

A HUMAN writer is never more honoured than by having one of his expressions adopted as a national proverb. We may almost measure the genius of a great orator or a great poet, by the number of proverbs which he has furnished for popular use. It always implies that a man has had a deep insight into human nature, a large share of human feeling, and a singular force alike of thought and of expression, if he is permitted, in this sense, to live after death, alike in the orations of the eloquent and in the household talk of the simple.

There is one Book which has furnished more of these popular proverbs than any other in the world: and that Book is the Bible. Sometimes it is quoted from irreverently: ludicrous turns are given to its serious sayings, and associations thus formed in the mind, which can never afterwards be broken. But, even where it is least meant, a tribute is thus paid to God's Word—to its force, to its insight, to its experience, and to its

[1] Preached on the Sunday after the Races.

wisdom—for which we must not be unthankful. If the Bible were quite the old-fashioned, obsolete, childish fable which scoffers would fain make it, they would not turn to it even to point their sarcasms or to wing their jests. And sensible men, even when not religious, are deeply conscious of the wisdom of God's Word, and use its brief sayings with respect at least, if not with reverence, and if not with love.

One of these Bible proverbs is contained in the text. It occurs in the midst of a chapter not often perhaps read by choice. It is one advantage of our Church Service, that, with reference to the New Testament at least, there is no picking and choosing of passages for public instruction. If we except the Revelation of St John—and I am sorry that we should have to except it —the whole of the New Testament is read through in regular order, where there is a daily service, three times in each year. And where there is only a Sunday service, each chapter still has its equal chance with others, and each is heard by every worshipper many times over in the course even of a brief life. And where is that chapter, however little popular be its subject, or however little attractive its general aspect, which does not contain within it some points of beauty and of interest; some passage, embedded perhaps in paragraphs of secondary importance, yet full itself, when brought to the light, of wise counsel, of touching pathos, or of sweet persuasion? It is thus with the words before us.

St Paul has said, in the verses immediately preceding the text, that, in such times of sorrow as he sees impending, he knows not how to recommend the formation of the ties of married life. He speaks, as he carefully reminds his readers, not by commandment, not as conveying a Divine precept, but in the way of advice, by his own judgment, and from a regard to the comfort of those whom he addresses. There is no sin, he says, in marrying and giving in marriage: only *such persons*, those who form such ties, *will have trouble in the flesh*, will have an increased amount of care, anxiety, and distress, *and* [not, *but*] *I spare you*: that is, I would fain spare you, my beloved friends, from that increase of sorrow. *But this I say, brethren*—this is what I say—this is the meaning of my words of warning—*the time is short*: more exactly, *the season*, that definite and destined period which yet remains to us of life before the end come, *the season is contracted: it remaineth, that both they who have wives be as though they had none; and they that weep, as though they wept not; and they that rejoice, as though they rejoiced not; and they that buy, as though they possessed not; and they that use the world, as not abusing it; for the fashion of this world passeth away. And I would have you without carefulness:* I would fain see you as free from unnecessary anxiety, arising out of the circumstances of life, as is compatible with the condition of persons living upon this earth.

And they that use the world, as not abusing it. The word properly expresses not so much an altogether wrong use, but rather a greedy, an engrossing, and an excessive use. To 'abuse' is, properly, and in its strict meaning, to 'use up.' It is not, necessarily, to use for a wrong purpose; to turn that which was meant for one use to another use: it is only, to use up, to use to the full, to use a thing so as to exhaust and to consume it. They who use the world ought not to use it to the uttermost; ought not to use it with too much of eagerness, too much of absorption in it, too much of addiction to it. That is the exact meaning of the word here rendered 'abusing.' And, so understood, does not the brief charge thus given convey a salutary and a timely caution to us all who are here assembled?

In endeavouring, by God's help, to press it upon your attention to-night, I will avail myself of the illustrations furnished in the context by St Paul himself, and ask you to notice its application to the three subjects, of the connections of life, the circumstances of life, and the possessions of life. In all these, there is a 'use' which is right, and there is an 'abuse,' that is, an inordinate use, which is not right but wrong. Let those who use this world, as all must use it, take heed that they abuse it not.

1. The connections of life. St Paul says, *Let those who have wives be as though they had none.* And the principle is of wide application. Let those who have husbands, let those who have parents, let those who have children, let those who have brothers or sisters, let those who have relations and friends, be as though they had none. Let those who use be all as not abusing. And in what sense? Is there no tie, no close, endearing tie, no tie of duty as well as of affection, in all these things? Is the meaning of the Apostle that which would contradict the plainest rules of Scripture and of morality, Regard these ties as if they were not binding, as if they were nothing for you? We need not answer that question. The tie of relationship was in St Paul's eyes one of sacred obligation: he has enforced it in many of his Epistles. The tie of marriage was in his eyes so solemn

and so indissoluble that on that very account he here urges men to hesitate before they form it in times of peril and of distress. Evidently his meaning is, Use, but abuse not. *Children, obey your parents in the Lord... Fathers, bring up your children in the nurture and admonition of the Lord...Wives, obey your husbands in all things...Husbands, love your wives, and be not bitter against them.* But remember in each case—rather to cement than to loosen each one of these ties—remember, and forget not, that the time is short. Hold not with too tenacious a grasp that which must soon be dissolved, by death, or by the Advent. Set not your highest affections on any one of these things. See that, however much you love one another, you love Christ, and love God, more. Take heed lest you so love any earthly person as to set the will of that person above the will of God, or aim at pleasing that person more than you aim at pleasing God. The time must soon come—soon, at the latest—when that tie will be broken; broken, never again to be re-formed on the same model: for in heaven, among the Angels of God, there is neither marrying nor giving in marriage, and they who shall be counted worthy to obtain that world, and the resurrection from the dead, must have learned here below the secret of that supreme and of that subordinate affection —the one towards God, and the other towards His creature—which alone can flourish or exist in heaven. Live now, St Paul says, in the recollection that the time is short. Let that thought arouse you to the discharge of every duty one towards another, as those who know that soon the very power to discharge that duty will be for ever lost and gone. Defer nothing that ought to be done, and allow yourself in nothing which one day you will wish undone. Let the words, *while we have time*, ring in your ears, and make you prompt for duty and intolerant of your own unfaithfulness. Soon will the husband be following his wife to the grave, and the son his mother: let no bitter thoughts of half-fulfilled or unfulfilled relations aggravate the sadness of that parting, or leave behind a deadly sting for the years of orphanage or of widowhood. *Let those that have wives be as though they had none*, not only in the subjugation of all idolatrous affections, but also in the faithful preparation for that time when every connection of life will be broken, and when for the fulfilment of every relative duty they will have to give account. *Use this world, as not abusing it.*

2. Again, in reference to the circumstances of life. St Paul says, *Let them that weep be as though they wept not, and those who rejoice as though they rejoiced not.* Joy and sorrow, elation and depression, sunshine and storm, the time to laugh and the time to weep, all are to be as if they were not. The Gospel does not say, It is wrong to weep, or, it is wrong to rejoice. The Gospel does not encourage that dead level of human feeling, which never rises into enjoyment and never sinks into sadness. It only says, When you rejoice, let it be as though you did not rejoice; and, when you weep, let it be with you as though you wept not. Use the circumstances of life as not abusing them. That is, use them not with an eager, a grasping, an absorbed and engrossed mind. In joy, remember sorrow: in sorrow, think of joy. Remember in either case that the time is short. Never let the joys of earth, and never let the sorrows

of earth—for either is possible—shut out or shut up your heaven. Never let a season of unusual enjoyment make you say to yourself, Now I shall never be cast down; now I have made my nest in the rock, and it shall nevèr be invaded again, and never despoiled again, for ever. And never let a time of calamity make you say to yourself, All is over with me: God hath forgotten to be gracious: nothing can reverse this black picture, nothing can people again this waste, this howling wilderness. These feelings are both alike exaggerations. If life be prolonged, you who are now mourning will be again comforted, and yet again mourning, many times over, before your great change come. If life be prolonged, you who are now prosperous will be again mourning, and yet again prosperous, many times over, before you go hence and are no more seen. Therefore let the light and the shade be duly commingled in your feeling, as assuredly they will ever be in your lot. Let the sun that is hidden shine still in your memory and in your hope: let the sun that is brightly shining be tempered by the knowledge that it must yet go down. In these things lies a great part of the discipline of life. It is in these alternations of joy and sorrow that God teaches man his chief lessons: and out of them grows for His children, in length of years, that calm and quiet spirit which is in His sight of great price. They have not ceased to rejoice, and they have not ceased to weep: but they have learned to do each even as though it were the other; to rejoice with a remembrance of weeping, and to weep with an anticipation of joy. Happy they who have so learned this lesson, that now, when sorrow comes, they can receive it as God's messenger; receive it with humility, receive it with composure, receive it without agitation and without murmuring; and, when joy, can see in it also a memento of that loving care which provides for the pilgrim refreshments to strengthen him for conflict, and refreshments to recruit him after conflict. Sorrow, as well as joy, has its extravagances and its excesses. Even sorrow may be nursed into a sin. It ought to be sobering, but it is often made enfeebling. It ought to remind us of sin, but it ought not to leave us in despondency: it ought to solemnize earth, but it ought not to obliterate heaven. *Let them that weep be as though they wept not, and them that rejoice as though they rejoiced not.* In this sense also, we must use the world as not abusing it.

3. Once more, and most obviously, the rule has an application to the possessions of life. And this in all degrees. All men have something: and all men, certainly all working men, whether high or low, are ever gaining something. For all these therefore it is written, *Let those who buy be as though they possessed not.* And well may it be thus written. How often have we seen men run into the error thus corrected. How often have we seen them buy as if they did possess, as if they were sure of enjoying. Sometimes a man has set his heart, all through life, upon one particular possession; some house or some land which his ancestors once owned, which his father lost, and which he has set himself to recover. Or, if not this; if this higher and tenderer motive has been wanting; still the object has been the same: a man has determined to gain this position or that, and to make himself, before he dies, great or rich or famous. And some men have done this successfully; and, viewed

only from earth, have gained that standing-place which others might envy. And O how safe have they thought themselves; how have they forgotten God in His gifts; how have they said, like the men in the Parable, *I pray thee have me excused*, to every call and every invitation of the Gospel; how have they said within their hearts, like the rich man in another Parable, *Soul, thou hast much goods laid up for many years: take thine ease, eat, drink, and be merry*. At last the stroke has fallen: God has said at length, *This night thy soul shall be required of thee*: and the whole fabric of human possession has fallen at once in ruins around them. This it is, to buy as if to possess. O what need have we all, with reference to small gains or greater, with reference to the little daily comforts which cheer the humblest home, to bear well in mind the inspired words, *And they that buy, as though they possessed not*. O what disappointments attend all human getting. How often is the thing got most unlike the thing sought, and the thing possessed most unlike the thing got. How do we deceive ourselves beforehand as to the thing which will make us happy. How often, when attained, it is found to be a mere shadow. How often, just when attained, and found to be something, it is snatched from us by an unexpected reverse, by a failure of health, or by the hand of death itself, and the whole of life has been a dream. There is no safety, and there is no happiness, for any man, but in living just for the day, thanking God for what he has, and fully prepared at any moment for its withdrawal.

Use this world, the Apostle says, *as not abusing it*. God has given us in it much to enjoy. He has given us many common, and He has given us many special blessings. To live at all in this beautiful world, with all its treasures of sight and sound, its things good for food and pleasant to the eyes, its comforts for the body and its means of information and improvement for the mind—this is enough, this ought to be enough, for any man, both to satisfy desire and to awaken gratitude. Let us not abuse the gift. Let us not use this world greedily; giving ourselves to its enjoyments in excess, intemperately, or sinfully. Let us not use it selfishly; catching all for ourselves, and thinking nothing of the wants, in soul and body, of those around us. Let us not use it unthankfully; seizing the gifts, and forgetting the Giver. Let us not use it blindly; having all our attention fixed on the near, the present object, and losing sight altogether of the higher and better, the enduring and the heavenly. In all these ways we may use or we may abuse the world.

Thoughts such as these, my brethren, common in themselves and obvious, could not but be strongly impressed upon Christian people by the events of the week just ended. Amidst the noisy and exciting scenes which have affected, in one way or another, our whole population, and from which it is too much to hope that no evil consequences will have resulted to any lives and souls, there is just one thing which has not altogether stood still: the course of sickness has not been arrested: the hand of death has not been stayed. I know nothing more impressive, more painfully impressive, than the contrast, at such times, between the street and the chamber of sickness. It is not the sight of health which is shocking to one ministering to sickness;

not the sight of health, not the sight of activity, not the sight of childish play or of manly relaxation; *but* the sight, in any sense or in any form, of sin. The sight of the drunkard, the hearing of the profane oath, the loud laughter of the abandoned woman driving shamelessly through our streets—these are the things which make a thoughtful man sick at heart, as they force upon his notice the bitter contrast, on God's earth, between sin in its triumph and that suffering which is its curse.

It happened to me, on one of those days of thronging crowds and abounding excitements, to visit the deathbed of a Christian man, known by name and sight to most of you, and now closing a long life of integrity, of industry, of honour, and of piety, by a death full of immortality. There he lay in his still tranquil chamber; and not a sound from the noisy neighbouring town could reach him through the open window which admitted in all their sweetness the bright cheering light and the fresh fragrant air of heaven. There he lay, calm, cheerful, thankful, loving; his work finished, his race run, his rest at hand. What a picture of *the righteous man entering into peace; resting in his bed,* as the same Prophet writes, still *walking in his uprightness;* yet trusting, not in himself or in his own blamelessness, piety, or charity, but only in the merits of his Lord and Saviour, whose name, even in moments of wandering and unconsciousness, was still and ever upon his lips. O, to return from that chamber of peace and blessedness, through quiet lanes and amidst the gathered fruits of an abundant harvest, to meet again, at the very entrance of our town, those who are dishonouring God by profaneness, by drunkenness, by temptation of others;

to see the Saviour Himself crucified afresh here, as He is glorified and honoured there; this indeed is a sad and painful contrast, awakening anxious thought and summoning to deep contrition.

Which of all us, my brethren, if spared, like that dying man, to the age of fourscore years, will have (to judge by the present) his retrospect of earthly life? first the discharge of every duty towards a father and a widowed mother: then a long and patient struggle with life's difficulties; those difficulties bravely encountered, and God remembered and honoured amidst all: then the promise well fulfilled, *Them that honour me I will honour*: and lastly, an old age spent in the firm yet humble maintenance of every Christian principle, and in efforts, as opportunity was given, for the spread of God's Word and of Christ's Gospel? O, my brethren, such a deathbed is not an isolated, separate, sudden thing: it is the result of such a life: and O suffer me to ask each one of you, Are you so living as to have any reasonable expectation of such a death? It comes of so using the world, as not abusing it: it comes of walking with God, of bearing the cross bravely, of living the life that now is by faith in Christ Jesus.

He of whom I have thus spoken belonged not outwardly in life to our communion: but such a man is not of a sect, he is of the Church of Christ; the Church, one and indivisible, now militant, soon to be triumphant. Such faith and such love are given to be our example. We, call ourselves what we may, need them for our own salvation: O have we found them? Little will it avail us, in the great reawakening, to have worshipped in the most beautiful of churches, to have used the most perfect of liturgies, or to have held and professed the most orthodox of creeds, unless we have also possessed that Spirit of Christ which is limited within no one communion, but works in the hearts of all those who seek the Lord Jesus Christ with earnestness and love Him in sincerity.

And if in some respects we can see blemishes—blemishes, as we venture to think, of an obvious and a serious kind—in the particular body of Christians of which he was one; yet let us confess, on the other hand, that to some Christian principles that body has sought to bear a bold and a consistent testimony: they have aimed in some points at a literal obedience, where others have been contented to follow more vaguely or more distantly: they have reproved the multiplication of needless and useless oaths: they have remonstrated against the wanton perpetuation of war: they have set an example of moderation and truthfulness of speech: above all, they have strongly maintained the need of a spiritual life and the reality of a spiritual presence, and have been able, in many instances, to say, not as the confession only of a true doctrine, but as the expression of a living faith, *I believe in the Holy Ghost.*

For these things we would thank them: for these things, so far as they have been consistently held, we would glorify God in them. Even from what we deem their excess of literalness, even from what we count their needless and unwise singularity, we can yet learn a lesson of self-humiliation, or self-correction, and of self-reproof. Most of all, when we see, in one of a communion not our own, such manifest tokens of a renewed heart and a devoted life, we can give thanks, beside his deathbed or his open grave, for the approach of that promised day when Christ shall gather together in one all the children of God who are here scattered abroad, and enable us to comprehend, with a clearness now impossible, what is the breadth and length and depth and height, and to know the love of Christ which **passeth knowledge.**

Seventeenth Sunday after Trinity,
September 22, 1861.

I.

IGNORANT PRAYERS.

St Mark x. 38.

Ye know not what ye ask.

AND yet the request was plain enough. Two of the disciples had asked that they might be allowed to sit on the right hand and on the left hand of their Lord in His glory. We might think this a vain request, an arrogant request, a presumptuous request: we might find many errors in it, and many faults: but the words themselves are distinct, plain, and expressive.

The answer however is, *Ye know not what ye ask.* You do not understand the meaning of your own words. You have no idea of that which is involved in them. Are you aware that a preeminence in glory presupposes a preeminence in suffering? Are you aware that, as your Lord Himself, so they who are to be nearest to Him in the kingdom of God, must drink to the dregs the cup of sorrow and be baptized with a baptism of fire and blood? That then is your prayer. When you say, *Grant that we may sit next to thee in heaven,* you say in effect, *Grant that we may drink of thy cup and be baptized with Thy baptism;* that cup which is gall and wormwood, that baptism which is immersion in a sea of blood. Can you bear this? *Yes*, they answer, in the ignorance of warm feeling and inexperienced zeal, *We can; we are able.* It was not our Lord's purpose at that moment to pursue the lesson into all its details: He leaves human confidence and young presumption to find itself out in time: He rather accepts the warm feeling of love and devotion which breathed in the request, and promises that share in His sufferings which they were not yet indeed, but in time should be, capable of enduring. *The cup which I drink*, He said, *ye shall drink, and with the baptism that I am baptized withal shall ye be baptized.* But even then, even after this life of suffering endured patiently for His sake, He could not promise that they should outshine all others, or enjoy that supremacy of glory which eternity, not time, must apportion. *To sit on my right hand and on my left is not mine to give, save to them for whom it has been prepared.*

Ye know not what ye ask. Were those words written only of the two sons of Zebedee? Do no ignorant requests go up now from earth into the ear of Christ? I propose, in the few words now to be spoken, to consider that question; to dwell with you upon the thought of ignorant prayers, adding such words of reproof, and yet of encouragement also, as we seem to find sanctioned in the teaching of our Lord Himself.

1. And let me say first, that ignorant prayers are not always and not necessarily unthinking, inattentive, much less irreverent prayers. Of some persons indeed in every congregation it must be said, in a tone wholly of reproof and warning, *Ye know not what ye ask.* When we see a person careless even of the external marks of

reverence in worship; not standing in praise, not kneeling in prayer; taking no part in the utterances of the congregation, whether in response or hymn; or looking around him in idle observation of others when every thought should be centred in himself and in the act which he has come hither to perform; well may the words occur to us in their gravest and saddest signification, *Ye know not what ye ask.* Little do you think what you are engaged in: little do you remember Him at whose footstool, in bodily presence, you are kneeling.

But the sons of Zebedee asked not in inattention or in irreverence, when their request was thus answered. And thus we are led to a further application of the words; one not entirely of rebuke, but rather of correction, of instruction, and at last of encouragement.

2. It is always an affecting thing to observe the devotions of a child. Simplify as you may the expressions in which you teach a child to call upon God; and alas, how few persons take that trouble! you must leave many which he most imperfectly comprehends. If we are not to begin to pray till we thoroughly understand every term employed and every subject introduced, indeed we shall never begin. In this respect the eldest of us all is a child still. What is there for which we ask, either here or in private, of which we really understand the whole meaning? It is not to the young only, though to them most obviously, that the words of the text may be addressed. The prayer of a congregation cannot be intelligible throughout and in all its parts to all worshippers equally. There must be young people present, and there must be uneducated people present, and there

may probably be persons of very inferior capacity present also, to all of whom much that is uttered, both in prayer and praise, is very little applicable or appropriate. And yet what they cannot *pray with the understanding* they may still *pray with the spirit*. There may be a prayer of ignorance which is yet a prayer of sincerity. Thus it was with the two disciples of whom the text speaks. Their request was an ignorant one: but it was made in simplicity, made in seriousness, made in love; and therefore He, the merciful Lord to whom it was addressed, did not refuse or repel, though He did inform and correct it. Let this be the encouragement of the young and of the ignorant who may be present in this place today. Do not think, we would say to them, that Jesus Christ rejects your prayers here because you do not understand everything which they contain. He looks at the heart; and if He sees you sincere and humble and earnest, using what you know and desiring to be taught, He will lead you on in the knowledge of Himself and of His truth, until at last the words shall in your case be made good, *Now I know in part; but then shall I know even as also I am known.*

3. Sometimes, again, we know not what we ask, because we mistake the character of the thing asked for; counting something good which is not good for us, or something evil which is not really evil.

These hearts of ours are all full of wishes: and it is the proper use of wishes, to turn them into prayers. It is the test of a wish, whether we can pray it. Sinful wishes refuse to be prayed; any wish which is not sinful should be at once moderated and consecrated by being made into a prayer. But when it is made into a prayer, how often may Christ say to us concerning it, *You know not what you ask.* Perhaps you are starting in the race of life, and the one thing which seems to you important is success. Or perhaps you have been considerably hindered and thrown back in life's competition: you have known what disappointment is: you have seen others pass you; others who set out with fewer advantages and with humbler hopes than yours: and now it is becoming a critical case; if success comes not now, if you do not make a stride or take an onward step now, life itself will have been for you a failure: and who can patiently bear that result? How natural, how right, that you should pray about these things. How natural, how right, that you should say, *Lord, if it be Thy will, give me success: Lord, if it be Thy will, save me from this blank of disappointment, from this shipwreck of my life: Lord, prosper, Lord, help, Lord, relieve me.* And yet has not Christ said, with reference to such matters, to many, in all times, of His faithful and cherished disciples, *In asking for success, in asking for prosperity, you know not what you ask? It is in failure that you are safest, it is in disappointment that you are closest to me and nearest to heaven: these things are of love; these things are for good: be patient, be of good courage; so shall you win your crown.*

Or perhaps there is some definite cause of annoyance at this time vexing you. You are tried by long-continued wearing, enfeebling discomfort of mind or body. Health is denied you: you never know what it is to be entirely free from pain: or you are daily oppressed with that indefinable but most perceptible sense of indisposition which makes exertion a severe struggle, and sometimes causes you to wish for that more decided condition of illness which might justify inactivity and constrain repose. Or the mind is suffering: some one is unkind to you: some member of your own household is wearying your spirit by daily irritability and ill temper: or some one whom you deeply love will not love you: or some friend whom you have borne with and served at the cost of much toil and self-sacrifice is repaying you with indifference and base ingratitude: and struggle as you may to be cheerful and contented under the trial, you cannot forget, you cannot shake off its yoke. How certain is it that, if you have any faith, if you be at all a Christian, you will pray about these things. You will say, *Lord, if it be Thy will, restore my health: Lord, if it be Thy will, remove this weight from me.* Yet here too the answer from your Saviour, not in word but in act, may be this, *You know not what you ask: your naturally high spirits might have run away with you, but for the drag which ill health has put upon them: your intense power of loving, your strength of human devotion, your delight in human sympathy, might have made you indifferent to a love altogether heavenly. I give you the one, seek not the other: it is I who have you in my charge; let me judge, let me prescribe, let me guide and keep you.*

You ask perhaps for the continued life, for the restoration from sickness, of one in whom your happiness seems to be bound up; a mother, a wife, a sister, a child: and behold, that life wastes and ebbs; your prayer for it seems to be cast out unheard: yet perhaps, could you see behind the veil, that long watching, that decaying hope, at last that bitter mourning, is to be to you the harbinger of a cloudless day; the desolation of a home below the very furnishing and peopling of a home above. Surely in all these things Jesus Christ may have been answering you as He answered on earth the petition of the sons of Zebedee, and saying, *You know not what you ask: let me exercise my judgment for you, instead of merely following yours.*

4. But we approach still more nearly to the original application of the text, when we speak of prayers offered in ignorance of the real meaning of the thing asked for, or of the processes by which alone it can be reached.

How little did the sons of Zebedee understand what was meant by sitting at the right hand and at the left hand of Christ in His glory. What a poor, carnal, earthly notion had they of the glory of which they spoke. What an ignorance is betrayed in the very words, of the spiritual blessedness for which a Christian ought to look in the world beyond death. Is it not even so with many of us? When we pray for heaven, for glory, for everlasting life, what do we mean, what do we understand, by these words? How little do any of us yet know of the joys of that world. To many members of this congregation the expectation of heaven is either a blank or else even a repulsive prospect. What is there in it which can possess for us a real attraction? Does the word *heaven* convey to us at present any more definite hope than that of an escape from hell? Just a safe state; just a painless state; just a state of reunion with lost friends: what else? what more? Who is there who thinks of heaven as his Father's home, as his Saviour's presence? Who is there who can say, like

St Paul, when he prays for life everlasting, *My desire is to depart and to be with Christ?*

And how much less were the sons of Zebedee aware, when they asked for the chief places in their Master's glory, by what processes alone, through what experience alone, they could hope to reach them. If they knew not what glory meant, much less did they know that the preparation for it was the cup of suffering, the way to it was through a baptism of blood. Is not this also true of us?

We hear many voices asking here for forgiveness; for mercy upon miserable sinners; for deliverance from the load of guilt by the application to the soul of the precious *blood of sprinkling*. Every night those who pray for little else ask, we doubt not, in private prayer for the forgiveness of their sins through the atonement made by Christ. Even with reference to that commonest and most elementary of all petitions, might not our Lord say to many of us, *Ye know not what ye ask? Are you aware*, He might say, *that to ask for forgiveness implies first of all a real sense of sin, and secondly a real regret, a real sorrow for it, and thirdly a real desire, a real purpose, to have done with it? Are you aware that forgiveness is not bestowed to take away the sting of sin, sin itself continuing, but rather to make sin itself hateful to you from a sense of its ingratitude? that I came to save you not in but from your sins; not to relieve the conscience from the discomfort of past guilt, but to cleanse it from sin's stain and sin's defilement, that so the heart might be set free for the future service of a living God?*

And we pray too, we have prayed already many times this day, for grace; for the grace of God; for the help of the Holy Spirit; for strength against sin, for progress in holiness; for deliverance from many particular sins, and for improvement in many particular points of duty. My brethren, these are good prayers, whoever utters them. *This is the will of God, even our sanctification.* It is the very object of all that He has done for us, to fulfil these very prayers. But even as to these prayers, yes, as to these prayers most of all, might not Jesus Christ say of many, in some degree of all of us, *They know not what they ask? Are they aware by what processes alone these desires are accomplished in any? Can they drink of my cup? can they be baptized with my baptism? Do they at all know by what sharp inflictions the spirit of obedience must be formed and practised? by how many thwartings and crossings the will of man must be thoroughly subdued to the will of God? by how slow a progress, through how many mortifications endured, after how many insurrections quelled, they must pass into this oneness of mind with Him whom they call their Father? Are they willing to be put into my furnace, to be refined like gold, and tried like as silver is tried?*

O, ye know not what ye ask: and yet it is right to ask. It is right to pray for forgiveness: it is right to pray for grace: it is right to pray for glory. Pray for these things as you can; ignorantly if ignorantly; anyhow if only somehow. It is a good thing to be on your knees before Christ for any purpose, with any hope, with any prayer. If you will only come to Him, He will do the rest: yes, and the very coming to Him is of Him. Yield yourselves to His call, to His influence, to His drawing: and what you are not now, and what you know not now, you shall be, *you shall know hereafter.* It is the reluctance to come to Him which makes us fearful for you. *Ye will not come to me, that ye might have life.* That is the condemnation, that is the misery. God give of His great mercy to many of us this will to come to Christ. He is no hard taskmaster: if He says to you, *Ye know not what ye ask,* it is not said to deter you, it is not said to make you feel that prayer is vain, or effort vain, or discipleship useless and impossible: it is said in all tenderness, to those who are seeking and struggling and praying on in spite of all. Christ does not meet you with formidable conditions; He does not daunt you with impracticable requirements: He does not present to you at once in open vision the whole of life, with all its difficulties, disappointments, temptations and falls, its sorrows and its sadnesses, its foiled efforts and frustrated hopes, and bid you take it all or none: rather He says to each of us, even as He said of old to His first disciples, *I have yet many things to say unto you, but ye cannot bear them now, and till you can bear I will not tell you them; and when you can bear them, I will tell you them, not all at once, but one by one; making you feel, as you surmount one difficulty, that you are ready for another, and that you can trust Him who has supported you through one to uphold you through another, and so on, one by one, even to the very last of all.* And though at present, in asking for forgiveness, or for holiness, or for eternal life, as all Christians do; in other words, for a conscience cleansed from guilt, and a heart from sin, and a life from self-pleasing and worldliness and vanity; you know not what you ask; know not, in particular, by what methods God may see it necessary for you to pass to the fulfilment of your prayer; yet remember, He will undertake, if you place yourself in His hands, to see you safely through; *He will not suffer you to be tempted above that you are able, but will with every temptation make a way for you to escape;* He will *guide you* step by step *with His counsel,* until at length He sees fit to *receive you into His glory.*

Ye know not what ye ask. The words are words of correction, but they are not words of displeasure. No, my brethren, ignorant prayers are not in themselves a sin: what is a sin, and the chief of all sins, and the root of all sins, is a state of no-prayer. Are there not some before me who pray not at all? pray not even when they are here in the congregation? pray not in the family, pray not by their bedside? While this is so, there can be no religion. It is not a question of progress: it is not a question of single acts of good: it is not a question of charitable or not charitable: it is scarcely a question yet of communicants or non-communicants: it is a more elementary question still; it is a question of saved or lost, a question of hope or despair, a question of heaven or hell. *Seek ye the Lord, while He may be found; call ye upon Him while He is near.* The time is short: upon some who hear me the gate of life is closing; upon some who hear me the eternal day is dawning. Let not all be in vain. Let not prayers and sacraments, means of grace and hopes of glory, the Word of Christ and the Spirit of Christ, all have been offered to you, pressed upon you, almost forced upon you—*that* they cannot be—in vain. Let this day witness in the case of some one long asleep, long *dead in sin,* that blessed sight, a sight which is *joy in heaven,*

BEHOLD, HE PRAYETH.

SECOND SUNDAY AFTER TRINITY,
June 9, 1861.

II.

CHRIST EATING WITH SINNERS.

Luke xv. 2.

This man receiveth sinners, and eateth with them.

THE words were meant as a reproach. *This man keeps bad company: this man has no dislike to the society of immoral persons: this man, if He were of God, would choose for His associates those who do God's will; we see whom He does live with.* It was thus that the self-righteous Pharisees of that day judged One whose holiness as far transcended theirs as the sun outshines a rushlight.

Many remarks occur to us on reading or hearing these few words from the Gospel for the day.

How much has Christianity done to change the prevailing estimate of men and things. Would any one think it a reproach now to a teacher or minister of religion, that he sought out the sinful? that he went among the lower and more degraded of his fellow-creatures, and acted on his Master's principle, *I came not to call the righteous, but sinners to repentance?* These things are understood now, thanks to the Gospel. There is such a thing as reflected light: and much of what we call humanity or good sense is in reality the effect of having long had Christ (as He Himself says) *teaching in our streets*.

And yet there is all the difference in the world between the reflected light and the direct light of Christ's Gospel. There is all the difference between having the light, whether we will or no, shining around us, and having the light, by our own free choice and earnest prayer, shining within, in the mind, in the heart, and in the soul. We do not now quarrel with a minister of religion for visiting the homes of vice and consequent misery; but we are still very cruel in our treatment of sinners in private and common life. How severely do we judge, when we ourselves are not at the bar. How scornfully do we censure, how malevolently do we repeat, enlarge, or invent calumnies, as though we even sheltered or fortified ourselves by pulling down the fortress of another's good name. What rules have we laid down for the punishment of offenders; rules arbitrary and most capricious; rules as unequal in their principle as they are harsh and mischievous in their operation. *To receive sinners and eat with them* is a crime still in Christendom.

And of course in some senses it would be a crime. If we prefer by our own choice the company of loose and immoral men; if we take for our personal friends those whose only recommendation can be that they will connive at or participate in our vices; if we are so indifferent to the wellbeing of society as to make it no bar to a person's reception that he or she has notoriously broken God's moral law; this would be a just reproach: in this sense *to receive sinners and eat with them* would be no virtue, but the very contrary. All depends upon the motive: if we would imitate Jesus in His treatment of sinners, let us see that we also imitate Him by His grace in His principle and in His motive.

We will first look at His conduct. And as we read, let us also pray for grace to make a right use of it, in the way of example, and in the way of encouragement.

It was quite true of Him when He was upon earth that He received and welcomed sinners. Wherever He went, the doors stood open, even while He ate, for the entrance of all comers. There was no guard set to keep out improper characters. There was no previous question asked as to life or conduct. Whosoever would, came to Him unchallenged. And strange to say, many very sinful persons did will to come. You would have thought that there was that in Him which would have deterred them. So saintly a life, so pure a conversation; on the other hand, so mean a station, so hard and needy a condition; each and all of these particulars might have been expected to repel rather than to attract such visitors. *Silver and gold had He none;* and what He had was of a coinage too spiritual, too heavenly, for these applicants. And yet, wherever He went, wherever He rested, He was surrounded by persons at whom the finger of disdain and scorn was pointed. *This man receiveth sinners, and eateth with them.* All classes of sinners came where He was. There was the publican; the man whose occupation was not only unpopular, as reminding his countrymen of their subjugation to a foreign power, but dangerous also and full of temptation to dishonesty and base gain; the man who, like the rest of his class, had yielded to that temptation, had defiled his hand with ill-gotten gold, and deserved but too well the execration which pursued him. That man came to Jesus, and was often allowed to eat with Him. And there was another class also of our fallen race: there was she who had sunk into the basest of all ranks; the woman who had cast away her one treasure of innocence and virtue, and was now before the eyes of the world marked out as a creature of shame and contempt, for whom earth had no hope left, and to whom, however repentant, the Pharisee could allow no room in heaven. She too came to Jesus. The dishonest man and the fallen woman met ever and anon in that presence. And when on one occasion it was sought to make our Lord pass sentence upon such an offender; when *a woman taken in adultery* was brought in and set down before Him, with the question, *What sayest Thou?* even then it was not upon her but upon her accusers that the Saviour pronounced judgment: He ratified indeed the divine declaration that *the soul that sins should die*, but He threw the office of the executioner upon *him that was without sin among them*, and when conscience had emptied the judgment-hall, uttered only those blessed words of mercy and of warning, *Neither do I condemn thee: go, and sin no more.*

And by that one saying He made it plain beyond contradiction why and with what purpose He thus received sinners and ate with them. It was not that He was indifferent, *I speak as a man*, to sin in itself, or to sin in its consequences. It was not that He sanctioned a lower standard of judgment than that which was prescribed in God's holy law. It was not that He cared less than the scribes and Pharisees for human rectitude or human purity. In His righteous soul there was a shrinking from, a loathing of sin and corruption, such as the holiest of the sons of men can never attain to. But mingled ever with that divine holiness there was a compassion, a tenderness, a solicitude for the sinner, which is the other half, with reverence be it spoken, of the Divinity of God Himself. And the sinner saw this and felt it, and was drawn by it in spite of himself towards One whom yet he saw to have no sympathy whatever with his sin. My brethren, does not that attraction work still? Is it not thus that you, whosoever among you care for Jesus Christ, is it not even thus that you also are drawn to Him? Is it not because you feel that He who hates the sin yet loves the sinner? because you feel that here and here only is that combination of opposites which is the want, the desire, the very agony of your soul; a holiness absolutely perfect, without which you could not trust, and a sympathy free, unfettered, inexhaustible, without which you could only say, *Depart from me, for I am a sinful man, O Lord?* You, my brethren, you, how many soever you be amongst us— and may God add to your number a thousandfold—you know from your own experience what it was in Jesus Christ which thus drew to Him the sinful, and justified the blessed reproach, the reproach which is His chief glory, *This man receiveth sinners, and eateth with them.*

For indeed they all felt, as they flocked around Him, that He who received them as sinners would not leave them in their sins. It was not only that He gave them the charge, however reasonable or however emphatic, *Go and sin no more.* It was not only that they saw how inconsistent and how ungrateful would be their continuance in that bondage from which He came to set them free. There was this, but there was more. In that presence sin itself loosened its hold. Though they saw not as yet the uplifted cross, and felt not the burden untie itself from their shoulders and roll itself away into the sepulchre below, yet there came forth from Him even then a virtue which carried with it cleansing: in Christ the Comforter *dwelt with them* though not yet *in them;* and the same faith which saved them from the guilt freed them even then also from *the law of sin and death.* The *Friend of publicans and sinners* was a friend who sang not to them a lullaby in their ruin, but stretched out the right hand of loving power to rescue them and *to pluck them from the burning.*

And he who would now be like Jesus in the character of a friend of sinners, must see that by God's help he be this and not that; not the friend of the sin but the friend of the sinner. Not the friend of the sin: he must never suffer in himself that evil habit of indifference which puts no distinction between vice and virtue, *between him that serveth God and him that serveth Him not.* Not for this was it that *Christ died and rose and revived,* that He might obliterate the boundary-line between the righteous and the wicked, or make God's law one whit less peremptory in its tone or less awful in its denunciations. We are not so to interpret the call of Christian charity—for if we did so interpret it, it would be charity no longer—as to show no displeasure at iniquity, or to hold out the hand of fellowship to one who is casting in his lot with evil. There is a spurious liberality in these matters, which uses the language and wears the garb of charity, but which is indeed *a lying spirit,* traitorous to the cause of Christ. This is one of the perils of these latter days, against which may God guard us all. He who would be like Christ at all must seek to be like Him altogether. The friend of the sinner must be, like his Master, the foe of the sin. Alas, we too often invert the rule, and are at once indifferent to the sin and unkind to the sinner. It does not really grieve us to see God dishonoured or the cross of Christ trodden underfoot by human transgression; and yet we hasten to spread everywhere the tidings of the sin, and shut out from our sympathy for ever the fellow-creature who has fallen. Where is he amongst us who acts upon his Saviour's rule, as given in the writings of His holy Apostle, *Brethren, if a man be overtaken in a fault, ye which are spiritual restore such an one in the spirit of meekness: considering thyself, lest thou also be tempted?* Where is he who, like his Master Himself, *received sinners and ate with them*, not that He might embolden them in evil, but that He might win them and influence them for good?

Thus much we need to learn for our guidance, as Christian men and Christian women, in our dealing with brothers and sisters who have fallen. But how can I throw into the background, this day more especially, the aspect of the text toward ourselves? Are there none in this congregation who have need to apply to themselves the encouragement here written for such as have sinned, in the record of the Saviour's mind towards them?

This man receiveth sinners, and eateth with them. His enemies cast this in His teeth: but what said He in answer? What have we heard in this day's Gospel, of His reply to that taunt? He bade them think of earthly things, things of common life, and judge from that reflection as to things heavenly. What does the owner of a hundred sheep feel and do on the occasion of the loss of one of them? What does the possessor of ten pieces of silver feel and do if one of them be missing? What does the father of a long-lost, long-erring son feel and do if at last after years of sorrow and separation he sees that son returning to him? Even thus it is with the great Lord and Possessor of heaven and earth, if sin enters His creation and takes away from Him so much as one of the souls which He has made. Even thus does He seek the lost: even thus does He welcome the found. *You count it a reproach that I receive sinners: little do you know of that parental yearning which goes forth after the weakly, the perverse, the self-ruined child, and which rests not in the joys of heaven, or in the contemplation of unfallen worlds, or in the safety of other souls that went not astray, so long as there be but one son or one daughter of the sinful race of man, forsaking the guidance of the All-wise or refusing the mercies of the All-gracious. If I am the friend of the prodigal, it is that I may reclaim the lost: if I receive sinners and eat with them, it is that I may win them back from ruin, and rejoice in the joy of their salvation.*

Today, my brethren, in an especial sense, Jesus Christ is about to eat with sinners. His table is spread: *all things are ready:* He waits but for the guests to take their places. *See that ye refuse not Him that speaketh.* Let none say, *He calls not me.* Let none say, *I am not worthy.* The call of the Saviour's feast is coextensive with the call of that Saviour's Gospel; both commensurate with earth. Are you a sinner? Then you He calls:

you He bids: you He receives. If you were not a sinner, you would not need this Sacrament: nay, you would not need the Gospel: you would not need a Saviour. Believe Him when He says that He desires not your death but your life. Believe Him when He says that He *came to seek and to save you*. We do not honour Him, we do Him great despite, when we frame conditions of admission and of exclusion which He has not imposed. Look at that humble meal at which He once reclined on earth. Mark that open door. See how the uninvited come and go freely. Observe how they throng and press; how they approach, listen, and touch Him. See that poor woman who stands behind Him weeping, washing His very feet with her tears and wiping them with the hairs of her head: was she sent away because she was a sinner? was she bidden to seek society more suitable to her sinful life, and to leave the sacred presence-chamber of the All-holy? Nay, listen to the gracious words which proceed out of His lips. Hear Him say, *Which of them will love him most? he to whom little or he to whom a heavy debt was forgiven?* See Him turn to the woman, and say of her, after dwelling upon her proofs of devoted love, *Wherefore I say unto thee, Her sins, which are many, are forgiven: for she loved much. Thy sins are forgiven. Thy faith hath saved thee: go in peace.* Were not all these things *written for our learning?* as though it had been said to us, *Ye too are sinful: one of you has contaminated himself with unlawful or doubtful gains; and one of you has indulged evil tempers and sinful desires; and one of you has even corrupted himself with wicked fleshly lusts: and yet the merciful Saviour stands and calls you; bids you draw near to Him without fear; bids you seek in His precious death your soul's pardon, and in His life after death your soul's strength and healing; bids you to believe and not doubt in your heart that God loves you, is your Father and your Friend, and will eternally bless and save; bids you cast away for ever the guilt which is behind, and walk henceforth in newness of life; yea, says of Himself, not with reference only to the history of His earthly sojourn, but with reference not less to the time of His heavenly glory, It was then, it is still, my good pleasure to receive sinners and to eat with them.*

THIRD SUNDAY AFTER TRINITY,
 July 6, 1862.

III.

GOSPEL RIGHTEOUSNESS.

Matthew v. 20.

Except your righteousness shall exceed the righteousness of the Scribes and Pharisees, ye shall in no case enter into the kingdom of heaven.

AND yet that righteousness of the Scribes and Pharisees was by no means destitute of pretension. The ordinances of the Law were numerous and weighty; and the Scribes and Pharisees had made them yet more so. They wearied themselves in the discovery of new particulars of duty, and could not subdivide too minutely, or multiply too largely, the requirements of a perfect obedience.

It is the fashion to regard the Pharisee as a mere trifler with religion, a mere pretender to sanctity, a mere deceiver towards man and a mere hypocrite (in the most vulgar sense) towards God. I think we may be too hard upon him. The Searcher of hearts might speak to him with severity; might pronounce decisively upon his motives, and, knowing these, upon his character as a whole in its condition and in its end. But I much doubt, my brethren, whether the Pharisee would not have passed muster, even in these days of Christian light, as a religious and as a devout man. If we saw him at his devotions here; if we spoke with him of duty; if we marked his deportment in the streets and at social tables; if we heard him discourse upon the wickedness of the world or upon the sinfulness of sin; if we traced him along his round of charitable visits through the lanes and yards of the town, reproving and rebuking vice, and setting a high standard of right and wrong before persons sunk in ungodliness and heathenism; I am much mistaken if we should not have been ready to exclaim, *That is indeed a good man: how I feel myself humbled in his presence: how does the very sight of him bring my sin to remembrance, and remind me of the stern realities of death, of judgment, and eternity.*

Now, if there be any truth in this remark, it also involves some serious inferences.

The Scribes and Pharisees were the religious people, the leaders of the religious world of our Lord's earthly day. They *sat in Moses' seat;* and *whatsoever they bid you observe*, He said of them Himself, *that observe and do*. They of whom He could thus speak did not bear upon their front, we may well suppose, the avowal of their own offensiveness in the sight of God. I draw from their condition, as it was towards man and as it was towards God, a reflection as to the possibility of there being unawares people like them amongst ourselves. If there be such persons, they will not know it, nor shall we. They will think themselves good, and we probably shall suppose them so. They will be found, if they exist at all, among the frequenters of Church and of the Sacrament, among the givers to our charities, among the maintainers of a good name and of a strict discipline.

It is of the essence of a Pharisee that he passes for a religious man. If there be Pharisees now, they will not be found among the blasphemers or among the profligate.

It is perhaps unavoidable, but it is much to be regretted, that we are so prone to study history, and especially sacred history, with *a veil upon our heart*, or through a glass which colours and distorts the picture. The good are made so very good, and the bad so very bad, that both alike part for us with their human likeness. Men full of infirmity are invested by our fancy with the faultlessness of angels, and men not destitute of the semblance at least of some virtues are painted to our eye as monsters of repulsive wickedness. Thus both ways we lose the benefit of divine instruction. The good are so good that they cease to be examples: the bad are so bad that they cease to be warnings.

But evidently our Lord deemed the righteousness of the Scribe and Pharisee to be one with which His people were in danger of contenting themselves. There was that in it which looked so like perfection, that His own disciples required to have the mask torn off lest they should admire and adore it. The radical unsoundness had no mark set upon it. If they were, as He told them, like graves full of corruption, they were at the same time either *whited sepulchres, beautiful outwardly*, or else so covered up that *the men who walked over them were not aware of them.* There was a risk therefore lest the righteousness of Christian men should not exceed the righteousness of the Scribes and Pharisees. And that risk exists still. Still year by year on this Sixth Sunday after Trinity we listen to the solemn charge of the Gospel for the day, reminding us that, except our righteousness exceed theirs, we shall in no case enter into the eternal kingdom. And He who thus speaks is the Lord of that kingdom, at whose judgment-seat all of us shall stand, and upon whose decision for good or evil will depend our admission into that glory. Therefore we have great need to try and to judge ourselves upon this point, while our destiny still hangs in the balance; and while He Himself who speaks still regards us as His people, and is still at hand not only to counsel, but also to guide, to influence, and to save.

We will mark, in two or three obvious points, the fatal defects of the Pharisaical righteousness.

1. The first of these was its formalism. The vigour of the plant was all thrown upwards: it had stalk and leaf, but it had no root, and therefore no produce.

There is perhaps no matter which makes a larger demand upon Christian wisdom and Christian discernment, wisdom in the teacher, discernment in the hearer, than the use and abuse of forms. It is evident that a religion which dispenses with forms breaks down eventually even in its spirituality. The experiment has been tried; tried seriously and confidently; tried by true Christians and with a high Christian aim: but the result has ever been this; in the second generation, if not in the first, a congregation or a sect or a school of professed Christians formed on the basis of a spiritual isolation, of a worship dispensing wholly with ordinances, has been proved by experience to have attempted an impossibility. It has sought to be *wise above what is written*, and it is fortunate if it can retrace its steps into a communion wisely *tempered together* in the recollection that the *man in Christ* is also at present a man in flesh. And yet that more sensible recollection has its own dangers too. At certain periods of the Church's history, we can almost forgive the impatience which sought to renounce altogether the influences of place and ritual, of sight and sound, in worship: so entirely had these influences overlain and smothered the spirit, and brought back the pure and heavenly revelation to a condition below that of the Mosaic law and of the *worldly sanctuary*. In fact, the history of the Church has been a perpetual oscillation between the too much and the too little in these respects; between a worship oppressed with carnality, and a worship extinguished in the effort to sublime it.

My brethren, I will not say that none of us may be in danger of despising forms: but I think I may say that we are for the most part exposed to a greater risk of resting in them. I can almost fear that there may be some here present, who will one day, lying on a deathbed, be telling their Minister that they were regular Church-goers, and building something of an eternal hope upon that slight and insecure foundation. And yet what is this hope in comparison with that of Scribes and Pharisees? Do you suppose that they satisfied themselves with an attendance once or twice on one day of the week upon the ordinances of God's worship? If your righteousness is to be of the same kind with theirs, take heed, as our Lord here warns you, that it exceed it in its degree.

But, alas, what is this hope, when we come to examine it? What do we Christians call these ordinances of worship here or elsewhere administered? *Means of grace*, that is their title: not grace itself; not something which by its very performance secures or works

God's favour: but opportunities of seeking and cherishing God's work within; valuable so far as in them we spiritually communicate with God through Christ by His Holy Spirit; valueless, worse than valueless, because illusory and deceptive, in so far as we trust in them as ends, or reckon them up as claims and titles to acceptance.

The spirit of formalism is a secret and a subtle thing: it creeps in where there should be everything to bar its entrance, and infects the devotion of many with a slow but fatal poison. Never put away from you, never regard as a wearisome truism, the caution which bids you to beware of it. The formalism of the Pharisee, his proneness to value himself upon the punctuality of his worship and upon the minuteness of his ceremonial obedience, should ever occupy in our minds a foremost place when we seek to lay to heart the warning voice of our Lord, *Except your righteousness exceed the righteousness of the Scribes and Pharisees, ye shall in no case enter into the kingdom of heaven. God is a Spirit: and they who worship Him must worship Him in spirit and in truth.*

2. Again, in close connection with the vice of formalism in worship, was that of literalism in doctrine. The spirit of the Pharisee was shown in a treatment of God's moral law at once most superficial and most arbitrary. *The commandments of God were made of none effect by their tradition.* Paltry evasions and quibbling distinctions, most unworthy of the greatness and of the wisdom of God, were introduced by the Scribes into the interpretation of Holy Scripture, and by the help of them they could make the oracles of God dumb

or contradictory at their pleasure, silent to themselves when inclination drew another way, oppressive to the consciences of others when the teacher would forbid that to which he himself had no leaning or attraction. In such hands the salt of truth utterly *lost its savour*, and revelation itself could no longer act as *a light to the path* of wayfaring and often erring men.

It was upon this network of puerile but burdensome trifling that our Lord Jesus Christ threw the light of a teaching at once lofty and simple, at once spiritual and practical, at once touchingly human and profoundly divine. The context of the verse before us deals with the righteousness of the Scribe and Pharisee in reference to its doctrine. They had entirely lost the spirit of the law in its letter. They had missed altogether the proper office of the teacher, which is to bring out the principle of a rule from beneath its form, the kernel of truth from the husk of language. When God said, *Thou shalt not kill*, He forbad the very first indulgence in the heart of that angry passion of which the full and unresisted developement is the sin of murder. When God said, *Thou shalt not commit adultery*, He forbad the sufferance in the heart of that first rising of lust, of which the latest yet most natural developement is the guilty act of the sensualist. And thus was it with all and each of God's commandments. If in one sense it is true that we shall be judged by our acts, in another sense it is equally true that we shall be judged by our thoughts. God sees the heart: He can do what man cannot; He can interpret the conduct by the motive, and view at one glance the mind which cherished the desire or which formed the design, and the hand by which the desire was fulfilled or the design accomplished. It is in this sense more than in any other that our Lord speaks in the text. It is as though He said, *The Pharisee looks at the act alone: look ye at the heart: out of it are the issues of life and death.* It is as though He had said, *Ye who would be my disciples must live evermore in the clear and full light of my Father's presence: mind and heart, thought and word, act and habit and life, all lie open before Him: remember and forget not that to please Him there needs not the obedience only of doing or of forbearing, but the obedience also of the will and of the soul, and that the righteousness of those who keep only the letter must be carried on and perfected in you by a righteousness of the spirit also.*

And where is he in this congregation who needs not to be reminded of that eye which is upon the heart of man? O, if the hearts of those present before me were suddenly laid open, who, *who could abide it?* Where is he who has so spiritually read God's Law as to have brought the very thoughts of his heart into obedience to the will of Christ? Where is he in whom appearance and reality are indeed at one, so that what he seems to man he is to God? In how many would that revelation of heart be absolutely condemning; as fatal to human esteem as to the hope of a blessed immortality.

3. The spirit of the formalist and of the literalist was also, in the last place, a spirit of self-satisfaction and of self-conceit. It is the natural effect of a low standard of duty to foster spiritual pride. A man who shuts his Bible may soon think himself perfect. A man who *compares himself*, as St Paul expresses it, only *with himself*, or only with a few neighbours and friends

taken into his intimacy because they suit or resemble him, is sure to *think of himself more highly than he ought to think*. This is one of the evils of what we call a contracted sphere: it is one of the inherent faults of a small society; of a family that lives entirely within itself, or of a town limited in numbers and unconnected with more important communities by the ties of trade and commerce. Such a society can scarcely escape being self-conceited. One of the faults of the Pharisees is almost necessarily theirs. The Pharisees formed a clique, and lived within it. Their very name denoted exclusiveness and isolation. Their very name said, *Stand apart: we are holier than thou*. It was this sort of pretension which drew down upon them the severest censures of *the Lord the righteous Judge*. *If they had been blind*, He told them, *they had not had sin:* if they had felt themselves to be in need of light, that one admission would have been a sign of grace. But, *saying, We see, their sin remained:* it was sealed upon them hopelessly and fatally.

My brethren, the one gate into Christ's kingdom is humility. Except in this sense ye be the very opposite of the Scribes and Pharisees, *ye cannot enter into the kingdom of heaven*. You must stoop very low, if you would ever rise high. So long as you have a good opinion of yourself; so long as it never occurs to you to doubt your own judgment or your own conduct, your own standard or your own attainment; so long you have not taken the very first step towards heaven. Heaven is for the humble; salvation is for the lost: hope is for them that have first feared; *the praise of God* for them that have despaired of themselves. My brethren, the thing which Christ could not away with in the Pharisees was their conceit. Does he like conceit better, think you, in His people? When He hears us laying down the law one to another, sitting in judgment one upon another, assuming to ourselves the attributes of Omniscience and of infallible justice, how must it grieve Him. O that assumption! O that arrogance! O that self-confidence and self-esteem! O that *justifying of ourselves* and *despising others!* how offensive must it be in heaven, where the chief joy is in man's repentance, and where He is present who both reads the heart and knows the history. Would that amongst us who are here present this day a work real and effectual might be wrought in this one respect by the Holy and Almighty Spirit. If we could only be brought low in our own eyes, only made to feel our own ignorance and shortsightedness and inconsistency, our own unfitness to judge, our own need of forgiveness; if from our several hearts there could arise the one hopeful cry, *God be merciful to me a sinner;* all would be well: *He who had begun a good work in us would indeed perform it against the day of Jesus Christ.* But, alas, the spirit of the Pharisee is strong in us, and even in our words of self-abasement there lurks the adder of self-righteousness. We are proud of our knowledge, we are proud of our uprightness, we are proud of our religion; at last we go one step further, and are proud of our humility. We know so well the Gospel doctrine of the sinfulness and depravity of man, that we have added yet this also to our catalogue of virtues, that we call ourselves *miserable sinners*, and are proud still.

Do I speak today to any who are not so? Is

there here one poor, self-accusing, self-condemning sinner? one *who knows the plague of his own heart*, and is crying out, *O wretched man that I am! who shall deliver me from the body of this death?* Then to him, or to her, *is the word of Christ's salvation sent. How beautiful upon the mountains*, in the judgment of that one soul, *are the feet of them that preach the Gospel of peace and bring glad tidings of good things.* Draw nigh by faith to Him who once said on earth to a sinful woman, *Thy sins are forgiven thee, go in peace;* and doubt not, but earnestly believe, that you too shall in no long time hear those words inwardly from the Lord and Giver of life. *For thus saith the high and lofty One that inhabiteth eternity, whose name is Holy: I dwell in the high and holy place, with him also that is of a contrite and humble spirit, to revive the spirit of the humble, and to revive the heart of the contrite ones.*

SIXTH SUNDAY AFTER TRINITY,
July 27, 1862.

IV.

FOUR THOUSAND MEN TO BE FED IN THE WILDERNESS.

Mark viii. 4.

From whence can a man satisfy these men with bread here in the wilderness?

A HUNGRY multitude surrounded our Lord, attracted by the interest of His teaching and by the fame of His miracles. For three days they had been with Him, and any supplies which they might have brought with them had long been exhausted. His compassionate heart was touched by the thought of their distress. He who regarded not the wants of His own bodily frame, when they came into competition with *His Father's business*, never overlooked or underrated the privations or sufferings of one human being; never pretended to say that the necessities of the body are trifling matters, or that the soul alone is worthy of the attention of an immortal being. He knew how in this life the soul and the body act and react upon each other, and how futile must be the attempt to divide man into his two parts and represent one only of those two parts as requiring or demanding his regard. He who for Himself refused to turn stones into bread, or to put forth His divine power in relieving want or averting pain when that want or that pain was His own, never refused to stretch out the arm of Omnipotence in aid of another's craving body or another's tortured mind.

On this occasion our Lord called the attention of His disciples to the condition of the multitude around them, in the tone of one who proposed a difficulty and asked its solution. *I have compassion on the multitude, because they have now been with me three days, and have nothing to eat; and if I send them away fasting to their own houses, they will faint by the way: for divers of them came from far.* In a similar case recorded in the Gospel of St John, He expressly appealed to one of the disciples, in the words, *Whence shall we buy bread, that these may eat?* saying this, as the Evangelist adds, *to prove* the faith of His Apostle, and not from any uncertainty on His own part *what He would do.* In both instances He received a discouraging reply to His appeal. Philip could only answer by magnifying the difficulty. *Two hundred pennyworth of bread is not sufficient for them, that every one of them may take a little.* And the disciples in the text could only reply in a similar strain, *From whence can a man satisfy these men with bread here in the wilderness?* In each case the inventive mind as well as the effective hand must be that of the Lord Himself and of none other.

My brethren, the difficulty urged by the disciples is one not of bygone times only. I would ask you to ponder it this morning. It is a difficulty arising from numbers, and it is a difficulty arising from place.

1. You have witnessed within the last few days a

spectacle[1] which may assist you in understanding the scene of this miracle. *About four thousand men* were on this occasion the recipients of our Lord's bounty. You have seen what four thousand men look like when they are gathered in one spot. It is not everywhere that we could speak of such an assemblage with the hope of being understood. Many villages, many towns, have never seen four thousand men in one place at one time. It seems as though you were to be specially enabled to enter intelligently into that occurrence in our Lord's life which was to form the Gospel for this Sunday. You have seen that which enables you to sympathize with the disciples when they said, *From whence can a man satisfy four thousand men with bread here* on this common or in this desert? You know what preparations were necessary in order to secure a sufficiency of provisions last week for four thousand men; what forethought and what calculation and what arrangement and what toil it required to do that which our Lord by the exertion of His divine will alone was able to effect for that multitude.

The difficulty arising from mere numbers is one which presses heavily from time to time upon the mind of a nation and of a Church.

When from any unhappy cause, such as that terrible and lamentable war which is at this time raging in the new world, the supplies of trade and commerce are suddenly cut off from a large portion of our countrymen, how sad a meaning is given even in a literal sense to the enquiry in the text. What a burden is thrown upon

[1] A Review of four thousand Volunteers on the Race Common at Doncaster.

private charity, what a burden is thrown upon the public resources, by a cry for bread, for the food of the body, going up from destitute thousands. Then it is that we feel how nearly allied on earth are strength and weakness; how an overflowing population, which in time of prosperity has furnished hands to work and heads to plan, has amassed wealth for merchant princes, and revenue (by a comparatively light taxation) for the country our common mother, may become an absolute curse in seasons of adversity, when its chief direct effect is in multiplying mouths to eat. At such times the sense of mere numbers may lie upon a nation's heart with an absolutely crushing weight. *From whence can I satisfy all these my children with bread in this wide district which can no longer work for its supply?* is a question easier to ask than to answer; a question which the wisdom of legislators and statesmen is at this moment anxiously and even fearfully pondering.

And are there not some among us capable of feeling the same weight of difficulty in reference to things spiritual? We all know that there is One who calls Himself *the bread of life, the living bread which came down from heaven, that men might eat thereof and not die.* Every miracle which He wrought for men's bodies was designed to attest His mission in behalf of men's souls. We believe, if we are Christians, that not only is Christ a Saviour, but the Saviour of mankind; that *there is none other name under heaven, given among men, whereby we must be saved.* It is not only that one who believes in Christ enjoys a higher privilege or a deeper happiness than he who neglects or is ignorant of Him: we believe that in Him alone is salvation: and while we doubt not that *the Judge of all the earth will do right*, in His judgment upon those who have had no choice to exercise because they have never heard of Christ's Gospel, yet we feel also that the one hope of fallen man depends upon his hearing of Christ; depends upon his being brought under the influence and into the light of His Gospel. Now, my brethren, if this be so, how terrible becomes the weight of numbers in reference to the prospect of eternity, to the hope of heaven. Who does not kneel sometimes before his Saviour with the anxious question, *Lord, from whence can a man satisfy with the living bread all this multitude?*

Here are we gathered by hundreds within this sacred building, to pray to God and to commune with Him through His Son Jesus Christ. This is the picked portion of our population. We are they who have heard of Christ Jesus; and not only have heard of Him, but believe also; believe that in Him alone is eternal life, and that they only who seek through Him shall find it. But are even we, beloved brethren, all satisfied, in deed and in truth, with the living bread? Have you all eaten of it this morning? Are you all preparing to eat of it at that Holy Table? Does not even the thought of you our best friends, our most hopeful hearers, lie heavily sometimes upon our hearts? Even with regard to you does not the minister sometimes ask his Lord, *How shall we satisfy all these men with the bread from heaven?* Even with regard to you there is a sense of embarrassment arising from insufficiency; from a disproportion between the means at command and the end sought. How then must it be when we look beyond these walls? How must it be when we reflect that of our sixteen thousand probably not sixteen hundred worship at all in this Church on the Lord's Day, and a far smaller number in any other? Do we not feel then the weight of numbers, when we remember the hundreds and thousands who worship nowhere, save in some idol's or some demon's temple of drunkenness and lust, on this holy day? when we reflect upon the poor feeble efforts which we are making to reach this mass without, and upon the huge immeasurable obstacles which lie in our way in making them?

And when our thoughts take a wider range, and pass to towns and cities in our own land where the population is counted not by hundreds, but by tens of thousands; when we think of that aggregate of ignorance, ungodliness and sin, which a population of a hundred thousand or of a million of souls must present to the eye of a holy and heart-searching God, and then compare with it the few faithful ministers and servants of God who are set to dispense the bread of life amongst that mighty multitude; see them struggling first within against the infirmities of the flesh and of the spirit, and then passing forth without their own doors, to do battle with a host of separate evils of which the name is legion; see them failing to arrest attention, put aside with any pretext of business or of preoccupation, unable in many cases to point to one earnest enquirer, to one undoubted convert, to one new communicant, to one earnest warm-hearted consistent friend, amongst the masses which they have sought to penetrate in their Master's name; indeed, my brethren, it is all that we can do to withhold the cry, *It is in vain: we want a new Gospel, for the old is worn out: a few little loaves, a few small fishes, what are they among so many?*

Now without pursuing the enquiry into other fields where a scene yet more hopeless, if it be possible, is presented to us, I would draw from this part of the subject one earnest question for ourselves, as to our own reception, and as to our interest in the reception by others, of that which we profess to regard as a living and life-giving food. What should we have thought if the disciples themselves had refused on this occasion to accept their Lord's miraculous gift? if they had said, *It is of no use; seven loaves can never feed four thousand men: I will take no part in diminishing by my act a provision so paltry: still less will I mock the hungry multitude before me by taking any part in the delusive ceremony of ministering to them of this scanty store?* The least we expect of the disciples is their own faith, their own obedience. If the prospect is discouraging, it must not be made more so by the faithlessness of the faithful: they at least must eat of Christ's bread, and assist Him in the distribution (so far as it will go) to others. To fold the hands because discouragements are many, is to play the traitor to His cause whose servants, whose disciples, perhaps whose ministers and messengers we are. My brethren, let us eat of His bread ourselves. Let us by an earnest and real communion strengthen ourselves out of His exhaustless fulness. Let us press around Him with all eagerness, eat ourselves of the living bread, and drink ourselves of the living water. And then see whether He will not also use us as His distributors; whether He will not give to one a little loaf, to another a morsel broken off from it, to carry to another soul that needs. See whether now and then there may not be given to one and to another some *token for good* in ministering to his brethren, within his own doors and also without them; enough to encourage if not enough to elate; redounding to his Saviour's glory, if also (as is probable) to the humiliation and downfall of pride and self.

2. We have spoken of the difficulty arising from numbers; from the disproportion between the men to be fed and the materials for their supply. We have to think also of the difficulty arising from the place; from the disparity between the scene which was before them and the food which was wanted. *Bread here in the wilderness.*

When we apply this to spiritual things, two remarks will suggest themselves.

i. There is an apparent contrariety between heavenly supplies and our earthly condition. We are here in a wilderness. We would not exaggerate the trials of life: we would not be unthankful for life's many blessings. But it is no exaggeration to say that *here we have no continuing city:* it is no unthankfulness to say that here we have no entire satisfaction. To some of us more than to others, but to all in some degree, life is a time of unsettlement and of unrest. Some of us have had experience of its strippings and of its uprootings; of its changes, its separations, its lonelinesses, its sorrows. And some of us have had experience of its disappointments; its fallacious prospects, its blighted hopes, its broken promises. Now this sort of experience of life makes us almost suspicious of an offer of happiness. When Christ stands in the midst of us, and says,

Come unto me, and I will give you rest, we are almost ready to say, *Can a man be satisfied with bread here in the wilderness? Shall God prepare a table in the wilderness? Can He give bread also here below, and provide real food for His people?* There is an incongruity between the place and the promise. Rest in a changing world, happiness in a troublous world, the ideas are inharmonious and discordant.

But I trust and believe that I can appeal to some of you, my brethren, to testify that, though there may be contrariety in the ideas, there is no contradiction. Some of you have found that, though all else changes, *God changes not;* that, though all else is unrest, in Christ there is peace. You can already attest the truth of His words, *These things I have spoken unto you, that in me ye might have peace. In the world ye shall have tribulation: but be of good cheer, I have overcome the world.*

ii. Finally, and with especial reference to the service of Holy Communion to which we are this day invited, I would remark that there is an apparent incongruity between outward elements and spiritual grace, between the food of the body and the food of the soul. In the Sacrament of the Lord's Supper we are invited to eat bread and drink wine in this holy place; and to an act thus in itself common we are taught to annex a special spiritual promise. It has occurred, I doubt not, to many minds, *How can this bread of the wilderness satisfy man's soul? How can I derive spiritual nourishment from natural supplies?* The answer is that which met the question also of the text. *From whence can a man be thus satisfied? From the word and will, from the act and living grace, of Christ.* He multiplied the seven loaves, so that they fed four thousand men. He uses the sacramental bread so as to make the food of the body minister to the soul. He has been pleased in great compassion to make the human senses of sight and touch and taste minister to the invisible realities of a soul *living because He lives*, of a Holy Spirit sustaining, quickening and animating the spirit of a creature and of a sinner. It is the will of God. It is the grace of Christ. It is the presence of the Holy Ghost. *Doubt ye not, but earnestly believe.* Draw near with faith, and an unseen hand shall work in the visible. The body and the soul are knit together by many intangible and insensible links: this is one of them. Thus would He who feels for man's difficulties bridge over for him the great gulf between faith and sight. This ordinance of eating bread and drinking wine in the Lord's House could never have existed were there not in deed and in truth a Saviour who once trod this earth of ours and then rose for us into a world unseen. When we eat and drink at His Table, we assure ourselves of, we proclaim one to another, *the Lord's death, till He come.* We declare one to another, we rehearse to ourselves, the fact of that death, and its purpose, and its efficacy. We remember also that He who died also lives, lives for evermore, and lives for us; that we feed here not upon a dead victim but upon a living and life-giving Bread: we enter after Him through the veil which hangs between earth and heaven, that we may tell Him our weakness and receive from Him of His strength. When we ask in the infirmity of nature, *From whence can a man thus be satisfied?* He answers, *Make the men sit down:* He takes the loaves and blesses and breaks them; gives them to His ministers, and they to His people; until all the believing *have eaten and are satisfied,* thank Him for His great goodness and *go on their way rejoicing.* Thus may it be with us. May a large and growing number gather with us around that Table, and may it be ever with a surer faith, a livelier hope, and a more abundant blessing.

SEVENTH SUNDAY AFTER TRINITY,
August 3, 1862.

V.

MISMANAGEMENT OF ETERNAL INTERESTS.

Luke xvi. 8.

The children of this world are in their generation wiser than the children of light.

THE steward of a rich landowner was on the point of being dismissed for dishonesty. He was ordered to give in his account, in preparation for the loss of his stewardship. Beggary stared him in the face. Without income and without character, what was before him? In this extremity, he runs over in his mind the possible alternatives. *What shall I do, deprived of my stewardship? For manual toil I have no strength: to live on charity is disgraceful. Let me try a different course. Yes, I will make friends. I will secure to myself a number of homes, in exchange for the loss of one.* The plan adopted was as successful as it was unscrupulous. He turns to his account-books, and scans the names of his master's debtors. Summoning them one by one before him, he enquires of each the exact amount of his liability. One who declares his debt to be *a hundred measures of oil* is desired to *take his bill*, the memorandum (we may suppose) of his obligation in his own handwriting, and to change the hundred into fifty. Another in like manner, owing *a hundred measures of wheat*, is desired to falsify his note of hand by substituting eighty for a hundred. By this fraud he has interested a number of persons in the success of his own villainy. Tidings of what he has done reach the ears of his injured lord. And he, deeply as he might have suffered from the device adopted, cannot refrain from admiring the adroitness shown by the dishonest steward. It is he, the master of the steward, and not the righteous Saviour who utters the Parable, who is said in the verse now before us to *commend the unjust steward because he had done wisely*. A careful reader notices that the word *lord* begins here with a small (not a capital) letter, to show us that it denotes the master of the steward and not our Lord Jesus Christ. It is in the following verse that He first speaks in His own behalf. *And I say unto you:* I who commend not the fraud of the steward, I who counsel no man to quit the straight and narrow road of perfect honesty, I who know the sinfulness of sin, and must one day execute God's judgment upon it in the person of the sinner, can yet draw from the case one lesson of advice and warning to my disciples : *I say unto you, Make to yourselves friends of* (that is, *by*) *the mammon of unrighteousness;* use the wealth less or greater of this world—that money which is so often acquired by wrong and so often used for wrong that it may be designated even in Christian hands as the very *mammon of unrighteousness*—use the wealth of this world, in whatever measure it may fall to you, so as to make to yourselves friends; not, like the friends of the wicked steward in the Parable, who may receive you in your distress into an earthly home, but rather friends who, *when it fails*, when you die, *may welcome you into everlasting habitations.* So use your portion of earthly goods in benefiting the souls and the bodies of your fellow-men, that in the great day, when God shall reckon with you for deeds done in the body, there may be many to *rise up and call you blessed;* many whose glad and thankful voices shall hail you as a benefactor and a friend as you enter the golden gates and tread the glorious streets of the celestial city.

And now let me ask your attention to one clause of the Parable, that which I read to you as the text. *The lord*, the master of the dishonest man described, *commended the unjust steward, because he had done wisely*, prudently with a view to his own selfish interests: *for the children of this world*, our Lord adds by way of comment upon that commendation, *the children of this age*, of this present time as opposed to the eternity beyond, *are more prudent than the children of light*, than Christian people, *unto*, as regards, or with a view to, *their own generation.*

The children of this world are in (for) their generation wiser than the children of light.

No doubt this celebrated maxim is verified in its most literal sense. Worldly people are more quick-sighted than Christians as to worldly interests. It is not often that a true Christian is a match for a cunning and unprincipled negotiator in the affairs of this life. His very goodness is against him. Unwilling to think evil, he is unready in counterworking it. His principles forbid him to be suspicious of others or crafty for himself. And if he so far departs from his principles as to become for the moment either the one or the other, the chances are greatly against the success of his inconsistency. He must be a worldly man all over, not for once or in one respect, if he is to be as wise in his generation as those who live for it. Thus it comes to pass that the world has often its laugh against the Christian; and the Christian, if he be a Christian indeed, will scarcely grudge it its triumph. He remembers *that world*, and can almost let *this world* go. *I shall be satisfied* one day, *when I awake, with Thy likeness*.

But I will confess to you, my brethren, that it was not in this light that I specially designed to set the text before you. I would rather read it—so the following verse, I think, directs us—as a serious reflection upon the ordinary management of a Christian life. Not only is a Christian less wise for his generation than the man of this world: that, if that were all, would scarcely be a reproach. It might be, as we have seen, his very Christianity which made him so. But I fear it means also that the children of light are less prudent in the pursuit of their object than the children of this world are in the pursuit of theirs. That he who professes to be living for eternity does not act as wisely with a view to that high and glorious end, as he who scarcely aims at anything beyond time acts with a view to that comparatively low and poor ambition. *The children of this world*, we may read it, *are wiser for their generation than the children of light are for their eternal hope*. A few plain remarks upon this comparison may be of use, by God's help, to all of us.

The wisdom here spoken of is (as the word imports) not an intellectual but a practical quality. It denotes what we call prudence, good sense, intelligence in adapting means to an end, in pursuing a definite object in a judicious way.

There are many definitions which might be given of a Christian; of him whom our Lord here designates as *a child of light*. But the one naturally suggested by the topic before us will suffice for our present purpose. A Christian is one who lives for eternity. He is one for whom *life and immortality* have been *brought to light by the Gospel*. For him therefore *heaven* as we term it, the state of everlasting blessedness beyond death, is what earth, the present life, the condition on this side the grave, is to others. If he means anything by being a Christian, he means this; *I seek a country: I look for a city which hath foundations: I look for the resurrection of the dead, and the life of the world to come*. That is the aspiration, that is the hope, that is the faith, of a child of light.

And these are in fact the only two classes of men amongst us. There are the children of this world. First the common multitude, who ask only, *What shall I eat, and what shall I drink, and wherewithal shall I be clothed?* whose whole life is occupied in the pursuit of a maintenance, in getting and spending, in the enjoyment or else the waste of health and strength, the heaping up of riches or else their improvident and selfish squandering. And far above these, yet also bounded in reality by the horizon of this life, there are the men of thought and mind, the merchants and statesmen and philosophers of the world; men of skill and calculation, men sometimes of large views and great endeavours; men who forget nothing except their own souls, and expatiate through everything save only the regions opened to us by the revelation of Jesus Christ. All these, differing all but immeasurably one from another, are yet combined in one vast aggregate by the universal absence amongst them of a single characteristic; namely, the definite pursuit and the well-grounded hope of an immortal life in heaven. And yet it must be added that even of these many have a religion: many accept the Bible as true, and habitually worship in the name of Jesus Christ. The point of difference is therefore in many cases perceptible only to the eye of God, who sees by an infallible intuition which world each man is living for, this world or that, the world of time or the world of eternity. If the former, they are its children; *children* our Lord calls them *of this age:* if the latter, they belong to the other class, designated in this Parable as *the children of light*.

But along with this higher and truer aim of life there comes not always, our Lord says, a corresponding wisdom in the choice of means. The children of this world know the way to their end, and they tread that way earnestly. They know that, if they would be rich, they must be diligent; they must allow nothing to distract them from the shop or the counting-house; they must make their ventures skilfully, and they must choose their counsellors warily. And they know that, if they would be honoured, they must be respectable: they must maintain a character for uprightness, for decent morality and for tolerable liberality. And they know that, if they would enjoy pleasure, they must make themselves pleasant: they must not disgust their friends by moroseness or churlishness; they must never lose an acquaintance, and they must be always widening their circle. Among the children of this world these things are well understood: and though there are many who from defects of temper, or infirmities of will, or the strength of unruly passions, start aside from the direct path of worldly success, and are pointed at by the finger of scorn as men of shipwrecked hopes, yet this very fact shows that the world scarcely reckons these among its children: they did perhaps once in its judgment *run well*, but some adverse influence *has hindered* them that they should not win their prize. On the whole, the true children of this world are not wanting in wisdom, as our Lord says, for their generation.

But how is it meanwhile with the children of light? True, their aim is far higher; and so far it is well with them. But how is it with their aiming? how is it with the accuracy of their eye, the steadiness of their hand, and the strength of their effort? A Christian is one who looks for eternity: how does he live for it? does he act wisely in the prospect of it? is he prudent, is he sensible, in relation to that great object? or does he show such a want of these qualities as would sometimes make a bystander doubt whether he had any definite aim or any sure hope at all?

For purposes of self-examination I will guide you to three topics of enquiry.

1. Do you show your wisdom as a child of light by *the accuracy of your eye* in reference to eternal things?

You profess to be looking for the life of the world to come. And you know that this profession requires of you that that should be your one object. You know that, as you *cannot serve two masters, God and mammon*, so neither can you really live with two objects, earth and heaven. Now can you live that knowledge? Are you enabled really to refrain from looking off from your real object to some secondary or fallacious one? What? are none of us allowing the world, in some form or other, to distract and divert our eye from things above, from things beyond death? Is there no heart in which, this very day, some secret desire is working and reigning, entirely inconsistent with the pursuit of heaven? Yes, *the heart is deceitful above all things: who can know it?* And yet I do believe that there is some heart, here open before God, from which the confession is wrung by my question, *Alas, I care far, far more at this moment for some temporal, yes or for some forbidden thing, than I care for all God's love or for all the joys of heaven.* Child of light, thou art not living *wisely*. What would a worldly man gain, which of all his objects, wealth, pleasure, or power, if he were thus desultory, thus loose in his aim, thus inconsistent in his purpose? He is *wiser in his generation* than thou art, or we could scarcely call him a child of this world. And thou, a child of light, a child of revelation, a child of the kingdom, a child of God, must thine eye be thus roving, thy forthright vision thus distracted? Repent and remember thyself quickly, lest perhaps against thee those terrible words should be fulfilled, *Ephraim is joined unto idols: let him alone.*

2. Again, I will ask, Is your wisdom, as a child of light, shown by *the steadiness of your hand?* Do you not only discern your object clearly, and suffer nothing else to distract your eye from it, but also keep a firm hand upon yourself in aiming at it? It is not enough to aim correctly, if the hand shakes so that it cannot

steady the arrow. It is thus with some Christians in their pursuit of heaven. They have no resolution. They see the object, but they have not firmness to make for it. They have no other object, and yet they cannot secure this. Thus the life of many persons is a constant missing of both worlds. They know what the true end of life is, and they are too clear-sighted to substitute another end for it; and yet they are at the mercy of a weak will, of an infirm purpose, so that they *cannot do the thing that they would.* In some cases, it is an evil temper, or an inability to stand alone, or a depression arising from the repeated experience of past failure, which shakes and at last palsies the hand of self-denial and self-control. And these are very sorrowful cases. Combined oftentimes with true instincts and genuine impulses of good, with warm affections and holy desires and lofty aspirations, there is a warp and bias in the nature which makes all else nugatory and fallacious, until the man whose eye is set on heaven is seen drifting helplessly and hopelessly down the stream of time, and at last engulfed in those deep waters from which there is no outlet for ever. My brethren, if I address any this morning who read in this description their own likeness, let them pray earnestly for grace to recover, in the strength of God's Spirit, that self-mastery without which devotion is impossible and hope delusion. *Resist the devil, and he will flee from you: draw nigh to God, and He will draw nigh to you.*

3. Lastly, I would enquire of you, Is your wisdom, as a child of light, shown by *the strength of your effort?* I ask now, not whether there is any other object in your view, not whether there is any unsteadiness in your self-

control, but whether your endeavours after heaven are at all worthy of the thing aimed at; whether you are in any degree showing that earnestness and strength of exertion which a child of light ought to manifest, and which a child of this world so often does manifest, in *running the race set before him.* It is here, even more than elsewhere, that a Christian often fails and falls behind. He does not, like the children of this world, try one expedient after another in the pursuit of his end. He is not inventive, because he is not resolute. He acquiesces in poor results, because he is not intent upon great successes. By degrees, he begins to suppose that great successes are not for him. He makes a difference to himself, which Scripture does not recognize, between that measure of faith which is enough for safety and that measure of faith which is enough for happiness. He despairs altogether of beginning his heaven here. He postpones the first glimpses of immortality till that time when death shall be in the past. And thus he lives immeasurably below his privileges, if those privileges can be estimated by St Paul's experience, when he wrote, *To me to live is Christ.* The children of light are less wise in their generation than the children of this world, if for this reason only, that they do not hope and therefore that they do not strive like them. Faint expectations and great exertions seldom go together. It is so in things earthly. Give a man hope, and you give him zeal: make success doubtful, and you destroy endeavour. My brethren, let us believe God, let us believe Christ, when He says, *I will have you to be saved;* when He says, *My grace is sufficient for thee;* when He says, *Be thou faithful unto death, and I will give thee the crown of life.* Believe this, not for others only, but believe it for yourself; and then in you will the words in due time be realized also, *I have fought a good fight, I have finished my course, I have kept the faith; henceforth there is laid up for me*—I can see it in the distance—*a crown of righteousness.*

Ninth Sunday after Trinity,
August 17, 1862.

VI.[1]

THE DIVINITY OF WORK.

John v. 17.

My Father worketh hitherto, and I work.

THE first Sunday in September is appropriated by the pious custom of this Church to a Sermon on *the genuine tendency of the Christian Religion to lead its professors to industry and diligence in business.* And the preacher is required to have specially in view the case of those young persons who are just entering upon a life of responsible duty in the shops and warehouses of this town, aided by the charitable benefaction of one who, while he lived, *cared for the poor*, and by the munificence of his last bequests to them, *being dead, yet speaketh.*

There is no occasion throughout the year on which I should more unwillingly be absent from the pulpit. I speak today as a working man to working men on the duty, the dignity, and the blessedness of working. I speak as one whose day of life is already past its meridian, to those whom the great Householder is *early in the morning* calling and *hiring into His vineyard.*

[1] This Sermon was preached before the young men apprenticed under Quintin Kay's charity. See Sermon xvi. in the former part of this Volume.

Ought I not to be able to say something to them—not in my own name but in His—on the important practical topic which is thus suggested to me?

It is but a fragment of the subject, which can be grasped at one time. If life be spared, other portions of it may be presented year by year in their season. But for the present I would confine your thoughts to one (perhaps the grandest) of the various considerations involved, that of *the divinity of work;* how in working we are made like God; how in working we are conformed to the likeness of our Lord and Saviour; even as He Himself says in the words just read to you, *My Father worketh hitherto, and I work.* Some of you may have thought of work as an evil. You may have found this among the clauses of the original curse upon fallen man, *In the sweat of thy face shalt thou eat bread, till thou return unto the ground.* And you may have hastened to the conclusion that but for sin there had been no work; that before sin entered work was not, and that, when sin is finally purged, work will cease with it and be no more. These inferences would be unfounded and erroneous. Little as we can understand of the state of man as he was created, before *sin entered into the world and death by sin;* little as the word of God itself tells, or perhaps could intelligibly or profitably tell, of that condition in soul and body so unlike and opposite to our own; there is just this written of him in his original uprightness, that *the Lord God took the man, and put him into the garden of Eden to dress it and to keep it.* There was work therefore even then. And in the revelation, equally scanty and to us equally mysterious, of the things that shall be when sin and death shall be no more, there is nothing which implies that work will have no place in heaven. I nowhere read that work, like death and hell, shall be cast into the lake of fire. I read, it is true, that *pain shall be no longer, nor sorrow, nor crying;* that *God shall wipe away all tears from the eyes* of His people, and that *He Himself will be with them and be their God:* but it is nowhere written—and we would thank Him for it—that the life of the blessed will be a life of inactivity, a life of passive enjoyment or of inert repose. If it is said that *the children of that world* shall be *equal unto the Angels,* yet we remember that it is one glorious characteristic of Angels to *excel in strength,* to *fulfil God's commandments, hearkening to the voice of His words.* The Angels themselves are *ministering spirits, sent forth to minister to them who shall be heirs of salvation:* and it will be one chief part of that salvation when it is at last achieved and accomplished, that in heaven, as never below, *God's servants shall serve Him.*

Work is not in itself the curse of man. Work was before the Fall: work shall be after the restoration. No curse which could have been devised for human sin would have been so formidable as that of a compulsory idleness. If God had sought only punishment, this might have been its nature; a perpetual and an inevitable inactivity. But God, even *in wrath remembering mercy,* designed the curse of man to be remedial yet more than penal. And therefore He deprived him not of occupation. The punishment was not that labour should cease, but that labour should become (1) more severe, and (2) less productive. Hitherto employment had not passed into toil, nor work into pain: now *in the sweat of thy face*, with effort more than moderate and exertion more than healthy, *thou shalt* oftentimes have to *eat thy bread*. Nor shall this excessive, this often painful toil be always remunerative. *Cursed is the ground for thy sake. Thorns also and thistles shall it bring forth to thee*. Labour shall too often be a disappointment: a man shall *look for much, and bring in little*. Excessive toil shall also oftentimes be fruitless toil. In these two respects a curse has fallen upon labour. Work itself is salutary, is honourable, is blessed: but painful work, and fruitless work, is a memento of our degradation, a consequence of our fall.

I address many this morning who have had experience of the thing described. You work often to weariness. You work beyond the point of healthy fatigue. When work is ended, an over-wrought brain forbids speedy or sweet repose. And you work sometimes in vain. All your labour fails to satisfy your employer, or fails to bring you in a just return. It is as though your very ground would bear only thorns and thistles. You say, it is all very well for the rich to talk of the blessedness of labour: for your part, you would willingly eat, drink, and take your ease. And others who hear me today are just entering upon a life of labour; and the prospect before them, little as they can see of it, looks already to them dull and monotonous. They too feel work burdensome: they too regard its fruits as inadequate and uninviting. And we also, who speak of the blessing of work, are not unaware of its accompanying drawbacks. We know that it is often excessive: we know that it is often disappointing. We do not deny that there is that in work which savours of the Fall and of the curse. We do not ask you to call the curse a blessing: but we ask you to bear the curse meekly, and not to disparage the blessing which lurks within it. In short, we would have you thankful for work, and submissive to toil. We would have you look forward to a work which shall be all pleasure, and patient meanwhile, by God's grace, of a work which is sometimes painful and never satisfying.

Jesus answered them, My Father worketh hitherto, and I work. Toil may be human, but work is divine. Bear the one, and love the other.

Jesus had performed a great miracle of healing on the Sabbath-day. For thirty and eight years a man had lain under a painful infirmity. At the word of Jesus he had risen in newness of life. *Behold, thou art made whole,* Jesus could say to him: *sin no more, lest a worse thing come unto thee;* a worse thing than eight and thirty years of disease and suffering. Out of this act of divine humanity the perverse ingenuity of the enemy could extract a cavil and a calumny. It was the Sabbath-day when the man was bidden to carry off his couch in sign of healing. The words above written were the answer to this charge. *My Father worketh hitherto.* Ill were it for the natural world, if the hand of the Creator were withdrawn from it for the Sabbath: that ceaseless working, in preservation and in providence, is essential to the order of nature and to the very life of man. *My Father worketh hitherto,* on six days and on the seventh; and ye yourselves owe life and being to that unwearied activity. *My Father worketh, and I work: what things soever the Father doeth, these also doeth the Son likewise:* and the ceaseless beneficence of God the Creator must have its counterpart below in the ceaseless beneficence of God the Redeemer. *The Son of Man* must be *Lord even of the Sabbath.*

With the particular application of the words to works of mercy done upon the Sabbath we are not now concerned. But the words themselves exhibit to us this marvellous feature in the life of God above, that it is a life of unwearied, of unintermitted, of incessant work. Once indeed God is said to have rested: *on the seventh day God rested from all His work which He had created and made.* And He speaks of that rest as designed also for His people. He bids us take heed lest any of us should fail to enter into the rest which *remaineth* in Him and with Him *for the people of God.* But, when we consider it, that rest itself must be a rest of action. Satisfaction in the thing made would have soon ended, if the hand of the Sustainer and the Upholder had not taken up the work of the Originator and the Creator. Do we imagine that the mighty fabric of nature and of animal life, like a clock wound up for its week, would have gone on without the perpetual sustentation of Him who first formed it? Is it in your own power to keep yourself in being for one single day, or to fix for your own lifetime to what point it shall go, and where it shall stop and find its limit? If you then *cannot do that thing which is least,* where is the wisdom of so speaking as if you could dispense with the agency to which you owe all things? A Creator implies an upholder. If the world was not at first by chance, neither by chance is it now. If a Divine Person was necessary to its creation, so a Divine Person is necessary to its preservation.

And when we think what preservation means, we can at least humble ourselves under the sound of the Saviour's saying, *My Father worketh hitherto.* By what other term can we express the agency of a God of Nature, a God of Providence, and a God of Grace? It would lower rather than heighten the impression, if we were to presume to explain or to illustrate. Rather let us allow the three departments (as we understand them) of the Divine activity to press upon our minds in their vast extent, in their marvellous complexity. Nature—Providence—Grace—what must He be who can carry on the machinery of any one of these?

Think of the administration of one Empire such as our own; think of the variety of its interests; think of the intricacy of its business; think of the multitude of human minds and human lives devoted to its management; think of its trade and commerce, of its arts and sciences, of its fleets and armies, of its legislation and its embassies, its home affairs and distant dependencies; and imagine, if you can, a single mind planning, and a single hand conducting, all these agencies: yet what will this be to the charge of a Universe, in which not our own country, but our own planet itself, is but a speck and an atom?

Or think of a single human life, with its growth, maturity, and decline, its varied fortunes, its joys and sorrows, its commonplace incidents and strange reverses, its amount of anxiety, of perplexity, of complication; and believe, as a Christian believes, that there is a thread running through it all, and a hand holding that clue and tracking that labyrinth, arranging everything with minute as well as general direction, and guiding everything to an end; and then extend your thoughts from one such life to many, and from many to thousands and to myriads and to millions; and remember that each one of these is seen as a whole, that no one obscures or outshines another, that, though each is at a different point in its progress from any other, yet there is no confusion and no entanglement and no mistake in the accurate management of any one: will not the result of such a contemplation, feeble and inadequate as it must be in itself, at least be this, to make you bend low before God's footstool, even as the God of Providence only, and to give you a more solemn impression of the words of the text, which say to us in Christ's name, *My Father worketh hitherto?*

Or think, once again, not of a single life, but of a single soul; think of yourself in your spiritual being; think of the various operations of your own heart as they lie open in the sight of God; think of your varied experiences (if you be a Christian at all) of depression and hope, of deadness and liveliness, of repentance and resolution; think but of your prayers, of the things which you deprecate and which you ask for, of the subjects of interest and anxiety which you bring with you, yourself alone, before the throne of grace; and believe, as every Christian believes, that God is cognizant of all these things, that He is a God who heareth prayer, and *knows what is the mind of His Spirit* as *He makes intercession, according to His will,* not only *for,* but in *the saints;* and then, once again, reflect upon the unnumbered human hearts, in this and every land, in which these processes of desire and supplication are daily (and this day more especially) realized and carried on; and remember that each one of these hearts has its own secrets and its own history, to which the answers of prayer must have a just and accurate relation, not to be confused or intermingled with any other: think of these things, possess your minds with them: and again I would ask, do they not show us what the work of God must be in heaven, and how truly our Lord might say of Him, in His one character as the God of grace, *My Father worketh hitherto, and I work?*

And I work. Yes, the work of the Son is even as the work of the Father. Last year I spoke of Him to you as He was in this respect on earth; of His early manual toil as the carpenter of Nazareth; of His later and not less assiduous labour as the prophet and the instructor and the physician of Israel. Truly His work on earth was as that of no other man. In the daytime *there were many coming and going, and He had no leisure so much as to eat.* And as His days were given to toil, so His nights to prayer. For Him, as for us, yet far beyond us, earth was a place of toil.

But what is heaven to Him? Does He rest there? Yes, *in Thy presence is the fulness of joy; at Thy right hand there are pleasures for evermore.* But that joy, those pleasures, are not found in inactivity. The life of Christ in heaven is a life of work. All that has been said of the Father has been said of Him. For is He not the doer of all the works of God? Has He not said, *I and my Father are one?* Is it not He who *made the worlds?* Is it not He who *upholdeth all things by the word of His power?* Is it not He who hears and answers prayer, and ministers to His people of His

Spirit? Is it not He, above all, who *ever maketh intercession for us*, with a knowledge of want as minute as the power to relieve it is infinite?

Yes, it is not we only who have to work: our Saviour works, and our God works, also. Weekday and Sunday, week by week, month by month, year by year, through years counted by the thousand and then not exhausted, has God Himself, the Father and the Son and the Spirit, set us the example of the work to which He calls us. Never despise work as your reproach: never hate work as your curse. He who works not is contemptible: he who works not, high or low, rich or poor, has the mark of the curse—yea, of a curse which God never uttered—branded in fire upon his brow. Hand or head—there is that much of distinction and of difference—hand or head must work, in all of us, or we are mere *cumberers of the ground, fit neither for the land nor for the dunghill.* And He who bids us work works Himself. God our Creator, Christ our Redeemer, the Holy Ghost our Sanctifier—the very names show that each one works, yet more, far more, than we. Therefore let us look upward, and let us look onward. A day is coming, when all of work that is bitter shall be done away; its over-toil, its scant reward. But work itself shall never end for the Christian. In *the lake of fire* there will be no work; only uselessness, only suffering; only self-torment and mutual torment; the torment of the remorseful, and the torment of the taunter. But in heaven there will be work, when once the resurrection comes, when once the body is given back; work delightful and blessed; the work of unwearied praise, the work of unbounded knowledge, the work of indefatigable love. On earth work is our necessity: we can only shake it off through sin; we can only shake it off in misery. In heaven work will be our happiness: it will be the badge of the saved, the perpetual proof to us that we are redeemed and rescued and glorified. Let us so work now, that we may be permitted to work then. Let each day's business be duly consecrated, by prayer before, and by prayer after it. Let each day find each of you, more especially my younger brethren, on your knees at morning and at evening; happier if (like the Psalmist) *at noonday* also. Take no work ever in hand, on which you cannot ask for God's blessing. Let your employers find that upon you rests the blessing of the faithful Joseph, *The Lord was with him, and that which he did, the Lord made it to prosper.* This is the heritage of them that fear Him: may it be ours. *Lord, Thou hast been our refuge from one generation to another. So teach us to number our days, that we may apply our hearts unto wisdom. O satisfy us early with Thy mercy: that we may rejoice and be glad all our days. And the glorious majesty of the Lord our God be upon us: prosper Thou the work of our hands upon us, O prosper Thou our handywork.*

TWELFTH SUNDAY AFTER TRINITY,
September 7, 1862.

VII.

THE GRADUAL MIRACLE.

Mark viii. 24.

I see men as trees, walking.

VARIETY is one mark of God's working, as order is another. Variety without discord; variety essential to harmony; *many members in one body;* many means to one end; *diversities of operations, but the same God working all in all;* this is the law which runs through all that is truly God's, whether in Nature or in Providence, whether in Revelation or in Grace.

And *what things soever the Father doeth, these also doeth the Son likewise.* When He was upon earth, witnessing for God, bringing God into all things, and impregnating human life with an all-pervading divine influence and presence, the same characteristic was observable in His words and in His works. There was a fertility of resource, and a diversity of administration, which bespoke the agency of One who *from the beginning was with God and was God,* the Doer of all God's acts and the Partner of all God's counsels.

It was so in His miracles. With scarcely one exception, with no one real exception, they were all miracles of mercy; of beneficence not of judgment; of soothing not of terror. And in all cases the condition of His healing was one and the same: faith on the part of the recipient, or at least on the part of those who brought him to Jesus. But with these two points of resemblance, all else was most various. Sometimes He wrought by means, sometimes without means, sometimes even against means. Most often He wrought readily and with words of spontaneous blessing: once He wrought as it were reluctantly, and, though with a gracious purpose, yet with expressions almost of harshness. Most often He wrought instantaneously and completely; the word or the touch was followed immediately by a perfect cure: once, and the example is today before us, He wrought gradually, and by two successive operations carried the work of healing to its accomplishment.

We often say that our Lord's miracles were all parables too. And is it not so with this miracle; the gradual healing, the healing not at once but at twice, of the blind man at Bethsaida? My brethren, the history has been read to you this morning: did not some of you feel it to be your own? God grant that it may be yours in both its parts, as it certainly is in one.

When the healing hand was first laid upon this blind man, the result was imperfect and inconclusive. Till now he had been in utter darkness: now he can not only see the light, but he can perceive objects. And yet it is but partially and incompletely. He *sees men as trees, walking*. He sees something, and he can see that it is in motion: but the characteristics of the human form and human face are not yet discernible. To his half-enlightened eye a man might be a tree: the walk of the one might be but the sway and swing of the other. Thus was the process of healing made to conduce at once to a sense of thankfulness and a sense of dependence. Something, much, was given: something, more still, was to be looked for. It was a great boon to have blank nothingness exchanged for light peopled with objects: in the first transport of the wonderful vision a man might almost forget that the cure was still imperfect. He could now control his own movements and guide his own steps: he was transferred from helplessness into independence, and from a life of dull monotony into a life of conscious vigour and of sweet enjoyment. But when he is asked to put his experience into words, he is constrained to acknowledge that there is still a want and an imperfection. I see men; and I see that they are walking: but as to details of figure and feature a man might be anything else as well. *I see men* but *as trees, walking.* And the merciful and gracious Lord, all whose works, like those of the original Creation, are, not halt and maimed but *very good,* designed not to leave him in that incompleteness. He would have Himself remembered and trusted in, not as One who can half heal, but as One whose power and whose love is infinite. Therefore *He put His hands again upon his eyes; and now he was restored, and saw every man clearly.*

You will perceive at once the use that I would ask you to make of this singular and exceptional miracle, this gradual cure, this healing not at once but at twice. This particular miracle is the parable of our times. Instances of immediate and perfect cures are the types of sudden and yet permanent conversions. In the earliest age of the Church such manifestations of Christ's spiritual

Omnipotence were rather the rule than the exception. Such were the operations of the great day of Pentecost; such the experience of Lydia of Thyatira and of the jailer of Philippi; such the spiritual history of one greater than either, the holy and blessed Apostle St Paul himself. And such have been from time to time the operations of the same Holy Spirit in later days, even amongst those who had grown up in the knowledge and profession of Christian truth, but had never apprehended its power till a season graciously vouchsafed of inward and effectual visitation. These things have been; and *the Lord's arm is not shortened* that they may not be again. But if we were asked to name a miracle which was the more probable pattern of our own spiritual experience, we should turn, every one of us, to the healing of the blind man of Bethsaida. The hand of Christ may have been laid upon us, not only in the institution of forms and sacraments, not only in the bringing us within the sound of His Gospel and the strivings of His Spirit, but also, let us hope it, in some deep inward convictions and earnest wrestlings of our own; in true repentance for sin generally and for sin particularly; in hearty prayer for pardon and amendment; and in resolutions, neither faint nor self-confident, for *walking in newness of life.* All this there may have been; and if we did not hope this with respect to many, we could scarcely gird ourselves to the exercise of this ministry: but is not the condition even of these, the more hopeful of the congregation, best to be described in the words of the blind man of Bethsaida, who, when he was asked *if he saw ought,* was constrained to reply as he looked up, *I see men as trees, walking?* The spiritual eye is not utterly closed nor utterly darkened; but its sight is confused, its discernment of objects both misty and inaccurate.

1. It is so in reference to the things of God.

We can speak but for ourselves: but who has not known what it is to say, *I cannot make real to myself one single fact or one single doctrine of the Bible? I can say indeed—and I bless God even for that—Lord, to whom else can I go? where, save in the Gospel of our Lord Jesus Christ, is there either the hope or the peradventure of healing for a case like mine? And therefore I can cling to the Christian Revelation with the tenacity of a shipwrecked sailor whose one 'broken piece of the ship' is his only possibility of escape: I can just float upon that fragment, knowing that, torn from it or washed off from it, I am lost: but if the question is, whether I really see ought; whether I can discern with the mind's eye the sacred and blessed forms of a Father and a Saviour and a Comforter who are such to me; whether, when I kneel down to pray, I can feel myself to be apart with my God; whether, when I approach Christ's Table, I feel myself to be His guest; whether, when I ask to be kept this day from all sin, I feel myself to be the temple of a Holy Spirit whose indwelling is my safeguard and my chief joy; then I must answer that my hold upon all these things is precarious and most feeble; that seeing I see but scarcely perceive; that my God is too often to me like the gods of the heathen which can neither see nor hear nor reward nor punish; that I too often conduct myself towards Him as though I thought wickedly that He was even such an one as myself, equally short-sighted, equally fallible, equally vacillating, equally impotent.*

More especially is this the case in reference to the distinctive doctrines of divine grace. How little do any of us grasp and handle and use the revelation of an absolute forgiveness. Those comforting words which follow the general confession of sin in our daily service; that solemn assurance, in God's name, by His authorized minister, that He does actually pardon and absolve; how little do we take it to our hearts! how few of us go away as forgiven men, to live and to act that forgiveness in the spirit and conduct of the day which follows. And so is it with the sister revelation of that Holy Spirit whom God has promised to all who ask Him. We pray indeed (who does not pray?) for grace to live as we ought, in the careful avoidance of known sin and the diligent discharge of known duty: but do we seriously expect an answer to this prayer? Do we in our inmost hearts believe that an influence, a guidance, a control, a suggestion, a presence—call it what you will—is vouchsafed, is maintained, is continued, day by day, and through each day, as the direct reply of God to this petition? What can we say more, in regard to all these things, than that at best we *see men as trees, walking?* that we have a dim, dull, floating impression of there being something in them, rather than a clear, bold, strong apprehension of what and whom and why we have believed?

2. And if this be so in the things of God, in matters of direct revelation and of Christian faith, it is scarcely less true in reference to the things of men; to our views of life, the present life and the future, and to the relations in which we stand to those fellow-beings with whom the Providence of God brings us into contact.

We all profess as Christians to be *looking for the resurrection of the dead, and the life of the world to come*. And yet, when we examine our own hearts, or observe (however remotely) the evident principles of others, we find that in reality the world that is holds us all with a very firm gripe; that what stirs us, what excites us, what makes the pulse beat and the heart glow, is not the prospect of a speedy *departure to be with Christ;* not the nearer hope of communion with Him, of opportunities of access to His presence more frequent or more effectual; not the communication to the soul within of a livelier faith or a more ardent devotion: none of these things: but rather some surprise of worldly success, some accession of fortune, some opening for larger gain, some promise of professional advancement, some new tie of domestic happiness; in short, some one of those occurrences which make earth and the present more powerful and more attractive, which give an added reason for *desiring life that we may see good days* below, and which in the same proportion put heaven further off, and make the gulf between it and earth wider, deeper, and more impassable. This, I repeat, is the practice of the man whose profession it is to *have here*, and to desire to have here, *no continuing city, but* rather to be ever *seeking one to come.* And then for the many who have no such stirs and no such excitements, whose life below is dry and monotonous, to whom existence, and the support of existence, is all that earth at its best can promise; yet is it found, as a matter of experience, that even these *see ought* of the true life which is *hidden with Christ in God?* Are not even these as dim-sighted with regard to heaven as if earth were ample enough to fill their whole field of vision? Are not they in constant danger of losing both worlds; of having nothing here, and yet of storing up no hereafter? Thus we say again, and say it sorrowfully, of both classes, of all classes, of Christian people, even as we see them at the best, that they are too much in the position of the blind man between the two applications of the healing hand, when he could just see that there was an object, but could so little discern relative or positive characteristics, that he *saw men as trees, walking.* We cannot appreciate the comparative dimensions of things heavenly and things earthly. The present is so real to us, and the future so unreal; outward advantage so evident, and a heavenly inheritance so veiled and so remote; the voice of men so loud and imperious, and the voice of God (as it is written) so *still and small;* that it is little to be wondered at if *seeing we see not and hearing do not understand;* if the objects which surround us assume an exaggerated stature, and the realities of heaven, being far above and beyond us, are proportionately diminished, dwarfed, and stunted.

The subject appears to suggest two words of application.

(1) First, to those who are truly in the position which I have sought by the help of this miracle to indicate. To those who are really under the healing hand of Christ, but upon whom as yet it has been laid incompletely if not indecisively. Many persons think themselves quite healed, when they are at best but half-healed. Many, having experienced a first awakening, and sought with sincerity the gift of the divine forgiveness, rest there, *and count themselves to have apprehended.*

They never listen seriously for the voice which asks them if they indeed *see ought*. If they did, they would have to take counsel with themselves, to try the measure of their attainment, to test the range and accuracy of their vision, and thus to arrive at the honest confession, *As yet I only see men as trees, walking.* And they could not surely think that, while this was all, the cure was perfected. They must feel that the object of sight is discernment, the distinguishing of things that differ; and that he who cannot yet know a man from a tree can scarcely be said to have regained sight. And my object this morning, as regards these persons, is to impress upon them the importance of going forward in the process of the healing; of not going away half-healed, but of waiting and asking for the second application of the touch of Christ, that which shall restore them wholly and enable them to see all things clearly. It is not a question only of inclination, of comfort, or of usefulness. It is indeed a question of safety and of life for all of us. I say not whether a man half-healed might, if he were indeed in Christ's hand and still under healing, get to heaven if death came upon him before the cure was complete: but I do say that a man who rests in the half-healing, who is satisfied with it, who turns away and goes about his own matters, regardless of the progress unto perfection, has upon him that fatal sign of indifference, of self-complacency, and therefore also of self-deception, which is Laodicean in its character and (if it be not repented of) must be Laodicean also in its end. Let us arouse ourselves, and (if it might be so) one another also, to count nothing done while ought remains; to *forget the things behind and reach forth unto the things that are before*, and so to *press toward the mark for the prize of our high calling in Christ Jesus.*

(2) Secondly, and finally, a word of caution must be added, to those who are too easily assuming that they are even half-healed. My brethren, the hand of Christ is not laid—alas, it must be spoken—even for the first time upon every man; not even upon every member of His outward Church; not even upon every worshipper in His House or (it may be) at His Table. The hand is not laid without our knowing it, nay, nor without our seeking it. The blind man must first come to Jesus, and come in faith: and which of all us has done so? It needs a desire to be saved, and it needs a willingness to be saved in Christ's way, and it needs a consciousness of deep defilement, and it needs a conviction that His blood cleanseth from all guilt, and that His Holy Spirit can set us free from all sin, to bring a man under the healing touch even once. O try and examine yourselves, my brethren, *and that not lightly and after the manner of dissemblers with God*, but honestly and in earnest, that ye be not, in the great day, *condemned with the world*. Even the first act of healing is a gift *above gold and precious stone:* despise it not. Power out of weakness, peace out of warfare, light out of darkness, sight out of dim, groping, creeping blindness, this it is to be the subject of the first healing. God enable us all to come for it to Him who is still on His throne of grace to grant repentance and to grant forgiveness. And let him who has this *follow on to know* the second. Then shall *a peace which passeth understanding* enter his heart; and at last his eye, once blind, long dim, shall receive

strength and clearness to *see the King* Himself *in His beauty,* and to *behold* as though full and close in view *the land that is very far off.*

SIXTEENTH SUNDAY AFTER TRINITY,
October 5, 1862.

VIII.

THE GOSPEL A FIRE.

Luke xii. 49.

I am come to send fire on the earth.

HE who thus speaks is called in Prophecy *the Prince of Peace*. The object of His coming was *to guide our feet into the way of peace*. The song which greeted His birth-night was the angelic hymn, *Glory to God in the highest, and on earth peace*. Amongst the latest words which He spoke to His disciples before He suffered were such as these, *Peace I leave with you; my peace I give unto you. These things I have spoken unto you, that in me ye might have peace*. And His first words to them after His return from *the grave and gate of death* were still these, *Peace be unto you. Then were the disciples glad, when they saw the Lord*. And yet here He says or seems to say the very opposite. *I am come to send fire on the earth. Suppose ye that I am come to give peace on earth? I tell you, Nay; but rather division. Think not that I am come to send peace on earth: I came not to send peace, but a sword.*

This apparent contradiction has never, I believe, perplexed or distressed any one. We all understand the difference between the intention and the consequence of an action; between the object of a thing and its result; between the effect of the same thing upon one person and upon another: an effect depending oftentimes not upon the mind of the doer but upon the spirit of the receiver.

The Gospel is in itself all peace. It is a message of love from God to man. It tells of reconciliation and atonement between a sinful creature and a justly displeased because forgotten and despised Creator. It says, not only, *Return unto me, and I will return unto you;* but also, *I have cast all your sins behind my back: I have laid upon a holy yet suffering Saviour the iniquities of you all. Mercy and truth* in that message *have met together: righteousness and peace have* indeed *kissed each other.* What can the intent of such a message, what can the purpose of such a messenger be save this, to give us peace? peace first with God, and then also peace with man? Whatever He may say or seem to say elsewhere, we cannot believe but that He came to give peace on earth.

And we go further and say that not only the object but the effect of the Gospel is to make peace. All the bickerings which disturb families, and all the wars which desolate kingdoms, spring out of that very want which Christ came to supply, out of that very disease which Christ came to heal. *Whence come wars and fightings among you?* Come they of the Gospel? come they of Christ? Nay, they all spring ultimately out of hearts defiled by sin and estranged through the sense of guilt from God. Let the Gospel come into a heart, taking away the dread of God, and so making peace within; and you all know that its instant effect is to make the spirit amiable and the life peaceable; to reconcile differences and to repair breaches; to make the man a follower of his Master not more in purity of conduct than in benevolence and gentleness of soul. And if this last result does not follow from a professed conversion, Christians sorrow over the inconsistency, and the world itself notices it, saying one to another, *That man can be no Christian, because he does not love.*

The conviction of these things has led some persons to seek a different meaning altogether for the words of the text. They have called to mind that St John the Baptist spoke before Christ's coming of His mission to *baptize men with the Holy Ghost and with fire;* and they have supposed our Lord Himself to be here speaking of that glorious gift which purifies and cheers and illuminates the heart upon which it has descended. No doubt this is an erroneous interpretation. Because fire is sometimes an emblem of the Holy Ghost, it does not follow that it can never have a different meaning. Because fire sometimes warms and cheers, it does not follow that it does not sometimes burn and desolate. And when the text has thus been softened down and explained away, there still remain the words, *Suppose ye that I am come to give peace on earth? I came not to send peace, but a sword.*

Therefore we believe that our Lord does here say, in the plainest sense of the expression, that, while the object of His coming is to give peace, the effect of His coming will too often be to send fire on earth. *And what will I,* He adds, *if it be already kindled? Does it astonish, does it perplex, does it daunt me, if the fire which is to result from my coming is already, during my own life below, kindled into activity? What if already, what if even towards myself, what if in those nearest to me by nature and by choice, symptoms of this fiery discord are already visible?* And yet, He proceeds to say, *before this or any other consequence of the Gospel Revelation can be fully manifested and realized, there is one thing to be accomplished. I have a baptism to be baptized with; a baptism of immersion in deep waters; a baptism of outpoured blood,* a baptism of inauguration and initiation into that office of the High Priest of man with which death alone, death and consequent resurrection, can invest me. And although flesh and blood may shrink and cower in the prospect of that fearful encounter, yet a soul conscious of its glorious mission thirsts rather and pants for its arrival. *How am I straitened till it be accomplished!* Till that last ordeal is over, He may have followers, but He cannot have a Church; He may teach, but He cannot redeem; He may attract, but He cannot save. *Except a corn of wheat fall into the ground and die, it abideth alone: but, if it die, it bringeth forth much fruit.* It is only *if I be lifted up from the earth* that I can *draw all men unto me.* And *this He said, signifying what death He should die.*

And then after this glimpse at the prospect of His approaching sufferings and of *the glory that should follow,* He resumes the subject of this particular consequence of His coming. *Suppose ye that I am come to give peace on earth?* to bring about an immediate reign of tranquillity and universal happiness? *I tell you, Nay; but rather division.* The Sabbath of the sin-ruined race is not yet. Long must the defiled and wearied earth wait for the restoration of its Paradise. The Gospel itself will seem at times to have rather postponed than hastened that glorious consummation. *For from henceforth there shall be five in one house divided, three against two, and two against three. The father shall be divided against the son, and the son against the father; the mother against the daughter, and the daughter against the mother; the mother-in-law against her daughter-in-law, and the daughter-in-law against her mother-in-law.*

The subject thus introduced may seem to some of my hearers to be not only a discouraging but an unprofitable one; a consequence of the Gospel rather to be endured than exhibited; to be mourned in secret rather than avowed before friends and foes. But these, my brethren, are the words of our Saviour, and, like all His words, full of instruction, if God give us the tongue to speak and the ear to hear. May it be so now, He being our helper.

1. The text calls the Gospel a fire. And the first remark upon it must be, that a fire is a power. Many of those who hear me can testify, from recollections not yet ten years old[1], what a reality, what a vitality, what a sweeping and resistless strength, resides in that element of fire. How it spreads, and glows, and rages, and devours. How it strides from point to point, from wood to stone, from gallery to wall, from floor to tower, licking and devouring and consuming, while a whole population cowers before it, and can only stand idly by, beholding and weeping over its work. Now I say that, when the Gospel is called a fire sent upon the earth, we shall do well to remember that a fire is a power; not a

[1] The Parish Church of Doncaster was destroyed by fire on the 28th of February, 1853.

name, not an idea, not a poor faint creeping thing which may be disregarded and let alone because at any moment human exertion can interpose and put it down, but a great, an active, at last a victorious and irresistible force, against which all the skill and all the strength in the world is as powerless as an infant's touch. Never suppose that the Gospel is an insignificant or despicable thing: whatever else it is or is not, it is certainly not that. The Gospel is a fire: and what a fire is, you know and you have seen.

2. But then we must admit, and we do so with sorrow, that there are places, as there are hearts, in which the Gospel is not a fire. And here we reach a very anxious and a very critical question. A fire, we have said, is a power. Our Lord is here speaking of the Gospel as a power for division. He says that one effect of His coming upon earth, one effect of His leaving a Gospel to be proclaimed when He was gone back to heaven, would be a spreading and desolating conflagration in human families. And He tells us how this will act. There may be a family, He says, of five persons. The Gospel gets into that household. One of the family has fallen in with the true living Word of God; perhaps from a minister casually heard; perhaps from a friend accidentally met; perhaps on a bed of sickness, or in a providence which has constrained reflection. Sin is now felt as a sore burden too heavy for man to bear. And the Saviour of sinners has at last revealed Himself as taking away and cleansing from all sin. Deep gratitude has taken possession of the relieved and tranquillized spirit; a gratitude which lives and moves within, and which cannot be let or stayed from working. Now

therefore it cannot be altogether a secret, that something has happened to that one of the five. With no wish to obtrude upon the rest either his new conviction or the experience through which he has passed to it, he cannot, if he would—and he would not—be precisely as in days of ignorance and thoughtlessness: he must do some things, and he must forbear from doing some things, which before were left undone, or which before were done, *according to the course of this world, according to the spirit that still worketh in the children of disobedience.* And at such a change, however carefully and modestly and delicately indicated, the spirit of the old nature ever revolts and takes offence. Added kindness and gentleness and patience and forbearance is no security, no safeguard, against this offence. Of all things perhaps it is the most irritating to the natural heart. To be angry, and yet to have no vent for that anger; to feel oneself condemned twice over, first by the piety, and then by the charity, of one of your own household; to have conscience goading you within by an example at once lofty and humble, and yet to be resolved not to yield to it; this is what fallen human nature must feel and resent, and no pains and no prayers can altogether avert the consequences. In that house henceforth there is division, discord, disunion; and the Gospel is the cause of it. Henceforth the only alternative of union in that house must be, the backsliding of the one, or the conversion of the rest. Christ *came to send fire upon the earth;* and in that house at least *it is already kindled.*

You observe that it is just because the Gospel is a power, that this effect is produced by it. So long as the Gospel was not (in that particular case) a power, so long it was not a fire; it caused no breach and no disunion. Therefore we are constrained to wish, even against our wish, for such signs of its working. If Christ does not send fire upon the earth, neither can He send peace into hearts. The fire is the sign of the peace. Because the sweet influence of the Gospel has entered a heart, therefore division has entered a household. If we are contented, in any town or in any house, to let the Gospel die out as a power; if, that is, we are satisfied with an orthodox belief, a regular worship, a decent conduct, and a practically worldly life; there will be no fire certainly: the Gospel itself will be a mere balm, a mere soporific, a mere lullaby of the soul. It is only at a later stage than this, when one here and another there has been thoroughly awakened and aroused by the personal call of Christ, that the prophecy will begin to be fulfilled, *I came not to give peace but a sword: I am come to send fire upon the earth.*

3. Now therefore let us bring the matter home to our own hearts; and see what the lesson of the text is for each one of us.

(1) I address myself no doubt this morning to some happily united families. You have come hither today to worship, bringing affection with you, and secure of finding it on your return. Who does not congratulate you? Who can wish sword and fire for your peaceful home? Yet *suffer*, brethren, even you, *the word of exhortation*. Suffer me to ask of you whence this concord springs? Has Christ anything to do with it? Are you all agreed together in *following Him whithersoever He goeth?* Does family prayer begin and end your day? and is it well understood amongst you that each one

separately is serving Christ, in all earnestness, in all purity, and in all diligence? Is this the secret of union? Is it an understood thing among you, that you are each walking heavenwards; and that, if you talk not much about it, it is not because it is an uninteresting but because it is a heart-deep subject? O, if you are not sure of these things, settle them. Let not family love be a mask for ungodliness and self-conceit. If you are all walking one way, let it not be doubtful which way that one way is. Let natural affection prompt you to see that you are *one in Christ.* Try to prevent the fire of Gospel light from being in your household a fire of discord, by seeing that it be to each one a fire of cleansing and a fire of quickening and a fire of devotion.

(2) It may be feared that in every congregation there are instances of an opposite kind. There are in all places disunited disorganized homes. And as I asked of united households, What has united you? so now I would ask of divided households, What has divided you? In the one case, Was it Christ? In the other case, Was it Christ? Was it the peace of the Gospel which cemented? Was it the fire of the Gospel which severed? In other words, Is this the cause of disunion, that two of the household are with Christ and three of the household are against Christ? Is it for conscience sake indeed, is it because of a greater love to Christ, that you, a neglected sister, that you, an unloved daughter, are thus treated? Is it because *the love of Christ constraining* you made you postpone even natural affection to the stronger mandate of duty? Is your unhappiness due to this, and to this alone, that you could not con-

sent to forget, to dishonour, or to disobey your Saviour? O search and look whether there be not another and a less worthy cause for this disunion: see whether no unmortified temper, no wilfulness or perverseness, no unruliness and insubordination of spirit, be at the root of your loveless life: whether therefore it be not rather Christ's enemy than Christ Himself who has sowed discomfort and discord in your home. If the Gospel be a fire, see at least that it burn only with a pure flame, only with a sanctifying if condemning brightness.

(3) And for those who may heretofore have allowed human prejudice, or some worse cause still, to make them intolerant of others' devotion or piety or self-sacrifice, and so to expose themselves to the terrible charge of being hinderers of Christ's little ones in the difficult work of salvation; let me earnestly and affectionately entreat them to look to it that they do not die thus; that they in the great division of this life be not divided against Christ, lest in the greater division of the life that shall be they be divided from Christ and therefore from happiness for ever. *It must needs be* that the Gospel divide: but woe still to them by whom that division comes. Wheresoever that division comes, it comes not of good but of evil. It comes by reason of human sin resisting the will of God that all should be saved. It comes not of the Gospel, though it come through the Gospel. If all would receive the truth in the love of it, division would be ended for ever, and the Gospel fire be only brightening, only comforting, only transforming.

(4) It is in this last sense that we desire to spread the Gospel through the lanes and yards of this town.

We do not wish to spread division by the Gospel: but, even if this be the effect, we recognize there one of the signs of the work of grace. If the Gospel divides men, it is because some heartily receive it. It is a sign that life is there, if some think it worth fighting against and others think it worth suffering for. There is an end, in that house, of the fatal lethargy which has so long numbed men to their ruin. We would indeed that all would receive; but we can *thank God and take courage* if there are even some. It is the work of the ministry to bring the Gospel home. It is something that it be preached in our Churches: it is more if it can be preached in our homes; if men can there be *reasoned with of righteousness and temperance and judgment to come*, till they not only say, but act upon the resolution, *We will go into the house of the Lord: there will we hear of a Saviour who died for us: there will we seek a Comforter and a Sanctifier: there will we unbosom our cares and sorrows before a God who cares for us and will save: there will we forget for a while the troubles and miseries of this sinful world in the anticipation of an inheritance incorruptible, undefiled, and unfading, reserved in heaven for us, and ready to be revealed in the last time.*

NINETEENTH SUNDAY AFTER TRINITY,
October 26, 1862.

IX.

THE UNCHANGEABLE WORDS.

Luke xxi. 33.

Heaven and earth shall pass away: but my words shall not pass away.

So then in this changeful world there is just one point of rest. All else passes away; youth, health, strength, human life; the tranquillity and plenty and prosperity of nations; the very *kingdoms of the world* themselves, as well as *the glory of them;* at last, for so we read our Lord's words here and elsewhere recorded, at last heaven and earth as at present constituted and circumstanced; all these things shall pass away, even as a dream that is dreamed or *a tale that is told.* But the words of Christ Himself, spoken once on earth, and now handed down to us in the Scriptures of truth; these words, the very things which we might have thought most transitory, most fleeting, most fugitive; mere sounds, uttered by the help of that breath which is most of all evanescent, of those lips over which death exercises so powerful a dominion; these words, these sounds of the voice, these marks of a pen on the pages of a perishable book, these words of Christ Himself shall never pass away.

There is something remarkable, we all feel, in such a

claim, in such an assertion. It is what no genius, however lofty or however self-confident, would have dared to make. Arrogance, presumption, ignorance, vainglory, would have been the least of the charges which such a statement would have drawn down upon any human writer who had ventured it. And yet we read it here, day after day, and century after century, without any disposition to cavil; may I not say? without any doubt of its truth. Thus far certainly the declaration has come true. If heaven and earth have not yet passed away, certainly the words of Christ have not perished yet. They are still the support and comfort of thousands; as fresh in their vitality as when He first spoke them. We cannot read the future: but certainly our experience of the past eighteen centuries gives us good reason to believe that to the end and through the dissolution of all created being the saying will still be verified, that, though heaven and earth shall pass away, the words of Christ shall not pass away.

The holy season which we are now keeping reminds us of that last end which shall be brought in by the second Advent of *the Lord from heaven*. We talk of that event as *the end of all things*. And doubtless to each one of us it will indeed be an end of all things of which we are thinking when we thus speak. Human rivalries and jealousies, human distinctions and ambitions, no less than human wants and cares and oppressions, will then have ceased for ever. And St Peter tells us of a deluge of fire which shall sweep across the face of this fair earth, as though to cleanse it from the defilement of sin's footsteps, and to prepare it for the use of a race which shall know only righteousness.

But we must not so speak or so think of that great consummation, as though it would indeed efface every mark of the present. We shall live through it, and enter upon an immortal life beyond. And the attributes of God Himself will live through it, only exalted and brightened by that final justification of His ways to men. And the work of Christ and of the Holy Ghost will live through it; the one and the other being only accomplished and perfected in the safety and blessedness of the before veiled and hidden but now revealed and manifested sons of God. In all these senses the end will be also a beginning. There are things which the end itself will *not destroy but fulfil.* Happy is he who has a firm hold of these things, these unchangeable, these indestructible verities. *My words*, Christ says, *shall not pass away*.

This is true in every sense.

1. And first, the revelations of Christ shall not pass away. When He *came down from heaven*, as at the approaching season of Christmas, *for us men and for our salvation*, it was, in part at least, as the Revealer of God. *No man hath seen God at any time: the only begotten Son, who is in the bosom of the Father, He hath declared Him. He that hath seen me hath seen the Father: and how sayest thou then, Show us the Father?* My brethren, what God is, He is for ever. *I am the Lord: I change not.* Have you ever reflected upon the disclosures which Jesus Christ has made to us of the character of God? That which He says God is, that we shall find God to be, and to be to us. Do not expect that there will be one God for you, and another God for me. Do not expect your case to be made an exception; so that

there shall be for you a waiving of precedents, and a modification of rules, and a mitigation of consequences, such as there is not, such as you know there is not, for any other. Have you ever thought of those words, so formidable yet so soon forgotten, *It is a fearful thing to fall into the hands of the living God?* Why fearful? Because the holiness of God, and the truth of God, and the justice of God, must be *a consuming fire* to all that has set itself up against these attributes. Because he who will keep his sin, he who will trifle with Christ's mercy, he who will neglect and despise the day of grace, he who has thus throughout life (in the Scripture sense of that term) *tempted God,* tried experiments, that is, upon His power and upon His discernment and upon His truth, must find himself at last scorched and consumed by that intolerable light which is the concentration of all the separate rays of the sun of God's glory. Christ came to reveal God: and Christ's words of revelation shall not pass away.

2. And thus is it with the predictions of Christ. One of His offices is that of the Prophet; of the Prophet not in the larger only but also in the more restricted sense, as the foreteller or predicter of future events. The text occurs at the end of a chapter of predictions. He has been telling how the temple of Jerusalem would be laid in ruins, and how a wrath of unexampled severity should light upon the land and upon the nation. He has spoken of a period briefly designated as *the times* (or *seasons*) *of the Gentiles,* during which Jerusalem itself should be trodden down by other nations, its own people being scattered, in captivity or exile, over the face of the earth. And He ended by

saying that that very generation would not pass away till all this was fulfilled. Within seven and thirty years from the time of His thus speaking, the prophecy was literally accomplished. His words did not pass away. Neither shall they pass away in that other and yet more solemn meaning which we believe to lie under the other throughout this prophecy. We believe that, although the destruction of Jerusalem and its temple was a fulfilment, it was not the only nor the chief fulfilment, of the words in which it was foretold. We have not yet seen what we believe to be the highest and deepest sense of the words, *And then shall they see the Son of Man coming in a cloud with power and great glory.* Here as elsewhere there is both a minor and also a complete fulfilment of prophecy. The fall of Jerusalem was the minor fulfilment: the second Advent will be the complete, the exhaustive accomplishment. And though we cannot expect to satisfy the minds of hasty or prejudiced readers on a subject requiring beyond most others humility and patience in its investigation, yet we believe it to be according to the sure method of Scripture to find thus a prophecy within a prophecy; a prophecy which has both a real though partial fulfilment, and also a fulfilment both real and perfect; the earlier accomplishment turning into a new ground of confidence in the realization of the later in its season. *Heaven and earth shall pass away: but my words shall not pass away.* Every prediction shall be not only verified but fulfilled; so that men shall say, in the retrospect of time, that *not one thing hath failed,* not one word has to be softened down or explained away: *hath He said, and shall He not do it? or hath He spoken, and shall He not make it good?* Do you suppose that when Jesus Christ foretold His own Advent in glorious majesty, He meant nothing more than a gradual improvement of the world in knowledge and obedience? nothing more than a future period of happiness and holiness, brought about by the diffusion of Gospel light or the reformation of national habits? O, He would not have spoken thus, or suffered His Apostles thus to teach, if it were not indeed one of those words of His which shall never pass away. Meanwhile, if we take Him for our Master, let us receive Him wholly. When He says, *Behold, I come quickly;* when He says, *The Son of Man shall come in His glory;* when he says, *Watch therefore; for ye know neither the day nor the hour wherein the Son of Man cometh;* let us take Him at His word, and not doubt. Let this holy season quicken in us the expectation of that coming, that coming of a Person, even of our Lord Jesus Christ Himself, which is as much the hope of the Church as it is the prediction of the unchangeable Word.

The words of Christ never pass away. So is it with His disclosures of God: so is it with His predictions of things to come: so is it also, yet more especially and practically, with His grave warnings and with His gracious promises.

3. The warnings of Christ are manifold. But they may be summed up in two; His warnings against sin and His warnings against carelessness.

(1) Great need have we to lay to heart that expression of the Epistle to the Hebrews, *Lest any of you be hardened through the deceitfulness of sin.* What a misleading, what a seducing, what a blinding power is

there in sin; that is, in our own sin. The sins of others look very black to us; we can all exclaim against them, we can all condemn them; we can all say, *Look at the folly, look at the perverseness, look at the infatuation, look at the madness of that drunkard, of that adulterer, of that dishonest, that profane, that wicked man; how is he in love with his own ruin; no remonstrance, no remorse, no punishment, seems to avail anything with him.* But when the case is our own, what palliations, what excuses, what reasons for wrongdoing, do we discover in a moment. And therefore I say that it is not without cause that Jesus Christ addresses so many of His warnings to definite sins; speaks to us so plainly, so by name, of those special sins to which we are liable; leaves us with no pretence for thinking that we can perhaps keep a small sin or two and yet be saved; forewarns us, on the contrary, that any one sin cherished—in other words, any one sin yielded to, allowed, suffered, in heart or in life—must exclude a man from God's kingdom; that, hard as it may appear, hard as it may be, to expel, to eradicate a sin, it is harder still (and the only alternative) to *dwell with everlasting burnings;* and expressly admonishes us, not only that our *sin will* most certainly *find us out*, but that it is the very battle-field of that great struggle, the issue of which, for every one of us, must be life or death.

Such is Christ's warning against sin. And of it too He says that His words never pass away. They are verified, over and over again, in every age and in every generation of man. There are those lying now on their deathbeds who are echoing their truth with cries and groans. They find that His words do not pass away.

The word which He spoke eighteen hundred years ago is judging them and passing sentence upon them here and now. And there are those still walking abroad on the face of the earth, with no mark set upon them in the sight of man, who are witnesses to themselves that Christ's words never die: they have found them true: they have obstinately done the thing which He hates, and they perceive that His brand is inwardly upon them, torturing and tormenting them before the time. God save us all, beloved brethren, if it be not too late, from this living death. Or if it be already upon us, may He, by the exercise of that almighty strength, that strength superhuman and absolutely infinite, which, however men in health and pride may scoff at miracle, is yet in sorrow and despair the one, the only hope of every man, pluck us yet from that burning, tearing off from us *the garment spotted by the flesh.*

(2) But some amongst us are saying in their hearts, *I thank God, I am a moral man: I thank God, I am not like many; not like this neighbour or that friend: I never yielded to the demon of sensuality or passion or lust: I can hear Christ's warning unabashed, unterrified. Be not highminded,* my friend, *but fear.* There is a warning against general carelessness as well as against definite sin. Nay, you must remember some of these unchangeable imperishable words of Christ, which make a self-satisfied, indifferent, unhumbled condition even worse than that of one who is tied and bound by sin. *The publicans and the harlots,* He said on one occasion, *go into the kingdom of God before you;* before the worldly-minded, before the proud, before the self-righteous Pharisee. The latest warning of this very

discourse is addressed to you. The very words which follow the text are these. *And take heed to yourselves, lest at any time your hearts be overcharged with surfeiting and drunkenness and cares of this life*, the distractions and anxieties even of a lawful calling, *and so that day come upon you unawares. They did eat, they drank, they bought, they sold, they planted, they builded; they married wives, they were given in marriage; until the day that the flood came and destroyed them all: even thus shall it be in the day when the Son of Man is revealed.* It was not a criminal course on which these had entered: the ordinary occupations of life, its natural enjoyments, were all that could be laid to their charge: and yet they were surprised and overwhelmed by the approach of Christ's Advent. Surely it is not in vain that this thought is presented to us yet once more today: do we not need it every one of us? Christ's warning against carelessness, even as before His warning against sin. *Watch ye therefore, and pray always*, thus He sums up the discourse for all alike, *that ye may be accounted worthy to escape all these things that shall come to pass, and to stand before the Son of Man.*

4. And if the warnings pass not away, but are ever sure, ever stedfast, so also is it, in the last place, with the promises. *Heaven and earth shall pass away: but my words shall not pass away.* Christ who came to reveal, and to predict, and to warn, came also to promise. In the name and by the authority of God Himself, He stood upon the earth, and made engagements. He pledged Himself, He pledged the veracity of God, to the fulfilment of certain promises. Have you thought of His words in this aspect? For example, He

said this: *I say unto you, Ask, and it shall be given you; seek, and ye shall find; knock, and it shall be opened unto you. If ye, being evil, know how to give good gifts unto your children, how much more shall your heavenly Father give the Holy Spirit to them that ask Him?* That was a promise, distinctly made: it was one of Christ's words here spoken of as never passing away even though heaven and earth should perish: Christ said, speaking in the name of God, *Ask, and ye shall have: God will give His Holy Spirit to them that ask Him.* My brethren, where should we be, and what, without that great fundamental promise? I know not that we could have learned it for certain elsewhere: and think what it is to be thus solemnly, thus positively assured of the power of prayer. So is it when Christ stood on that last, that great day of the feast, and said among the crowds flocking to the beautiful and instructive ceremonies of the Feast of Tabernacles, *If any man thirst, let him come unto me, and drink.* No other condition: only this: *Do you thirst? Are you full of unsatisfied longings for something which may really bring you peace? Are you vainly saying, Who will show me any good? My soul is thirsty, and has no water; hungry, and has no meat? Then come unto me; to me who am as near to you as your own soul; always hearing, knowing all things, yea, even the very secrets of your inmost being; come unto me, and drink: come unto me, and be satisfied. Him that cometh to me I will in no wise cast out.* And so it is, once again, when He cried aloud to all who would listen to Him, yea, even to those whom He had just been reproving for their ungodliness and unbelief, *Come unto me, all ye that labour and are heavy laden, and I will give you rest.* That also was a promise: and Christ's promises never pass away. Who can tell how often that promise has been fulfilled during these eighteen centuries? Who can tell how many disconsolate lives it has cheered, how many desolate hearts it has comforted, how many deathbeds it has illuminated with a hope full of immortality? Yes, there are those here present today, who can say of these promises of Christ that they have never yet passed away. They can accept the disclosures of Christ, they can trust the predictions of Christ, they tremble at the warnings of Christ, were it only because they have found the promises of Christ sure and stedfast, a light to lighten their darkness and a lamp to guide their way. From what they have experienced they can infer what they see not: from what they have received they can judge of what they wait for. And shall not others also be drawn by their testimony to make trial of the truth of Christ? Let them see whether they also, honestly calling, are not answered; whether they also, asking for the living water, are not in some measure and in due time satisfied. So shall this Advent season be a time of refreshing indeed in this place and in this congregation. And as you believe that all Christ's words are stedfast and may be relied upon, so believe that the word which bade us eat bread and drink wine in remembrance of Him *until His coming again*, was a word of truth and of life also. Gather round His holy Table with earnest and waiting hearts; ask Him, with reference to His own promise, to feed you personally with the living bread; even with that communication of Himself to your soul, in which even now is eternal life, and in the fruition of which through unending ages is the very joy and rest of heaven.

SECOND SUNDAY IN ADVENT,
December 7, 1862.

X.[1]

THE OFFENCE OF CHRIST.

St Matthew xi. 6.

And blessed is he, whosoever shall not be offended in me.

IT is a common saying, None of us know what we are, till we are tried. What strange revelations are sometimes made—I say not now to other men, but even to ourselves—of unsuspected workings of evil within, under strong and sharp temptation. Deeds or words or desires concerning which we should have been ready to say at other times, *Is thy servant a dog, that he should do or say or conceive this thing?* have been found not only possible but actual when the subtle enemy presents them to us at what is (for him and his devices) a fitting and a suitable time. And then we wake from the dream of self-righteousness and self-conceit, to find ourselves fallen indeed: happy if we do not draw from this humiliation an inference of absolute hopelessness and blank despair.

Now to this class of human experiences belong those sudden failures of faith, of which some sound and even eminent Christians have had to complain. The very

[1] This Sermon was preached also in the Chapel Royal, St James's Palace, on the 8th of February, 1863.

rock under their feet has seemed to be crumbling into fragments, or *sinking like lead in the mighty waters.* They have looked upward through the darkness, and seen no light. They have felt after their Saviour, and He was not; they have cried aloud to God, and He did not answer. This has been the case more especially in seasons of inaction and solitude. Work is a great bracer of faith: it proves that there is some faith, and it reacts upon the faith out of which it springs. And Christian companionship is a great comforter of faith: that in which others around me are surely believing seems to me the more credible and the more certain. But take away both these things, work and companionship; shut a man up in prison, and leave his mind (as we powerfully describe it) to prey upon itself; and see what his faith may dwindle to then. We find then that a Christian in this life is not soul only, but body also: the animal spirits have a powerful influence upon the action if not upon the existence of grace: and one of the strongest proofs of the Fall, as well as one of the most humbling mementos of the need of patience, is found in the fact that the withdrawal of all external influences is no aid to the inward condition: *from within, out of the heart of man,* at such times more especially, *proceed evil thoughts;* thoughts, if nothing worse, of doubt, of faithlessness, of unbelief; thoughts which call in question *things most surely believed,* and demand an unreasonable evidence of truths which God has revealed.

To such causes I would trace the enquiry of John the Baptist recorded in this day's Gospel. In days of vigour and activity he had borne a noble and self-denying testimony to the person and mission of the

Saviour. Again and again he might himself have assumed Christ's position: he was plied with the question, *Art thou the Christ?* and he had stedfastly answered in the negative. He had pointed to Jesus as the Lamb of God; had declared that he was himself but *a voice crying in the wilderness, Prepare His way;* and when his own disciples would have sown the seeds of jealousy between the messenger and the Master, he was firm and resolute in the reply, *He must increase, but I must decrease: He that hath the bride is the bridegroom; but the friend of the bridegroom, who standeth and heareth him, rejoiceth greatly because of the bridegroom's voice: this my joy therefore is fulfilled.* And yet here we find him sending to ask whether Jesus is indeed *He that should come*, the promised Saviour of Israel and of man.

The key of the difficulty is in his circumstances. John was now in prison; soon to exchange confinement for martyrdom; at present lying, for he knew not how long, under the arbitrary sentence of a wicked and tyrannical king. I can suppose that doubts visited him, even him, in that solitude, in that inaction. He heard indeed of Christ's works; the fame of these reached him in the prison: but there was much to surprise him in the resolute adherence on the part of Jesus to a position of humility and comparative privacy: John may have shared the common feeling of his countrymen, *If Thou do these things*, if Thou claim by Thy mighty works to be the Messiah, the Son of God, *show Thyself to the world.* At all events, even if doubtful and unbelieving thoughts did not thus embody themselves within, there was a wish (can we call it an unnatural wish?) for a little more light, a little more certainty, a little more explanation of motives, and reconciliation of acts with claims. Who cannot enter into it? Can we not all hear him saying, *I know there can be no mistake and no illusion: He that sent me to baptize with water, the same said unto me, Upon whom thou shalt see the Spirit descending, and remaining on Him, the same is He which baptizeth with the Holy Ghost; and I saw, and bare record that this is the Son of God: and yet, and yet, I could like another proof of it; I could be the happier and the better for one more sign, for one more assurance: go, my friends, visit Him for me; ask of Him yet a token of His Messiahship; tell Him that His poor kinsman after the flesh, His witness and His forerunner, now lying in prison for the testimony of the truth, and vexed with many a trying thought in his solitude and his inactivity, would fain hear one more answer, be it ever so brief, to the great, the all-important question, Art Thou indeed He that should come, or must we look still onward, onward still, for one who shall do greater deeds, speak wiser words, or live a holier life than Thou?*

Thus we take the enquiry literally, and yet do not press it too far into its consequences. We read it as John's question for himself, and not only as his question for the satisfaction of his disciples. And yet we do not infer from it more than the natural longing of a faithful yet depressed man for an additional ray of the light of God's truth. We feel with him in that longing: we can ourselves, with all our hearts, echo that prayer.

And it is instructive, and comforting too, to observe how Jesus answered it. He did not, as some modern teachers using His name might have done, repel the enquiry as a sin. He did not reprove the message and let the messengers return unanswered. No: there was the same compassionate heart, the same wise mind, the same divine *goodness and forbearance and longsuffering*, which at a later time, under circumstances widely different, allowed a doubting Apostle to enjoy the very proof which he demanded, and yet, in the act of doing so, pronounced a double blessing upon those who rest satisfied with that evidence which God deems sufficient, and are contented, by God's grace, even without seeing, to believe.

St Luke tells us that *in that same hour He cured many of their infirmities and plagues and of evil spirits; and unto many that were blind He gave sight.* And then, having suspended His answer to John's question until He had furnished this special evidence to his messengers, *then Jesus answering said unto them, Go your way, and tell John what things ye have seen and heard.* Our Lord well knew and tenderly considered the case to which He was ministering. If the messengers could return and say to their master, *Not only did we hear on all hands marvellous accounts of His healing power, but we ourselves saw Him exercise it; we saw Him heal many persons of painful and terrible diseases; we saw Him give sight to the blind, and power of motion to the paralytic; we heard ourselves the gracious words which proceed daily out of His mouth, and noticed how the poor flocked around Him to listen;* if this might be their report, not a tale of hearsay, but the evidence of ocular proof, He knew that it would carry conviction with it: the poor prisoner would listen, and feel his hope revive and his heart expand with reassurance; he would wait the appointed time in patience, and receive the martyr's crown with thankfulness.

Such, my brethren, were the signs of His Messiahship which our Master Himself deemed then the most convincing. We live in an age which scoffs at miracle. And we are aware that the cogency of the argument from power is necessarily weakened by distance. Our Lord Himself, no doubt, felt this, when He vouchsafed to John's disciples a present proof, that they might carry it home to their master in all its life and freshness. The record of miracles, read in a book eighteen hundred years afterwards, is a less lively evidence than the sight of their accomplishment at the time. And we should be most unthankful if we did not remember that God has given to us of this age evidences of the truth of the Gospel which the first hearers of it necessarily lacked. Evidences of its influence upon the lives and deaths of true believers through many centuries are now abundant and notorious where in the first age of all they were necessarily wanting. The whole history of Christianity was then a page unread, unwritten. And we should be doing also a great dishonour to the Gospel if we denied that it does make its appeal to the reason and to the conscience and to the heart of man. If it really contradicted or outraged any one of these, it would not be a Gospel. But when men make this last the whole of the Christian evidence; when they say, *Judge of Christ's words and of Christ's history entirely by your own feeling; what does not satisfy your understanding, treat as if it were not; take what you will, and leave what you will, and if you only do it honestly, you will be right;* then we must answer, You are dissociating things which God has joined together; power and wisdom and goodness are His three seals; no one of these is complete without the others; your reason needs each one of these for its satisfaction; and when Jesus Himself said to the messengers of John, *Go and show John again those things which ye do hear and see*, He spoke as much according to the exigencies of all time as for the satisfaction of the time then present.

And well indeed might He add, in the words of the text itself, *And blessed is he, whosoever shall not be offended in me*. To be *offended*, in the Scripture sense of the term, is to be staggered, to be tripped up, to be caused to stumble and fall, by some obstacle lying in the way of our steps. Especially is it applied to the work of temptation or sin in overthrowing the constancy or destroying the consistency of one of Christ's disciples. Thus it is written, *Woe unto the world because of offences; for it must needs be that offences come: but woe to that man by whom the offence cometh.* In something of the same sense our Lord here speaks of the blessedness of that man who allows nothing, no impediment, no stumblingblock, of mind or life, to shake the stedfastness of his faith in Him. *Blessed is he, whosoever shall not be offended*, caused to stumble, *in me*, in the case of me, of my doctrine, or my person, or my demands. As if He had said, *You see by this example how tender a plant is grace in man's heart: my own faithful friend, my own honoured herald, craves some new or some further assurance of my being that which he himself has boldly proclaimed me: how must it be with others? How many are the obstacles to a true, a constant, and a consistent faith. Happy is he, blessed for time and for eternity, who so assures himself of my credentials and of my evidences, that he can run with patience to the very end the race set before him, and enter at last, loved and loving, into the very rest and joy of his Lord.*

Blessed is he, whosoever shall not be offended in me. There was one principal cause in those days, and there is one principal cause in these days, of men being offended in Jesus Christ.

1. In those days the chief hindrance to faith was the lowliness of Christ's position. The Old Testament Scriptures seemed to speak of a Prince and a Conqueror; of One who should make Jerusalem the pride of the earth, and exalt her people to universal dominion. So they read them. And having once formed this conception of *Him that should come*, they gave no heed to other declarations of the same holy Book, which as plainly indicated a previous humility and suffering. *Ought not Christ*, our Saviour asked, appealing to their own Scriptures, *to have suffered these things and to enter into His glory?* That is, do not the *holy men of old, speaking as they were moved by the Holy Ghost*, evidently predict a suffering as well as a glorified Messiah? Is not this the very burden of their writings, *Suffering first, then glory?* But they did not so read them. Like us, their successors in the infirmities of nature as well as in the privileges of grace, they were too apt to read the Bible with a prejudgment; settling first what it ought to say, and then making it say that and that only. Thus, when Christ came, He *stood among them*, as John the Baptist expressed it, and they *knew Him not*. O the force of prejudice; its power, and its peril! Christ Himself stood there among them, and they knew Him not.

They were *offended in Him*. He ought to have been this; and not being this, they would none of Him. He was a Man: they knew His father and His mother; His sisters, they said, and His brothers: they could tell whence He was; from remote Galilee, from despised Nazareth: all this was wrong—how could this be the Christ? Where was His royal robe? where His victorious banner? where the magnificent prospects of the house and throne of David? They were offended in Him. It was a very natural prepossession; but, like many other things called natural, it was the opposite of spiritual, it was the opposite of true.

Now I do not say that there is no danger in these times of a precisely similar kind of offence. There are many in these times, as in those, who can see and even admire *the Man Christ Jesus*, but who cannot rise from that contemplation to the true faith of the Son of God Most High. They talk of the beauty of His character, of the wisdom of His doctrine, of the holiness of His life: but they cannot believe in His proper Incarnation, His proper Divinity, or His proper glory. Are there any such amongst us? God give them a better mind: a truer discernment of things that differ; a juster because a higher estimate of their Lord and their God.

2. But when we speak of the peculiar danger of these times, in reference to the offence of Christ, we shall think less of His lowliness than of another characteristic, the holiness of Christ. For one man amongst us who rejects Christ (in His true character) because he cannot understand how a Man could also be very God, a thousand probably refuse His salvation because He is

too strict for them in His example and in His enforcement of holiness. In short, sin is the stumblingblock, rather than incredulity. There is an elevation, and a purity, and a practical character, in Christ's teaching, which keeps off from Him those who love and will retain their sin. It is very sad to see men who so evidently want Christ, and who have so much that should make Christ attractive to them, yet standing aloof from Him because of that one little subtle bosom sin which must go if He comes. Yes, if we could only make up our minds to part with that; that one evil temper, that one sinful indulgence, that one harmful miserable deadly lust; how happy should we be: how should we welcome Jesus Christ; how should we fall down before Him, and pray Him to let us be with Him. How light would the heart then be, how sweet the home, how bright the life. How should we become conscious of a new joy; the joy as of a first love, of a new existence. But there it is: it is there, and we cannot dispossess it: we have found by experience how it has sometimes seemed to go, and come back again; how it has relaxed its hold, and then tightened it; so that now, when it takes leave, we can see it behind the door, mocking our freedom, watching for its return: and we are too sincere, too candid, too honest, to come to Christ with pretences, with promises not to be kept, vows sure to be broken: and thus it comes to pass that we dally, all our life long, with a salvation which would be our happiness and our heaven, because Christ is holy and we are unholy, because if Christ would save He must also cleanse, and because we cannot answer in the affirmative that one heart-searching preliminary question, *When Jesus saw him lie, and knew that he had been now a long time in that case, He saith unto him, Wilt thou be made whole?* Thus we also, like the Jews of old, though for a different reason, are *offended in Him.* God of His infinite mercy roll away this stone from the path of some of us today, make us *willing in the day of His power,* and fulfil in us this word of gracious benediction, *And blessed is he, whosoever shall not be offended in me.*

Blessed is he. Why this earnest, this emphatic benediction? Does it not tell of the tenderness of Christ, of His consideration for human weakness, of His appreciation of human difficulty? Does it not say this to us? *I know that faith is not easy: I know that it is far easier to walk by sight than by faith: I know that the hindrances to faith are many, and the objections to the Gospel neither few in number nor light in weight. The days will come when men born in a Christian land and nurtured amidst Gospel light will count themselves learned in proportion as they are unbelieving, and make rational another term for sceptical. And many more will listen to these disputants without understanding them; will imitate the manner and adopt the tone of the caviller, ignorant, all the time, of the grounds on which he proceeds, and incapable of trying aright the assumptions which he parades. Men will accept the assertion, easily made and difficult to be refuted, yet, like every such assertion, demanding care and watchfulness in its acceptance, that science contradicts the Bible; when perhaps it is their ignorance of science which makes the statement formidable, and when oftentimes the most truly scientific man has also been the most believing. Yet none the less will the assertion be made, repeated, and entertained; none the less will it shake the resolution of the feeble, and keep out of many hearts which are athirst for it the healing and the comfort and the satisfaction of the Gospel. All this I know: and therefore I say, Blessed is he, whosoever shall not be offended in me. Blessed, because it is easy to be offended; because reasons for offence lie everywhere on the surface, and because it needs a wise and experienced judgment to separate between the precious and the vile. Blessed, because many are they who judge hastily and judge timidly and judge presumptuously, and few by comparison they who search long, dig deep, and cleave immoveably to the truth once found. Blessed, because in that search not the reason only, but the heart also; not the cold and scoffing intellect, but the soul with its wants and its aspirations, its instincts and its intuitions; is the appointed guide, the sure companion; and because many men will seek to dissever what God has joined, and to take with them in the discovery of truth only one half, and the worse half, of that immortal being to which God has given the responsibilities of life. Blessed, above all, because he who findeth me findeth life, and they who gather not with me must for ever scatter.*

Therefore He with whom we have to do shows in this, as in all things, that He both knows us well and can feel for us tenderly. Be not ye *shaken in mind, nor be troubled;* but *cleave to Him with purpose of heart.* Leave Him not till you have found a better: leave Him not till some one else can tell you *words of eternal life.* Then go: then part with Christ: but till then part not with that one *anchor of the soul, sure and stedfast,* which alone even professes to *enter into that within the veil.* So holding fast by Christ, you will find in due season that you have held by One who is as much the Truth as the Life; One who made and therefore can satisfy the understanding, as much as He made and can therefore fill the soul. *What I do thou knowest not now, but thou shalt know hereafter:* and if in anything you be still in darkness, *God shall reveal even this unto you.* Blessed in the end will he be, and he only, who has not suffered himself to be offended in Christ.

THIRD SUNDAY IN ADVENT,
December 14, 1862.

XI.

THE VOICE CRYING IN THE WILDERNESS.

John i. 23.

I am the voice of one crying in the wilderness, Make straight the way of the Lord.

WE read last Sunday of the Baptist in his weakness: today we read of the Baptist in his strength. Like Elijah in whose *spirit and power* he came, he had his season of depression. Elijah fled into the wilderness, in the reaction (as it were) of his great triumph on Mount Carmel, and complained of his desertion; said that he was *left alone* in God's service, and even *requested for himself that he might die:* and God was pleased to reassure him by an appropriate word of comfort and by a wholesome commission of duty. The Baptist, by no fault of his own, was in a condition, at the close of life, of solitude and inactivity: he was a prisoner, soon to be a martyr, *for the testimony of the truth:* and in that position, though we read not that his faith actually deserted him, we read at least that he desired a new token, a sealing evidence, of its reasonableness and of its truth.

But if we would judge a man justly, we must look at him in his health and in his activity. That is what this day's Gospel enables us to do with regard to John. It sets before us in few words both the messenger and the message; both the herald and his proclamation. And each of these two things will have a lesson for us, which may God give us all grace to lay well to heart.

The report of John's ministry caused no little anxiety in Jerusalem. Those who then *sat in Moses' seat* could not leave unexamined so remarkable a mission. A solemn deputation was sent to interrogate him. Was it possible that in this extraordinary man they were to recognize the Messiah Himself? The language of Prophecy seemed to point, however obscurely, to this time, or about this time, as the period of His Advent: and there was much assuredly in the person, and much in the doctrine, and much in the excitement occasioned by both, to make it at least an open question whether perhaps this might not be indeed the very Deliverer of whose arrival all Israel, and in a certain sense all the world, was at this time in a mingled state of desire and apprehension.

But to this enquiry the Baptist gave a simple and a negative answer. He might no doubt have assumed to himself, and borne without exposure, the title thus suggested. In some respects he was more what the people looked for in their Messiah than Jesus Himself. At all events the field was open, and there was none as yet to contest it. But it was one great feature of that holy character, that the Baptist *constantly spoke the truth.* He would never take to himself anything that was not his due. *A man can receive nothing, except it be given him from heaven. He confessed, and denied not, but confessed, I am not the Christ. What then? Elias?*

that great prophet himself, who was once taken up from earth without dying? No: *I am not he:* sent perhaps in his spirit, and to do in this age a similar work to his; but not the very man, as you expect him, come back in person to the earth. *Art thou* then *the Prophet?* He of whom Moses spoke when he said, *A prophet shall the Lord your God raise up unto you of your brethren: Him shall ye hear?* No: that prediction spoke of the Messiah Himself; and again I tell you, I am not He.

Not the Christ; not Elijah; not the Prophet: *who* then *art thou?* We must carry back an answer: *what sayest thou of thyself?*

The true bold man is as ready to speak the truth in positives as in negatives. He had told them what he was not: now let them hear what he is. *He said, I am the voice of one crying in the wilderness, Make straight the way of the Lord, as said the prophet Esaias.*

My brethren, this is a day of Ordinations throughout the Christian world. One of your own Ministers is today to receive a step in the sacred profession, from the Deaconship to the Priesthood. And two others, of those whom you have seen for some months going in and out among you in this place in preparation for Holy Orders, are this day receiving their first Ordination, while our hearts are much with them. Therefore I cannot think it unseasonable, or uninteresting to any of you, to reflect a little upon the topic now before us; that of the Christian messenger and his message, as set before us in the case of St John the Baptist.

1. And first, what does he say of himself? What is he? a great man, exalted above his brethren, whom

all are to look up to, and all to admire and to reverence?

(1) *He said, I am a voice.* As much as to say, *You are not to think at all about me: who I am, is no matter to you: except indeed that I must watch and pray always lest any word or act of mine give occasion to the enemies of the Lord to blaspheme: beyond this, beyond anything that I must take heed to be or not to be as your example, you are not to regard, you are not to think of me: I am a voice.*

So you see, my brethren, there is a sound in your ears, of which we are but the instruments. If that sound be true; in other words, if God sends it; you will not be absolved from its binding force by any inadequateness or by any unworthiness of those who utter it. For his own admonition, the minister does well to say to himself, *I am a man; I live before my people; my example is one which many will satisfy themselves with following; if they are as good as I am, in speech and act, they will count themselves safe: and therefore it is a very serious, a very solemn, a very momentous thing, for them as well as for myself, what I am:* but, when he addresses himself to his people; when he thinks of his ministry; when he ponders the grave issues which depend upon its exercise; he can scarcely do better than take up the words of his Lord's own forerunner, and say, *Do you ask what I am? I am a voice.* It is the answer of humility, and it is the answer of truth. *Think not of me, but think of my message. If I had not a message, I should be nothing. I am a voice, and nothing besides.*

(2) But again, I am the voice *of one crying.* The

word denotes crying aloud, calling out, vociferating. The voice of God within, the voice in which He speaks in conscience, in conviction, in His Holy Spirit, is *a still small voice:* man cannot use that voice; it is God's own; it is the secret voice in which He communicates with a man's soul; it may be quickened instrumentally, made persuasive, made powerful, by the other; but itself is beyond our use: *no man may deliver his brother*, and no man can borrow, for his brother's deliverance, the still small voice of God Himself. *I am the voice of one crying aloud, of one shouting, in the wilderness.* My brethren, the messenger of God must not be a timid man. He ought to be humble: if he is God's messenger, he will be humble: but he ought not to be timid. He ought to be convinced of the truth, and he ought to be convinced of the importance, of his own message; and then he will rise out of himself, out of all thought of misplaced modesty and misgiving and diffidence, just while he delivers it. In the pulpit, if nowhere else, he must speak with authority. His *trumpet* must *give* no *uncertain sound.* He must obey the direction of the same Prophet Esaias, *Cry aloud, spare not, lift up thy voice like a trumpet, and show my people their transgressions, and the house of Jacob their sins.*

(3) Once more, I am the voice of one crying *in the wilderness.* St John the Baptist was this literally. *The word of God came unto John the son of Zacharias in the wilderness. John did baptize in the wilderness. In those days came John the Baptist, preaching in the wilderness of Judea.* The stern strong call of his ministry was unsuitable to the haunts and homes of business or of pleasure. If he was to make such a call audible, he

must summon men to him: he must take them apart to listen to him. A total change of life, an entire revulsion of feeling, a true and deep repentance for all that we have done and for all that we are, can scarcely be wrought in any man save in a wilderness: he must find or he must make for himself a seclusion and a solitude to learn it. We all know how great is the advantage which a physician derives, in the treatment of a patient, from having him under his own roof, where he can not only give his orders, but see them obeyed; where he can attend at once to diet and to medicine, watch the effect of each, apart from all counteracting influences, and modify or vary them at his discretion. Just so it was with the Baptist in his wilderness of Judea. There he had the whole man with him; not a few fragments only of his attention, but the whole of it: there without let or hindrance he could observe each symptom of the spiritual case, and try this or that remedy according to the need of each.

The minister of God, my brethren, in these days, cannot literally speak to you in a wilderness. You are all surrounded by a thousand cares and interests, in the midst of which, if at all, you must hear the voice of God. It is only when distress or sickness enters a house, that the voice can sound (in any sense) in the desert; and even then, so subtle is the enemy of our souls, so complicated the machinery of human thought, so difficult, alas, at all times the work of salvation, that no man is ever stripped quite bare of adjuncts and circumstances, or left without any sound whatever in his ears save that of conscience and the Gospel. In this world of busy interests and abounding temptations lies the daily life of each one of us. In it, if anywhere, we must hear and we must obey the call of God. But, that we may do this effectually, every one of us every day must seek the wilderness. Privacy at certain times, for morning and evening prayer, for a few moments at least of reflection and meditation, is the want, is the necessity, of each one of us: and if we cannot get it otherwise, let us see that at least we get it here, in God's house: why not (very many of us) each day of the week, in that quiet service which is here daily offered? But at all events on this holy day, this weekly festival of Creation and of Redemption, this day which is God's special gift to the souls as well as the bodies of His sinful creatures, let us come together with that deep reverence, that intense devotion, that *hungering and thirsting after righteousness*, which of itself secures as well as indicates the presence of God, and makes a privacy for the soul even amidst the thronging multitude of God's worshippers. *I am the voice—of one crying—in the wilderness.*

2. And now what does the voice cry? This being the messenger, what is the message? The text answers the question. *Make straight the way of the Lord.*

(1) *The Lord* here is God Himself. The words are quoted from the 40th chapter of the Prophecy of Isaiah: and there you will observe, the capital letters indicate that *the Lord* means Jehovah, the High and Holy One Himself, God the Father. It is thus also in the parallel prophecy of Malachi. *Behold, I will send my messenger, and he shall prepare the way before me: and the Lord, whom ye seek, shall suddenly come to His temple, even the messenger of the covenant, whom ye delight in: behold, He*

shall come, saith the Lord of Hosts. The messenger prepares the way before God Himself, *the Lord of hosts;* and then the Person who actually comes is *the Lord whom ye seek*, the Lord Jesus Christ, in whom alone God reveals Himself to man. *Make straight the way of Jehovah: and* then *the Lord* Jesus Christ *shall come.*

(2) In the next place, *the way of the Lord.* That is, in so many words, to say, *The Lord, God Himself, is coming.* That is a frequent description of God, in the Book of Revelation more particularly: *Grace be unto you and peace from Him which is and which was and which is to come; Him that cometh.* I beg you to observe that it is a title of God, of the Father. God Himself is known and revealed to us in Christ as *He that cometh.* Is it not calculated to give a very solemn impression of what is before us all? *The Lord Himself,* God Almighty, *cometh out of His place, to punish the inhabitants of the earth for their iniquity.* Do not think to escape, O sinner, whosoever thou art, that hardenest thyself in thy sin. Not the despised Saviour only, but God Himself, is coming: that is our Advent call to you.

(3) Well then, *make straight the way of the Lord.* If a great Conqueror or mighty Sovereign was approaching at the head of his armies, through uncleared forests or across rugged mountains and deep rocky dells, a multitude of men would precede him, to cut or hew the way. There must be no delay, and there must be no obstacle, when and where he comes. Now that is what the voice cries, with reference to God's Advent. *Make straight the way. Every valley must be filled up, and every mountain and hill must be brought low,*

and the crooked must be made straight, and the rough places plain. Whichever of God's comings we speak of; whether the one which John the Baptist personally heralded, the coming of Christ as at this season *in great humility;* or the coming of God to the individual soul in this life through Jesus Christ by the Holy Spirit; or the glorious Advent for which we are still looking, when *the dead shall be raised incorruptible,* and *all nations shall be gathered* for judgment before the *great white throne;* whichever of these Advents be our subject, the cry of the voice is still the same, *Make straight the way.* And observe, it is to men that it calls: it is not to the preacher, it is not to the Church collectively, it is to individual men: *Make ye straight,* all and each of you, *the way of God.* He is coming: you are His pioneers: it is your business to remove obstacles, to rectify crookednesses, and thus, in each case, to straighten the way, that, when God comes, He may find all smooth, and all direct. Now what does this say to us, when we try to turn the charge from figure into reality? *Make straight the way of God.* It is plain that it is with ourselves that the work must begin; in ourselves that the call must be obeyed.

i. And this, first, by cultivating sincerity. *Straight* is the opposite of *crooked.* We must harbour no hypocrisy and no guile. We must deal plainly and truly with our own hearts. We must say to ourselves, *If what I hear at Church is true—and I suspect it is—then I must not hear only, but do. If Christ is really coming again, or if Christ did come once, I must live accordingly: it cannot be right, it cannot be safe, to say one thing at Church, and do another and an opposite thing at home.*

Now let me see what there is in my conduct which wants altering. Is there anything wrong in my language, in my heart, in my morals? Is my house ready for Christ's Advent? Is mine a family which remembers God and orders itself by God's rule? At any cost, at any risk, I must make all straight: my profession and my practice must be at one: I must not go on calling Christ my Lord, and not doing the things which He says. The least I can do is to be sincere; to act up to my light; to have no dark places in my heart, and no crooked by-paths in my life.

ii. Again, we must not only cultivate sincerity; which, if it stood alone, might perhaps be done by giving up all Christian profession, and lowering our belief to the level of our practice; but also we must diligently follow after repentance. John the Baptist, our Church Collect says, *was sent to prepare the way of our Saviour by preaching of repentance.* And so it is still. Repentance is as much the preparation for the second as for the first Advent of Christ. Repentance, you know, is a change of mind. It is a new mind towards sin and towards God. It is not remorse, it is not depression, it is not sorrow or crying; it is a changed mind. Perhaps we have thought that it must be a gloomy thing: we think of a penitent as of one who has done with happiness, and is constantly lashing himself for his past sins. Learn a better lesson, my friends, lest you be blind for ever to your truest joy. Repentance is the return of the exile to the land of his birth and the home of his father. Repentance is the recovery from long sickness; the revival from a living death. Repentance is the recovery of sight and hearing, of touch and taste, by one who has long been deprived of every faculty and every sense. Repentance is the being set free to be happy; the being introduced into enjoyments before unknown, and invested with capacities hitherto torpid and spell-bound. But why use many words in describing that which must be felt if it is to be known? Arise, thou desolate and outcast, arise and go to thy Father, and thou shalt know it. *Awake, thou that sleepest*, ask Christ to *give thee light*, and thou shalt know it. Let this Advent, let this Christmas, be to you, be to all of us, by God's grace, the beginning indeed of a new year, even of *the acceptable year of the Lord*. The voice crying in the wilderness says, *Make straight the way of God*. He is coming, coming quickly: prepare His way. Seek Him now by prayer; *know Him now by faith;* serve Him now with diligence and watchfulness: and thou shalt *be found of Him in peace*. O cast out, while yet there is time, the abominable thing which He hateth; the vile affection, the sinful lust, the hateful passion, against which His presence is *a consuming fire;* lest, when He comes, thou perish with it. Let the light of His spiritual coming so shine within thee as a fire to cleanse, to cheer, and to enlighten, that thou mayest see without terror the rising of that Advent day which shall disclose *the hidden things of darkness*, and *burn up on every side the enemies of God*. *Christ came* first *not to judge but to save:* know Him now as thy Saviour, and then it shall be thy one comfort, that He and none else is the Judge.

FOURTH SUNDAY IN ADVENT,
December 21, 1862.

XII.

THE GRACE OF MEDITATION.

Luke ii. 19.

But Mary kept all these things, and pondered them in her heart.

IT is no part of the object of Holy Scripture to attract either wonder or adoration to the person of our Lord's mother. *Highly favoured, blessed among women*, in being made the link of connection between the Deity and the humanity of Christ, she is yet never presented to us as herself more than human, or invested with anything of awe or of mystery beyond what is inseparable from the whole idea of the Incarnation of the blessed and eternal Word of God. When once her sacred office was accomplished, she stepped back into the rank of holy and pious women, and became only so far an object of attention to the Church below as she exhibited in spirit and conduct an example for their imitation. When on one occasion, at the opening of our Lord's ministry, she suggested to Him, by implication at least, the propriety of His interposition, she was reminded by Him in terms grave and decisive that in the affairs of His Messiahship His only prompting was from above, and that no earthly tie—not even that nearest of all ties, which He had so tenderly cherished through thirty years of domestic privacy—could be recognized as any plea for seeking to regulate the manifestation of His glory. And when at the end of all, after those bitter days of His last mortal suffering, and those strangely exciting scenes which followed His Resurrection, she is shown to us for one moment before she disappears for ever from the page of Inspiration, it is but as one among the *hundred and twenty* worshippers in that upper room in Jerusalem which was the cradle of the Church of all lands and all times: *these all continued with one accord in prayer and supplication, with the women, and Mary the mother of Jesus, and with His brethren.* How needful was this reticence of God's Word concerning the Lord's mother, how needful alike the absence of exaltation and the presence even of rebuke, the later history of the Church has well testified. If out of such materials the Church of a large part of Christendom has contrived, by a vague theory of developement, to frame a system of divine honour for the human mother of the Saviour, what might not have been the prevalence and the exaggeration of such an error, how could even we ourselves have hoped to escape it, if the Word of God had so dwelt upon her position or her virtues as even to appear to give the weight of its authority to a doctrine so fanciful yet so attractive?

But we must not, from a fear of deifying the Lord's mother, of exalting her *above what is written* and above what is true, fall into the opposite error of setting aside or treading underfoot her bright example. This holy season appears especially suitable to the contemplation of those graces with which it pleased God by His Holy Spirit to equip and adorn her for the blessed office of bringing into the world of man the only-begotten and eternal Son of God. Most of all to Christian women, yet not to them only, would we commend, in God's name, the study of this holy character.

We can scarcely fail to see that the text itself, taken from this day's Gospel, gives more than a mere feature of that character; that it presents to us that which was the main, the distinctive quality, of her of whom it speaks, that which made her so appropriate a type of the perfection of woman, and therefore so suitable a parent of Him who came to elevate and to ennoble that half of our race, while He redeemed and renewed and saved the whole. *But Mary kept all these things, and pondered them in her heart.*

Kept, and *pondered*: these are the two parts of the description. We can understand both of them.

How marvellous had been to her the experience of that one year. Think of the terms of the Annunciation itself. *The Angel said unto her, Fear not, Mary: for thou hast found favour with God. And, behold, thou shalt bring forth a son, and shalt call his name JESUS; He shall be great, and shall be called the Son of the Highest: and the Lord God shall give unto Him the throne of His father David: and He shall reign over the house of Jacob for ever, and of His kingdom there shall be no end. The Holy Ghost shall come upon thee, and the power of the Highest shall overshadow thee: therefore also that holy thing which shall be born of thee shall be called the Son of God.* And then, as the time drew on, and at a distance from home she was delivered of the promised Son; and, as He lay a helpless child in the manger *because there was no room for them in the inn*, they were visited by shepherds, reporting the angelic announcement of that *great joy* which a Saviour's birth was to bring *to all people*, and the heavenly song which followed it, *Glory to God in the highest, and on earth peace, good will toward men;* well can we understand that she, His blessed and honoured mother, kept all these sayings in her heart; lost not the remembrance by day or by night, but treasured it in her inmost soul as that which could not pass nor be forgotten.

And as she kept, so also she pondered. The word denotes that putting together, that process of combining and harmonizing, which is a first condition of all true knowledge. Much indeed was there in her case which needed such harmonizing. Great and growing must have been the wonder with which she contemplated her destiny. Who and what was she, that this mysterious connection should be given to her with divine things, with a Divine Person? And who indeed was He? Could it be that in this little child there was the presence not of man but of God? that in this little child she held Him who *made the worlds*, and who came to remake that world which had lost and destroyed itself by sin? How must she have been first startled and then comforted by those superhuman utterances which sometimes came forth from One usually so natural and always so obedient. What a process of combining, of harmonizing the seen and the unseen, the human form and the Divine Spirit, must have been going on in her secret heart from His birth onward; a process not ended when His ministry began, but still exercised while she stood by His cross and communed with Him after He was risen. When we think of it our only wonder is, not that she long pondered, but that she ever believed. The very possession of the earthly presence must have impeded rather than facilitated the realization of the heavenly.

My brethren, the words are to us not historical only, telling us what she did, but practical also, telling us what we have to do.

There are many things from which we all suffer; many causes which contribute to our slowness and backwardness in the race of eternal life. There is the solicitation of things that are seen, ever drawing us aside both from faith and duty. There is *the sin which doth so easily beset us;* that particular form of evil, whatever it be, which happens from the constitution of our nature to be for us the most powerful and the most seductive. Of these things we have often to speak with you: from these things we derive our chief difficulties and our bitterest sorrows. But I know not whether even these hindrances and these distresses may not be traced up to a higher and more fundamental. My brethren, we do not follow the example here set before us: we do not *keep all these things*, and we do not *ponder them in our heart*.

Of late we have been called to reflect upon those very things which were the subject of her meditation. We have been keeping the feast of the Nativity, recalling the scenes of our Saviour's first Advent, when He *took upon Himself the form of a creature, and was made in the likeness of men.* If these events were full of significance ever, they are so still. If Mary felt that to have any part in such transactions was an honour and a blessing beyond thought or word, that was because the transactions themselves were the most momentous that were ever wrought on earth, and involved consequences absolutely infinite in the eternity beyond.

But we need not limit too closely the things or the sayings to which we would apply, in our case, the language of the text. We see in its full compass the whole of God's Revelation: we look on, as Mary could not then, from Bethlehem to Calvary, from the cradle to the cross and to the crown. All God's dealings with us, as a race, and as individuals, are presented to our view together. On this first Sunday of a New Year we can review each one for himself his own little history; can take account both of the way by which, and of the point to which, we have been led by God's Providence in life's journey; can judge of that which is, and of that which has been, and (to a certain extent) also of that which shall be; can estimate our spiritual condition, and infer from it both the grounds of hope and the grounds of fear which it suggests to us for the great future. My brethren, have we entered at all, during this season, into such reckonings? or have we surrendered ourselves, without reflection, without apprehension, to the enjoyments, few or many, which the season has brought with it, and never listened to the warning voice accompanying them, *Know thou that for all these things God will bring thee into judgment?* Till we have done this, the example here proposed can scarcely be applicable: we must first feel these things, before we can either keep them or ponder.

This age, like every age, has its special dangers, for those who are, and for those who are not, in some sense Christians indeed. Few will deny that one peculiar risk of our age, for all who live in it, is the temptation to neglect reflection. Everything is in motion: there is no rest for any man but in the grave. How different from the still tranquil life of the villages or the hillsides of Palestine. How different even now the whirl and the turmoil of European excitement from the stagnant sameness and indolent apathy of the East. How opposite the spiritual dangers resulting from each. If the one is in peril of a dreamy inaction, the other runs an equal risk of a giddy and unreflecting dissipation. In the latter peril our lot lies: against it our chief struggle must direct itself. We are in danger of hearing and reading and doing many things, and of thinking and reflecting and judging little. We are in danger of listening to many Sermons, and of joining in many Services, without carrying away with us the lessons or the fruits of any. We are in danger of dissipating even religious thoughts, of drowning the very voice of conscience, in the multitude of our professions and the variety of our doings. When God works a conviction in us, we often satisfy its demand by adding another attendance at Church or another religious reading at home, without ever drawing nearer to Him *whom to know*, not to hear about, *is eternal life*. If our presence here is regular, if our family prayer is duly observed, if we give of our superfluity to feed the poor, if we now and then run hither or thither on some errand of charitable ministration, we think that all must be well with us: and yet, my brethren, that regular worshipper, that giver of alms, that respectable and decent liver, may not have all the time one spark of true piety, which is true communion with God, in his whole being;

XII.] *The Grace of Meditation.* 371

he may *have a name to live, and be dead:* and why so? Because the growth of the seed in him is all upward; because he *has no root in himself;* because he has not yet chosen and prized the *one thing needful;* because, whatever he may seem and whatever he may profess, he does not really *keep all these things, and ponder them in his heart.*

It makes us sad to reflect upon the opposite and equal impediments on which faith may make shipwreck. Certainly our Lord warned us most earnestly against feeling without acting; against that sort of listless and timid piety which never comes forth either to *confess Him before men* or to minister to men in His behalf. But we cannot forget how decided was His preference of that faith which *sat at His feet and heard His word,* over that activity which spent itself, root and branch, in deeds of bustling service. *Thou art careful and troubled about many things; but one thing is needful; and Mary hath chosen that good part which shall not be taken from her.* Our path lies, steep and narrow, between opposite risks: on this side a morass, on that a precipice: here a yawning pit, and there a consuming fire. But He whom we serve will be our Guide through all, if we only cleave to Him stedfastly, and listen with reverence to His grave counsels, while He adapts them with loving wisdom to the care and to the circumstances of each. Today He speaks to us of the need of reflection; tomorrow He may tell of the necessity of diligence: let us hear *every word that proceeds out of His mouth,* and submit ourselves, alike in this and in that, to His gracious and compassionate discipline.

Cultivate then, beloved brethren, let us all do so, the

peculiar grace which shone in the Lord's mother. If we read little, let us *keep* it well: if we read much, let it be because we have time to *ponder*. Haste, in divine things, is ever a sign of heartlessness: if our time for thought is scanty, let us use it the more calmly and the more thoughtfully. Every one surely in this congregation might secure to himself by proper care a few moments at night and morning (who not at midday also?) for self-recollection, self-correction, and earnest communing with God. One moment so spent is worth hours even of sacred reading without it. One moment so spent—with the windows of the heart set fully open towards the heavenly temple, so that the light and the air and the warmth of the very city of God may reach it in its inmost corners and recesses—is so full of hope, so full of promise, yea, so full of blessing, that it makes a man say, as he retires from it, *Behold, the Lord is in this place, and I knew it not. This is none other but the house of God, and this is the gate of heaven.*

The test of true religion lies, for every man, in this secret thing; this thing which is a secret between him and God alone. Does he keep the things which God teaches, and ponder them in his heart? Without this there may be punctuality of worship and propriety of life: but without this there cannot be a heart right with God, nor a mind set resolutely upon things above. Where an interest is felt in God's truth, it will be shown, as in other matters, by a frequent recurrence to it: when the body is separated from their study, the soul will run upon them: *The desire of our soul is to Thy name and to the remembrance of Thee. With my soul have I desired Thee in the night; yea, with my spirit within me have I sought Thee early. My soul waiteth for the Lord, more than they which watch for the morning; I say, more than they that watch for the morning. Mary kept all these things, and pondered them in her heart.*

And where there is a want of this pondering, of this musing and meditating over the things of God, of this guarding and this putting together of the several truths learned from the study or ministry of His Holy Word, there can be but a feeble and tentative hold upon realties *most surely believed among us*. We do not really know God's revelation because we are familiar with its sound: that very familiarity may lead as much to spiritual ignorance as to intellectual knowledge. Nothing in God's Word can come fresh or new to us; we know it all; we have known it from childhood; we have been noted perhaps for our acquaintance with its blessed teaching: in the same degree have we reason to fear lest we *know nothing* of it *yet as we ought to know*, and lest, if it be so, we may be *ever learning and never able to come to the knowledge of the truth*. It evades us when we seek to grasp it: beware lest, when we lie down to die, there be nothing left of it either to support or to console. *Behold, my servants shall eat, but ye shall be hungry; behold, my servants shall drink, but ye shall be thirsty; behold, my servants shall rejoice, but ye shall be ashamed; behold, my servants shall sing for joy of heart, but ye shall cry for sorrow of heart, and shall howl for vexation of spirit.* From that terrible awakening to find our very knowledge a dream, may God of His infinite mercy save us all, by writing in our hearts betimes her holy example, who *kept all His sayings, and pondered them in her heart*.

There are many ways of practising this grace of meditation: firm resolute self-examination is one of these; and earnest steady contemplation of God and Christ and the Holy Spirit as revealed to us in the Scriptures is another of these; and praying over a verse or two of the Bible on the strength of their being true, and in reference to their spiritual teaching, is another of these; and there are others beside. But of all these none is so impressive, and none so effectual, to all those who approach it in a right spirit, as that act of Holy Communion to which you are called today in the Sacrament of the body and blood of Christ our Saviour. There we ponder His truth in His presence; there in an especial manner the Master is with His disciple, and the Revealer with His word.

If there be, as I well know, some, yea, many, amongst you, who desire to *grow in grace and in the knowledge of the Lord and Saviour;* who reproach themselves bitterly for their backwardness, their sluggishness, and their earthly mind, in reference to the things of God; let them *draw near* now *with faith, and take this holy Sacrament to their comfort;* praying especially that God will make it His instrument in their case for correcting lightness and deciding doubt and removing unbelief; for enabling them at last, if never before, truly to *keep all His sayings,* and deeply to *ponder them in their heart.*

SECOND SUNDAY AFTER CHRISTMAS,
January 4, 1863.

XIII.

YEARS OF PREPARATION.

Luke ii. 49.

Wist ye not that I must be about my Father's business?

ON this one Sunday in the year we are taught to contemplate the childhood and the youthful life of Jesus. The Word of God, our only guide in these matters, has told us but little of it. The Gospels are chiefly occupied with His ministry; with the three years during which He was teaching and working miracles amongst the people, and more especially with those last few days of bitter anguish which closed His sorrowful and toilsome life below. It was perhaps to be feared lest some superstitions might connect themselves, as with the person of her of whom we spoke last Sunday, His human mother, so with the scenes and incidents of that period during which He was gathering strength in secret for the *contradiction of sinners against Himself; increasing in wisdom and stature, and in favour with God and man.* There was to be no historian of His youth; no dragging into publicity, even for the example of later times, of that long season of progress and preparation through which it pleased Him to pass humbly and patiently to the manifestation of His glory and the accomplishment of human Redemption.

Nevertheless, my brethren, there must be no forgetfulness on our part of the marvellous fact that our Lord Jesus Christ did spend on earth some thirty years before He wrought one miracle or held one public discourse as God's messenger or man's Redeemer. We need that fact, every one of us, for our instruction and for our admonition. The details of that period are lost to us; God's wisdom has so appointed it: but the fact that there was such a period, and the reason of it, and the principle on which it was passed through, is full of divine lessons, some few of which I would ponder with you on the occasion now presented.

1. And first we should notice the importance of this fact to a right conception of our Lord's work for us as a whole.

Some persons never speak of anything but the death of Christ. The whole of the Gospel is for them the one fact of the Atonement. And that one fact rightly understood is indeed the sum and substance of the Gospel. We blame no man for making much of it. It is impossible to overrate it. But to the right understanding even of the Atonement it is essential to bear in mind how and through what stages He passed to it. The sufferings of the last week, intense and incalculable as they were, formed but a small part of His whole humiliation. The death must not be detached or severed from the life. The life was first given for us, and then the death was borne for us.

An unbeliever cannot appreciate the argument here suggested. We must first be convinced in our inmost souls that Christ was not a mere man; that He was indeed very man, but that He was very God also. This sustaining and life-giving conviction is wrought in us instrumentally by the study of His works and words below. Not until it is ours can we understand either the death or the life. Not until it is ours can we feel either the poignancy of the sufferings or their remedial virtue. Others may have endured in disease or in martyrdom a bodily anguish as terrific. Others may have lingered as long—the malefactors crucified with Him lingered yet longer—under the gradual infliction of a cruel and torturing execution. But it was the divine in Him which made the human suffer. It was the hidden Godhead which both enabled Him in that anguish to bear sin, and made that sinbearing so intolerable. If He had not been God also, He would have suffered vainly, but He would have suffered less.

Even thus is it with the life of Jesus. We should despair of so picturing to any man the early years of the Saviour as to make him feel them as a part of His passion, if we did not first ascertain that that man believed in Him as God, and read each line of the page by the light of that conviction. If he can do that, I will venture to say that the thirty years of common life will bear comparison in their painfulness with the three years of ministry and suffering. The thirty years will then be felt as an integral part both of the sacrifice and of the example.

When the Apostle Paul says that He who was originally in the form of God *made Himself of no reputation*, or (more exactly) *made Himself empty, and took upon Him the form of a servant, being made in the likeness of men;* he teaches us no doubt that there was an entire subordination in Him of the divine to the human; that He laid by and disused, for the time, the original and inalienable Deity, and submitted to every condition of growth, both mental and bodily, to which man himself is subject. We do not presume therefore to say that there was, throughout the infancy and boyhood of Jesus, a distinct and equable consciousness of the condescension to which He was submitting Himself. Yet even this rather heightens than diminishes the effect of that condescension when gazed upon in retrospect. And we do feel that, marvellous as was the patience of our Lord under calumny, insult, and torture, it was not greater, it was even less wonderful, than His patience through thirty long years of obscurity and silence.

Think of Him—if you believe in His Divinity—as an infant in the arms of His mother in the crowded inn at Bethlehem. Think of Him as a young child, practising the first powers of speech and motion in a humble home at Nazareth. Think of Him as a boy, increasing in common knowledge under the instruction of some village teacher, supplemented only by some casual aid (such as this day's Gospel describes) from a periodical visit to Jerusalem. Think of Him as a young man, learning His reputed father's trade, that the sacrifice of the body might go along with the sacrifice of the soul in His obedience to the will of God for man. Think of Him thenceforth for ten or for fifteen years working in the shop and at the trade of the carpenter, burying deep within those mighty, those burning thoughts of *His Father's business,* of man's Redemption, which, *when the fulness of the time should come*, were to spend themselves in consuming toil, and at last in an obedience perfected in death only. Lay these things together—and call in, as you must do, the aid of a faith mighty even to remove mountains, that you may not stagger nor be offended at a contrast and a combination above man's intellect to conceive—and you will say that the great step in Christ's humiliation was when He incorporated Himself in the family of man, when He deigned to begin that long series of condescensions, of which weakness and neglect and misconstruction were items, and to look forward through a long vista of dull monotonous years to a prospect marked only by reproach and pain, by a cross uplifted and an opened grave.

We have spoken thus far as though there may have been an unconsciousness on His part, during early years, of the glory from which He had descended and to which He should return. We enter here upon mysterious subjects: we do well to remember in all such questionings that *the place whereon we are standing is holy ground.* The words of the text prove that, by flashes at least if not continuously, there shone forth from within Him even in childhood a glorious light. They suggest to us that, however combined with opposite characteristics, there was in Him from earliest years the sense of a mission, and the resolute purpose to fulfil it. *How is it that ye sought me? wist ye not that I must be about my Father's business?* He had then consciously a Father in heaven, and in that Father's affairs He Himself was consciously concerned. Well may it be written that she whose love was nearest to Him below, she who watched with a mother's eye every indication of that mysterious, that superhuman life, *kept all these sayings in her heart—kept all these things and pondered them in her heart.* God grant us all grace to *go and do likewise.*

2. For indeed, my brethren, these thirty years of silent preparation had more in them than a mere condescension or humiliation. Both in what they were not, and in what they were, they contain for us all a serious and a comforting lesson.

(1) What do they say to men or to women whose whole life is obscurity and monotony? Is not that the description of most lives? How many in any congregation are persons of mark and note? persons whose lot in life is one of interest, distinction, or wide-spread usefulness? These things may be for the few: the many toil on without observation and without success. What to these would have been the life of Christ as an encouragement or as an example, where for these His sympathy as in a life actually and personally known, if all His years had been passed in a round of public duties, if His childhood had been one of premature publicity, if in youth or early manhood He had taken to Himself the office of the Prophet of His people? The bulk of His life was spent even as yours. He too, the Creator of all things, was for all but the whole of His earthly sojourn an obscure, an unknown, an unregarded man. It was His will, in taking man's nature upon Him, to take it in its least attractive and therefore in its commonest form. Even obloquy and opposition, even envy and hatred, are less hard to bear, for many characters, than total forgetfulness and disregard. And therefore He chose to endure the latter as well as the former;

thereby teaching us that great and small in earthly positions are to the eye of God distinctions without a difference; that a lofty aim can elevate the lowliest, and a true self-devotion consecrate the commonest. *What God hath cleansed, that call not thou common.* Do thy work, however dull, however obscure, as for God, as in God's strength and by God's appointment, and it shall be marked for thee at every turn with Christ's footsteps, as much in its monotonous humility as in its occasional anxiety and distress.

And do not these same thirty years say this to us also; that every life's work needs a preparation, and that nothing is to be counted lost which is given to it? This is not the place—but there are places—in which a serious admonition is needed on this topic with regard to the most sacred calling. Is it not too true that, whereas no lawyer and no physician would be tolerated in the practice of a profession which he had never learned, for clergymen on the contrary, for expounders of God's law, for physicians of men's souls, no preliminary training is oftentimes judged necessary? that men can rush into the cure of souls without discipline and even without forethought? Great need have we to reflect upon the thirty years now under notice, in reference to this subject. If ever there was one who might go early, and go untrained, into God's ministry, surely it was He who was not man only. Yet He deemed it no superfluous scruple to shrink from presenting Himself, even at the complete age of maturity, as the Prophet and the Shepherd of Israel. He toiled on still in the workshop, revolving and maturing in silence the glorious plans of a Messiahship and a Redemption. And did He not thereby teach us, as the need, so also the nature, of a due preparation for the ministry? Did He not say to us, *There is no need of the desert or of the cloister to equip a man for the holiest ministry: the true training-place for the ministry of souls is the soul of the minister: amidst manual toils, in the workshop of the carpenter, no less than in haunts of learned study, that discipline may be carried on: see only that you be conversant with human life and human character; see that you acquaint yourself thoroughly with the true wants and the true sorrows of humanity; see that you be imbued with that knowledge of man, in yourself and in others, which is the one requisite for man's instructor, healer, and comforter: and consider that every month and every year spent in that preliminary training is worth many a year—if it were possible, many a lifetime—of a crude and ignorant and therefore profitless ministry without it?*

(2) But if these thirty years are thus full of instruction in their negative aspect; I mean, by their obscure and by their preparatory character; do they not teach also by direct example? We cannot forget, at this time least of all, that we minister in this place to many still young, still dwelling in a parent's home, and finding a large part of their daily struggle in the duty of cheerful obedience. Look back, my young friends, upon your Saviour's home in Nazareth. See how He *went down* thither with His parents, from His visit to Jerusalem of which you have heard today, *and was subject unto them.* See how He consented to abide there, still a son, a faithful and an obedient son, long after He came to man's estate. You do not read in Him of any ambition to be independent: you do not find Him remonstrating

or murmuring against the restraints of home, and beginning to remind Himself or others that the time was come for self-management and self-concern. There He continued, in that dull home, in that stagnant village, through thirty long years, until the time actually came for *His showing unto Israel.* Shall not the son, shall not the daughter, of a Christian home deem that good enough and great enough which a Saviour, who was also the Creator, thought happy enough and honourable enough for Him?

Let these records of His example *sink down into your hearts*, not to be idle there, but daily fruitful. And add yet to them this one; how amidst all the docility and all the obedience of His early home-life our Lord yet surrendered not into others' keeping the responsibilities and the sanctities of His personal being. You are taught by His example to be obedient in all things: but you are taught also to cherish the remembrance that your life can neither be lost in that of others, nor surrendered (in its deeper mysteries) into another's keeping. You yourself have a life within, and a life above, and a life beyond, which you cannot delegate to other management, nor shift to other accountability. *Wist ye not that I must be about my Father's business?* was the question asked of His parents, at the age of twelve years, by Him who in all things was subject to them, and in all things dutiful. Alas, we too often invert the rule of duty, and are both insubordinate and unreflecting; struggling against the yoke of home authority, and yet not from any sense of responsibility to an authority higher still.

It is not often, God be praised for it, that our duty to

a parent comes really in these days into conflict with our duty to God. If it ever does so, we know that *we must obey God rather than man.* But we must be quite sure that God has spoken, when we enter into this painful alternative of duty. More often he who kicks against parental authority is in the very same degree resisting also the authority of God. Ask yourselves from early years, *Am I about my Father's business?* and you will find that the work of the Father above is generally in full harmony with the requirement of the father below.

Wist ye not that I must be about my Father's business? What is that? What is it for us? Surely it is the setting forward on earth, in our own little sphere, that *kingdom of God* which is *righteousness and peace and joy in the Holy Ghost.* To be doing that; to be in evident sympathy, because in real sympathy, with God's will for us and for all men; to be evidently, because really, on the side of God in the great conflict between truth and falsehood, between right and wrong, between sin and holiness; to be doing what in us lies to make Christ better known, more honoured and more loved, by those around us, because we have first learned to honour and to love Him in our own souls; to count nothing troublesome which can do good to a fellow-man and fellow-sinner, because we remember what Christ thought it no burden to do for us; thus, *by patient continuance in well doing,* undismayed by opposition, undaunted by difficulty, unwearied even by failure, to seek for an immortality beyond, in which *God's servants shall serve Him, shall see His face, and bear His name in their foreheads;* this is, for each one of us, young and old, rich and poor, to be indeed *about our Father's business:* for this no one is too poor, and no one is too young, and no one, by Christ's grace, is even too sinful: for this *to live is Christ*, and for this *to die is gain*.

FIRST SUNDAY AFTER THE EPIPHANY,
January 11, 1863.

XIV.

OBEDIENCE THE CONDITION OF HELP.

John ii. 5.

Whatsoever He saith unto you, do it.

WE have spoken lately on these occasions of the fore-runner of Christ, and of the mother of Christ; of His own childhood and youth and early manhood, of those thirty years of common and uneventful life through which He passed to His work as the Messiah and the Redeemer. Today we are to speak of His *beginning of miracles;* of the first of those *signs* by which (as St John expresses it) He *manifested forth His glory.* Not for nothing, assuredly, was His first miracle wrought at a marriage-feast *adorned and beautified* (our Church says) *by His presence.* He came not to take men out of the world, but to guide and to bless them in it; He *came eating and drinking,* that He might show men how even to *eat and drink to the glory of God.* He came not, like John the Baptist, to summon us into the desert, but rather to teach us how in the commonest calling and amidst the most secular business we may yet in His strength *abide with God.* He came not to forbid *buying and selling, marrying and giving in marriage,* but rather to remind us that in the very midst of these things His final Advent will be upon us, and that therefore they who would be safe in them then must watch in them now.

But apart from these more general lessons to be learned from the *beginning of miracles* now before us, there is much in the details of the narrative, which may well impress and instruct us.

A failure of wine as the feast went on drew from the Lord's mother what was designed no doubt as a hint that His intervention would be seasonable. She had learned, during these thirty years of silent observation and pondering, to understand something of the prophetic announcement, *He shall be great, and shall be called the Son of the Highest.* Whether she had ever before, in the privacy of the home at Nazareth, called in that divine aid and found it effectual, we know not: we only read that now, in a moment of embarrassment, she at once turned to Him, and said, in a manner which clearly implied a request, *They have no wine.*

His answer was grave, though (need it be said?) not wanting in respect or courtesy. The name by which He addressed her, and which jars perhaps a little upon our ears, was applied, in the language in which it is here written, not to parents only but even to sovereigns. It was used as a term of respect and of reverence. It had been more to the taste perhaps of modern readers, if instead of *Woman* the English Bible had given *My mother.* But is not this one of the thousand instances in which the plain speaking of the Bible is, when well considered, its beauty and its glory? *Man, thy sins are forgiven thee. O woman, great is thy faith. Woman, behold thy son.* We are men and women before we are anything else; before either earthly station or human relationship has come in to modify or add to nature. And the Holy Scriptures remind us, over and over again—thus, perhaps, not least—that there is a dignity and a nobility in humanity itself, which nothing of man's adding can materially increase.

The mode then of our Lord's address is entirely respectful. But the object of it is no doubt reproof. *Woman, what have I to do with thee? Even thou, my mother, must be taught, that in the concerns of my heavenly Father's business flesh and blood can bear no part. Even thou and I must here stand separate. I alone must judge when and how it behoves me to put forth the powers of my Messiahship. And in this instance mine hour is not yet come. The time for my interposition is not yet. Even thou, I know, wilt submit to wait for it.*

The words which follow show how entire was her acquiescence in the will of Him who was at once her Son and her Lord; her Son *as touching His manhood*, her Lord *as touching His Godhead*. *His mother saith unto the servants, Whatsoever He saith unto you, do it. Let no word of His escape you: if it should please Him to say anything, wait not to doubt or to discuss, but obey instantly. Let the command be ever so difficult or ever so improbable; if it should bid you to offer water to one who calls for wine; if it should bid you to draw wine from a cask which you know to be empty; still, whatsoever He saith unto you, do it.* How well the charge was obeyed; how these servants in ready unquestioning submission first filled the waterpots with water and then unhesitatingly drew it forth as wine; and how in the act of doing so they found themselves the agents of a miracle; all this we know; we have again read today the simple record of it; a record, puzzling indeed beyond explanation to the pride of human intellect, but intelligible as well as beautiful to all those who recognize in Jesus Christ the Almighty Creator, and believe that, *whatsoever the Lord pleases, that does He in heaven and in earth, and in the sea and in all deep places;* believe that it did please Him on this occasion to prove that He was working, working with a purpose, and working to an end.

Whatsoever He saith unto you, do it. That is in this instance the condition of a miracle. If you would see one of Christ's signs, you must implicitly follow Christ's signal. If the palsied man is before Him, hoping for a cure, he must not remonstrate against the order to do that which is impossible; to stretch forth that very hand whose healing is in question. In obeying comes strength. The power to obey is given in the endeavour; and without the endeavour there is not the power. We see it both ways. We see how faith can remove mountains; and we see how unbelief can even arrest the arm of Christ. *He could there do no mighty works because of their unbelief.* He could not, consistently with his principle. He could not, because more harm than good would be done by thus overbearing and overwhelming unbelief. That was what the Pharisees asked: *First show a sign, and then we will believe: first give the proof we prescribe, and then ask our allegiance.* No; God gives enough, but He does not give all we wish, not exactly that which we wish, in the way of evidence of truth. The mind which refuses the proof given would equally deal unthankfully with the proof demanded. It is not the will of God so to demonstrate His Son's Gospel as to make incredulity impossible. The promise is only this; *If any man will do*, is willing and desirous to do, *His will, he shall know of the doctrine, whether it be of God.* Therefore, in preparation for such satisfaction, the rule of the text is the one thing needful for us, *Whatsoever He saith unto you, do it.* Stand ready; argue not; remonstrate not, but stand ready; and then, in His own good time—He says it is not yet His time— He will speak, and thou shalt know.

We, my brethren, are not expecting, any of us, what is commonly called a miracle. And yet what is God's work of grace in any human soul, but a wonderful, a supernatural, an omnipotent work? St Paul seems to say in his Epistle to the Ephesians that it is of the same nature as the Omnipotence required to raise the dead. *What is the exceeding greatness of His power to us-ward who believe, according to the working of His mighty power, which He wrought in Christ when He raised Him from the dead.* Now many of us, all of us as we are by nature, need that work, that preternatural, that supernatural work, to be wrought in us. And I know that there are some here present who feel that that work of grace has not yet been wrought in them. There are those who see clearly with the eye of the mind what grace is, what are its signs, and what its effects; and see as clearly that they themselves are not yet the subjects of it. And while many, even of these, are content to be as they are, others (God grant it) are bitterly accusing themselves, and longing with all their hearts to know the power of that grace which they know not. I address myself to these last, and say, Perhaps His hour is not yet come: perhaps He may keep you waiting for that clear light, for that perfect day; but meanwhile, *Whatsoever He saith unto you, do it:* if there is anything in your conduct, or if there is anything in your language, or if there is anything in your spirit, which you feel to be contrary to His will and word, set yourself to correct it: do not say it is impossible; do not say, because it is a perversion of truth to say, *I cannot do it till grace comes;* remember the words, *In the way of Thy judgments, O Lord, have we waited for Thee:* it is not that you are to be holy first, and then Christ will save you; but it is true that we must set ourselves towards Him by honest purpose and sincere effort or we shall never reach Him: therefore we say again, *Whatsoever He saith unto you, do it;* and first surely among these acts of obedience will be the humble earnest prayer, to Him who has promised that those who ask shall have, that He will be pleased, according to His most true promise, to work powerfully in your heart; not to leave you to yourself, but to make you what He would have you; yes, so to influence you by His Holy Spirit, that you may neither *sin on with Christ in sight*, nor perish in the very light of a heaven opened. To you Christ has already spoken; He has already made you a promise, He has already bidden you to expect its fulfilment: let your first effort be the acceptance of the promise, that *whosoever shall call upon the name of the Lord*, call honestly, call earnestly, call perseveringly, *shall be saved.*

Such is the lesson of the text for those who are waiting and watching for the grace of God within.

Like the servants in this miracle, they must stand ready to obey His call, whatsoever it be; they must set themselves at once to such duties of act and of devotion as are already known to them from Christ's word, and they must be ready to move in any direction at His first call and summons. Then will He speak to them. Then at last will He reveal Himself, not as to the world only, but as to His own called and chosen and faithful.

But the words of Scripture are manifold in their application, and we all feel that we have not yet exhausted these.

Whatsoever He saith unto you, do it.

1. One of you has long had upon his mind a duty which he shrinks from. A young person has something hidden which ought to be revealed; some misconduct which a parent should know; some debt, perhaps, which is weighing upon him like a millstone; some secret of folly or imprudence, which nothing but frank confession can ever remove from the conscience. A parent has a right to the confidence: it is God's own medicine for the conscience-wounds of youth: the effort once made, peace returns, and with it hope, and with it strength for duty. But no: pride forbids, and courage fails, and the command itself becomes less peremptory to the dallier: week after week slips away, and at last he says that the time is gone by; what was not told early cannot be told late; the secret has settled itself in the inner being, and must work there, and worry there, till at last it wear itself out, or be succeeded. If such a person be here before me, let me urge him or her to act forthwith and decisively upon the golden rule of the text, *Whatsoever Christ saith unto you, do it.* Be brave

to face a moment's shame, that you may obey Him who *knoweth all things*.

And not the young only, but the middle-aged also, and the gray-headed also, are tempted sometimes to feel, with regard to one of Christ's commands, *This is a hard saying; who can hear it?* who can act upon it? Take a single example: the duty of forgiveness, of reconciliation, of Christian concord. One of you has long cherished a grudge, a dislike, an envy or a contempt, towards some acquaintance, friend, or relative. He has allowed it to sink so deep, that even the advances of the other rather aggravate than soften it. It has become a part of himself. He nurses his grievance, ponders, reviews, and dwells upon it, till even its first dimensions, while it was fresh and recent, are exceeded by the present. He persuades himself that it was too grave an injury, or too wanton, or too ungrateful, to allow of its forgiveness; that it is an exception to the general rule, and that even without forgiving this he himself may be forgiven. Meanwhile the uneasy feeling within spreads and festers: there is a sore place in the conscience, which, before God at all events, cannot be forgotten: hence prayer becomes restrained and irksome, and the spiritual life languishes and withers. O, my brother, *whatsoever Christ says to you, do it.* Make the effort, though it be formidable: and He, He Himself, will both strengthen you for it, and visit you with His comfort after it.

2. Sometimes the commands of Christ are not only difficult, but improbable and unlooked for. So it was here. Wine was wanted, and the first process for procuring it was the order to fill six large waterpots

with water. What could be so unmeaning? might the human reason enquire: let me wait for a more intelligible, a more rational direction. The servants, warned by the Lord's mother, obeyed without arguing: and the miracle was wrought; Christ *manifested forth His glory*. But so, alas, do not we. How do we sit in judgment upon the reasonableness of Christ's appointments, and grudge if we see not in prospect every step of the way by which He is guiding us to His end. When He calls us to bear pain or loss; when He bids us to part with some cherished object of affection or of ambition; when He bids us with our own hand to sacrifice that which was too dear to us, that which might have enchained us to earth and made heaven itself distasteful; how apt are we to think that the command was unnecessary, that *the desire of our eyes* would have made us happy, and that our very souls will be the worse for this privation and for this cross. But he is not fit to do Christ's work here, or to see His face hereafter, who cannot implicitly trust Him, and in heart and desire at least *follow Him whithersoever He goeth*. Probable or improbable, expected or unexpected, reasonable or unreasonable as man judges, the command of Christ must be obeyed: whatsoever He saith unto us, we must do it.

3. And there is yet one other thing to be noticed. How small and trivial oftentimes are Christ's commands; how little it seems to signify whether they are done or left undone; how slight appears to be their possible influence upon our own or another's good. Is it not thus with most of the daily duties of every one of us? How little do they seem to bear upon God's work. How unnatural it seems to connect religion, the thought of

Christ, with such matters. What has the business of the shop or of the counting-house to do with my soul? What is the meaning of asking a blessing upon such common, such humble, such paltry employments? Nevertheless, my brethren, that, for you, for most of us, is Christ's work; that is *the calling wherein you are called;* and you must sanctify it as it is, or you will have no work for Christ at all. *What God hath cleansed, that call not thou common. Whatsoever He saith unto you,* though it be a small thing, though it be what any one could do, though it be entirely concerned in form with things that are temporal and perishable, *whatsoever He saith unto you, do it.* Be assured that there is no work in life, however sacred, of which a large part does not consist of things small and trivial. A clergyman often says to himself, *Why should I go today to that house or that school? I have often gone there, and nothing has come of it: I am weary, I am indisposed, the duty is even more trifling than it is irksome: tomorrow will be time enough; for today, for tonight, I will take my ease and postpone it.* And yet, perhaps, if he goes, he finds some opening, more than ordinary, for influence and for usefulness: and if he stays away, he finds afterwards that he has lost some important opportunity; a soul is gone to its account unvisited and unshepherded; guilt is incurred by the remissness, and the duty of tomorrow is found tenfold more repulsive for the negligence of today. In reference to little things as to great there is but one safe rule, but one principle which will *bring peace at the last, Whatsoever He saith unto you, do it.* If the command be difficult, He who gave it is Almighty, and He can make the *great mountain a plain* before those who serve Him. If the command be unexpected, if it seem to be inappropriate, He, *the only wise God*, knows better than we; in quiet obedience will be success and blessing. If the command in many of its details seem trifling, still He who does nothing in vain will turn it to good, perhaps to important ends; at all events will be with us in it, and *give us His blessing*. Thus in all things He shall speak and we will follow. Whether it be a sin to be conquered, or a duty to be done; whether it be a grace to be fostered, or a soul (our own or another's) to be sought and saved; still the charge of the text is for each one the rule alike of safety and of happiness, *Whatsoever He saith unto you, do it. With Thee is the well of life: and in Thy light* alone can we ever *see light*.

And indeed, my brethren, each day reminds us that the time is short. Soon *the night cometh when no man can work*. Old and young are quickly passing away: this winter has made strange havoc in this place of well known and much honoured friends: last night's bell told you of the departure of one who but a few Sundays ago was among us as a worshipper; one who, in years at least, was the father of our congregation; one whose life stretched back from one American war to another, and included easily in its span the three revolutions of France. He is gone, respected and honoured, to the home of the departed: and we are all following in that long procession, the destination of which is the grave and the judgment. Quickly is the rising generation becoming the chief occupant of the field of life, and the vigorous men and the known men and the leading men are stepping back into the weakness and obscurity of the aged. God grant that we may all have grace so to *serve our generation* in this our day *according to His will*, that, when we *fall on sleep* and are *laid unto our fathers to see corruption*, ours may be the repose of the faithful, and ours *the resurrection of the just*.

SECOND SUNDAY AFTER EPIPHANY,
January 18, 1863.

XV.

FAITH THE MEASURE OF HELP.

Matthew viii. 13.

As thou hast believed, so be it done unto thee.

THIS is one of those brief sayings in which lie hid whole volumes of truth. May God give us grace so to read and to ponder it, that it may be for our life.

The Gospel for this day, from which it is taken, is made up of the record of two miracles.

A leper, excluded from the society of men and from the worship of God by reason of a loathsome and incurable disease, has ventured to draw near to the compassionate Saviour, and to address to Him the memorable words, *Lord, if thou wilt, Thou canst make me clean.* Words soon spoken; but, when closely examined, marvellous in their meaning. *That disease for which there is no remedy; that disease which the Law of Israel has placed under the inspection, not of the physician, but of the priest alone; that disease which makes a man an outcast from all domestic, social, and sacred life; I believe that Thou, to all appearance a man like one of us, canst remove it at Thy pleasure: I believe that Thou, by the mere application of Thy healing hand, canst, if Thou wilt, make me whole and clean from this plague.* That was faith. It was the rising above things seen and natural, into the region of things unseen and divine. It was the expression of a deep conviction that the Person addressed, though a man like other men, was also something more; was One by whom God spake and wrought, and in whom, as in no mere man, God Himself dwelt. Such faith was never yet sent empty away. *Jesus put forth His hand, and touched him, saying, I will; be thou clean. And immediately his leprosy was cleansed.*

A centurion, having a servant in his house paralyzed, meets Jesus at the entrance of the town of Capernaum, with a petition, implied if not expressed, for His gracious intervention. That, again, was faith. It was the persuasion that Jesus Christ had the power of God; that He who was no physician, He who was nothing if He was not more than man, could at His pleasure restore a helpless and hopeless sufferer to the fulness of strength and health. Here then was the condition of help satisfied. Here was that faith which Jesus required of all who came to Him for healing. And He said at once, *I will come and heal him.* But the faith of the applicant rose higher still. Others had believed in the power of Christ to *come and heal;* to stand by the sickbed, and bid disease and suffering flee. But this man saw that even presence was not necessary; that He who possessed an almighty power here must possess an almighty power there; that nearness or distance could make no difference in the exercise of a divine authority; and that, if He *spake the word only,* spake it in absence, without coming under a roof unworthy to receive Him, the effect must be the same: *my servant shall be healed.*

This centurion was a soldier: he knew, he said, what discipline was: he *was under authority*, a subaltern and subordinate himself: and he also possessed authority; he *had soldiers under him*: which of those men would hesitate to obey his word of command? If he said to one, *Go*, or to another, *Come;* if he said to his servant, *Do this;* in any case obedience was certain. And if he, a common man, thus obeyed and was obeyed; if he could depend upon the execution of an order, whatever its nature, by men of free will and free action like his own, under the influence of a merely human discipline; how much more—such is his argument—how much more will disease and suffering obey the voice which speaks by the right of the Creator, whether that voice speak near or far off, whether that right be exercised in one manner or exercised in another manner. The question was almost exactly that of the prophet; *Am I a God at hand, saith the Lord, and not a God afar off? When Jesus heard it, He marvelled, and said to them that followed, Verily I say unto you, I have not found so great faith, no, not in Israel.* Clear and unanswerable as the reasoning was, it was a higher exercise of faith than that which trusted in Him in presence. And in the same degree it was more acceptable. It was an earnest too of that ingathering of the Gentiles, which was to result in due time from the operation of the same divine faith. *Jesus said unto the centurion, Go thy way; and as thou hast believed, so be it done unto thee. And his servant was healed in the selfsame hour.*

Faith, my brethren, is the one principle of our Reformed and Protestant Church. By it, instrumentally, a man is justified. By it a Christian man lives; by it he dies. All that is ever good in us comes, instrumentally, by faith. A man who has no faith, no true, no living, no working faith, is a lost man. With faith goes hope: and a man without hope, what is he in a sinful, a suffering, and a storm-tossed world? Thus there is no topic on which we require to be more clearly instructed, more often questioned and exhorted and warned, than this one, of a true faith; what it is, how it may be known, and who (in the true sense) possesses it.

There are many wrong definitions of faith, and many counterfeits of it. Many persons are *made sad* by misrepresentations of it, *whom God has not made sad:* and many, we must fear, are strengthened in evil ways by an idea of the nature of faith which God's Word has not sanctioned and God's judgment cannot confirm. Let us seize the opportunity this day given us, and correct or apply (according to our need) our conception of this essential grace.

Faith, in general, is the opposite of sight. *We walk by faith, not by sight.* Faith is spiritual sight, as opposed to bodily. Faith is seeing the invisible. It is *the assurance of things hoped for, the proof of things not seen.* In a lower sense it operates in everything. It is the basis of every process of husbandry, and of every step in education. He who sows for a harvest sows in faith. He is acting upon a sight of something invisible. He sees in his mind a day some months distant, when this grain of corn which he is dropping upon the earth will be reappearing in a strangely altered, in a now at last practical form. That is faith, in things natural and earthly. Therefore let not a Christian be called an enthusiast simply because he walks by faith. Where would the world be without faith? What a standstill of all things useful and serviceable for the life that is, if faith is to be discarded. Faith is the sight, the mental or spiritual sight, of things unseen.

But thus far it has no Christian aspect. Faith in a harvest may quicken dependence upon God, and thankfulness to God, and other moral and religious feelings; but it does nothing more towards *the saving of the soul*.

Christian faith is seeing Christ; seeing Him with the mind's eye; seeing Him when He is out of sight: seeing Him as He really is, in His person, in His character, in His work for us, in His resurrection life and power. It was not seeing Christ in the body which healed the leper or the centurion's servant. It was the passing through the bodily sight of Him to the spiritual. It was the conviction that this Man standing before them was something else too. Depend upon it, it was the very same grace with that faith to which we are called. It was not an easy thing to see God in the form of a Man. It was just as difficult as to see God now in Christ, when there is no form before us. Faith in Christ then, and faith in Christ now, is one and the selfsame thing; the being convinced that He is, and is what He is; the being convinced that He, our Lord Jesus Christ, lives now, at this moment, and *has all power in heaven and in earth;* lives after death and resurrection, after bearing our sins and taking them away; lives as our High Priest, as our Intercessor, as our Mediator and Advocate with God.

Perhaps you will say, Many people are convinced of

this and are none the better for it. You will recall the words of St James, who says, *The devils also believe, and tremble.* It is true: there is a dead faith, as well as a living; and a dead faith will save no man. But, to speak more correctly, a dead faith is none. Faith is seeing the invisible. Does a man see the invisible, does a man see the unseen Saviour, is a man convinced in his heart of the being and of the work (past, present, and future) of our Lord Jesus Christ, whose every word and work is a denial of that faith? Does a man believe that his house is in flames, who will not even rise from his bed to alarm others or save himself? It is a mere question of names, whether we shall give the title of faith to a thing which neither lives nor acts. St Paul takes it for granted that the faith to which he ascribes such marvels is a living not a dead thing. No man talks of meeting a man when he meets a corpse. Faith in the Christian sense, is a real conviction of Christ. Do you suppose that a man whose very soul sees Christ, sees Him as his Saviour and sees Him as his Judge, will be careless about pleasing Him? careless how often or how insolently he wounds Him or *crucifies Him afresh?* No; faith, which is the sight of the unseen Saviour, must work and act; it cannot help it: if it does not, it is not faith. When the leper had this kind of faith, it brought him to Christ for healing. When the centurion had this kind of faith, it brought him to Christ in behalf of his servant, and made him say, *Speak the word only, and my servant shall be healed.* So will it be with us. That faith which is the sight of the unseen Saviour in His true nature and office will certainly bring us to Him with all our sins, all our griefs, and all our wants.

And this is the faith which justifies. I spoke of misrepresentations and counterfeits of faith. One says, *Faith is the assurance that Jesus Christ loves me personally, has forgiven my sin, separately and individually, has a purpose of favour and salvation towards me specially.* And one reproaches himself, and is despised by others, because he cannot yet say this. And another, in the midst of a very inconsistent and even sinful life, is cheerful and almost reckless, because he either has now, or once had, a persuasion of his own forgiveness and his own acceptance. Alas for the day when every false hope shall be swept away by the reappearance of Christ. I do not find that this leper had a previous conviction of Christ's intention to heal him particularly. His words are, *If Thou wilt, Thou canst.* And the centurion's words are like these. *My servant lieth at home sick of the palsy: speak the word only, and he shall be healed.* This was true faith; the conviction, not that Christ certainly would, but that, if He would, at least He could. And that is true faith still. The comfortable assurance, *He has willed to heal me*, is one of God's good gifts to those whom He has first healed: but the preliminary condition is only this, *I believe that, if He will, He can.* That sort of faith, bringing a man in earnest prayer before Christ for forgiveness and for grace, is saving faith, however long the other be delayed; nay, if it never come at all in this life. Many a Christian man has never had a full certainty, to his dying day, of his own salvation. But he has had what was essential; a sight of the unseen; that is, a conviction of the power of Christ to save, and an earnest daily application to Him for his own salvation. Saving faith is the conviction that Christ can save, and the resolute, determined, unflinching prayer that, as He can, so He will also, save me.

And now many are accusing themselves, as they listen, of a great weakness and deadness of faith as thus described. It is not only that they do not feel themselves to be yet saved; but it is that they have many doubting unbelieving thoughts even about Christ's salvation; perhaps about His divinity, perhaps about His atonement, perhaps about His accessibility, perhaps about His readiness to receive such as they are, so sinful and so doubting. In these days so many things are written without fear, and said without shame, in the way of disparagement of Him, that a person with no great knowledge and still less self-confidence is in danger of being quite shaken in mind as to the very foundation of the Christian hope. This is our trial; one of the greatest of the trials of the age in which our lot is cast. But I desire to say an encouraging word to those who are too much cast down and distressed by these misgivings. I suppose that you wish to believe: I suppose that you have not given up your own anxious desire to be a Christian and to die a Christian in the distinctive sense of that word. And I suppose, further, that you do, even amidst doubt and misgiving, and much vacillation and uncertainty, make your daily prayer to or through that Saviour who is the one object of our Christian faith. If this be so, what comfort may we derive from our Lord's own reception of one whose application could only express itself in those deeply touching words, *Lord, I believe: help Thou mine unbelief.* How wonderful a combination. *I believe: help Thou mine unbelief.* How strangely does it anticipate the very state of mind which we are seeking to characterize. Yes, a person who will bring his unbelief with him to Christ cannot be entirely or chiefly an unbeliever. In that praying amidst doubt, in that dragging of our unbelief into Christ's presence, we recognize, however disguised, a positive act of faith. It is the conduct of one who is not loving his sin, not wrapping himself in his incredulity, but rather treating it as his enemy and coming with it to the light to get it reproved. It is the very case of him who, when asked by Christ Himself whether he also would go away, answers, *Lord, to whom shall we go? Thou hast the words of eternal life.* He who must go somewhere, and has nowhere else to go, is indeed *not far from the kingdom of God.*

But O, my brethren, let us rise even from this, and go on unto perfection. If we have nowhere else to go, let us go to Christ. Let us not be contented with the knowledge of this only resource: let us also use it. Faith grows, even like hope, even like love, by habit and by converse: let it be so with ours.

Be assured that one deep heartfelt prayer to Christ, on the basis of His being and of His atonement, is worth whole months and years of study of evidences apart from this contact. It is for want of this that many men live and die doubters. It is for want of that intercourse, of soul with soul and spirit with spirit, that we continue speculators in truth, instead of living members of Christ's body. If by means of the weak words now spoken one person in this congregation should be led, through God's grace, to cast himself upon the salvation which is in Christ only; to ask of God, in hearty prayer, the forgiveness of his sins, simply because of Jesus Christ; to ask of God His mercy and grace, His fatherly hand over him and His holy Spirit with him, only because he reads in the Gospel that such was the promise which Christ made, and such the hope which He died to ratify; then indeed this morning's work will have been well done and richly blessed: new seals of the Gospel will be impressed, broad and deep, upon this congregation, and God through Christ Jesus will be glorified in them.

Faith grows, like hope, like love, by converse. Yes, brethren, it is not an easy thing to see the invisible. It is not an easy thing to get the seen outshone by the unseen, and the temporal overborne by the eternal. That is the task set before us. We must learn so to live as that the will of Christ shall be stronger in us than the self-will, and the word of Christ more persuasive than the word of the world and of the devil. If we live not this life, which is the life of faith, how can we die that death, which is the death of the faithful? We must know Christ well now, or we cannot hope to have Him for our stay in the dark valley. And therefore I call you to a diligent use of those things which are tenderly and lovingly given to us as *means of grace*. Prayer, and meditation, and reading God's Word, and attendance at Christ's holy Table, are changed from irksome duties into attractive invitations, as soon and in proportion as we can regard them as means of *growing in grace and in the knowledge of our Lord and Saviour Jesus Christ*. If they are neglected, or listlessly and thanklessly and grudgingly used, it is because we are looking upon them from the wrong side; because we do not long for a stronger faith and a clearer light in things heavenly, or do not believe God's love to us in providing ordinances of strength and comfort for His feeble and fainting and flagging children. Let us use each as His gift to us; His gracious gift of a new opportunity of communing and conversing with an unseen Friend and Saviour; of growing in the personal knowledge of Him *whom to know* for ourselves *is eternal life;* and assuredly *the place will be too strait for us*, and the time too short and too rare, of hearing and worshipping: *the desire of our souls will be to the Name of God and to the remembrance of Him.*

According to your faith, Christ says, *so be it done unto you.* That is His rule. *According to your faith.* Much faith, much help: little faith, little help: no faith, no help. God keep us from the last alternative. May we so use the little given, as to have more abundantly. At last, may ours be that faith which is all but sight, and which waits but for the drawing aside of a thin veil of earthly atmosphere, to translate us into *the inheritance of the saints in light*, where *we shall see Him as He is*, and *be satisfied, when we awake, with His likeness.*

THIRD SUNDAY AFTER THE EPIPHANY,
January 25, 1863.

XVI.

VAGUE PRAYERS.

St Luke xviii. 41.

What wilt thou that I shall do unto thee?

THE poor blind man had no difficulty in answering that question. He could not for an instant forget or mistake the nature of his want. He, when he heard that Jesus of Nazareth was passing by, had cried to Him for mercy, because he felt a particular want, and because he believed that Jesus only could supply it. He, when the companions of the Saviour, little knowing His compassionate heart, *rebuked him that he should hold his peace*, only *cried so much the more*, because he felt that this was his only chance, and that it was quickly passing and escaping him. And therefore, when Jesus actually stopped, and commanded him to be brought to Him; and then, on his near approach, asked him the definite question of the text, *What wilt thou that I should do unto thee?* he, without hesitation, and without delay, mentioned that malady which was making his life a life of darkness and of helplessness, and said, with a steady and unfaltering utterance, *Lord, that I may receive my sight.* Faith itself was here supplemented by an accurate knowledge of the heart's plague and sorrow, and He who waited but for this avowal said at once in reply to it, *Receive thy sight: thy faith hath saved thee.*

My brethren, it happens to every one of us, each week, and (I trust) many times in each week, to be kneeling as this blind man knelt, in the presence of Jesus Christ, and calling to Him for His mercy. We have done it today. The very words of the blind man have been upon our lips: *O Son of David, have mercy upon us.* But now suppose Him stopping on His daily round of spiritual ministration to the Churches, and turning His earnest heart-searching gaze upon some one—yes, for it is true, upon each one—of this gathered congregation, as He puts this grave personal question, to the soul within, *Thou sayest, Have mercy on me: now what wilt thou that I shall do for thee?* are we all ready with the answer? Does each heart so know its own bitterness, in its point and in its sting, as to be able at once to reply, *Lord, that I may receive from Thee just this or just that?* On the contrary, is it not too certain that many of us, thus suddenly confronted with the Saviour whom we have professed to seek, would be constrained to answer, *I called not: I meant not to be thus taken at my word: I came hither for form's sake, not with a purpose: depart from me yet a while; come not to torment me before the time?* And might not others amongst us, with whatever impulses and yearnings after good, still feel themselves at a loss as to the particular thing which they desire, and find themselves silent, if not from indifference yet from confusion and embarrassment, when the definite question sounds, however lovingly, in their ear, *What wilt thou that I should do for thee?*

Thus the Gospel for this day serves the important purpose of reasoning with us as to the loss and the danger of vagueness and unreality in prayer.

It is true, there is such a thing as what we may well call simple communing with God; that mere interchange (with reverence be it spoken) of thought and feeling with God through His Son Jesus Christ, without any special request or petition, which is one of the chief privileges and chief blessings of the Christian life below. But in such intercourse there would be little difficulty in replying to the question of the text. *Lord, that I may be with Thee; Lord, that I may grow in grace; Lord, that I may practise for heaven; Lord, that I may know Thee better and love Thee more;* such an answer as this would have in it nothing of that vagueness, nothing of that unreality, which the text, in its spiritual application, is sent to reprove.

It is not of such communing with God that we would speak in terms of disparagement. But we have all known something of a vagueness and unreality in prayer, the very reverse and opposite of this.

1. Here, for example, and in private also, we are wont to begin our devotions with an act of confession. We speak in strong terms—we could scarcely use stronger—of our depravity and corruption, of our unworthiness and our misery, of our omissions of duty and our commissions of sin. The language of the most familiar of all forms of confession, that which opens our ordinary public worship, is of this character. And just because it is so, just because it uses strong terms to characterize our sinfulness and our vileness, it is suitable to the case of all who know themselves, and large

enough to admit within the compass of its sympathy those who need everything to assure them that they can possibly be objects of divine regard. And this language, in a public service, must of necessity be not only strong but general. If it were made particular, it would become unreal. If we were all to confess, when we meet here, that we have done this or that particular sin, the words would, as a matter of course, be untrue, be false words, for many. But now suppose that our Lord Jesus Christ Himself, hearing one of us describe himself in this strong manner as *a miserable offender*, as *having erred and strayed from God's ways like a lost sheep*, as *having left undone what he ought to have done, and done that which he ought not to have done*, were to accost him particularly, and say, *What wilt thou that I should forgive thee?* or, in other words, *What hast thou done so much against me?* might it not be found that some of us had meant nothing by their strong self-accusations? might we not, some of us, answer, *I know nothing against myself; I have always done my duty: I thank God I am not as other men are?* What a conflict then, what a collision, between our language of confession and our real inward thoughts. We have nothing to answer when Christ says to us, *What did I hear thee say?*

Let us practise ourselves, my brethren, in meaning something by our confessions of sin. If here, in God's House, we must be contented with summaries of our condition; with calling ourselves miserable sinners, in whom there is neither health nor hope; let us take heed that we prepare for such confessions by diligent self-examination at home. We have no right to use these words in Church—true as they are, and (when rightly understood) comforting as they are—unless we do know something against ourselves, which, in our secret prayers at all events, we confess particularly. Let us habituate ourselves to a distinct and definite review of sins that are past. In the evening let us consider with ourselves what we have said, what we have done, wrong, on the day that is ending; what we have left unsaid and left undone which ought to have been either done by us or spoken. And indeed we shall find enough, every one of us, to make us ashamed and to make us sorrowful. What day in our past lives has been indeed lived aright? What relation has been properly fulfilled, what duty thoroughly done? What act of worship has not been full of sin? What prayer has not been, more or less, either from coldness or from wandering, an affront to the holy God to whom it was addressed? If we will only thus judge ourselves, we shall bring with us hither, week by week or day by day, such a catalogue, stamped upon the memory, of shortcomings, inconsistencies, backslidings, and sins, as shall make the words of public confession no longer vague to us, but most definite: if our Lord should ever say to one of us, *What meanest thou by this language of self-condemnation?* we shall be ready to answer, *Lord, I mean by it that today and yesterday and the day before I said and I did this which I ought not: Lord, I mean by it that the experience of a past lifetime has shown me what I am, and taught me an overwhelming lesson of unprofitableness, vileness, and sin. Lord, be merciful unto my sin; for indeed it is great.*

The confession of sin, and its natural accompaniment, the prayer for forgiveness, is one part, the earliest and a most indispensable part, of all worship. It has respect to the time past; to that irretrievable, that ineffaceable past, which is the millstone round the neck of all of us. God be praised for that *unspeakable gift* of an atonement and propitiation for sin, which enables us still to endure under a load so burdensome and so oppressive. May He give us grace to *lay hold upon the hope* thus *set before us*, and so to use the promise of pardon as that it may indeed *sprinkle our hearts from an evil conscience*.

2. But the other part of all prayer has respect rather to the future. *That we may obtain mercy;* that is one thing: *and find grace to help in time of need;* that is the other. With regard to this latter, even more than with regard to the former, there is a risk of vagueness, of unreality, in our prayers. The petitions which we seem to bring with us to the throne of grace may be neutralized by our inability to answer the searching enquiry of our Lord, *What wilt thou that I shall do for thee?*

There are those, it must be feared, who at the end of this Service will have literally asked nothing of the Lord. There are those whose whole occupation within these doors is the dwelling upon things which have passed or are to pass without them; whose hearts are never really withdrawn from the world, even while they are apparently praying to God or singing His praise. I know of no proof of our Fall more decisive than this. While we are speaking to God, our thoughts are absent. Not only is faith weak, or zeal intermittent, or interest faint and flagging: attention itself is wanting. And this while we are worshipping. What must it be at other times? *If the light that is in thee be darkness, how great is the darkness.*

But not only thus. There are those who give some heed to the words of prayer and praise here uttered, some who are even devout in their utterance, who yet cannot answer the question, *What wilt thou?* Let each one of us seriously say to himself as he quits the Church this morning, *What have I asked today? What definite boon, what special grace, have I prayed for? what definite boon, what special grace, am I now expecting in consequence to receive?* I fear that the first answer will be, in many cases, *I know not: I have asked nothing. The exercise of worship or of communion may act favourably upon the frame of my mind or the temper of my soul: I may be soothed and tranquillized and encouraged by the opportunity of approaching God through His Son Jesus Christ: this I hope; this I may be: but I cannot say that I have asked anything, or that I look for anything, from the Lord.* And then, from a self-examination of this kind, which is all condemning, we shall pass, by God's grace, to the endeavour to amend in this respect our worship for the future. We shall make it a special and (I am sure) a profitable part of our preparation for worship, to reflect upon particular wants; in other words, to review our condition as it has been or as it is, and to make up our minds to ask of God through Christ just that definite thing which we find ourselves most to need.

One of us will discover that, in the most simple sense of all, he needs deliverance from sin. He has fallen again and again, for months and years past—perhaps (for besetting sins are not only obstinate but generally life-long) from his very youth up until now—into some particular offence against his duty towards God or towards man. It may be temper, it may be vanity, it may be frivolity, it may be indolence, it may be worldliness, it may be some sin of language, or some habit of intemperance or evil lust. He has struggled, or intended and resolved to struggle, against this temptation, many times over, in his own strength: now and then he has fancied it overcome; the house was *swept and garnished*, and he hoped that the wicked spirit might never return. And sometimes he has even prayed against it; and has been disappointed to find that prayer itself gave no immediate safeguard against sin: he has first fallen for want of prayer, and then he has fallen in spite of prayer. These things make many a man sad and sick at heart: more souls than we dream of are *tied and bound with the chain of sin:* and to these, above all, the thought of Christ, with His power over evil spirits and His readiness to exercise it, ought to be dear: these, above all, when He comes and says to them, *What wilt thou that I should do for thee?* ought to have no difficulty in answering, *Lord, that I may get rid of this particular sin: Lord, that I may receive strength from Thee to break off the fetter and go free: Lord, that I may so abide with Thee and in Thee, that the enemy himself, when he cometh, may find nothing in me.* I would earnestly beseech any such persons, if such there be before me, to set before themselves, when they here pray for God's grace, the particular sin to which they are prone, and to ask deliverance from it, not (as we are too apt to do) in a faint and feeble way when the temptation itself is close at hand or already assailing them, but rather in the lull and suspense of its warfare, while they can call in Christ's almighty aid with no misgiving or sinking courage to let and to counteract it. It is in the far distance, not when the enemy is upon us, that we best apply to Him who is our hope, and gain from Him the fortifying armour which alone can *withstand in the evil day.*

Another, in the prospect of worship, will feel that the thing which he most needs is a general increase of faith. The world is too much with him: he cannot see the invisible; he cannot *look up to heaven, and by faith behold the glory that shall be revealed.* He finds himself grovelling in the things that are present, and incapable of lifting up his soul to things heavenly, things eternal. When Christ asks him, *What wilt thou that I shall do for thee?* no answer could be so suitable as that of the blind man himself, *Lord, that I may receive my sight. What I need is, not so much deliverance from a particular kind or form of sin, but rather the power to apprehend those great realities of heaven and of eternity, of God and Christ and the soul, in which alone consists the permanence and perpetuity of human existence. And when in preparation for worship I am thinking over what special want and distress I shall bring most prominently to the Lord for healing, I can think of nothing so appropriate as this which seems to be of all the most general; an increase of that vital gift of faith by which alone I can either see Christ or live to God.* The Apostles themselves *said* once *unto the Lord, Lord, increase our faith.*

But let us all, beloved brethren, bring something, whatever it be—something real, something definite, something learned by experience and examination—whenever we profess to approach God's mercy-seat with the prayer for healing, help, or grace. The very endeavour to do this will give point and meaning to our worship. If we all come hither, week by week, with a known and felt want to be satisfied out of Christ's fulness, there will be a force and an energy and a concentration in our worship, which is commonly too much lacking. Then will the question of the text sound in our ears with less of reproof than of encouragement; and when the Saviour asks, as the preliminary to healing, *What wilt thou that I shall do for thee?* we shall be ready, all of us, with the definite response, *Lord, that mine eyes may be opened: Lord, that I may receive my sight.*

QUINQUAGESIMA SUNDAY,
February 15, 1863.

XVII.

FAITH TRIUMPHANT OVER REFUSAL.

Matthew xv. 23.

But He answered her not a word.

THE Gospel for this day shows our Saviour in an unwonted character. For once the good Physician seems to be unwilling to heal. And yet this is the one narrative of the Gospels to which we should refer for encouragement and comfort any one who was most fearful and most desponding. How is this? Whence this strange combination, of repulsion and attraction, of a forbidding form and an encouraging sense?

Our Lord on this one occasion had overstepped the limits of His own country. He had left the Holy Land, and gone into *the borders of Tyre and Sidon.* Whatever other purposes this journey may have answered, such as a brief intermission of His usual toils, or a passing change of scene and society, this at least must be admitted, that there is no record of any other event or any other act of His during it, save only that which is described in this one passage itself. We can almost believe that the sole object of our Saviour in this excursion into the coasts of Tyre and Sidon was the working of that very miracle which seemed, but seemed only, to be wrought reluctantly and as it were unwillingly.

He did not thus diverge from His usual course, for the purpose of proclaiming His salvation in a land of strangers. This would have been contrary to His principle: and St Mark expressly says that it was not so. *He entered into an house, and would have no man know it: but He could not be hid.* People who had pressing wants could not be kept from Him. The prosperous and the self-righteous could dispense with Him, could even cavil at and blaspheme Him. But let a pain or a sorrow cut deep; let other resources fail, and the physician of the body confess or show himself defeated; and there was that in the Saviour of sinners which even upon earth could *draw all men unto Him.* It was so then, and it is so now.

Thus it was in the case before us. A woman of Canaan—*a Syrophœnician woman* St Mark calls her— was suffering under one of the most cruel distresses that could befall a mother: she had at home a young daughter possessed with an unclean spirit. We know not precisely in what this possession consisted; but we can imagine that its symptoms were as distressing, as fearful, as the very worst case that was ever witnessed of absolute raving madness. Here then was an example of a known and felt want, about which there could be no mistake, and for which there was no human remedy. That person could answer the question, *What wilt thou that I should do for thee?* There was no vagueness in her conception of the distress from which she was suffering. And by whatever means she had become acquainted either with the Saviour's power to heal, or with His presence in her country, the fact was so; she knew that He was there, and she knew that He could, if He would, do for her even this thing which lay entirely outside the province of human strength.

How must it have grieved and astonished her, knowing what she did of His usual readiness to help and save, to find herself received with an immovable and most chilling silence: to find her anguish treated with disregard, her entreaty repulsed, not by a kind and reluctant refusal, but by a stern and rigid and hopeless silence: *He answered her not a word.* The disciples themselves, who were not always (in those days) ready to second the petitions of their Master's suppliants, were touched by the piteous and unregarded cries of this Canaanite mother. *Send her away*, they said to Him, *for she crieth after us. Grant her prayer, and let her depart. Her importunity is wearisome, as well as pitiable: let it avail with Thee, and let us be rid of it.* That which He had not given to her, He gave to them; a word of reply; an answer, whether this or that. But it was an answer of refusal. *I was not sent, save to the lost sheep of the house of Israel: and she is not of Israel; she is a stranger and a foreigner, beyond the pale of my commission. The time is not yet, when all nations shall be freely welcomed within the gate of God's Church: I came to seek first the lost sheep of Israel: not until after my departure shall the Gospel of the kingdom be preached without distinction among all the nations.*

She then who had believed without hope, must now (even as it is written) *believe against hope.* The silence is broken, but only to make the case more desperate. He is sent only to Israel, and she is a Gentile. Where is that faith to be found, which shall believe still? He Himself has shut out hope: let her return to her home now doubly darkened, and watch on, as she may, through sorrow and anguish, the tortures, in soul and mind and body, of her who is dearer to her than life. So would many have argued; so, my brethren, should we, I fear, have argued: but thus did not she. She felt, we may imagine, that the Saviour of sinners could not but be merciful to human sorrow; that there must lie beneath this show of sternness a heart of compassion and loving-kindness: at all events—and this is the truest lesson—that here alone, that in Him alone, lay even the peradventure of assistance; that, if He did not help, help there was none for her; and that therefore in His presence, at His feet, even if unheeded, even if repelled, even if refused and rebuffed, she must still linger, if she would not see the candle of hope put out for ever in darkness.

But her trial was not yet ended. When she drew still nearer, and renewed her cry for help, she was told, in yet severer accents, that she was not one of those to whom as yet Christ came to minister. *It is not meet*, He said, *to take the children's bread, and to cast it to dogs.* To extend the special privileges of Israel to the Gentile world without, was like taking the food of the children and throwing it to the dogs. Thus doubly repelled and rejected; denied in the matter of the answer, and affronted in its form; surely she will renounce hope, and bear her grief henceforth as she may. The words themselves leave no loophole either for cherishing hope or persisting in entreaty. Thus would indeed everything have judged save that faith which is strong even to remove mountains. But that faith was hers. And that faith can perceive even in refusal a mysterious consent. That faith can say, *Truth, Lord; Thou hast rightly described us; we are dogs, fit only to be spurned and trampled upon and cast out; we are unclean, we are vile, we are unworthy of the least of all Thy mercies: yet, Lord, even as the dogs under an earthly table are suffered to pick up the crumbs which drop from the children, so, without claiming to ourselves one promise or one privilege or one prerogative of Thy chosen, we, even we, the nations that know Thee not and have wandered furthest from the light and from the consolation of Israel, may be allowed, in Thy grace, to gather up here and there something of the overflow and abundance of their blessings, not enough to make Israel one whit poorer, yet enough to make us unspeakably and incalculably the richer.*

And now *the trial of faith, more precious than of gold that perisheth*, is gloriously ended: the Saviour who gave the grace has *magnified and made it honourable*: He has left on record for the latter days of His Church one of the noblest triumphs of that marvellous, that invincible gift: and He closes the trial with those words of blessing which sufficiently show what had been throughout its purpose and its design, *O woman, great is thy faith: be it unto thee even as thou wilt. And her daughter was made whole from that very hour.*

We have often of late seized the opportunity of speaking of the nature and working of that great and fundamental Christian grace, of which it is written that *the just shall live by his faith.* And today assuredly we shall not fail to lay to heart that characteristic mark of true faith which the history before us is so well calculated to illustrate. Let us look at it once more in its parts.

1. Here is, first, the Saviour leaving the usual scenes of His ministry, and passing into a land to which He had as yet no message. As soon as He reaches it, He makes it plain that He did not come there for purposes of public ministration. He came there, I think we may say, for the sake of one soul. He would leave on record just one example of His care for those who were not yet His own. He would make one exception, even thus early, to that general rule which restricted His ministry to the Jews. Thus would He warn them that God's blessing might escape them altogether, if they gave not the more earnest heed. Thus would He show that He, the Almighty and the All-wise, is not tied and bound by rules of procedure. *When and as He will*, such is the law of His working. And they who would find Him must watch for Him. Into the coasts of Tyre and Sidon He comes but now and then, or He comes but once; and they who have their griefs waiting for Him must lose no time in producing them while He is near. Soon the visit ends, and she who has procrastinated has lost the opportunity.

2. Again, how many are the heart's sorrows. How often are they connected with family life. How often is it the son or the daughter, the sister or the brother, the wife or the husband, whose pain or whose sin awakens in us that sense of need, that unrest, that disquiet, that longing and yearning, which is to be to us, if we rightly use it, the memento of the unseen and eternal. This Canaanite mother was brought to Christ by a daughter's misery. Happy they whose family sorrows

bring them to the same place for healing; to the feet of Christ, to the throne of grace. Have any of you, my friends, left behind you at home this day some object of solicitude or distress? *The heart knoweth its own bitterness:* but these things are of common experience: there are sad and aching hearts in every congregation; and One *who is greater than the heart and knoweth all things* sees them and feels for them.

3. But at all events, if the home be ever so bright, if the life be ever so cloudless, there is a want deep down within, which is either keenly felt, or, if not felt, tenfold more urgent. If not for a child *whom Satan hath bound,* yet at least for ourselves we have all need to approach Christ with the prayer, *Have mercy on me, O Lord, Thou Son of David.* In some of us there is by habit a possession of the evil one: in all of us there is by nature a taint and an infection of sin. What shall we say of this, be it which it may? Is it not a real matter? more real than anything which is visible? Is it not a malady, is it not a disease, is it not a misery, to be so *tied and bound by the chain of sin,* that, even *when we would do good, evil is present with us?* to be so biassed towards wrong, and so averse from good, that we, who are God's creatures, and who must one day stand before Christ in judgment, can yet live as if we were immortal below, nay, cannot, even when we would, remember ourselves and turn readily and believingly to God? The very least of our maladies in soul is greater than the very greatest of our maladies in body or in circumstance. The very least of our spiritual maladies is an indisposition to duty, an averseness from God; could we name a disease more alarming or more deadly? What shall

they who live and die in this state do in that world in which *God shall be all in all?*

4. Thus then we have all of us occasion to approach Him who has turned aside to visit our coasts. We have all a malady which needs healing, and for which He alone, alone in heaven or in earth, even professes to have a remedy. The less we feel, the more we need. Has the Gospel call reached some hearts—we know that it has—in this congregation? Are there some who do feel their spiritual disease, and who, feeling it, have sought the presence of Christ for healing? Yes, we believe—or we could scarcely bear the weight of this ministry—that many hearts here present are turning day by day to the *Lord of all power and might* for *that thing which by nature they cannot have;* a comfort not their own, and a strength not their own, to be perfected in earthly distress and in human weakness. But have all these at once found that comfort and found that strength? If each one of them were closely questioned this morning, as they sit here in God's House of Prayer, as to their confidence of personal forgiveness, and their experience of practical help in overcoming evil and in doing good, how many could return an answer of peace? Must they not rather say that, when they have seemed to pray most earnestly, Christ has often *answered them not a word?* that, when they have most desired to pray, the very heart has seemed to die within them, and the cry for compassion could scarcely rise from their lips? Have they not often seemed to hear Him answer, *My grace is for others: it is not for thee? My sheep hear my voice, and thou hast disregarded it? My table is spread for the children, and thou art not of them? It is not*

meet to take the children's bread, and to cast it unto the dogs? Yes, the sense of utter unworthiness sometimes almost frames itself into a refusal and a repulse. We say perhaps to ourselves, *It is true: I am rightly named: I am all this: I am vile, I am unholy, I am outcast and rejected, and I deserve it all:* and then we go on to make a most opposite use of this knowledge to that which this miracle of healing should suggest to us. She, the Syrophœnician mother, accepted the description and yet turned it into a plea for grace. She made not His discouraging words a reason for departing, but rather a reason for drawing yet nearer and crying yet more importunately. And so ought we to do. The more we find ourselves or fancy ourselves repulsed, the more ought we to pray on and not faint. We have not heard, as she heard, from the Saviour's own lips, the words of refusal and of disdain: and yet those very words were taken by her as an argument for renewing her supplication. My brethren, we do not believe that any real prayer was ever cast out for the unworthiness of the asker; and certain we are that, if our prayer be cast out, we have none else to go to: there, in Christ's presence, at Christ's footstool, yea, at the foot of Christ's cross, we may well kneel and kneel resolutely, saying, *Lord, to whom shall I go? Thou, and Thou only, hast the words of eternal life. Lord, I believe: help Thou mine unbelief.*

5. And doubt not, but earnestly believe, that, as this miracle describes us in some of its parts, so shall it describe us also in all. It was written to teach men this lesson; that refusals, even if they were uttered in words from the heavenly places, are at the very worst

only trials of our faith. *Will we*, that is the question, *pray on through them?* If we will, then are we of those whom Christ hears; of those whom Christ regards as His faithful, His called, His chosen. No sounds ever reach us from on high, save those of encouragement, of sweet and gracious invitation: we cannot say that Christ ever said to us, *I am not sent to thee:* but even if He did say so, still, by the example of this woman, it would be our duty to pray on and not to faint. There ought to be in our hearts, as in hers, an assurance of His character even deeper than any words; a conviction that He, whom the Holy Scripture sets before us as the Physician of the sick and the Saviour of the sinful, must, whatever He may seem to say, have an under-purpose of love towards all who seek Him. Even if there were any isolated and disjointed words to be found in our sacred Book, which might seem to repel, we must nevertheless read them by the light of the general purpose, and be assured that He who *came into the world to save sinners* cannot really intend to daunt or to deter even the most sinful. God grant us all this faith beyond hope, or this faith against hope, according to our need.

6. And assuredly, this morning, we may take the history before us as a strongly encouraging call to Christ's holy Table. True, we are not worthy to sit there as His guests; *not worthy*, as our own Service says, borrowing the words of this miracle, *so much as to gather up the crumbs under it:* still He who here blessed and crowned the faith which acknowledged unworthiness and yet craved the boon, will not refuse any of us who, with a sincere desire to approach and to find Him, draw near in self-renouncing faith, and cast themselves on

His mercy. May a large and growing number thus *seek Him while He may be found, and call upon Him while He is near.* Soon, too soon, will He grant the petition of those who *pray Him*, as the natural heart prays Him, *to depart out of their coasts:* easy is it to lose sight of Him; easy in the act, and bitter in the retrospect. So may it not be with us. May we seek on, and also find. May we bless Him for not having yet *dealt with us according to our sins, nor rewarded us according to our wickednesses.* And may the sense of past mercy quicken in all of us, by God's grace, the pursuit of His love and of His salvation.

SECOND SUNDAY IN LENT,
March 1, 1863.

XVIII.

THE DUMB SPIRIT.

Luke xi. 14.

Jesus was casting out a devil, and it was dumb. And it came to pass, when the devil was gone out, the dumb spake.

It is thus still. The miracle is fulfilled in our experience. While the devil still has possession, the man is dumb: only when the devil is cast out by the word of Jesus, can the dumb speak.

The tongue of man is called in Scripture his glory. *Wherefore my heart was glad, and my glory rejoiced. Awake up, my glory; awake, lute and harp; I myself will awake right early.* Speech is the index of reason. In one great language of antiquity there is no distinction between the two ideas: there is but one word for the reason within and the expression of it without. Reason is speech in its source; and speech is reason in its utterance. You have all seen many times, and whenever you have seen you have pitied, the children of a benevolent Institution in this place, when you have chanced to follow them in a walk, and to mark that unnatural silence, or else that more painful babbling, by which they give notice to every passing stranger of that great deprivation with which it has pleased God to afflict them. You know both how much Christian love and Christian patience can do to repair this loss, and, alas, also what it cannot do; how far skill and toil can go in remedying, and where both must stand aside and bow before God's mysterious yet irresistible and (we doubt not) all-wise will. You can well understand, as you observe that spectacle, why the organs of human speech should be called in their perfection man's glory.

This great gift of speech is ours, my brethren, without let or hindrance. What we will, we can ask for: what we think, we can say: what we purpose, we can announce. Has any one of us ever stopped to give God thanks for this gift of speech? The more we ponder it, the more we marvel. That any one of us should be able to put into words any one thought; that it should be natural to us, as we grow out of the merest babyhood, to speak a language; that in the strength of this power we should be able not only to inform one another as to ourselves, but even to affect and influence one another towards the thinking or saying or doing either this or that; that a faculty of mutual communication, far, far more wonderful than any art of signal or of telegraph by which we seek to apply or to extend it, is thus bestowed upon human life, rendering help and cooperation and sympathy possible, and making coexistence and society not a burden but a delight; these things are prodigies, when we reflect upon them, beyond any that science discloses or magic counterfeits; and I ask again, which of all us has ever either thanked God for the gift of speech, or reflected upon the responsibilities which that gift involves?

Jesus was casting out a devil, and it was dumb. The

poor frame, with its very organs of utterance, was tied and bound by an indwelling spirit of evil. The devil within held in thraldom the lips and the tongue. The indication (in this instance) of the possession was the silence. No act of kindness could elicit thanks. No eagerness of enquiry could extract information. No pain, no injury—stranger still—could draw from the possessed an answer even of complaint. It was the will of the possessing evil one thus to show his power and his presence. As the Psalmist *kept silence*, he tells us, on one occasion, *yea, even from good words;* so the devil in this instance made his victim to keep silence, yea, even from wicked words; from words of anger or rage or malice or blasphemy. These are among the freaks of Satanic agency; an agency nearer to us, and more real and powerful in its dealings, than some of us know or will acknowledge. I want to show you, my brethren, that there is a sense, and a very true sense, in which every natural man, every man who lets himself alone and lives practically *without God*, apart from Christ, *in the world*, has in him a dumb spirit, and can only lose that spirit under the healing touch of Christ.

1. I might speak—but it would not affect or be true of all who hear me—of that calamity, that curse, which we designate as a bad temper. Has any one here present a bad temper? Or has any one here present lived with a person of a bad temper? Have you not been reminded sometimes, in that experience, of the dumb spirit spoken of in the text? That sullen silence; that overcast brow; that gloomy, morose, most irritating reserve; that gathering, threatening, overhanging cloud

of dull, dark, speechless displeasure, by which a long evening has been rendered miserable, and upon which night and sleep have come without mitigation and without relief; that obstinate nursing and cherishing of an untold grudge, which wakens again in the morning to its last night's sullenness, and seems almost to pride itself upon its tenacity and its perseverance; was not this indeed an example of possession by a dumb spirit? Did not you yourself, if you have ever had in you this temper, feel as though you were not your own in indulging it? as though you had something or some one else occupying the citadel of your being, and refusing to release you from the bondage? as though the dissipation of your gloom were absolutely out of your power, and the retention of anger a sort of duty laid upon you by an authority to which you were subjected? Yes, it is true: you are at such times under a Satanic, a diabolical influence: you are possessed by an evil spirit, and that evil spirit is dumb.

2. But it is not only in noticeable cases of bad temper that we see the same power working. Mark that man—*his name* indeed *is Legion*—who lives what is called an entirely preoccupied and self-engrossed life; who has his business and follows it, has his interests and pursues them, has even his pleasures and enjoys them, but in all these has in reality no partner and no associate; looks to himself, as to all that most intimately touches him, and himself only; excludes from his true confidence alike friend and brother, alike child and wife; gives out in social converse the merest superficialities of his thoughts, and in domestic intercourse the veriest dregs and refuse of his being; locks up in his

own bosom the affections which God gave him for blessing, presupposes selfishness in others because he feels it in himself, and will trust no other soul with that confidence which he knows could have no reception and no reciprocity in his own. Does the description sound unamiable? It is so: this is not the ʻman for love, because love is not in him; not the man to awaken tenderness, because the spirit of compassion is a stranger to him. But does the description sound exaggerated? Has it no counterpart in human experience? O, my brethren, amongst these hearts lying open today before God who made them, there are many which God alike and man must call selfish: the world counts selfishness no crime; nature calls selfishness natural, and even glories in it: and of all these we must say that, so far as the deep realities of existence are concerned, its truest principles, its keenest feelings, the spirit of selfishness is evermore also a spirit of silence: the lips may speak, but the soul speaks not: the devil that possesses is not debasing only but dumb.

3. Let us approach more nearly to an universal experience. The cases hitherto described, however common, have exceptions. Some natural men are sweet-tempered: some natural men are benevolent and warm-hearted. But, when we think of the great purpose for which the gift of speech was bestowed upon us, we shall feel that there may be an absence, even in these, of that which makes speech man's glory. *Let your speech be always with grace*, St Paul says, *seasoned with salt*. It is made in Scripture both the duty and also the test of a Christian, that his speech be not only innocent, but beneficial; not only kind and frank, but

consistent also and edifying. His aim ought to be, to do good with his words; so to use this marvellous power as that others shall be the better for it, as that others shall have cause to thank God for having endowed him with it. To this end, a Christian seeks, first of all, to *be* what he ought to be; to *be* good, to *be* holy, to *be* charitable and thankful and humble; knowing that *out of the abundance of the heart the mouth speaketh*, and that he who is this will show it. But, even beyond this greatest of safeguards, he also exercises care and watchfulness in the use of speech. He does not, as some would do, undervalue and disparage it. He does not say, Be natural, be frank, be unstudied in your language, and it is enough. He does not, like some, laugh at the idea of influencing by conversation. He knows that there is such a thing—for he has himself (let us hope) sometimes felt it—as a power accompanying speech, and a positive good done by it. He desires and prays that he may exemplify it. He knows that there are persons in whose society he feels himself a better man, less worldly, less censorious, less ambitious, less trifling. Such would he be; one of those whose influence is for good in this mixed scene and battle-field of life. It is by speech, not least but most of all, that we influence and are influenced. Not indeed by speech which contradicts and is contradicted by the conduct; but yet by speech, if it be consistent with the conduct, even more directly and more powerfully (it may be) than even by the conduct itself. In such speech there will be seldom and sparingly an introduction of sacred names and sacred things. To talk about religion is not always to influence. It is not only, nor chiefly, by the actual introduction of holy things, that we ourselves have been most influenced towards holiness. It is rather by indication than by obtrusion of Christian principles; by an evident watch kept over the admission of vain and unprofitable things, by a firm faith cherished within, and a strong and stedfast charity maintained without, rather than by frequent introduction of the name of Christ or the precepts of the Gospel; that a Christian man will use his gift of speech in the service of his Master. But he does use it, and they who know not the cause feel oftentimes the effect.

Now, if this be so, by what name can we designate that use of speech which altogether overlooks or refuses this high object? Let us all look back, my brethren, this morning upon our past employment of the gift of language. What shall we say of it? Is not the review most disheartening? To whom can we point as having been benefited by our possession of this marvellous thing? Nay—for effects are God's, not ours—when did we ever set ourselves seriously to do good by our conversation? Alas, how idly have we entered the room in which our family or our friends were gathered together for food or converse. Not one word of prayer has gone before, of secret, earnest prayer, that we might be kept from doing harm, enabled to do good. Not one single-minded aim proposed to ourselves, or one resolute effort made to raise instead of lowering the tone of all. No thought has been turned to the seizing of opportunities; to the endeavour to minister to the satisfaction of the doubting, the establishment of the wavering, the softening of the morose, or the sobering of the careless. No plain unswerving principle has been maintained, in judging, with reference to the topics of the day, either of men or things. There has been no superiority in our talk to vulgar prejudices or to unfounded imputations. No real pleasure expressed at any triumph of good or any tribute extorted by the Gospel. No hearty admiration of deeds of heroism or of self-devotion; no honest sympathy with oppressed patriotism or suffering virtue. Therefore, I say it most sincerely, as to any value, any worth, contained in the gift of speech, we might as well have been bereft of it. In the judgment of Him who heareth as well as *seeth in secret*, the spirit which has possessed us has been no better than a dumb spirit.

4. It has been so towards men. We have done no good with our speech. And how has it been towards God? The text stands in immediate connection with a passage of Holy Scripture about prayer. Strong encouragement has been given to our halting failing faith, in reference to the duty of seeking God in prayer. A form of prayer has been given, in answer to the request of the disciples, *Lord, teach us to pray;* and words have been added, which show beyond all question that it is not in God but in ourselves that the work of prayer is straitened. Then follows immediately the brief narrative of the text: *Jesus was casting out a devil, and it was dumb.* If the possession of the evil one makes us dumb (as to all that is valuable) towards man, so also does it towards God. Strange it may well seem to us, that, with a throne of grace revealed, and a God seated thereon of whom it is one characteristic attribute that *He heareth prayer*, we should not all rush with one accord to offer up first the prayers of want and then the praises of gratitude. It is not so. Rich and poor, high

and low, old and young, one with another, all by nature hang back from prayer. Has God made prayer a command? We disobey it. Has He made prayer a privilege? We think scorn of it. Any excuse is enough to put aside prayer. Books which would neither amuse nor interest us at other times, are welcome to us if they come instead of prayer. That which we should regard as no reason for missing the most trifling engagement of earthly duty or pleasure, is a sufficient, an ample reason for postponing prayer. Every morning we have to lash ourselves to the exercise, by some dread of consequences or (at best) by a mere sense of dissatisfaction and of unrest. Happy they who even thus can be brought to it. My brethren, if I desired to impress upon any one's heart the meaning and the reality of Original Sin, I would speak to him of his prayers. I would say, Do not you perceive that your 'glory', as Scripture denominates your power of utterance, absolutely refuses to move in its highest, its noblest, and its most remunerative office, as the exponent of your thoughts and your wants in the ear of God? How can you doubt that you are in evil case, how can you gainsay the fact of your corruption and of your degradation, when you find yourself under the mastery of some malign influence which absolutely prevents you from holding communion with your Father and your God in heaven? Yes, you are possessed indeed by the evil one; and the devil that is in you is indeed, towards God as towards man, a dumb spirit.

The Gospel of our Lord Jesus Christ never leaves us in our low, our lost estate. If it unmasks us, it is that we may see what we are, and seeing may escape from it.

If it humbles, it is only that we may rise, gradually and consciously, out of all that is evil into all that is good. The text which condemns, also promises. *Jesus was casting out a devil which was dumb; and when the devil was gone out, the dumb spake.* It was even thus that He spake after His resurrection. *These signs*, He said, *shall follow them that believe: they shall speak with new tongues.* Has it not been found true a thousand times? They who once spoke profanely or in guile; they who once feared not to blaspheme God and His Word; they who once drew others downwards to their own level of ungodliness and vanity; they who at all events set before themselves no high object, and sought nothing in society save their own honour or their own amusement; they who cared not how infrequent was prayer, or how indolent and lifeless was praise; have been found again and again to speak with other tongues, as soon as the power of Christ's healing has begun to tell upon them. There is a magic in that contact, which is mighty to transform souls. Let a man be convinced of his own misery and of his own ruin; let him humbly and earnestly call upon the Saviour of sinners to save him; let him day by day, and many times in each day, seek the cross and throne of Christ to *obtain mercy* and to *find grace;* let him place himself on Christ's side, and determine to know Him for himself not less as his Master than as his Propitiation; and depend upon it, the light within will soon, more or less, shine through; the still small voice which sounds daily in the soul, will find an echo in the voice; he who was dumb shall begin to speak; and men will find there, in proportion as he drinks more deeply for himself of the water of life, not less a charm to attract than a power to influence. They will *take knowledge of him that he has been with Jesus;* and the words shall be fulfilled which say, *And it came to pass, when the devil was gone out, the dumb spake, and the people wondered. All the people, when they heard him, gave praise unto God.*

THIRD SUNDAY IN LENT,
March 8, 1863.

XIX.

THE LIVING SOUGHT AMONG THE DEAD.

Luke xxiv. 5.

Why seek ye the living among the dead?

THE words, my brethren, are Angels' words. They were addressed to those faithful and pious women who had carried their spices and ointments to anoint the Lord's body in its grave. Very early in the morning of that original Easter day, by the light of which every Sunday and every weekday of our Christian year shines and is glorified, they came to the sepulchre expecting to minister to the dead as they had once ministered to the living. Thoughts by the way had perplexed them concerning the great stone which they had seen rolled to the mouth of the sepulchre. To their astonishment this difficulty had vanished. The stone was rolled away, and they could enter freely. But how often is facility the prelude to disappointment. How often in life is the difficulty foreseen not the real difficulty. They entered in, but it was to find that entering vain. The sacred body itself was gone. *They entered in, and found not the body of the Lord Jesus.* They were not unnoticed in their distress. Two of those heavenly messengers whose office it is *to minister* below *to the heirs of salvation,* and who might well be awake and active on this morning which was the crisis of a world's redemption, presented themselves to the anxious and perplexed women with the question of the text, *Why seek ye the living among the dead?* There is a force and beauty in the original which is somewhat obscured in the Version. *Why seek ye the living One*, or, as the margin gives it, *Him that liveth, among the dead? He is not here, but is risen.*

The words are words of rebuke: but oftentimes rebuke is the surest vehicle of consolation. To be reproved for not believing a thing which it is misery to doubt; to be accused of unreasonableness in not accepting at once a truth which would be life to us from the dead; nothing can be so comforting. It is as good as to say, *You may be happy this moment if you will: do not forfeit by an irrational incredulity a mercy and a blessing which is yours if you will have it. Why seek ye the living One among the dead?* is, in other words, *The Lord is risen indeed; rise after Him, rise with Him: death has lost its sting, and the grave its victory.*

Why seek ye the living among the dead? Who, you will ask, does this now?

1. It is done, in the worst sense, by those whom Scripture calls *the children of this world.* If we look for our happiness below—whether in riches, honours, or pleasures, whether in ambition, self-indulgence, or love —we are, in the worst sense, seeking the living among the dead. This world is one great sepulchre, and the men that live for it are so many soulless bodies. This life, let it run its course for a few years, has been to each of us, or will be, the grave of many hopes, many beliefs, and many affections. How difficult is it, looking back even from middle life, much more from old age, even to

imagine to ourselves enjoyments which in some earlier stage of being were our all in all. Pursuits which we once lived for seem to us now mere insipidity and emptiness. Joys for which we would have sold a birthright are seen now as the mere mess of pottage. Friends, alas, whom we once idolized have forgotten us or have been forgotten. An eminence which we once panted to reach is gained and found a molehill. A renown which cost us health and comfort and perhaps a soul is grasped and found a shadow. We look back upon the infatuation with wonder. How could we thus misjudge our own interest? We awake, and, behold, it was a dream. But in all this there is a moral, and a grave one. That which the desires of youth seem to manhood, and that which the pursuits of manhood seem to old age, may not the interests of life itself seem to the departing soul, to the disembodied spirit? I know nothing below from which the operation of this law is excluded. The mere lapse of time, the mere change of circumstances—still within the limits of this life—makes everything that is behind seem insignificant, seem delusive: shall it not be thus when we advance one step further, and look back upon the world that is from the world that shall be? Let us listen betimes to the warning voice which says to us, Why seek ye the permanent in the transitory? *Why seek ye the living among the dead?*

2. The same question has its application to formalism in religion. And what do we mean by formalism? We mean that habit of resting in the means of grace as if they were ends, of regarding the ordinances of religion as if they were securities for acceptance, which is at once the oldest and the most obstinate of all human tendencies

in the things of God. A man thinks that he has done all that is required of him when he has brought his family to the house of prayer. If he adds to this a prayer at home, he is sure that all must be well with him. If his manner here is orderly, his response in the service duly made, and his attention to the sermon respectful and serious, he will write himself a religious man, and perhaps say on his deathbed that towards God as well as man he has always done his duty. And do not suppose, my brethren, that we are any of us able to dispense with or to disparage forms. Within the shell lies the kernel: he who throws away the one parts with the other also. We only say, Do not think that the handling of the fruit, and its eating, are necessarily one and the same. There is a resting in forms which actually separates you from the spirit. *The publicans and the harlots* may *enter the kingdom of God before* that man who has occupied his seat here for fifty or for seventy years, and who has never failed in his tribute of outward worship to the God who made him. There may not have been in that man one spark of real sorrow for sin, of real anxiety for salvation, of real wrestling in prayer, of real, honest, heart-deep gratitude to the Saviour who shed for him His most precious blood. And if it be so, if it be indeed so, then to him belongs, not in an encouraging but in a fatally condemning application, the grave question of the text, *Why seek ye the living among the dead?*

3. We approach more nearly to its first meaning, when we speak of its bearing upon the case of doubters. These women were reproved for perplexing themselves about the disappearance of the body, when they ought

rather to have regarded it as the fulfilment of His own prophecy of resurrection. They were losing by their want of faith all the comfort which they would have derived from accepting His own words in their simplicity. They were hanging over the place where He was not, forgetful of the place and the state in which He had declared to them that He would be found. *He is risen; He is not here: remember the words which He spake while He was still with you.* My brethren, there are some in every congregation whose prevailing fault is of this nature. They can follow Christ to the tomb, but they cannot get beyond it. They believe in the life; they admire the example; they are touched by the tenderness and by the authority of the teaching; they could weep over the sufferings, and they can adore the mind that shone through them. But they stagger at resurrection. Their minds have a sceptical turn, and the thought of what contradicts experience is to them impossible. Thus they flit around the grave, they feel it as holy ground, they bring their offerings of praise and of reverence to Him whom they have left lying therein. But they stop short of a hearty and a lively faith in Christ risen. They hope it may be so; they do not deny it; but it forms no part of their daily trust or of their daily motive. And thus they lose, and must lose, that which is distinctive and characteristic in Christianity. They cannot hold the Atonement, and they cannot hold the Divinity, of their Saviour. They cannot build upon Him, and they cannot live by Him. O for a voice, not of severity but of attraction, to ring in their ears the angelic remonstrance, *Why seek ye the living One among the dead?* Ye who reverence Him as a man, ye who believe that

He spake and that He did something at least of what is written in the Gospels, how is it that ye leave out of His words that which tells and tells again of resurrection, and out of His works that crowning miracle to which He ever appealed as the one sign of His Messiahship? Believe that One whose character is there before you would not speak presumptuously; that One whose life is there before you could not lack power. Apply to Him in your hearts by earnest prayer, as though He were alive from the dead: determine to cast in your lot with St John and with St Peter, with the holy women who saw and believed, with St Thomas who once had doubted, and St Paul who once had persecuted; determine to run the risk for eternity with men and women who could scarcely have been deceived and who gave life itself as their testimony; and depend upon it, you, in no long time, will be able to say, in the confidence of a sure conviction, *Now I believe, not because of their saying, for I have found Him myself, and know that this is indeed the Christ, the Saviour of the world. I have found Him in the comfort which He inspires and in the grace which He communicates, in the satisfaction of my wants, the correction of my faults, and the concentration of my affections; I have found Him sufficient for the life that is, and I will trust Him with my one deposit against the life that is to come. Why seek ye the living One among the dead? He is not here, but is risen.*

4. There is a different case, though in one point resembling this, to which I would make a last application of the words of the text. It is that of Christian people, true believers, firm holders of the Propitiation and the Mediation of Jesus Christ, but who yet never

XIX.] *The Living sought among the Dead.* 447

advance practically beyond the death, beyond the cross and the grave, into the clear light and full glory of a risen Saviour. They bring their sins for forgiveness, night by night, to the foot of the cross; they place no slight and no presumptuous trust in that *blood of sprinkling* which speaks peace to the conscience; and they pray for the grace of the Holy Spirit to keep them from treating as an unholy or a common thing that *blood of the covenant wherewith they were sanctified.* What lack they yet? Something there is yet beyond, might we but reach it, if St Paul's words read this day from the Epistle to the Romans and from the Epistle to the Colossians have any definite or substantial doctrine for the Church of all time. What means that contrast between being *reconciled by the death* and *saved by the life* of Jesus? What means that *law of the Spirit of life in Christ Jesus which makes us free from the law of sin and death?* What means that *life of Jesus* being *made manifest in our mortal flesh?* What means that saying, *I was crucified with Christ, and it is no longer I that live, but Christ liveth in me? To me to live is Christ?* Above all, what means the exhortation which we have heard today? *If ye then be risen with Christ, seek those things which are above, where Christ sitteth on the right hand of God. Set your affection on things above, not on things on the earth. For ye are dead, and your life is hid with Christ in God. When Christ, who is our life, shall appear, then shall ye also appear with Him in glory.* These and suchlike expressions tell of something beyond the death of Christ; beyond a trust in the Atonement; beyond a recurrence, however earnest or however constant, to the blood of sprinkling. They say to us, Be not for ever lingering in the sepulchre, though He who lay there was indeed slain for your sin. Remember, He is not there now: He is risen. Rise after Him. He is in heaven for you: He is there as your High Priest, He is there as your Intercessor, He is there also, and above all, as your life. He says Himself, *Because I live*, live after death and resurrection, *ye shall live also*. He says Himself, *I am the true vine... Abide in me and I in you... Without me ye can do nothing*. He says Himself, *He that eateth me*, he who day by day receives me into his heart by a real, living, spiritual communion, *even he shall live by me*. These things all point above and beyond a mere trust (though it be the first thing, and without it there is none other) in the death and the atonement. They all teach us, that the life upon which Christ entered, as on this day, by resurrection from the dead, is the life in which we must know Him, in which we must daily converse and commune with Him, from which our own life must draw its supplies, and in which our own life must as it were be hidden for safety, if we would ever know what is meant by *the salvation which is in Christ Jesus*. There is rest, there is security, there is comfort and strength and joy. Thither, to the heaven in which He dwells with the Father, must our eye ever be directed, if we would not be the prey of torturing doubt, of perpetual vacillation, of ever assailing and ever prevailing sin. *Leaving the principles of the doctrine of Christ, let us go on unto perfection; not laying again the foundation of repentance from dead works, and of faith towards God, of the doctrine of baptisms, and of laying on of hands, and of resurrection of the dead, and of eternal judgment. And this will we do, if God permit.* And then the Apostle rises into the glorious subject of the Melchizedec priest-

XIX.] *The Living sought among the Dead.* 449

hood, and calls his readers to rise with him into the contemplation of One who, *having neither beginning of days nor end of life, is able to save to the uttermost all who come unto God by Him, and to them that look for Him shall appear the second time without sin unto salvation. Why seek ye the living One among the dead?* Onwards not backwards, upwards not downwards, be the eye of your soul ever directed, if you would know *the inheritance*, the present inheritance, *of the saints in light*, or know the length and the breadth, the depth and the height, of His calling, who says, *I am the resurrection and the life: he that believeth in me, though he were dead, yet shall he live; and whosoever liveth and believeth in me shall never die. He is not here: He is risen.*

Thus let us today seek Him, as we gather round His holy Table. Let us see that we partake not of a dead but of a living Saviour; of One who not only died to reconcile, but lives to save. *I am the bread of life: he that cometh to me shall never hunger, and he that believeth on me shall never thirst.* Let us so remember the cross, as to seek the throne; so trust in the death, as to be saved by the life. And may He Himself look down upon us in His great compassion, humbling, quickening, guiding, comforting, by His Holy Spirit, according to our need, and drawing from all our hearts the tribute of the Easter adoration—

Unto Him that loved us, and washed us from our sins in His own blood, and hath made us kings and priests unto God and His Father, to Him be glory and dominion for ever and ever. Amen.

EASTER DAY,
    April 5, 1863.

XX.

THE CHRISTIAN DOUBTER.

Matthew xxviii. 17.

But some doubted.

JESUS CHRIST, risen as on this day from death, stood here before the eleven disciples: and yet they doubted. He had directed them to meet Him in Galilee; He had fixed the place; He had promised the meeting; they had obeyed, and He had appeared: and yet they doubted. They had known Him in life; they had followed Him hither and thither during more than three years; they had toiled with Him, and journeyed with Him, and suffered with Him; they had loved Him, they had been faithful to Him, save indeed during the few short hours of His trial and His passion, when the weakness of the flesh had triumphed over the resolution of the spirit: and yet, notwithstanding this intimate knowledge, and notwithstanding this devoted affection, and notwithstanding the obedience which they had exercised in now meeting Him, and notwithstanding the homage of reverence and worship which they were at this moment paying Him—notwithstanding all these things, some still doubted.

So extraordinary is the power of sympathy, of true fellow-feeling, over the heart and life of man, that these three words touch the soul of many with an influence denied to the protestations of a positive faith and the outbursts of an ardent devotion. If you wish to raise a man out of his sins, confess to him that you too are a sinner. If you wish to help a man out of his difficulties, confess to him that you too have doubted. Then he will feel that he can trust you; then he will say to himself, That man, like his Master, *has suffered being tempted*, and therefore, like his Master, he can feel for and perhaps *succour them that are tempted*. If you would be (in your humble way) a physician of souls, never pretend to be without disease yourself. The air of superiority may overawe: but it is the acknowledgment of weakness which softens, which teaches, which helps.

Something of this kind is at work in the words of the text. Visions of angels, evidences of power, instant acknowledgments of truth, and ready adorations of the Saviour, might seem to us, if they stood alone, rather glimpses of another world than illuminations of our own. But when we read that the very disciples who were nearest to Him, the very disciples who best loved Him, the very disciples who had gone into Galilee in obedience to His command and in expectation of His presence, yet themselves, even while they worshipped Him, in some cases doubted; then indeed we feel that there is reality, we feel that there is sympathy, we feel that there is help for us; we are drawn to the narrative, and to all that lies within it, as *by the cords of a man:* these people, we say, were like us; God grant that we by His grace may become like them.

That Book which writes on its pages, *But some doubted,* is a truthful book. It is not patching up, or propping up, some *cunningly devised fable:* if it were, it would say that so overwhelming was the proof that not one person to whom it was presented could for an instant doubt it. That Book itself seems to feel for us. It is as though it would say this to us; *A great demand is here made upon your faith: the matter presented to you is above nature; flesh and blood cannot receive it: be not surprised if you stagger at its strangeness: so did some of those to whom it first came; some of those to whose senses the proof appealed; some of those who became afterwards its messengers and its witnesses. Be not ashamed, be not terrified, if at first you receive the record with hesitation or amidst misgivings: of those to whom it first came, some doubted.*

It is by such indications of its transparent truthfulness that the Bible commends itself as much to the judgment as to the conscience of mankind. Little do its enemies know their own interest, when they point to the weaknesses and the inconsistencies of God's saints, to a biography chequered by faults and falls, by omissions of duty and commissions of sin, as arguments against the faith or against the revelation which the Book thus impugned offers as the instrument of human salvation. And little do the friends of the Bible know their own strength, when they evade or tremble before the argument thus enforced. It is because the Bible paints human nature as it is—as it is, *yea, even in the regenerate*—that we recognize in it the voice of Him who *knows what is in man* because He Himself created him. The words, *But some doubted,* show us that we are not reading of imaginary characters, or of persons whose natural character was placed under some violent compulsion or constraint to turn them into believers and witnesses of the Gospel; but of men like ourselves in all the workings of perception and of reflection; men who had to be convinced in reason before they could embrace and live the faith. That some of them once doubted turns for a testimony to that truth which at last they believed. Well has it been said, *They doubted that we might not doubt: God for the more confirmation of the faith suffered one of His holy Apostles to be doubtful in His Son's resurrection.* It was he who once said, *I will not believe*, who was the first to utter afterwards that memorable confession, *My Lord and my God.*

These are some of the thoughts which lie on the surface of the clause read as the text. But it is no part of the business of a minister of the Gospel to suggest doubts or to encourage doubts in his hearers. And he must be careful not so to speak as though doubting were either the necessary or the reasonable condition of a Christian. Some men nurse their doubts: some speak as if it were a sign of intellect, or a proof of candour, or else an interesting weakness, to be doubters all their days: and even of those who do not err in this direction, yet many, once again, use no decision with themselves, listen to no counsel and will adopt no regimen, for the removal or satisfaction of doubt, and thus show an ungoverned and a wayward spirit, most opposite to that which breathed in the first disciples and which still dwells in those who shall be heirs of salvation. And therefore, my brethren, having spoken generally of the encouraging aspect of the words before us, I desire now to mark more carefully the characteristics of these Gospel doubters, that we may not misuse the comfort nor miss the instruction which their case affords.

1. These persons were not doubters from any disposition to cavil. They did not think it an ingenious thing to find out difficulties in believing. Their minds were open to conviction, should sufficient evidence be vouchsafed to them. There was a difficulty in accepting the truth, and God had not yet given them all the proof which He designed for them. The evidences of Christ's resurrection were not yet complete. He who does nothing in vain designed for them some further light; and, till that light was given, it can scarcely be said with perfect reverence that doubt was excluded.

2. These persons were not doubters from its being their interest to disbelieve. They were not persons who had dark places in heart or in life, which they wished to keep dark. They were not cherishing bosom sins, and they were not treading underfoot known duties. If they had been in this condition, of course a holy Saviour could not have been welcome to them. Well might they have hoped that the Master and the Judge of man, once laid in His grave, might stay there and see corruption. Are we quite sure, my brethren, that in our doubts there is no lingering motive of this nature? At least I am persuaded that no source of doubt is so fruitful as a careless, inconsistent, Godless, sinful life; that no man is so likely to be beset with misgivings about the truth of Christ's resurrection or the authority of God's Word as he who has kept himself through early years out of the reach of Christ's inward voice; and that no retribution is more certain in its coming, or more just in

its infliction, than that which visits a long neglect of duty with a judicial incapacity for believing.

3. These persons did not make doubt a reason for not obeying or for not worshipping. They came at Christ's call into Galilee to meet Him; and when they saw Him there, they worshipped. There are degrees in doubt, as there are degrees in faith. Every doubt is not an adverse judgment. A man may obey though he doubts, and a man may worship though he doubts. Let me beg you to ponder this thought. To give up obeying, or to give up worshipping, is not to doubt, but to decide; it is to close doubt, and to choose unbelief. How different the spirit which expresses itself in those instructive words, *Lord, I believe: help Thou mine unbelief.* That man's faith could not stand the full test, *If thou canst believe, all things are possible to him that believeth:* that man doubted: that man knew what misgivings were, and what objections were, and what difficulties and despondencies were: but he brought his doubts with him, he brought his misgivings and difficulties with him, yea, he brought his unbelief with him, and came to Christ not so much in spite of as because of them; came as a sick man to the Physician, came as a lost man to the Saviour; and therefore he was heard, therefore he was succoured: He who *will have all men to be saved* saw in this man not one who loved his doubts but one who hated them, not one who cherished his unbelief but one who amidst all believed and trusted and had faith still. Just so was it with the doubters in the text. They obeyed though they doubted, and they worshipped though they doubted. They were doubters, they were not infidels. Between these two lies a whole

gulf, a whole sea, of distance and of difference. I would press it upon you, my brethren, with all earnestness, not to confound the two. You may doubt, and yet obey: you may doubt, and yet worship. There is no dishonesty in that: nay, there is no inconsistency in that. I am well persuaded that the greatest doubter in all this congregation has more reason to believe than to disbelieve. He has more reason to think that there is a Saviour than that there is not a Saviour. He may find difficulties in the Gospel: he finds more without the Gospel. He may doubt his Saviour's resurrection, or his Saviour's divinity, or his Saviour's power to hear, to answer, and to save. I am sure that this negative feeling does not outweigh the positive. I am sure that his heart and his conscience, if he ever listens to them, are more satisfied in Christ than his understanding or his reason can possibly be dissatisfied with Christ. Therefore his position, at worst, can be only that of a doubter; that of a man who does not feel certain of having a Saviour. What then? Shall he live at once as if there were none? Shall he discard reverence, and stifle prayer, and shut his Bible, and forsake the congregation? Is that the dictate of conscience? is that the direction of reason? Nay, that is to precipitate a decision in one direction, when as yet he knows not that it ought not to be in another. The balance of evidence is still in Christ's behalf. For the time then that balance is decisive. For the time he must behave himself as though Christ were true. It is thus that he would act in any one of the doubtful decisions of daily life. We act according to the preponderance of probability. To act against it is insanity. If we cannot be certain, we must doubt; but we must act still. Even so it is in matters of faith. I will venture to say that no person here present has one half or one quarter the reason for doubting that he has for believing. Therefore he who doubts is bound to obey and is bound to worship still. Alas, too often the first doubt shuts the Bible, and the second doubt stifles and strangles prayer. And then where are we? We have settled that question upon which we profess only to be in doubt. For he who cuts himself off from the ordinary influences of God's Holy Spirit has made it (if God's Word be true) impossible for himself to believe. Would he but have prayed on, and obeyed on, and sought on, there would in no long time have arisen upon him a marvellous light; the light not of a cold scoffing intellect, but of a warmed and transformed and invigorated heart. And he who allows conscience to speak within will find in this last experience a decision idly hoped for from the other.

4. A last word remains. These persons, as they did not allow doubt to drive them from Christ's service or from Christ's worship, so were turned from doubters into resolute believers by a nearer access to Christ, and by the revelation of His risen power. *When they saw Him, they worshipped Him: but some doubted.* He was already in sight, and they had bent the knee in homage. But now *Jesus came and spake unto them;* drew nigh, approached, came up to them; and talked to them, spake with them as a man talketh with his friends; *saying, All power (authority) is given unto me in heaven and on earth. Go ye therefore, and make disciples of all the nations, &c.* If these men, because they doubted, had

turned away; if they had said, It is dishonest to obey, it is a mockery to worship, till every doubt has vanished; what would they not have lost? They would have forfeited the fulness of faith, and the honour and happiness of service. While they stood afar off, while they paid Him only the distant homage of a doubting reverence, so long the very sight of Him was not conclusive: they must have seen that it was He Himself, long their Companion, their Friend, their Guide, their Master; but they allowed the thought of the difficulty, the thought of the cross, and the thought of the death, and the thought of the grave, to overbear that conviction of the senses: they fancied it almost less improbable that some one else should wear that loved form and personate that gracious Master, than that a victory so marvellous, so beyond former experience, should have been won over that last enemy before whom rank and wealth, before whom strength and sovereignty, alike bow down to rise up no more. But now when He drew nigh and spake to them; when they heard once again *the gracious words that proceeded out of His lips;* when they heard Him tell of the mystery of His kingdom, and bestow upon them with the living voice the commission of His representatives below; when He gave them a certain form of initiation into the membership of His Church, and promised His own divine presence to be with them till time should be no more; then at last they felt that to doubt on would be less a sin than a madness: He who thus spake could be none other than the Son of God Most High: before proof it was right to doubt, but after proof it would be impiety and blasphemy: and thus the understanding which had been in suspense was decided and satisfied, and the homage of a longing heart was fulfilled in the devotion of a life and of a death.

Such was the course of doubt, my brethren, in the case here before us: such its course, and such its end. Within ten days after the Ascension the miracle of Pentecost had ratified for ever the miracle of the Resurrection. He who so fulfilled such a promise must indeed be risen to die no more. He who could so work in man's heart, and so transform man's life; He who could thus change fear into courage, and wavering into stedfastness; He who could thus make one who had denied Him to escape the ridicule of a few servants *rejoice to be counted worthy* before rulers and priests *to suffer shame for His name;* could not indeed be *holden of death*, could not have remained in or been stolen from the rich man's sepulchre, but must be alive again for evermore in the glory and *power of an endless life*. That was the extinction of doubt, as this was its silencing.

My brethren, the Christian doubter—I use the term advisedly; there are Christian as well as unchristian doubters, and we have sought to characterize them this evening—the Christian doubter will derive guidance as well as hope from the example now before us. And that in three points.

(1) He will seek nearer access to Christ. As he feels that doubt is a sign of distance, so he will endeavour to remove doubt by nearness. Thus he takes precisely the opposite course to the merely intellectual doubter. His doubt drives him to Christ. If the Gospel is true, Christ lives, and has *all power in heaven*

and on earth. If the Gospel is true, Christ cares for men, and has a tender as well as devoted interest in the salvation of the most sinful. If the Gospel is true, Christ hears prayer, and is always more ready to listen than the best of us to pray. Therefore the practical test of the truth of the Gospel will be, not the cold discussion of its evidences, not the keen dissection of its doctrines, but the application to Christ, as a living Person, for instruction, for help, and for satisfaction. It was by His drawing near and talking to them that the doubts of the first disciples were removed. So must it be now. Therefore we who are perplexed and troubled with ceaseless doubtings must come wherever Christ is; must frequent the House of Prayer and the Table of Communion; must pray much at home, and study the Word of God with diligence; as the only means of resolving doubt, as the only reasonable method of arriving at conviction. But even this must be done in a patient and a waiting spirit. Christ nowhere promises to pour a sudden light upon darkened hearts. It is a trial of faith to which many earnest seekers have been subjected, that they seem to ask in vain; that they do not derive an immediate, or rather a conscious benefit, even from acts of devotion. More especially will this be so if they have long trifled with devotion; if in former days they have knelt without praying, sung without praising, read without interest, and heard without attention. There is a discipline in these things; a reaping and a sowing, in the things of the soul, which grace itself rather mitigates and overrules than sets aside or supersedes. The Christian doubter is patient as well as earnest. What he looks for is light at eventide, rather than light at noonday. *Then shall he know, if he follows on to know the Lord. It shall come to pass,* says the promise, *that at evening time it shall be light.*

(2) He will especially hail any sign of Christ's willingness to employ him. These doubters in the text were sent forth to evangelize and to baptize. Nothing soothes doubt so much as active service. Let Christ send a man, and the man will scarcely doubt whether Christ is. Therefore if I address tonight any persons who are tortured with doubt and misgiving as to their Saviour's resurrection or divinity or power to save, I counsel them, with prayer and watchfulness, to set themselves about doing something in His name: let them visit the poor, let them teach in the school, let them (if they can do nothing else) employ their hands in working for the needy; let them undertake some office of this kind, with hearty prayer for a blessing upon it to themselves; let them perform it, quietly and unostentatiously, as a commission from Christ: and though here also I must counsel patience; though here also I must remember that *God gives no account of His matters*, and must not be prescribed to as regards time or mode; yet I venture to assure them that He will approve and that He will bless the effort, and make it at least as comforting to the doer as beneficent to the receiver. If Christ owns His work in your hand by making it serve His own purposes of mercy and loving-kindness, there must be a Christ, He must be living, and He must be working.

(3) But last and above all, the Christian doubter must seek the illumination of the Holy Ghost. We have said that, though Easter might silence doubt, it

was Pentecost which extinguished it. A man who has the Holy Spirit working powerfully within, drawing his thoughts towards God and heaven, enabling him to conquer sin and to be strong for duty, cannot doubt whence this gift comes: he *has the witness in himself;* he believes not because of another's message, but because he has known Christ for himself, and found Him to be indeed a Saviour. For that Holy Spirit who proceeds from the Son and from the Father; who takes of the things of Christ, and shows them to His disciples; who helps their infirmities, and intercedes for them inwardly with yearnings which cannot be uttered; let us all pray earnestly and not faint. One victory over a besetting sin, achieved by faith in Christ crucified and Christ risen; a victory which we should not have assayed but for Christ, and which is granted as a direct answer to prayer offered in the name of Christ; is worth far more, as a personal and practical proof of the Gospel, than all the arguments of all the theologians. God multiply amongst us, in us, these evidences. And may He at last so *stablish and strengthen and settle* our faith, that we may be able to *fight the good fight* and *witness the good confession;* to *endure* through life *as seeing the Invisible,* and to tread the dark valley with *His rod and His staff to comfort us.*

EASTER DAY,
April 5, 1863.

XXI.

THE COMPANIONSHIP AND THE INDWELLING OF THE SPIRIT.

St John xiv. 17.

He dwelleth with you, and shall be in you.

I BELIEVE *in the Holy Ghost.* That is what we are met this morning to say in the ear of God. *I believe in the Holy Ghost.* That is what we are met this morning to say one to another, and to confess in the face of the world. Whit Sunday is the festival of the Spirit. Whit Sunday, like the other chief festivals of Christianity, has two objects: it commemorates a fact, and it testifies to a doctrine. The fact is, the descent of the Holy Spirit of God upon the first disciples; the fulfilment to them, ten days after the Ascension of Jesus, of their Master's most true promise, that they should *receive power* for their life's work by the entrance into them of the Holy Ghost in all His manifold gifts of strength and grace. And out of this fact springs the doctrine; that, as we also have work to do, and difficulties to encounter, and infirmities to overcome, and sins to vanquish and to eradicate, so to us also the same divine presence is promised for each one of these undertakings; a presence, not a mere communication; a personal agency within, not a mere providence or protection or assistance from without. The commemoration of an event is also the confession of a want and the claiming of a promise. *I believe in the Holy Ghost,* is not merely, *I believe that the Holy Ghost once descended,* but, *I believe that there is still such a Person, I believe that He still works and still lives in Christian men, I believe that I need His work and His indwelling, and I believe that to me, even me, that work and that indwelling is promised, is guaranteed, and shall be made good.*

Our Lord distinguishes, in the words of the text, between two kinds, or two degrees certainly, of the Holy Spirit's presence. *He dwelleth with you, and shall be in you.* Evidently He points to the difference between the condition of His disciples while He was with them below, and the condition of His disciples after His return into glory. While He was with them below, the Holy Ghost *dwelt with* them in His person. They saw in Him the presence of the Divine Spirit. His mighty works, His wonderful words, His perfect holiness and charity and self-denial and truth, all these things, daily witnessed by them and profoundly reverenced, were results of *the Spirit given to Him not by measure.* Though He was very God, yet He acted below within the limits (as it were) of a perfectly inspired humanity. It was of the essence of His humiliation, that He lived and acted, spake and wrought, during His earthly sojourn, as though He were only a Man full of the Holy Ghost. Thus, when He dwelt with them, the Holy Spirit dwelt with them; dwelt with them in a sense and with a fulness never realized in the case of any others. And the Spirit who was in Jesus kept them also in the truth by virtue of a controlling influence put forth upon them from Him. *While I was with them in the world, I kept them in Thy name.*

But this influence was to be withdrawn. When His work of obedience was completed in the work of suffering; when a life given was at last crowned by a death endured; and when, after a brief interval of converse after resurrection, sufficient to make them His witnesses, sufficient also to explain to them in some degree the mystery of a risen life, He departed from them till the season (yet future) of the Advent and the Judgment; how was their stability to be then secured? how were they then to be kept in their allegiance? how were they then to be qualified for their office, and preserved from the manifold temptations of this present evil world? The answer is given in the second clause of the text. *He shall be in you. That Holy Spirit who before dwelt with you in Jesus, shall now be in you by a presence personal and immediate of His own. He shall be in you to teach, He shall be in you to comfort, He shall be in you to direct, to regulate, and to transform. He shall be in you to make the doubter believing, the timid brave, and the inconstant resolute. He shall be in you to give energy to your exertions, persuasion to your preaching, and consistency to your life.* It was so. This day which the Church celebrates throughout her generations saw the fulfilment of the promise. The Holy Spirit did descend, as at this time, upon the first disciples, to be in them for ever. Then was seen the difference between the coexistence and the inhabitation which the text distinguishes. For then first was the carnal in them transformed into the spiritual, the ignorant, the timid, and the earthlyminded, into the wise, the courageous, and the heavenly. What the presence with them even of the Saviour Himself had failed to do was done perfectly and at once by the presence in them of the Saviour's Spirit. And the saying was fulfilled which He spake, *It is expedient for you that I go away; for, if I go not away, the Comforter will not come unto you; but, if I depart, I will send Him unto you.*

My brethren, I hasten through explanation that I may turn to application. I am jealous over you lest this Whit Sunday should be a form; the recollection of a fact, but not the expression of a conviction, and not the stirring up of a gift and of a grace.

1. *He dwelleth with you, and He shall be in you.* Are there any senses in which the Holy Ghost may be said even now, even when Christ's bodily presence is gone from us, to dwell with us rather than to be in us?

(1) Yes, He dwells with us in Church ordinances. Every time that we meet here for worship, every time that that holy Table is spread for Communion, there is a coexistence with us of the Holy Ghost. Do you doubt that there are those here present in whom the Holy Ghost is at this moment working? Do you suppose that His grace has died out from the Church? Do you imagine that sorrow for sin, do you imagine that a thirst for holiness, do you imagine that a lively love for the Saviour, do you imagine that an earnest wrestling and an effectual communing with God, are less directly wrought in man's heart by the Holy Ghost than they were in the days when Apostles preached or martyrs witnessed? Even in these familiar places, even in these

prosaic, these common days, the Holy Ghost works still, and works personally, in Christian ordinances. It is our fault, as well as our unhappiness, if that working of the Holy Ghost is external to any one of us. *Ye have not, because ye ask not.* But let us first grant this, that He works in some. The Holy Spirit is present here this morning; present really, present personally, though present secretly and by an individual not a promiscuous operation. At this moment, though amidst many infirmities and many sins, He is with us still.

(2) And He dwells with us, not here only, but in the haunts of common life. He dwells with us in Christian lives; in the daily sight and hearing of the conduct and language, of the acts and the words, of true Christian people. You well know that, scattered here and there through the houses of this town, there are noble examples of a consistent faith and a devoted holiness. I can almost believe that there is not one of you who does not know such a character. Is there no son, no brother, no husband, here present this morning, who lives in daily contact with such a life? You have seen day by day for years, till you have almost ceased to notice it, that steady, that unswerving piety, which seems but to shine the brighter for neglect, for discouragement, for isolation, perhaps for ridicule. You have seen that temper, which was perhaps by nature quick to wrath, gradually schooled and disciplined, till now an affront kindles no resentment, and a sarcasm provokes no retort. You have seen the progressive shaping and brightening and enlarging of that *ornament of a meek and quiet spirit which is in God's sight of great price.* You have seen sensitiveness pass into equanimity, cen-

soriousness into charity, frivolity into seriousness, and a regard for the world into the one pursuit of heaven. You have seen a care for others take the place of an indulgence of self, and a profound yet active sympathy cast out by degrees from the character and from the life the spirit of self-concentration, of self-seeking, and of self-esteem. And now you have learned to rely upon that person as one who cannot disappoint and cannot fail. To him, or more probably to her, you have for years carried with entire confidence all your selfish distresses and all your mistrustful cares. That face you have beheld *as the face of an Angel;* that presence was for you the sunbeam, it was the divinity, of your home. I say that in that Christian character the Holy Spirit dwells with you. And I say that nevertheless the Holy Spirit may not yet be dwelling in you. Yours may still be the condemnation of him who has the light, yet walks not in it; who avails himself of the safeguard of another, without seeking it for his own ; who sees the blessed influence of Christ's Spirit, sees it and in a sense rejoices in it, yet never sets himself to turn the co-existence into an indwelling, or the bright reflection of glory into a direct influx and contact of light.

(3) And we may go yet one step further before we cross the boundary line between the two states described. The disciples in the former condition not only lived with Him in whom the Spirit was, but also submitted themselves, in general intention at least, to the guidance of His example and the influence of His will. They were not (with one exception) either cavillers at Christ or traitors to Christ. With many remaining errors and many natural infirmities, they were yet altogether on

the side of good, even while the Spirit was rather with than in them. Even so it is still. There are many well-disposed persons in this congregation; many persons who would not knowingly cherish a sin or forego a duty; many persons who not only wish to *die the death of the righteous*, but are desirous in many respects to live his life. The words of the text have an application at once admonitory and encouraging to these. It says to them, Do not rest in the borders and confines of the light, but press on towards its manifested glory. Not yet have you drunk of the full fountain of the living water; not yet have you quite passed the limit between the life of nature and the life of grace; not yet are you what the disciples were after this Pentecost, though you are not far (it may be) from their state before it. Examine yourselves with all seriousness on this revelation of the Holy Ghost. What reason have you to think that that which is good in you is in any way due to the influence of the Holy Ghost? In other words, are you honestly praying day by day for the influence, the personal and abiding influence, of God's Holy Spirit within? Or is yours rather the amiableness of a nature from which creation's gifts are uneffaced by the fall? the beauty of a temple not demolished, though the presence of deity has departed from it?

2. God grant us grace, on this festival at least of His Spirit, to ponder deeply with ourselves the revelation of our need and of His promise; that so we may both find where we stand, and also repair our great want out of His fulness through Jesus Christ.

The time would fail us to tell of all the sinner's wants, or of all the Spirit's gifts to Christ's servants. Let us take the two referred to in this day's Collect. *Grant us by the same Spirit to have a right judgment in all things, and evermore to rejoice in His holy comfort.*

(1) *A right judgment in all things.* I suppose there may be men in the world who are vain of their judgment. Certainly there are those to whom other men instinctively turn for the guidance of conduct and of opinion. Nature has her gifts of wisdom: a sagacious intellect, a clear and dispassionate judgment, strong common sense, and a large experience of life, these things are found, it would be idle to dispute it, in men destitute of the Spirit. Nevertheless, where these gifts are dissevered from prayer and seeking after God, they are ever less than perfect. They will be found sometimes to break down somewhere. They rather witness to the Spirit's gifts than supersede them. They tell how beautiful are the fragments of that perfect man which was demolished by sin; how tenfold beautiful will be that reconstructed man which is the hope and the promise of the redemption. They go a long way, but they do not go all the way, towards supplying the want of the fallen and the sinful.

For most of us the want of *a right judgment in all things* is a grave and a pressing want. We feel it in things heavenly, and we feel it in earthly things. We feel it for ourselves, and we feel it as the advisers and counsellors of others.

How serious in these days is the responsibility of judging of doctrine. How fearful have we reason to be lest we err on the side of narrowness, or of latitudinarianism; of intolerance, or of indifference; of bigotry, or else of lukewarmness. Among those who have no time for study and little aptitude for thought, how anxious oftentimes is the desire to be right, and yet the helplessness of being so. And scarcely less, did we know all, among the Clergy—among those whose profession it is to teach, and with whom it is death to be blind guides—there is the same cry for light, and the same difficulty in finding it. *Give us*, they cry, *a right judgment, for indeed we are fearfully responsible, and yet ourselves most undecided.* I only touch upon these things today, as reasons why the doctrine of Pentecost should be deeply dear to us. *Grant us by the same Spirit, who as at this time taught the hearts of Thy faithful people, to have a right judgment in all things.* A right judgment in heavenly things is the gift of the Spirit. We do believe, not only that there is no truth to be found in God's revelations save by studying them in God; I mean, that, unless a man be a humble man and a believing man and a praying man, the Bible itself will be silent to him or worse than silent; but also that to him who does humble himself and does believe and does pray there will always *arise up light in the darkness;* there will be enough of light to guide him to heaven, even though his light may not be exactly his neighbour's, nor his grasp of truth so firm or so comprehensive as his brother's. And this kind of guidance, this enough of light for a man's own direction towards heaven, is peculiarly and above all others a gift of the Holy Spirit. It springs directly from prayer; directly from communication with God Himself in the soul that waits for Him. I commend this earnestly and affectionately to all persons who are in perplexity about doctrine, as an infallible practical remedy. A right judgment for himself, if for himself only, will be given, I firmly believe, to every man who seeks it as a gift of the Holy Ghost through prayer.

And how shall it be with things earthly? How much of life consists in the exercise of a judgment. How often in every day have we to decide whether to do this or that; whether to do this or not to do it; whether to use that free will which prescribes and which refuses, in this direction or rather in the opposite. And for others also; how often are we asked for counsel. How much of each day's occupation consists, in many professions, in one more especially, of advising and directing. In all this a man may be forgiven if he often feels himself very poor, very resourceless, very helpless. Often are two sides so evenly balanced; the choice between the two is so ambiguous; the reasons for doing this or doing that are apparently so nicely, so indecisively poised; that we could almost have recourse to the lot to end the perplexity of the judgment. And what has this to do with religion? Why speak of these things on Whit Sunday? Because, my brethren, it is here not least that the promise of the Holy Ghost has its place and its fulfilment. The judgment depends for its right exercise more than we suppose upon the heart. If the heart is right with God; if on a particular morning we have earnestly put ourselves, body, mind, and soul, into the hands of God; if we have calmed and tranquillized our weary and vexed spirit by bathing in the water of heavenly life and love; then every faculty and every element of our being falls of itself into its place; we can think and we can act, we can speak and we can judge, with a facility, with a self-command, with a decision and with a wisdom, at other times denied; men *take knowledge of us that we have been with Jesus*, and that Jesus is as much the All-wise as the All-merciful, the Almighty as the All-holy. Thus again and again is the prayer fulfilled to us, *Grant us by the same Spirit to have a right judgment in all things.*

(2) *And evermore to rejoice in His holy comfort.* We want judgment, and we want comfort. We are full of cares, and full of sorrows, every one of us. Who can guide, who can comfort us? I need not answer that question to any Christian who is here present. Where is that distress which is not the better for being carried straight to Christ's footstool? In what age, in what heart, has not the title of *the Comforter* been vindicated for Him whose work we are commemorating? *O taste and see how gracious the Lord is: blessed is the man that trusteth in Him.*

And who shall not bless God for this one thing yet above all, that He has interposed one and but one condition between the want and the gift? *God will give His Holy Spirit to them that ask Him.* Blessed words. You can ask: you know you can ask: what else could you do? could you earn, could you merit, the gift? But to ask; to kneel down and say, *O God, give me Thy Holy Spirit for Jesus Christ's sake;* this you can do: and he who does this does all. May God of His infinite mercy grant that this prayer, so simple yet so all-availing, may arise this day from many contrite hearts, from many long-sealed lips. So shall a *peace which passeth understanding* spring up gradually within; and this blessed festival of Whit Sunday be marked for ever with the brightest of memories, as the day on which the wandering child resought his Father's home, and the sanctuary long desolate, long desecrated, long defiled, was filled once again with that marvellous brightness which is *the light of the knowledge of God's glory in the face of Jesus Christ.*

WHIT SUNDAY,
May 24, 1863.

XXII.

TRINITY IN UNITY.

St John iii. 9.

How can these things be?

THE question is answered by another. *Art thou a master (teacher) of Israel, and knowest not these things?* The question, *How can these things be?* is met by another question, *How canst thou be ignorant of these things?*

And yet, my brethren, the question asked by Nicodemus is one which all thoughtful persons have asked a thousand times, and it had respect to matters which lie far above out of the sight of man. It was with regard to the working of the Holy Spirit in man's heart, to turn him from flesh into spirit, and so to make him meet for admission into the heavenly kingdom, that this enquiry was addressed to our Lord by Nicodemus, *How can these things be?* Were these things indeed so easy of apprehension that an enquirer should be rebuked for not understanding them?

We have read this question today as a part of the Gospel for Trinity Sunday. And the day itself is eminently suggestive of such thoughts. It presents to our view that great mystery of our religion, the doctrine of the *Trinity in Unity;* of the three Divine Persons in the one indivisible Godhead. How many in all times have asked with reference to this doctrine the very question of the text, *How can these things be?* Was it a wrong question? Was it wrong to feel the doctrine to be a mysterious one, and to wish for instruction in it? Was it wrong to feel the doctrine a difficult one, and to crave for some additional light upon its meaning, its consistency, and its use? None of these things, my brethren. God is not honoured by a tame, dull, torpid acquiescence in the revelations of His truth. He would have us not only attend with interest, but enquire also with intelligence. He counts not any man to know who has not first learned; learned, as all men learn, by enquiry, by search, perhaps through much doubting, certainly through many processes of combination and reconciliation of truth. He only bids us ask in a right spirit, and ask in the right way.

Now I will suppose a person to read for the first time, or for the first time to notice, such a verse in Holy Scripture as that in which our Lord thus addresses His disciples on the night before He suffered.

I will pray the Father, and He shall give you another Comforter, that He may abide with you for ever; even the Spirit of truth.

Or this:

But the Comforter, which is the Holy Ghost, whom the Father will send in my name, He shall teach you all things, and bring all things to your remembrance, whatsoever I have said unto you.

Or this:

But when the Comforter is come, whom I will send

unto you from the Father, even the Spirit of truth, which proceedeth from the Father, He shall testify of me.

Or yet once more:

Howbeit when He, the Spirit of truth, is come, He will guide you into all truth: for He shall not speak of Himself; but whatsoever He shall hear, that shall He speak: and He will show you things to come. He shall glorify me: for He shall receive of mine, and shall show it unto you. All things that the Father hath are mine: therefore said I, that He shall take of mine, and shall show it unto you.

Must not a man so reading say this to himself? These words are written in Holy Scripture. They not only form a part of the faith of the Church, but they also form a part of our Lord's own words, and of our Lord's last words, to the disciples whom He had chosen, and whom He was now about to send abroad into the world as the instructors of all nations in His truth.

And they are not single words; torn from the context, and twisted into unnatural shapes, so that the statement itself can scarcely be recognized in its inferences. The words occur naturally, in the midst of a most comforting and a most affecting discourse: and they occur repeatedly, in many varieties of form and of expression, but with an emphasis, a fulness, a harmony, and a precision, which forbids me to say that I have either misread or misinterpreted them.

I approach them more closely; and I see this on the very surface, that three Persons are spoken of. There is *I*, the speaker, the Lord Jesus Christ Himself. There is *the Father*, known from the whole tenor of our Lord's discourses to denote the Holy and Almighty God, the Author of all being, and the Lord and Judge of the souls which He has created. There is also another Person spoken of, as *the Comforter, the Holy Ghost, the Spirit of truth:* and to Him, as to the Father, and as to the Saviour also, are attributed the acts and the resolutions of a Person; *He shall teach, He shall testify, He shall speak, He shall take, He shall show.* I cannot but feel, as I read, that it is not a mere influence of which Christ speaks; not a mere operation and not a mere effect; but, if there be any meaning in words, a personal Agent; as truly and distinctly a personal Agent, as the Father from whom, or as the Son by whom, He is promised and sent.

And when I look into the words themselves, I cannot but observe that, as they speak of Persons, so also they speak of Divine Persons. Of Himself the Lord Jesus Christ here says, to quote but one expression, *All things that the Father hath are mine:* could any language more positively assert the Divinity of the speaker? He who claims as His own all that is the Father's, and speaks of another as glorifying Him by showing it, does indeed say, in more than mere words, *I myself am God.* What else do we mean by Deity, than the possession, the ownership, of the universe? What does not grow out of this one attribute, as to the majesty, the omnipotence, and the omnipresence of God? And if, again, the Holy Spirit is here spoken of as proceeding from the Father and the Son, as exercising an almighty influence within the souls of men, as revealing things to come, as taking of the things of God and displaying them to the soul, what is this but an act of Deity? what is the inference from this, but that the Person spoken of is also a Divine Person?

These are some of the wonderful, the astounding inferences which a candid reader must draw from the verses brought before you. They speak of divine acts, and they ascribe those acts to distinct Persons. Christ prays, the Father gives, the Spirit comes, and teaches, and testifies, and glorifies. We cannot help, we cannot evade, the conclusions: there are three Persons, each one of whom *by Himself is God and Lord.*

And yet reason and conscience and revelation all cry out against the inference that *there are three Gods or three Lords.* The absolute Unity of the Godhead is a first principle of all religion. *Hear, O Israel: the Lord our God is one Lord.* If anything in our doctrine denies that first principle, that thing must be erroneous; from true premises, it may be, but certainly a false conclusion. The same Scripture which speaks of the three Divine Persons, speaks also no less positively of the One God. Hence the effort of the Church to embody, if it be possible, in one phrase the two parts of the revelation. *There is but one living and true God:* that must be held fast as the axiom of all religion. *In unity of this Godhead there be three Persons, of one substance, power, and eternity; the Father, the Son, and the Holy Ghost:* this also must be admitted as the sure inference from the plainest words of Scripture. Tritheism must be repelled as a fearful idolatry; yet room must be found in Monotheism for the divinity of our Lord and the personality of the Spirit. The Trinity in Unity, the Triunity of God, is the form devised by man for the combination of the two halves of this all-important revelation.

Now when this is done, and when, as on this day, the Church comes together in one place to acknowledge and to adore the great mystery of our religion, the three Divine Persons in the but One God; are there not some, even (it may be) in this congregation, who would meet us with the question of the text, *How can these things be?* And how far is this a right question? and where does it begin to err? It may err in spirit, and it may err in direction.

1. Sometimes it is the question of mere haste, indifference, impatience, petulance, or vanity. A man who has not had one serious thought, nor breathed one earnest prayer; a man who has never given himself to the study of divine truth, or so much as opened for information the sure word of Revelation; will say to you, with a positiveness which on any other subject would be felt to be ludicrous, *I never can believe in the doctrine of the Trinity: I never can believe that there are Three Persons in One God: it is a contradiction in terms to say that Three are One or that One is Three.* In vain do we urge upon him the plain words of Scripture with reference to the divine attributes of Christ, and to the distinct agency of the Holy Spirit. In vain do we remind him of the inadequacy of human language to express matters so far beyond our comprehension. In vain do we assure him that *Person* and *Substance* are admitted to be most imperfect expressions of that distinction which is yet felt to be both scriptural and reasonable. In vain do we entreat him to use what words he will to express better than we have done the thing itself, the eternal, the essential verity, which lies under the Church's enunciation of the Christian doctrine

concerning our God. To all such explanations he turns a deaf ear, and has no answer but one to the faith in which ages and generations have lived and died, *How can these things be?* We venture to say that that man has erred in spirit. He has not brought to the consideration of the things of God a preparation which all would judge essential to the understanding of the things of man. He has sat in judgment upon the most profound subject on which the thought of man can be exercised, without one hour's real preparation or one moment's honest study. If that man had read with anxiety and prayer that one discourse of our Saviour from which we have quoted, he would have seen that it was impossible to disregard the phenomena which it presents. He would have seen that the language there used makes it futile for any Christian theology to turn aside from the mystery which it presupposes. He might say that the word *Trinity* is a term of man's invention; it is so: he might say that it is an imperfect definition; it is so: he might say that he knows a better expression for bringing together in one the two sides of the truth; let us hear it: but, if he professes to regard the New Testament as his guide to Christian doctrine, it is idle for him to ridicule, or to pass by unnoticed, the marvellous revelations of the Divinity of the Son and of the Personality of the Spirit. The question, *How can these things be?* is on his lips the confession of his incompetency and the parade of his presumption. God keep us evermore from that spirit in the investigation of His truth.

2. But the error of the question may be an error not of spirit, but, as we have called it, of direction. A

person who says concerning the revelation of the Trinity, *How can these things be?* may possibly be guilty only of mistaking the direction in which we ought to seek God's truth. We may be expecting to understand, not the fact, but the method, of the coexistence of the three Divine Persons in the one essence of God. We may be sincerely desirous of light; we may be refusing no word of God; we may be studying the Bible diligently, and availing ourselves of every help to that study which we can find or make. The mistake is, that we do not think it honest to accept a revelation till we can comprehend it. Or let me rather say—for indeed we cannot believe that which we do not in some degree understand—the mistake is, that we are not satisfied to receive what God has told us for one purpose, till we can receive it for another and a different purpose; not satisfied, for example, to believe that our Saviour is Almighty and All-holy and All-merciful, and therefore is God, until we can understand how it is that He can be at once Divine and human; at once God from eternity, and yet also a crucified and a risen Man, exalted by the Father to a glory which yet was His unchangeably from the beginning. Or not satisfied, once again, to believe that the Blessed and Holy Spirit of God is a present and an indwelling Person, sent to us by our Saviour from the Father to guide us into all truth, to keep us from sinning, to comfort us in sorrow, and at last to raise us from death; and yet also Himself one with the Father and with the Son, partaker in that inalienable and incommunicable Deity which is ever one and but one. In short, we may be demanding a power of comprehension where the power of apprehension should suffice. We may be refusing to accept what God tells, till we ourselves can include in that acceptance what God does not tell. If a man announces to me that a poor neighbour is dying of a frightful disease, I accept the announcement as a reason for hurrying to his bedside, though I know neither the nature of the malady nor the possibilities of its cure. If a vessel is wrecked on my coast, I hasten to minister to the surviving passengers, though I know nothing either of the laws of navigation or of the principles of the tides[1]. All human knowledge, certainly all spiritual knowledge, is practical in its aim. If God reveals to me in His Holy Word that He so loves me that He gave His only-begotten Son to die for my sins and to rise again for my justification, I do not stay to ask, *How can these things be? what is meant by the Sonship of Christ, or how and in what way was that atonement and that justification connected with the gift of the Son?* I seize upon the great fact; I was lost without Christ, and with Him I am found. And if God is pleased to go on to tell me things which show that this Saviour is absolutely Divine; that He has all power in heaven and in earth, that all that the Father hath is His, that He hears and answers prayer, that He intercedes for sinners in God's presence, and is able to save to the uttermost those who come unto God by Him; I do not stay to ask, *How can these things be? how can One who is in some sense separate from the Father yet be coequal with Him and coeternal? how can One who intercedes with God be God Himself? how can unity be consistent with distinct*

---

[1] See Dr Arnold's Sermons, "Christian Life, its Course," &c., Sermon XXVII.

personality, or how can the one only God exist in a plurality of Divine Persons? I understand God to mean that I may lean upon Christ with all the weight of my sins and of my sorrows, because He is not man only; because though He is man in all sympathy, He is also God in all power. There is much around the revelation which is left in deep shadow, but the light shines full and free upon the great practical revelation itself. Even thus is it if God be pleased to tell me, as in the context of the words now before us, that there is a Holy and Blessed Spirit whom He is ready to give to all who ask Him, and whose influence is essential to every living man to turn him from darkness to light, from a man of mortal flesh into a man of immortal spirit. I perceive at once that this means that I must ask for His help. I do not wait to enquire, *How can these things be? how can Spirit act upon spirit? how or in what manner does the Holy Spirit act upon those in whom He dwells? by what reality and by what exercise of His presence does He live and move and operate within?* I understand that the object is to make me call for His help; and, if I do so, I find by degrees that that help has come. It is no necessity of mine to understand the nature of the agency, any more than to understand the way in which food nourishes or wine cheers or air refreshes. The purpose of revelation is practical, not theoretical. If I refuse to act upon God's Word till I can explain to the satisfaction of the intellect all that surrounds and all that bears upon and all that is connected with the life-giving truth itself revealed, then indeed I shall die before I know, and be lost before I have set myself to seek salvation.

And what if in this state of our knowledge, in this condition of persons not so much informed as directed, not so much illuminated in understanding as guided and led into right, we must yet frame to ourselves expressions of doctrine which shall at least not mislead? What if we would incorporate in a few brief particulars that which God has told us of Himself? What if, for the convenience of creeds and confessions, we would just put together so much as we know, and yet not pretend to know more than God has spoken? Could we do better than speak, in terms at once clear and ambiguous, of a *Trinity*, a *Trinity in Unity?* and declare this (as we have done today) to be *the Catholic Faith, that we worship one God in Trinity, and Trinity in Unity?* Yes, the words are sound words, as much in the mysteries which they leave, as in the mysteries which they reveal. Only let us take heed, every one of us, that the doctrine of this day be to us a real not a fallacious, because a practical and not a theoretical doctrine. *What to me*, let each one ask himself, *is the doctrine of the Father?* Is He my Father? does my heart so cry to Him? does my life so represent Him? *What to me is the doctrine of the Son?* Is His divinity my stay? is His humanity my comfort? *What to me is the doctrine of the Spirit?* Is His presence my soul's life? is His operation my life's holiness? *And what to me is the doctrine of the Three in One?* Do I so trust in the Son as never to sever Him from the Father? and so trust in the Spirit as to seek Him ever through the Son? This if I do, I am already walking in the light, and hereafter I shall see it. This if I do, though I cannot yet answer the question, *How can these things be?*

I can at least give a reason for the hope that is in me, and believe that what I know not now I shall know hereafter. The noonday of my illumination is not yet: but already the Sun of righteousness is risen upon me, and life and immortality are brought to light by His Gospel.

Trinity Sunday,
May 31, 1863.

Messrs MACMILLAN AND CO.'S PUBLICATIONS.

WORKS BY THE VERY REV. C. J. VAUGHAN, D.D.,
Dean of Llandaff and Master of the Temple.

The Prayers of Jesus Christ. A Closing Series of Lent Lectures delivered in the Temple Church. Crown 8vo. 3s. 6d.

St Paul's Epistle to the Romans. The Greek Text with English Notes. Seventh Edition. Crown 8vo. 7s. 6d.

The Epistle to the Hebrews. The Greek Text with Notes. Crown 8vo. 7s. 6d.

University Sermons, New and Old. A Selection of Sermons preached before the Universities of Oxford and Cambridge, 1861—1887. Crown 8vo. 10s. 6d.

Memorials of Harrow Sundays. Sermons preached in the Chapel of Harrow School. Fifth Edition. Crown 8vo. 10s. 6d.

Temple Sermons. Crown 8vo. 10s. 6d.

Lectures on the Revelation of St John. Fifth Edition. Crown 8vo. 10s. 6d.

Lectures on the Epistle to the Philippians. Fourth Edition. Crown 8vo. 7s. 6d.

Lessons of the Cross and Passion. Words from the Cross. The Reign of Sin. The Lord's Prayer.—Four Courses of Lent Lectures. New Edition. Crown 8vo. 10s. 6d.

Authorised or Revised? Sermons on some of the Texts in which the Revised Version differs from the Authorised. Crown 8vo. 7s. 6d.

Heroes of Faith: Lectures on the Eleventh Chapter of the Epistle to the Hebrews. Second Edition. Crown 8vo. 6s.

St Paul's Epistle to the Philippians. The Greek Text, with Translation, Paraphrase, and Notes for English Readers. Cr. 8vo. 5s.

Epiphany, Lent, and Easter. A Selection of Expository Sermons. Third Edition. Crown 8vo. 10s. 6d.

Twelve Discourses on Subjects connected with the Liturgy and Worship of the Church of England. Fourth Edition. Fcap. 8vo. 6s.

Notes for Lectures on Confirmation. With Suitable Prayers. Fourteenth Edition. Fcap. 8vo. 1s. 6d.

The Church of the First Days: The Church of Jeru- salem, The Church of the Gentiles, The Church of the World. New Edition. Crown 8vo. 10s. 6d.

Christ satisfying the Instincts of Humanity. Eight Lectures delivered in the Temple Church, Lent, 1870. Second Edition. Extra fcap. 8vo. 3s. 6d.

MACMILLAN AND CO., LONDON.

The Two Great Temptations. The Temptation of Man and the Temptation of Christ. Lectures delivered in the Temple Church, Lent, 1872. Second Edition. Fcap. 8vo. 3s. 6d.

Addresses to Young Clergymen, delivered at Salisbury in September and October 1875. Extra fcap. 8vo. 4s. 6d.

Rest Awhile. Addresses to Toilers in the Ministry, delivered at Charterhouse in September 1879. Extra fcap. 8vo. 5s.

The Solidity of True Religion, and other Sermons, preached during the London Mission in 1874. Second Edition. Extra fcap. 8vo. 3s. 6d.

The Book and the Life, and other Sermons, preached before the University of Cambridge, 1861—1862. Third Edition. Fcap. 8vo. 4s. 6d.

Life's Work and God's Discipline. Three Sermons preached before the University of Cambridge, 1863. Third Edition. Extra fcap. 8vo. cloth. 2s. 6d.

The Wholesome Words of Jesus Christ. Four Sermons preached before the University of Cambridge in November 1866. Second Edition. Fcap. 8vo. 3s. 6d.

Foes of Faith. Sermons preached before the University of Cambridge in November 1868. Second Edition. Fcap. 8vo. 3s. 6d.

Counsels for Young Students. Three Sermons preached before the University of Cambridge in October 1870. Fcap. 8vo. 2s. 6d.

The Young Life equipping itself for God's Service. Sermons preached before the University of Cambridge, 1872. Sixth Edition. Extra fcap. 3s. 6d.

"My Son, Give me thine Heart." Sermons preached before the Universities of Oxford and Cambridge, 1876—78. Extra fcap. 8vo. 5s.

The Epistles of St Paul. For English Readers. Part I. containing the First Epistle to the Thessalonians. Second Edition. 8vo. 1s. 6d.

The Lord's Prayer. Second Edition. Extra fcap. 8vo. 3s. 6d.

Sermons preached in the Chapel of Harrow School (1847). 8vo. 10s. 6d.

Nine Sermons preached for the most part in the Chapel of Harrow School (1849). Crown 8vo. 5s.

Rays of Sunlight for Dark Days. A Book of Selections for the Suffering. With a Preface by C. J. VAUGHAN, D.D. New Edition. 18mo. 3s. 6d.

MACMILLAN AND CO., LONDON.

CPSIA information can be obtained
at www.ICGtesting.com
Printed in the USA
LVHW081504040523
745899LV00010B/111